THE GLOSSARY OF
MARKETING
MANAGEMENT

Compiled & Edited By:
Manasi Pathak

Rhythm

Independent
Publication

THE GLOSSARY OF MARKETING MANAGEMENT

Compiled & Edited By:
Manasi Pathak

ISBN:9798861399777

9798861399777

Published by:
Rhythm Independent Publication,
Jinkethimmanahalli, Varanasi, Bengaluru, Karnataka, India - 560036

For all types of correspondence, send your mails to the provided address above.

The information presented herein has been collated from a diverse range of sources, comprehensive perspective on the subject matter.

A/B Testing

A/B testing is a methodical approach used in the field of marketing management to evaluate and compare two variants of a marketing element, such as a webpage, email campaign, or advertisement, in order to determine the version that generates better results.

The process involves creating two versions of the marketing element, typically referred to as the "A" and "B" variants. These variants are nearly identical, except for a single variable, known as the variable being tested or the independent variable. The purpose of A/B testing is to evaluate whether the changes made to the variable being tested have a significant impact on the desired outcome, also known as the dependent variable.

The A and B variants are then presented to a selected sample of the target audience, who are randomly divided into two groups. The performance of each variant is monitored and measured, typically by tracking metrics such as click-through rates, conversion rates, or sales. Based on the results, statistical analysis is carried out to determine which variant generates better outcomes.

A/B testing allows marketers to make data-driven decisions by offering objective insights into the effectiveness of different elements. It helps identify the most optimal version of a marketing element, leading to improved customer engagement, higher conversion rates, and ultimately, increased return on investment (ROI).

AI In Marketing

AI in marketing refers to the use of artificial intelligence systems and technologies to enhance and streamline various aspects of marketing management. It involves leveraging machine learning algorithms and advanced analytics to automate and improve marketing strategies, customer targeting, campaign optimization, personalization, and overall decision-making processes.

AI in marketing has revolutionized the way businesses connect with their target audience. By analyzing vast amounts of data, AI systems can provide valuable insights and predictions, allowing marketers to make data-driven decisions and create more effective marketing campaigns. AI-powered tools and platforms can segment customers based on their behaviors, preferences, and demographics, enabling businesses to deliver personalized and targeted messages to specific customer segments.

Furthermore, AI in marketing can automate repetitive tasks, such as data analysis, content creation, email marketing, and lead scoring, freeing up marketers' time to focus on strategy and creativity. AI algorithms can identify patterns in customer behavior, predict future trends, and recommend the most relevant content or products for individual customers.

The integration of AI in marketing management also extends to customer experience management. AI-powered chatbots and virtual assistants can provide prompt and personalized responses to customer queries, improving customer satisfaction and loyalty. Additionally, AI systems can closely monitor social media and online platforms, analyzing customer sentiment and providing real-time insights for reputation management and customer service enhancement.

In summary, AI in marketing management enables businesses to drive more relevant and personalized interactions with customers, optimize marketing campaigns, boost efficiency, and improve overall marketing performance.

AIDA Model

The AIDA model is a widely-used marketing communication tool that outlines the four sequential stages a consumer goes through during the promotional process: Attention, Interest, Desire, and Action. This model serves as a guide for marketers to create effective communication strategies and engage consumers in a step-by-step manner.

The first stage of the AIDA model is Attention. At this stage, marketers aim to grab the attention of their target audience by creating compelling advertisements or promotional messages. This can be achieved through eye-catching visuals, catchy slogans, or intriguing headlines. It is crucial to create a strong initial impact to ensure that consumers notice and become aware of the product or service being promoted.

The second stage is Interest. Once marketers have captured the attention of consumers, they need to build interest in the product or service. This can be done by highlighting the unique features or benefits, demonstrating how the product solves a problem or fulfills a need, or providing testimonials or case studies. Marketers aim to create curiosity and engage consumers, encouraging them to learn more about the offering.

The third stage is Desire. Here, marketers aim to evoke a desire in consumers to own or experience the product or service. This can be achieved by showcasing the product in action, presenting it as a status symbol, or offering exclusive discounts or incentives. Marketers aim to create an emotional connection and appeal to the desires or aspirations of the consumers.

The final stage is Action. At this stage, consumers are encouraged to take action and make a purchase or engage with the brand. Marketers provide clear, concise, and easy-to-follow instructions on how to proceed with the purchase or desired action. This stage also involves overcoming any potential barriers to conversion, such as offering flexible payment options or providing guarantees.

AR Marketing Campaigns

AR marketing campaigns refer to advertising and promotional strategies that leverage augmented reality (AR) technology to engage and interact with target audiences. This approach integrates virtual content into the real world, allowing users to experience products, brands, or services in a more immersive and interactive way.

AR marketing campaigns aim to captivate and entertain consumers by creating a novel and engaging brand experience. By superimposing computer-generated images onto the physical environment, AR enhances the user's perception of reality, enabling them to experience products or services in a more personal and meaningful manner.

Above-The-Line (ATL) Advertising

Above-the-line (ATL) advertising refers to a strategy in marketing management that involves promotional activities and campaigns that are aimed at reaching a wide audience. This type of advertising is typically conducted through mass media channels such as television, radio, print, and outdoor advertisements.

The key characteristic of ATL advertising is its focus on creating brand awareness and building a positive brand image. It aims to reach a large number of consumers and create a broad impact. This is in contrast to below-the-line (BTL) advertising which focuses on targeted and personalized communications with specific segments of the target market.

ATL advertising is particularly effective in generating awareness about new products or services, as well as reinforcing existing brand perceptions. It is a powerful tool for reaching a broad customer base and creating top-of-mind brand recall. By using mass media platforms, companies can achieve wide coverage and create a strong presence in the market.

However, ATL advertising can be expensive compared to other forms of advertising, and its impact on sales and ROI can be difficult to measure directly. Therefore, it is crucial for marketing managers to carefully plan and evaluate the effectiveness of their ATL campaigns and ensure that they align with overall marketing objectives.

In conclusion, ATL advertising plays a critical role in brand building and reaching a broad audience. By leveraging mass media channels, companies can increase brand awareness and create a strong market presence. However, it is important to balance the costs and benefits of ATL advertising and integrate it with other marketing strategies to maximize its effectiveness.

Above-The-Line (ATL) Marketing

Above-the-line (ATL) marketing, in the context of Marketing Management discipline, refers to a promotional strategy that utilizes mass media channels to reach a wider audience and create brand awareness. It involves activities aimed at targeting a large market segment through traditional advertising methods such as television, print media (newspapers, magazines), radio, and outdoor advertising (billboards, posters).

The key characteristic of ATL marketing is its ability to reach a broad audience, allowing companies to communicate their message to a wide range of potential customers. It focuses on building brand recognition and creating a positive brand image, rather than directly driving sales. By using high-reach media channels, ATL marketing aims to generate consumer interest, attract attention, and establish a brand's prominence in a competitive market.

ATL marketing campaigns often rely on creative and engaging advertisements that capture the attention of viewers and leave a lasting impression. These campaigns can be expensive due to the high cost of media placement, production, and creative development. However, by targeting a large market segment, ATL marketing can have a wide-reaching impact and generate long-term brand loyalty.

In conclusion, above-the-line marketing plays a crucial role in Marketing Management as it allows businesses to promote their products and services to a larger audience through mass media channels. By leveraging traditional advertising methods, brands can create brand awareness, generate interest, and establish their presence in the market.

Account-Based Marketing (ABM)

Account-Based Marketing (ABM) is a strategic approach to marketing that focuses on targeting individual organizations, or accounts, rather than broad market segments. It involves identifying key accounts that align with the company's target audience and personalizing marketing efforts to cater to the specific needs and characteristics of those accounts.

The ABM approach requires close collaboration between marketing and sales teams to identify, engage, and nurture high-value accounts throughout the entire customer journey. Unlike traditional marketing methods that focus on attracting a large number of leads, ABM aims to build strong and lasting relationships with a select group of accounts.

Ad Auction

Ad Auction is a competitive process that takes place in online advertising, where advertisers bid for ad placement on a publisher's website or in search engine results. It is a key component of digital marketing strategy, as it enables advertisers to reach their target audience effectively and efficiently.

In an ad auction, advertisers compete against each other by submitting bids for a specific keyword, audience demographic, or ad placement. These bids reflect the maximum amount that the advertiser is willing to pay for each click, impression, or conversion. The ad with the highest bid is typically displayed first, followed by the ad with the second-highest bid, and so on.

The bidding process in an ad auction is often facilitated by an ad platform or an ad network. The ad platform determines the winning bid based on factors such as bid amount, ad relevancy, and quality score. Advertisers can set a daily or campaign budget to control their ad spend, and the ad platform ensures that the daily spend does not exceed this budget.

Ad auctions are designed to be fair and transparent, with the goal of delivering the most relevant and engaging ads to users. The ad platform takes into account various factors, including the ad's relevance to the user's search query or browsing behavior, to determine the ad's quality score. A higher quality score can lead to a lower cost per click or a higher ad position.

Overall, ad auctions play a crucial role in online advertising, allowing advertisers to target their ads effectively, publishers to monetize their websites, and users to discover products and services that align with their interests and needs.

Ad Campaign

An ad campaign is a strategic marketing initiative that involves creating and implementing a series of advertisements or promotional activities in order to achieve specific marketing goals and objectives. It is a carefully planned and coordinated effort that aims to communicate a specific message to a target audience and influence their buying behavior.

The main purpose of an ad campaign is to increase brand awareness, generate leads, and ultimately drive sales. It typically includes various elements such as print advertisements, television commercials, radio spots, online banners, social media posts, and email marketing. These different forms of advertising are used to reach different segments of the target audience and to reinforce the overall campaign message.

An effective ad campaign begins with thorough market research and analysis, which helps identify the target audience, their needs, and preferences. This information is used to develop a clear and compelling campaign message that will resonate with the intended audience. The campaign strategy should also take into account the competitive landscape, current market trends, and the overall marketing objectives of the organization.

Once the campaign message and strategy are finalized, the creative team develops the actual advertisements and promotional materials. These materials are then deployed across multiple channels and media platforms to maximize reach and impact. Throughout the campaign, the effectiveness of the advertisements is measured and evaluated using various metrics, such as sales figures, brand recognition, and customer feedback.

In summary, an ad campaign is a comprehensive marketing effort that involves the strategic planning, creation, and implementation of a series of advertisements and promotional activities. It is designed to communicate a specific message to a target audience, increase brand awareness, and drive sales.

Ad Copy

Ad Copy refers to the written or verbal content used in advertisements to promote a product, service, or brand. It is a crucial component of marketing management, as it is responsible for capturing the attention, interest, and desire of the target audience, ultimately leading to action or purchase.

The primary goal of ad copy is to communicate the unique selling proposition (USP) of the product or service, which sets it apart from competitors and appeals to the needs and wants of the target market. Effective ad copy takes into consideration the target audience's demographics, psychographics, and behavior, in order to craft messages that resonate with them.

Ad copy should be concise, compelling, and clear, using persuasive language and techniques to quickly and effectively deliver the message. It often employs emotional appeals, storytelling, humor, or other creative tactics to engage the audience and leave a lasting impression.

Moreover, ad copy should align with the overall marketing strategy and brand image of the company. It should reflect the brand's values, personality, and positioning in the market, ensuring consistency and reinforcing brand identity.

In addition to written copy, ad copy can also include visual elements such as images, graphics, or videos to enhance its effectiveness. However, regardless of the format, the ultimate aim of ad copy is to drive consumer behavior and generate a positive response, whether it is making a purchase, requesting more information, or engaging with the brand in some way.

Ad Exchange Networks

Ad Exchange Networks are platforms that facilitate the buying and selling of online advertising inventory in an automated and real-time manner. These networks work on the principle of programmatic advertising, where the buying and selling of ad space is done through a series of real-time auctions.

The primary goal of ad exchange networks is to connect advertisers, who want to promote their products or services, with publishers, who have available ad space on their websites or apps. Advertisers bid on the ad space available on different publishers' platforms, based on their target audience, budget, and other criteria. Publishers, on the other hand, offer their ad space to the highest bidders through the ad exchange network.

Ad exchange networks operate on a real-time bidding (RTB) model, where advertisers can bid on available ad impressions as they become available. This allows for highly efficient and targeted advertising, as advertisers can reach their specific target audience in real-time, based on various demographic, behavioral, and contextual factors. Ad exchange networks also provide advertisers with valuable data and analytics, allowing them to optimize their campaigns and improve their return on investment (ROI).

In summary, ad exchange networks play a crucial role in the world of digital advertising, enabling advertisers to reach their target audience efficiently and publishers to monetize their ad space effectively. These networks leverage programmatic advertising and real-time bidding to connect advertisers and publishers, ensuring that the right ad is delivered to the right user at the right time.

Ad Exchange

An ad exchange is a digital marketplace that enables the buying and selling of online advertising inventory. It acts as a platform where advertisers and publishers can connect and trade advertisements in real-time.

Ad exchanges automate the process of buying and selling ad placements by utilizing real-time bidding (RTB) technology. Advertisers can bid for available ad spaces that match their target audience, while publishers can list their inventory and set prices for each impression. The exchange facilitates the transaction, ensuring that the highest bidder's ad is displayed on the publisher's website.

Ad Impressions

Ad impressions, in the context of Marketing Management, refer to the number of times an advertisement is displayed or shown to users. It is a metric used to measure the reach or exposure of an ad campaign to the target audience. Ad impressions are usually counted each time an ad is loaded or rendered on a web page, mobile app, or any other advertising medium.

Ad impressions are an essential component of performance measurement in digital advertising. They provide insights into the potential audience reached by an ad and are often used alongside other metrics such as click-through rate (CTR) and conversion rate to evaluate the effectiveness of an ad campaign.

Ad Inventory

Ad inventory refers to the available space or slots on a platform or medium where advertisements can be displayed or served. It represents the total number of advertising opportunities that can be used by advertisers to reach their target audience.

In the context of marketing management, ad inventory management plays a crucial role in optimizing advertising campaigns and maximizing campaign effectiveness. It involves strategic planning, coordination, and analysis of available ad space to ensure that advertisements are efficiently and effectively placed to reach the right audience at the right time.

Ad Monetization

Ad monetization refers to the process of generating revenue by displaying advertisements on a platform or through a digital medium. This marketing management strategy aims to maximize the earning potential from advertisements by strategically placing them in front of a target audience.

The primary objective of ad monetization is to convert website visits or app engagement into ad views and subsequent clicks, leading to increased revenue for the platform or digital medium. This is accomplished through various methods such as banner ads, interstitial ads, native ads, video ads, and sponsored content. Advertisements are typically sourced from businesses seeking to reach the platform's audience and are often displayed based on an algorithm that considers the viewer's preferences, behavior, and demographics.

To effectively monetize ads, marketing managers must consider several factors. These include optimizing ad placement to ensure maximum visibility and engagement, striking a balance between ad frequency and user experience, and selecting relevant advertisements that resonate with the target audience. Furthermore, proper ad targeting and retargeting strategies should be implemented to deliver personalized and contextually relevant ads to individual users.

Successful ad monetization can be measured through key performance indicators such as click-through rate (CTR), cost per mille (CPM), and revenue per mille (RPM). By analyzing these metrics, marketing managers can fine-tune their ad monetization strategies, ensuring optimal revenue generation while maintaining a positive user experience.

Ad Network

An ad network is a platform that connects advertisers with publishers, enabling the distribution and display of advertisements across multiple websites or mobile apps. It acts as an intermediary between advertisers, who want to promote their products or services, and publishers, who have available ad space on their digital properties.

Ad networks provide a marketplace where advertisers can choose specific demographics, geographies, or interests to target their ads. They offer a wide range of ad formats such as display ads, video ads, native ads, and mobile ads. The network's technology allows advertisers to manage their campaigns, monitor performance, and track key metrics like impressions, clicks, and conversions.

Ad Position

The term "Ad Position" refers to the placement and location of an advertisement on a webpage or in a media platform. It is a crucial element in marketing management, as the position of an ad can significantly impact its visibility and effectiveness.

The ad position is determined by factors such as bidding strategies, quality score, relevance, and competition. It is typically defined by a numerical value or ranking, with higher positions indicating greater visibility and exposure to potential customers.

Ad Relevance Scoring

Ad relevance scoring is a metric used in the field of marketing management to determine the suitability and effectiveness of an advertisement in relation to the target audience. It measures the extent to which an ad aligns with the interests, needs, and preferences of the intended audience.

The process of ad relevance scoring involves analyzing various factors such as keywords, ad copy, landing page experience, and historical performance data. By examining these factors, marketers can evaluate how well an ad meets the expectations and demands of the target audience.

Ad Relevance

Ad relevance, in the context of Marketing Management, refers to the level of correspondence between an advertisement and the target audience's interests, needs, and preferences. It measures the extent to which an ad aligns with the target audience's expectations and resonates with their motivations and desires.

Effective ad relevance is crucial in marketing as it directly impacts the success of advertising campaigns. When ads are relevant, they have a higher likelihood of capturing the attention of the target audience, engaging them, and influencing their behavior positively. On the other hand, irrelevant ads can be easily ignored or even perceived as intrusive, leading to wasted resources and a negative brand image.

Ad relevance can be achieved by employing various strategies. Firstly, a thorough understanding of the target audience is crucial, including their demographics, behavior, and preferences. This knowledge enables marketers to tailor their ad content to suit the specific needs and interests of the audience. Additionally, leveraging data-driven insights and analytics can help in identifying and targeting relevant audiences accurately.

Furthermore, relevance can be enhanced by optimizing ad formats, placement, and timing. For instance, displaying ads in the right context and on appropriate platforms ensures that they reach the intended audience when they are most receptive. Personalization and customization techniques, such as dynamic ad content, can also contribute to higher ad relevance by delivering more personalized messages to individual consumers.

Ad Retargeting

Ad retargeting, also known as remarketing, is a marketing strategy that involves targeting online advertisements to users who have already shown some level of interest in a particular product or website. It is a method of reaching out to potential customers who have previously visited a website or interacted with a brand, in an effort to encourage them to return and complete a purchase or conversion.

Ad retargeting works by placing a pixel or a tracking code on a website, which then collects information about visitors, such as the pages they visit or the actions they take. This data is used to create custom audience segments, which can be targeted with specific advertisements that are relevant to their previous interactions. These ads are displayed to the users as they navigate through other websites, social media platforms, or search engines, keeping the brand or product top of mind and increasing the chances of conversion.

Ad Revenue Models

An ad revenue model refers to the method by which companies generate income from advertisements displayed on their platforms or distributed through their channels. In the context of the Marketing Management discipline, ad revenue models play a significant role in the overall marketing strategy and financial sustainability of a business.

There are several different types of ad revenue models that companies can employ, each with its own unique characteristics and advantages. One common ad revenue model is Cost Per Click (CPC), where advertisers pay the platform or channel based on the number of clicks their ads receive. This model is often used in search engine advertising and display advertising networks. Another popular model is Cost Per Impression (CPM), where advertisers pay based on the number of times their ads are viewed by users. This model is often used in display advertising and social media advertising.

Ad Revenue

Ad revenue refers to the income generated from advertisements displayed through various marketing channels. In the context of marketing management, it is a crucial metric that measures the financial performance and effectiveness of advertising campaigns.

This revenue is primarily derived from advertisers who pay for the opportunity to showcase their products or services to a targeted audience. The amount of revenue generated is typically based on the number of ad impressions or clicks received by these advertisements.

Marketing managers play a vital role in maximizing ad revenue by identifying and implementing

7

strategies to attract advertisers and increase the visibility and reach of the advertisements. They analyze market trends, consumer behaviors, and competitor activities to create effective advertising campaigns that can generate higher revenue.

Furthermore, marketing managers also focus on optimizing the monetization of advertising space. They negotiate pricing models, such as cost per click (CPC) or cost per thousand impressions (CPM), to ensure maximum profitability for the advertising inventory.

Overall, ad revenue serves as a key performance indicator for marketing managers, providing insights into the effectiveness of their advertising efforts. By constantly monitoring and analyzing this metric, they can make informed decisions to enhance their advertising strategies, attract more advertisers, and ultimately drive revenue growth for their organization.

Ad Scheduling

Ad scheduling, also known as ad timing or advertising scheduling, refers to the strategic planning and implementation of when advertisements will be displayed or aired to reach the target audience effectively. It is a critical aspect of marketing management, as it helps organizations optimize their marketing campaigns and allocate resources efficiently.

Ad scheduling involves determining the specific time periods, such as certain days of the week or specific hours of the day, during which advertisements will be shown to potential customers. This decision is based on factors such as consumer behavior patterns, market research, and competitor analysis.

The primary objective of ad scheduling is to ensure that advertisements are displayed when the target audience is most likely to be receptive and responsive. By studying consumer behavior, marketers can identify peak times when potential customers are more engaged, such as during specific TV programs, online browsing patterns, or commuting hours.

Implementing ad scheduling allows marketers to optimize their advertising budgets by avoiding unnecessary expenses during non-peak periods. By strategically selecting the timing of advertisements, businesses can increase their reach, maximize exposure, and enhance the overall effectiveness of their marketing efforts.

Ad Spend Allocation

Ad Spend Allocation refers to the process of determining how to distribute a company's advertising budget across various marketing channels and campaigns in order to maximize the effectiveness and efficiency of the advertising efforts.

The goal of ad spend allocation is to ensure that the allocated budget is used strategically to reach the target audience, generate awareness, drive sales, and achieve the desired marketing objectives. It involves analyzing historical data, market trends, consumer behavior, and competitive landscape to make informed decisions regarding where and how much to invest in different advertising channels or platforms such as television, radio, print media, online advertising, social media, and direct marketing.

The allocation process typically begins with setting the overall advertising budget, which is determined based on factors such as company's financial resources, marketing goals, target market, and industry benchmarks. Once the budget is set, marketers need to consider various factors such as reach, frequency, target audience profile, cost per impression, and return on investment (ROI) potential of each advertising channel or campaign.

By intelligently allocating the ad spend, marketers can optimize the reach and impact of their advertising messages, ensure optimal utilization of resources, and achieve the desired marketing outcomes. It is crucial for marketers to continuously monitor and evaluate the performance of each marketing channel and campaign to make necessary adjustments in the ad spend allocation strategy and maximize the effectiveness of the advertising efforts.

Ad Spend

Ad spend, also known as advertising expenditure, refers to the amount of money a company invests in advertising activities to promote its products or services. In the context of marketing management, ad spend plays a crucial role in determining the success of marketing campaigns and achieving the desired business objectives.

Ad spend is a key component of the marketing budget, and it involves the allocation of financial resources towards various advertising channels such as television, radio, print media, online platforms, and social media. The purpose of ad spend is to create awareness, generate interest, and influence the target audience to take the desired action, such as making a purchase or subscribing to a service.

The allocation of ad spend is based on various factors such as the company's marketing objectives, target market, competition, and the effectiveness of different advertising channels. A well-planned ad spend strategy involves conducting market research, analyzing consumer behavior, and evaluating the performance of past advertising campaigns.

Marketing managers need to optimize ad spend to ensure maximum return on investment (ROI) and achieve the desired marketing outcomes. This requires monitoring and analyzing the performance of different advertising channels, tracking key metrics such as reach, frequency, click-through rates, and conversions.

In summary, ad spend refers to the financial resources allocated towards advertising activities to promote products or services. It is a crucial aspect of marketing management, influencing the success of marketing campaigns and achieving business objectives.

Ad Targeting Optimization

Ad Targeting Optimization is a marketing management technique that aims to enhance the effectiveness and efficiency of advertising campaigns by identifying and reaching out to specific target audiences. It involves the use of data analytics and advanced algorithms to analyze consumer behavior, demographics, and preferences, as well as existing market trends and patterns.

The primary objective of Ad Targeting Optimization is to deliver the right message to the right audience at the right time. By identifying and understanding the characteristics and interests of different consumer segments, companies can tailor their advertising messages and choose the most appropriate channels and platforms to reach their target audience.

Ad Targeting Options

Ad targeting options refer to the various methods and criteria used by marketers to select and reach their intended audience with their advertising messages. These options allow marketers to deliver their ads to specific groups of people who are more likely to be interested in their products or services.

There are several ad targeting options available in the field of marketing management. Demographic targeting is one such option, where marketers choose specific demographic characteristics such as age, gender, income, education, or occupation to target their ads. This helps ensure that the ads are shown to the right people who are more likely to have an interest in the product or service being advertised.

Another ad targeting option is geographic targeting, which enables marketers to display their ads to people in specific locations or regions. This is particularly useful for businesses with a physical presence in certain areas or for those targeting specific markets or regions.

Behavioral targeting is another popular ad targeting option. It involves analyzing and understanding user behavior, such as browsing history, online activities, or purchase patterns, to deliver relevant ads. By targeting users based on their past behavior, marketers can increase the chances of their ads being seen by people who are more likely to convert into customers.

Ad Targeting

Ad targeting is a marketing strategy that involves tailoring advertisements to a specific group of consumers based on their characteristics, preferences, and behavior. It is aimed at delivering the right message to the right people at the right time, maximizing the effectiveness of advertising campaigns and reducing wasted ad spend.

By using various data sources and technologies, marketers can identify and segment their target audience into different groups based on demographics, interests, location, online behavior, and purchasing habits. This allows them to create personalized ads that resonate with the specific needs and desires of each segment.

The process of ad targeting begins with market research and data analysis to gain insights into consumer behavior and preferences. This information is then used to define target audience profiles and develop advertising strategies that will appeal to these segments.

Ad targeting can be implemented through different channels and mediums, such as search engines, social media platforms, websites, and mobile apps. Marketers can choose to target their ads based on specific criteria, such as age, gender, income level, education, marital status, interests, and browsing history.

Benefits of ad targeting include increased ad relevance and engagement, improved conversion rates, higher return on investment (ROI), and reduced advertising costs. By reaching the right audience with the right message, marketers can significantly improve the effectiveness of their campaigns and achieve their marketing objectives more efficiently.

Ad Tracking Tools

Ad tracking tools are software or technologies used in the field of marketing management to monitor and analyze the performance of advertising campaigns. These tools provide valuable insights into the effectiveness of various ad campaigns, allowing marketers to optimize their strategies and allocate resources more efficiently.

Ad tracking tools are essential for measuring key metrics such as click-through rates, conversion rates, impressions, and engagement levels. By tracking these metrics, marketers can determine which ads are driving the most results and identify areas for improvement. This data-driven approach helps in making informed decisions about budget allocation, targeting options, and creative optimizations.

Ad Tracking

Ad tracking, within the context of Marketing Management, refers to the process of monitoring and measuring the performance of advertising campaigns in order to gain insights and make informed decisions. It involves the collection and analysis of data related to the effectiveness of various advertisements and marketing initiatives.

The primary objective of ad tracking is to assess the impact of advertisements on consumer behavior and determine their contribution to overall marketing goals. This involves tracking key metrics such as click-through rates, conversion rates, sales revenue, and return on investment (ROI). By tracking these metrics, marketers can understand the effectiveness of their strategies, identify areas of improvement, and optimize their advertising efforts.

Ad Viewability Rate

Ad Viewability Rate refers to the percentage of ads that are actually seen by users on a website or digital platform. In the context of Marketing Management, this metric is used to measure the effectiveness of an ad campaign and the potential reach of an advertisement.

Viewability is important in the world of digital advertising, as advertisers want their ads to be seen by users in order to generate brand awareness, engagement, and conversions. Ad Viewability Rate helps marketers understand how many impressions resulted in an ad being viewable to users.

Ad Viewability

Ad viewability refers to the measurement and evaluation of whether an online advertisement is successfully seen and displayed by the intended audience. It is a key metric used in the field of Marketing Management to assess the effectiveness and impact of online advertising campaigns.

The concept of ad viewability gained prominence with the rise of digital advertising and the need for marketers to ensure their ads were actually being seen by users. The ability to measure viewability provides insights into ad impression quality, helping advertisers understand the value they are getting from their investments. Additionally, it allows them to make informed decisions about optimizing their ad placements and creative strategies.

AdWords

AdWords, a term in the field of Marketing Management, refers to an online advertising platform developed by Google. It enables businesses to create and display ads on Google's search engine results pages and across its vast network of partner websites. AdWords operates on a pay-per-click (PPC) model, where advertisers only pay when users click on their ads.

This platform offers advertisers a variety of targeting options to reach their desired audience. They can target specific keywords, geographic locations, time of day, and even demographics. Advertisers have the flexibility to set their advertising budget and bid amount for each click. Google's sophisticated auction system determines the ad placement based on the bid amount and quality score, which is a measure of the ad's relevance and click-through rate.

AdWords functions through two main networks: the Search Network and the Display Network. The Search Network focuses on text-based ads that appear alongside search results when users enter relevant keywords. On the other hand, the Display Network showcases visual ads, such as banners and videos, on partner websites that are related to the advertiser's target audience.

AdWords provides advertisers with comprehensive analytics and reporting tools. They can track the performance of their ads, measure click-through rates, conversion rates, and return on investment. This data allows advertisers to refine their campaigns, optimize their keywords, ad copy, and targeting strategies to improve their advertising results and drive more relevant traffic to their websites.

Advertising Agency

An advertising agency is a company that specializes in creating, planning, and executing marketing and advertising campaigns for businesses and organizations. It is involved in various aspects of marketing communication, including market research, creative development, media planning and buying, and campaign management.

The primary goal of an advertising agency is to help its clients reach their target audience effectively and efficiently. This involves understanding the clients' products or services, identifying the target market, and developing strategies and tactics to convey the intended message to the audience. The agency works closely with the client to determine the most appropriate media channels, such as television, radio, print, or online platforms, and creates engaging advertisements that resonate with the target audience.

Advertising agencies employ professionals with expertise in different areas, including account management, creative development, media planning, and market research. These professionals work collaboratively to develop creative concepts, design advertisements, negotiate media placements, and evaluate campaign performance. The agency acts as a liaison between the client and various media outlets, negotiating rates and placements to ensure maximum reach and impact within the specified budget.

Overall, an advertising agency plays a crucial role in helping businesses and organizations promote their products or services to their target audience. By leveraging their expertise and resources, they help clients develop and implement effective advertising strategies that can drive awareness, generate leads, and ultimately contribute to business growth.

Affiliate Marketing

11

Affiliate marketing is a performance-based marketing strategy where a company, known as the advertiser, partners with individuals or other companies, known as affiliates, to promote their products or services. This form of marketing allows the advertiser to reach a wider audience by utilizing the affiliate's online platforms, such as websites, blogs, or social media accounts, to generate leads and drive sales.

The concept of affiliate marketing is centered around the principle of revenue sharing. When an affiliate successfully directs a visitor to the advertiser's website who then performs a desired action, such as making a purchase or filling out a form, the affiliate is rewarded with a commission. This commission is usually a percentage of the sale or a fixed amount agreed upon by the advertiser and the affiliate.

Affiliate marketing benefits both the advertiser and the affiliate. For the advertiser, it provides a cost-effective way to expand their reach and increase brand exposure, as they only pay when a desired action is completed. It also allows them to tap into the expertise and influence of the affiliate, who can provide valuable insights and recommendations to potential customers.

On the other hand, affiliates benefit from affiliate marketing by earning passive income from their online platforms. They can monetize their content by promoting products or services that align with their audience's interests. Additionally, affiliates have the flexibility to choose which advertisers to partner with and how they promote their offerings, enabling them to create a business model that suits their preferences and strengths.

Affiliate Program Management

Affiliate Program Management refers to the strategic planning, implementation, and monitoring of an affiliate marketing program by a company or organization. It is a crucial aspect of Marketing Management that focuses on driving sales, increasing brand awareness, and generating revenue through partnerships with affiliates.

In an affiliate marketing program, a company or organization forms partnerships with affiliates who promote their products or services on their platforms. These affiliates are typically individuals or other businesses with established online presence and target audiences that align with the company's target market.

The role of Affiliate Program Management is to effectively manage and coordinate these partnerships to maximize the program's success. This involves recruiting affiliates, negotiating and setting commission rates, providing marketing materials, tracking affiliate performance, and ensuring timely payment of commissions.

Additionally, Affiliate Program Management includes monitoring the program's performance and making adjustments as needed. This may involve analyzing affiliate sales data, identifying high-performing affiliates, and implementing strategies to optimize performance or address any issues that may arise.

Effective Affiliate Program Management requires strong communication and relationship-building skills, as well as a deep understanding of the company's products or services, target market, and industry trends. It also involves staying up-to-date with the latest affiliate marketing strategies and technologies to maintain a competitive edge.

Affiliate Program Networks

An affiliate program network, in the context of Marketing Management, refers to a platform or entity that connects advertisers (companies or individuals who want to promote their products or services) with publishers (website owners or influencers) who are willing to promote those products or services in exchange for a commission.

These networks act as intermediaries, facilitating the relationships between advertisers and publishers. They provide the necessary infrastructure and tools to track and measure the performance of affiliate marketing activities. Additionally, they handle the financial transactions, ensuring that publishers are properly compensated for their efforts.

Affiliate Program

An affiliate program is a marketing strategy in which a company establishes partnerships with individuals or businesses (known as affiliates) who promote the company's products or services on their platforms. In this program, affiliates receive a unique referral link or code that tracks their efforts and enables them to earn commissions on sales generated through their promotional activities.

By participating in an affiliate program, affiliates act as brand ambassadors, using their platforms and networks to spread awareness about the company's offerings and drive potential customers to make purchases. This form of performance-based marketing leverages the affiliates' existing audience and influence to boost the company's reach and sales.

Affinity Marketing

Affinity marketing is a strategic approach in marketing management that involves establishing partnerships or collaborations between companies or brands that share a similar target audience or customer base. This type of marketing taps into the existing relationship and trust between the affiliated brands to create a mutually beneficial marketing campaign or promotion.

The goal of affinity marketing is to leverage the trust and loyalty that customers have with one brand to introduce and promote another brand or product. By aligning with a compatible partner, companies aim to increase brand awareness, drive customer acquisition, and generate sales opportunities.

Agile Marketing

Agile Marketing can be defined as a marketing approach that emphasizes flexibility, collaboration, and rapid iteration in order to respond quickly to changes in the market and customer needs.

In the context of Marketing Management, Agile Marketing is a methodology that borrows principles from agile software development and applies them to the marketing process. It involves breaking down marketing tasks into small, manageable chunks (known as sprints), and continually reassessing and adjusting marketing strategies and tactics based on real-time data and feedback.

This approach allows marketing teams to be more adaptive and responsive to changing market conditions and customer preferences. By continuously testing and measuring the impact of marketing initiatives, Agile Marketing enables marketers to make data-driven decisions and optimize their campaigns for better results.

Agile Marketing also emphasizes collaboration and cross-functional teamwork, as it involves regular communication and coordination among team members, stakeholders, and other departments. This promotes a culture of transparency and helps to align marketing activities with overall business objectives.

The key benefits of adopting Agile Marketing include improved speed and efficiency in marketing execution, increased ability to prioritize and focus on high-impact activities, enhanced customer engagement and satisfaction, and the ability to quickly adapt to market trends and competitor actions.

Algorithmic Marketing

Algorithmic Marketing refers to the use of mathematical algorithms and data analysis techniques to inform and optimize marketing strategies and tactics. It involves the application of advanced analytics, machine learning, and artificial intelligence to extract insights from large volumes of data and make data-driven marketing decisions.

By utilizing algorithmic marketing, marketers can effectively analyze customer data, segment audiences, personalize messages, and predict customer behavior. This enables them to deliver more targeted and relevant marketing campaigns, enhance customer engagement, and ultimately drive business growth. Algorithmic marketing also enables marketers to optimize various marketing activities such as pricing, product recommendations, content customization, and media planning.

Algorithmic Personalization

An algorithmic personalization in the context of Marketing Management is a technique that uses algorithms and data to tailor marketing experiences and messages to individual consumers. It involves analyzing a wide range of data points, such as the consumer's demographics, browsing behavior, purchase history, and preferences, to create highly targeted and personalized marketing campaigns.

This approach aims to enhance the consumer's experience by delivering relevant content and offers that align with their needs and interests. By utilizing algorithms, marketers can automate the process of personalization, ensuring scalability and efficiency in reaching a large customer base.

Algorithmic Recommendation

An algorithmic recommendation in the context of Marketing Management is a data-driven suggestion or decision made by an algorithm to optimize marketing strategies and activities. It is based on the analysis of large volumes of data to identify patterns, trends, and insights that can improve marketing outcomes.

Algorithmic recommendations are designed to assist marketing managers in making informed decisions by providing them with actionable insights and suggestions. These recommendations can be related to various aspects of marketing, such as campaign targeting, budget allocation, message optimization, customer segmentation, pricing strategies, and more.

To generate algorithmic recommendations, advanced analytics techniques and machine learning algorithms are used to analyze large sets of data, including customer demographic and behavioral data, market trends, competitor analysis, and historical campaign performance. These algorithms can identify correlations, connections, and predictive patterns that may not be readily apparent through manual analysis.

By leveraging algorithmic recommendations, marketing managers can enhance the effectiveness and efficiency of their marketing initiatives. These recommendations can help optimize marketing budgets by identifying the most lucrative target audience segments and determining the most effective marketing channels. They can also assist in personalizing marketing messages and experiences based on customer preferences and behavior.

In conclusion, algorithmic recommendations in Marketing Management leverage data analysis and machine learning techniques to provide data-driven suggestions and decisions that can improve marketing performance and outcomes.

Alternative Media

Ambassador Marketing Strategies

Ambassador marketing strategies refer to the marketing techniques that utilize individuals who have a strong connection and loyalty to a brand to promote and endorse it to their own networks and communities. These individuals, known as brand ambassadors, act as advocates for the brand, sharing positive experiences, generating word-of-mouth recommendations, and influencing the purchasing decisions of their peers.

An ambassador marketing strategy involves identifying and recruiting brand ambassadors who embody the values and image of the brand and align with its target audience. These ambassadors can be customers, employees, influencers, or industry experts who have a genuine passion for the brand and a considerable following or influence in their respective communities.

The key objective of ambassador marketing is to leverage the credibility and trust that ambassadors have built with their audience to increase brand awareness, enhance brand reputation, and drive sales. Brands often provide ambassadors with exclusive access to new products, discounts, or incentives in return for their advocacy and promotional efforts.

A successful ambassador marketing strategy requires ongoing engagement and support for ambassadors, including regular communication, training, and resources to ensure they have the knowledge and tools to effectively represent the brand. Brands can also track and measure the impact of their ambassador marketing efforts through metrics such as engagement, reach, conversions, and customer feedback.

Ambassador Marketing

Ambassador marketing is a strategy employed in the field of marketing management to leverage the influence and reach of influential individuals, also known as brand ambassadors, to promote a product or service. These brand ambassadors are typically respected professionals or celebrities who are trusted and admired by a specific target audience.

The main objective of ambassador marketing is to create a positive association between the brand and the ambassador, in order to enhance brand awareness, build trust, and drive customer loyalty. The use of brand ambassadors can add credibility, authenticity, and social proof to a brand, as consumers are more likely to trust the recommendations and endorsements made by someone they admire or respect.

Ambassador marketing campaigns often involve a combination of offline and online activities. These may include the use of social media platforms, such as Instagram or YouTube, where ambassadors share their experiences and opinions about a brand or product. They may also participate in events, product launches, or other promotional activities to engage with their followers and generate buzz around the brand.

In addition to amplifying brand visibility, ambassador marketing can also be used as a valuable source of feedback and market research. By closely monitoring the responses and interactions generated by brand ambassadors, marketers can gain valuable insights into consumer preferences, perceptions, and trends, which can inform future marketing strategies and campaigns.

Anchor Text

Anchor text refers to the clickable text in a hyperlink. It is the visible and descriptive text that provides context and information about the content of the link. In marketing management, anchor text plays a crucial role in search engine optimization (SEO) and improving website visibility.

When search engines crawl and index websites, they analyze anchor text as an indicator of the relevance and authority of the linked page. Well-optimized anchor text helps search engines understand the content behind the link and improves the likelihood of the linked page ranking higher in search engine result pages (SERPs).

Marketing managers strategically select anchor text to enhance the visibility and ranking of their websites. They use relevant keywords and phrases that accurately describe the linked content to maximize the SEO value of the anchor text. The text should be concise, clear, and informative, providing users and search engines with a contextually relevant summary of the linked page.

However, it is important to strike a balance when using anchor text. Over-optimization or excessive use of keywords can be considered spammy by search engines and result in penalties. Moreover, anchor text should be diversified to include a mix of branded, exact match, and partial match keywords to avoid algorithmic devaluation.

In marketing management, optimizing anchor text involves understanding the target audience, conducting keyword research, and analyzing the competition. By effectively deploying anchor text, marketing managers can improve their websites' visibility, increase organic traffic, and ultimately, achieve their marketing goals.

App Store Optimization (ASO)

App Store Optimization (ASO) is a strategic process in the field of Marketing Management that aims to improve the visibility and discoverability of mobile applications in app stores. It involves various techniques and tactics to optimize the app's metadata, design, and performance in order to increase its ranking and organic downloads.

The primary goal of ASO is to enhance the app's conversion rate by attracting more users to download and install it. This is achieved through a combination of keyword optimization, compelling app descriptions, engaging screenshots and videos, and positive user reviews. ASO also takes into account factors such as user engagement, retention, and app ratings, as these influence the app's ranking in search results and top charts.

ASO is essential for app developers and marketers to ensure their app is highly visible among the millions of apps available in the app stores. By improving the app's rank and visibility, ASO helps increase organic downloads, reduces user acquisition costs, and boosts the overall success of the app. It is an ongoing process that requires continuous monitoring, analysis, and optimization to adapt to changes in user behavior, trends, and algorithms employed by app stores.

In summary, App Store Optimization is a specialized practice within Marketing Management that focuses on optimizing various aspects of mobile applications to increase their visibility, attract more organic downloads, and ultimately drive the success of the app in the competitive app marketplace.

App Store Optimization Tools

App Store Optimization (ASO) tools refer to a set of software or platforms used by marketing managers to optimize mobile applications in app stores such as the Apple App Store and Google Play Store. ASO tools are designed to improve the visibility and discoverability of mobile apps, ultimately leading to increased organic app downloads and user engagement.

ASO tools encompass a range of features and functionalities that aid marketing managers in analyzing, monitoring, and optimizing various aspects of an app's presence in app stores. These tools provide valuable insights and data on keywords research, competitor analysis, app ratings and reviews, and app performance metrics.

With ASO tools, marketing managers can perform keyword research to identify the most relevant and high-traffic search terms for their app. They can track their app's rankings for specific keywords and adjust their ASO strategies accordingly to improve visibility. Additionally, these tools allow managers to analyze the metadata of their app, including app title, description, and screenshots, to optimize them for better conversion and user experience.

Competitor analysis is another crucial aspect of ASO, and these tools provide insights into competitors' keywords, rankings, and strategies. By analyzing competitors, marketing managers can make informed decisions and fine-tune their own ASO strategies to stay ahead in the market.

ASO tools also enable marketing managers to monitor and respond to app reviews and ratings. The tools provide notifications for new reviews and facilitate easy management of user feedback, helping managers to maintain a positive brand image and improve user satisfaction.

In summary, ASO tools are an essential part of marketing management for mobile apps. These tools empower marketing managers to optimize their app's presence and performance in app stores, leading to increased organic app downloads and user engagement.

Attention Economy

The attention economy is a concept in marketing management that recognizes attention as a scarce resource in today's digital age. It refers to the competition among various entities to capture and retain the limited attention of consumers. As consumers are bombarded with an overwhelming amount of information and stimuli, their attention becomes a valuable commodity.

In this context, marketing managers must devise strategies to effectively capture and maintain consumer attention amidst the noise and distractions. They need to create compelling and relevant content that resonates with their target audience, grabbing their attention and keeping them engaged. These strategies may include innovative and attention-grabbing advertisements, personalized messages, or experiential marketing techniques.

Furthermore, the attention economy also emphasizes the importance of building long-term relationships with customers. Marketing managers need to go beyond capturing initial attention and focus on sustaining attention over time. This can be achieved by delivering consistent value and engaging experiences, as well as by leveraging consumer data and insights to personalize interactions.

In the attention economy, attention is not a limitless resource. Therefore, marketing managers must be mindful of not only capturing attention but also respecting consumers' attention by avoiding intrusive or irrelevant marketing tactics. By understanding the dynamics of the attention economy and employing effective strategies, marketing managers can enhance brand awareness, improve customer loyalty, and drive business success in the digital era.

Attribution Modeling

Attribution modeling is a marketing management concept that refers to the process of determining the value or impact of different marketing channels or touchpoints on consumer behavior and the ultimate conversion or sale. It involves assigning credit or attribution to each touchpoint along the consumer's journey and analyzing their relative contribution to the overall marketing success.

In other words, attribution modeling is a way to understand and measure the effectiveness of various marketing efforts in driving customer engagement and generating desired outcomes. It helps marketers in deciphering which marketing channels or tactics are most influential in driving conversions or sales, and therefore, enables them to make informed decisions about allocating resources and optimizing marketing strategies.

Augmented Reality (AR) Ads

Augmented Reality (AR) Ads are a marketing strategy that utilizes augmented reality technology to deliver immersive and interactive advertising experiences to consumers. AR Ads blend virtual and real-world elements to engage and captivate users, while also promoting products and services.

AR Ads leverage the power of mobile devices, wearable devices, or dedicated AR devices to overlay virtual content onto a user's real-world environment. This technology allows advertisers to create unique and personalized brand experiences that go beyond traditional advertising methods.

Augmented Reality (AR) Marketing

Augmented Reality (AR) Marketing, within the context of the Marketing Management discipline, refers to the strategic utilization of augmented reality technology to create interactive and immersive marketing experiences for consumers.

AR Marketing involves the integration of digital content, such as images, videos, or animations, into the real-world physical environment. This technology allows marketers to overlay virtual elements onto the real world, enhancing consumer experiences and engagement with the brand.

By leveraging AR Marketing, companies can deliver unique and memorable brand experiences that effectively capture and retain consumer attention. Through the use of AR-enabled devices, such as smartphones or tablets, customers can interact with virtual objects or access additional information about products and services in real-time.

AR Marketing provides marketers with the opportunity to create personalized and targeted campaigns that resonate with consumers on a deeper level. By tailoring the virtual content to specific customer segments, companies can enhance the relevance and effectiveness of their marketing messages.

Moreover, AR Marketing enables companies to track and analyze consumer behavior and engagement with the virtual content. This data can be used to refine marketing strategies and optimize future campaigns, leading to improved overall marketing performance.

B2B Marketing

B2B Marketing, also known as business-to-business marketing, is a marketing strategy focused on selling products or services from one business to another. In this context, the "B2B" represents the relationship between the two businesses, distinguishing it from business-to-consumer (B2C) marketing. B2B marketing is a subset of marketing management that specifically addresses the unique challenges and characteristics of business-to-business transactions.

The main goal of B2B marketing is to establish and foster relationships between businesses, with the aim of generating sales and long-term partnerships. Unlike B2C marketing, which often focuses on emotional appeals and individual consumer needs, B2B marketing is more rational and logic-based, targeting key decision-makers within organizations.

B2B marketing strategies typically involve a mix of traditional and digital marketing techniques. These may include targeted advertising, content marketing, lead generation, email marketing, trade shows, and networking events. Additionally, B2B marketers often rely on market research and data analysis to identify and understand their target audience and develop effective marketing campaigns.

Given the complexity of B2B transactions, relationship-building and trust are crucial in B2B marketing. B2B marketers must strive to create value for their target businesses by offering tailored solutions, providing expertise, and demonstrating a deep understanding of their clients' needs and goals.

In conclusion, B2B marketing is a specialized marketing discipline that focuses on selling products or services from one business to another. It involves the development of targeted strategies and tactics to build relationships, generate sales, and foster long-term partnerships in a rational and logic-based manner.

B2B2C Marketing (Business To Business To Consumer)

B2B2C marketing, or Business to Business to Consumer marketing, is a marketing strategy that involves a company selling its products or services to other businesses (B2B) in order to reach the end consumers (B2C). It can also be referred to as B2B to C marketing.

This type of marketing approach is commonly used when a business wants to expand its target audience and reach a wider customer base. By partnering with other businesses, they can leverage their existing customer base and distribution channels to sell their products or services to the end consumers.

B2C Marketing

B2C Marketing, or Business-to-Consumer Marketing, is a fundamental aspect of the Marketing Management discipline that focuses on the strategies and tactics used by organizations to promote their products or services directly to consumers.

Unlike B2B (Business-to-Business) Marketing, which involves selling products or services between businesses, B2C Marketing involves targeting individual consumers as the end customers. The goal of B2C Marketing is to create awareness, generate interest, and ultimately drive purchase behavior among consumers.

In order to effectively engage with consumers, B2C Marketing utilizes a variety of channels and techniques, such as advertising, public relations, direct marketing, social media marketing, content marketing, and influencer marketing. These channels are employed to capture consumers' attention, generate brand recognition, and influence their decision-making process.

B2C Marketing heavily relies on market research and consumer behavior analysis to develop targeted marketing campaigns. Through the understanding of consumer needs, preferences, and motivations, organizations can tailor their marketing efforts to resonate with their target audience.

In today's digital era, B2C Marketing has evolved with the advent of e-commerce and online platforms. Online advertising, search engine optimization, email marketing, and personalized web experiences have become crucial components of B2C Marketing strategies.

Overall, B2C Marketing plays a vital role in establishing and maintaining strong relationships between organizations and their consumers. By effectively communicating the value proposition of their products or services and understanding the evolving consumer landscape, organizations can achieve market success and drive revenue growth.

B2G Marketing (Business To Government)

B2G Marketing, also known as Business to Government Marketing, refers to the marketing efforts and strategies employed by businesses to promote their products or services directly to government agencies or departments at various levels (local, state, or federal).

In the context of the Marketing Management discipline, B2G Marketing involves identifying and targeting government entities as potential customers and developing marketing campaigns specifically tailored to their needs and requirements. Unlike B2C (Business to Consumer) or B2B (Business to Business) marketing, B2G marketing focuses on selling to governmental bodies, which often have unique purchasing processes, regulations, and budgets.

Behavioral Advertising

Behavioral advertising refers to a marketing strategy that utilizes consumer data and online behavioral patterns to deliver targeted advertisements to individuals. It involves analyzing users' browsing history, search queries, and other online activities to understand their interests, preferences, and purchasing behavior.

By tracking and collecting information about users' online behavior, marketers can create personalized and relevant advertisements that are more likely to resonate with their audience. This approach allows advertisers to increase the effectiveness of their campaigns by delivering the right message to the right people at the right time.

Behavioral Economics

Behavioral economics is a field of study that combines elements of psychology and economics to understand and predict individual and group behavior when making economic decisions. It seeks to understand how people actually behave in real-world situations, rather than assuming rational decision-making.

From a marketing management perspective, behavioral economics plays a crucial role in analyzing consumer behavior and designing effective marketing strategies. It recognizes that consumers are not always rational and logical in decision-making processes. Rather, they are influenced by various psychological and social factors that can subtly affect their choices.

By studying behavioral economics, marketing managers can gain insights into consumer motivations, preferences, and decision-making processes. This understanding allows them to develop targeted marketing campaigns that are more likely to resonate with consumers and drive desired behaviors.

Additionally, behavioral economics helps marketers recognize common biases and cognitive shortcuts that affect consumer decision-making. For instance, the concept of loss aversion suggests that consumers feel the pain of loss more strongly than the pleasure of gain. Marketing managers can leverage this knowledge to craft messaging and pricing strategies that appeal to consumers' aversion to loss.

Overall, behavioral economics provides valuable tools and frameworks for marketers to better understand and influence consumer behavior. By incorporating psychological insights into their strategies, marketing managers can increase the effectiveness and impact of their marketing efforts, ultimately driving business success.

Behavioral Segmentation Analysis

Behavioral segmentation analysis is a marketing management technique that categorizes consumers into distinct groups based on their behavior patterns and actions. It involves analyzing and understanding consumer behaviors, such as purchasing habits, usage patterns, brand loyalty, and decision-making processes, in order to create targeted marketing strategies.

By segmenting consumers based on their behavior, marketers can better understand their needs, preferences, and motivations. This allows them to develop tailored marketing campaigns that are more likely to resonate with specific consumer groups. Behavioral segmentation analysis helps companies identify different customer segments, define their specific characteristics and requirements, and design marketing efforts that meet their unique needs.

Behavioral Segmentation

Behavioral segmentation is a marketing strategy that involves dividing a market into different groups based on consumers' behavior, preferences, and buying patterns. This segmentation approach is used by marketing managers to understand and target specific consumer segments in order to develop effective marketing strategies.

Behavioral segmentation is based on the idea that consumers' behavior and purchasing decisions are influenced by various factors such as their usage rate, loyalty, benefits sought, occasions, and their response to marketing strategies. By analyzing these behavioral patterns, marketers can gain insights into consumers' needs, wants, and preferences, and tailor their marketing efforts accordingly.

For example, a company may segment their market based on consumers' usage rate, dividing them into heavy users, moderate users, and light users. This allows the company to develop specific marketing campaigns and offers for each segment based on their consumption behavior.

Another example of behavioral segmentation is segmenting the market based on consumers' loyalty to a brand. The company can identify loyal customers and develop loyalty programs or incentives to retain their business, while also targeting non-loyal customers with persuasive marketing strategies to encourage them to switch to their brand.

Overall, behavioral segmentation is a valuable tool in marketing management as it allows marketers to understand consumer behavior and preferences in order to develop targeted marketing strategies, increase customer satisfaction, and ultimately drive sales and revenue.

Behavioral Targeting

Behavioral targeting refers to the marketing strategy that utilizes online consumer behavior data to personalize and tailor promotional efforts. It involves analyzing and tracking consumers' browsing patterns, preferences, and interests across various digital platforms, such as websites, social media, and mobile applications. This data-driven approach aims to understand individual consumer behavior in order to deliver relevant and customized content, advertisements, and offers.

In the field of marketing management, behavioral targeting plays a crucial role in improving the effectiveness and efficiency of marketing campaigns. By analyzing previous online activities and interactions, marketers can identify and target specific consumer segments based on their interests and preferences. This enables them to deliver personalized advertisements that resonate with consumers' needs and desires.

Below-The-Line (BTL) Advertising

Below-the-Line (BTL) advertising refers to a marketing communication strategy that utilizes non-traditional and direct promotional methods to reach a targeted audience. Unlike Above-the-Line (ATL) advertising, which focuses on mass media channels like television, radio, and print, BTL advertising employs more targeted and customized approaches to engage consumers.

A key characteristic of BTL advertising is its ability to create personalized interactions with customers. This approach often involves direct engagement through channels such as email, direct mail, telemarketing, and events. BTL advertising aims to establish one-on-one communication and build relationships with customers, as well as influence their purchasing decisions.

The primary objective of BTL advertising is to achieve specific marketing goals, such as increasing brand awareness, generating leads, driving sales, and enhancing customer loyalty. BTL strategies can be customized to suit the needs and preferences of different customer segments, allowing companies to effectively target specific groups of consumers.

Furthermore, BTL advertising often provides measurable results, enabling marketers to evaluate the success of their initiatives. By utilizing various tracking mechanisms and analytics tools, marketers can assess the impact of specific BTL campaigns and make data-driven decisions to optimize future efforts.

In summary, BTL advertising encompasses a range of tactics that directly engage with customers on a personalized level. This approach offers a more targeted and customized alternative to mass media channels, allowing marketers to establish meaningful connections and achieve specific marketing objectives.

Bid Management

Bid management in the context of marketing management is the process of planning, strategizing, and executing bids or proposals in order to secure new contracts, projects, or business opportunities. It involves creating compelling and competitive bids that address the needs and requirements of the clients or customers, while also aligning with the goals and objectives of the organization.

The bid management process typically starts with identifying relevant opportunities through market research and analysis. This includes identifying potential clients, understanding their needs, and evaluating the competition. Once a suitable opportunity is identified, the bid management team develops a detailed plan that outlines the approach, scope, timeline, and resources required for the bid.

During the bid preparation phase, the team gathers relevant information, such as technical specifications, pricing models, and legal terms and conditions. They also collaborate with various stakeholders, including subject matter experts, sales teams, and legal and finance departments, to ensure all aspects of the bid are addressed.

Once the bid is ready, it is submitted to the client within the specified deadline. The bid management team may also be responsible for managing any negotiations or discussions with the client during the evaluation process. In some cases, they may need to revise or update the bid based on client feedback or changes in the requirements.

The ultimate goal of bid management is to win new business and secure profitable contracts or projects. It requires strong project management skills, effective communication and collaboration, and a thorough understanding of the market and the client's needs. Additionally, bid management often requires continuous improvement and learning from past experiences to increase the chances of success in future bids.

Big Data Analytics

Big Data Analytics refers to the process of examining and dissecting vast amounts of data in order to uncover valuable insights and patterns that can be used to inform marketing strategies and decision-making. In the context of Marketing Management, Big Data Analytics involves collecting, organizing, and analyzing large and complex datasets to identify trends, preferences, and customer behavior.

By leveraging advanced technologies and analytical techniques, Big Data Analytics enables marketers to gain a deeper understanding of their target audience, customer preferences, and market trends. It allows marketers to uncover hidden patterns and correlations, revealing valuable insights that can guide the development of effective marketing campaigns and strategies.

Additionally, Big Data Analytics empowers marketers to make data-driven decisions and predictions, enabling them to optimize marketing efforts, identify new market opportunities, and enhance customer experience. It provides marketers with the ability to personalize marketing messages and offers based on individual customer preferences and behaviors.

Furthermore, Big Data Analytics facilitates the measurement and evaluation of marketing efforts, allowing marketers to track the performance and effectiveness of their campaigns in real-time. By analyzing various marketing metrics and key performance indicators, marketers can gain valuable insights into the success of their marketing initiatives and make informed decisions for future marketing activities.

Blog Marketing Strategies

Blog marketing strategies refer to the tactics and approaches used by marketers to promote and market their products or services through blog platforms. In the field of marketing management, these strategies focus on leveraging the power of blogging to increase brand awareness, drive website traffic, and engage with the target audience.

One common blog marketing strategy is content creation, which involves regularly publishing informative and engaging blog posts that cater to the interests and needs of the target market. By delivering valuable content, marketers aim to position their brand as a thought leader and build trust with consumers. Additionally, content creation helps improve search engine optimization (SEO) by generating relevant keywords and backlinks.

Blog Marketing

Blog marketing is a marketing strategy that involves using blogs as a platform to promote products, services, or content. It is a form of content marketing that aims to attract and engage a target audience by creating valuable and relevant blog posts.

In the context of marketing management, blog marketing plays a crucial role in building brand awareness, driving website traffic, enhancing customer engagement, and generating leads. It is a cost-effective method that allows businesses to establish thought leadership and credibility in their industry.

Brand Activation

Brand Activation in the context of Marketing Management refers to the strategic process of creating awareness and building a strong connection between a brand and its target audience. It involves leveraging various marketing techniques and communication channels to engage consumers and encourage them to interact with the brand.

The objective of brand activation is to enhance the brand's visibility, generate positive brand experiences, and ultimately drive consumer loyalty and advocacy. It is a dynamic approach that goes beyond traditional advertising and focuses on creating meaningful interactions and relationships with consumers.

Brand Advocacy Programs

A Brand Advocacy Program is a strategic marketing initiative that aims to leverage the influence and enthusiasm of loyal customers to promote and endorse a brand or its products or services. It involves identifying and nurturing brand advocates who are passionate and loyal customers willing to recommend the brand to others.

These programs work by fostering a strong relationship between the brand and its advocates, creating a sense of loyalty and partnership. Brand advocates are typically provided with exclusive benefits, rewards, or incentives for their support and dedication. They may also be given early access to new products, opportunities to provide feedback and suggestions, or participate in brand events.

The primary objective of a Brand Advocacy Program is to harness the power of word-of-mouth marketing, as advocates often have extensive networks and can influence purchasing decisions of others based on their personal experiences and recommendations. By mobilizing brand advocates, companies can generate positive buzz, increase brand awareness, and drive customer acquisition.

Implementing a Brand Advocacy Program requires careful identification and selection of potential advocates, as well as ongoing engagement and support. Brands need to foster a genuine and authentic relationship with their advocates, ensuring transparency, and open communication.

Overall, Brand Advocacy Programs play a crucial role in creating a community of loyal and vocal brand supporters who voluntarily amplify the brand's message, values, and offerings. By tapping into the power of brand advocates, companies can establish credibility, enhance customer satisfaction and loyalty, and ultimately drive business growth.

Brand Advocate

A brand advocate, in the context of Marketing Management, refers to an individual or customer who actively promotes and supports a particular brand or company. This person not only uses the brand's products or services but also voluntarily shares positive experiences and recommendations with others, both online and offline.

The role of a brand advocate is vital in today's competitive market as they help drive brand awareness, credibility, and customer loyalty. Through their genuine enthusiasm and advocacy, brand advocates influence their social circles, peers, and followers to consider and trust the brand, ultimately leading to increased customer acquisition and retention.

Brand Alignment Strategies

A brand alignment strategy refers to the process of ensuring that a company's brand identity and messaging are consistent across all marketing channels and touchpoints. It involves aligning the brand's values, personality, positioning, and visuals with its target audience, market segment, and overall marketing objectives.

The goal of brand alignment is to create a cohesive and recognizable brand image that resonates with consumers and differentiates the company from competitors. It helps establish trust and credibility, enhances brand awareness and recognition, and ultimately drives customer loyalty and purchase intent.

Brand Alignment

Brand alignment refers to the process of ensuring all aspects of a brand, including its messaging, visuals, and customer experience, are consistent and in harmony with the brand's core values, goals, and positioning. It is a crucial concept in marketing management as it helps maintain a cohesive and unified brand image and identity across all touchpoints.

When a brand is aligned, it means that its various marketing activities, such as advertising campaigns, social media presence, and product offerings, are all in sync and reinforce the brand's core message. This consistency builds trust and familiarity with consumers, making it easier for them to recognize and connect with the brand.

Brand alignment involves a holistic approach that requires careful attention to every detail of a brand's communication and experience. This includes aligning the brand's visual elements, such as logo, colors, and typography, with its desired image and target audience. It also involves ensuring that the brand's messaging, including its tagline, value propositions, and product descriptions, are aligned with its intended positioning and desired perception.

Achieving brand alignment requires effective communication and coordination among different departments within an organization, including marketing, design, customer service, and operations. It involves defining a clear and consistent brand strategy and guidelines that all stakeholders can follow. Regular monitoring and evaluation of the brand's alignment are also essential to identify any inconsistencies or areas for improvement.

Brand Ambassador Management

Brand Ambassador Management in the context of Marketing Management discipline refers to the process of selecting, training, and coordinating individuals, known as brand ambassadors, who represent and promote a brand or product to the target audience.

The primary goal of brand ambassador management is to build and maintain a positive and authentic brand image by leveraging the influence and credibility of these ambassadors. Brand ambassadors can be employees of the company or external individuals who are passionate about the brand and its values. They act as the face of the brand and play a crucial role in engaging with customers, creating brand awareness, and driving sales.

Brand ambassador management involves several key activities. Firstly, it involves identifying and selecting individuals who align with the brand's values, target audience, and marketing objectives. Once selected, these ambassadors are provided with comprehensive training and guidance on the brand's messaging, product knowledge, and promotional strategies.

To effectively manage brand ambassadors, regular communication and coordination are essential. This includes providing them with the necessary marketing materials, tracking their activities and performance, and providing feedback and support. Brand ambassador management also involves monitoring and evaluating their impact on brand perception, customer engagement, and sales metrics.

In summary, brand ambassador management is a critical component of marketing management that focuses on recruiting, training, and coordinating individuals who act as the brand's representatives and promoters. It plays a vital role in building brand reputation, increasing customer trust, and driving business growth.

Brand Ambassador Program

A brand ambassador program is a marketing strategy in which a company recruits individuals (usually customers or influential individuals) to represent and promote the brand in a positive and authentic way. These brand ambassadors often have a strong online presence, such as a large following on social media platforms, and are able to reach and engage with a wide audience.

The main goal of a brand ambassador program is to increase brand awareness, build brand loyalty, and drive sales. Brand ambassadors act as advocates for the brand, sharing their positive experiences and recommendations with their network. They may do this through various activities, such as posting sponsored content on social media, hosting product giveaways, writing reviews, or participating in events and promotions.

By leveraging the influence and credibility of brand ambassadors, companies can tap into new markets and reach potential customers who may not have been aware of the brand before. Brand ambassadors are often seen as more trustworthy and reliable compared to traditional advertising methods, as their recommendations come from personal experiences rather than paid advertisements.

However, it is important for companies to carefully select and manage their brand ambassadors to maintain the authenticity and integrity of the program. They should choose individuals who align with the brand values and target audience, and provide them with the necessary tools and support to effectively promote the brand. Regular communication and feedback are also essential to ensure brand ambassadors stay motivated and continue to represent the brand in a positive manner.

Brand Ambassador Selection

A brand ambassador is an individual, typically chosen by a company, who serves as the face of the brand and promotes its products or services to target audiences. In the context of marketing management, the selection of a brand ambassador plays a crucial role in building brand awareness, establishing brand credibility, and driving customer engagement.

The process of brand ambassador selection involves carefully identifying individuals who align with the brand's values, image, and target market. These individuals should possess qualities, such as trustworthiness, authenticity, and influential social presence, which make them capable of effectively communicating the brand's message and influencing consumer buying decisions.

Brand Ambassador

A brand ambassador is an individual, typically a well-known personality or influencer, who is hired by a company to promote and represent their brand and products. They are responsible for creating a positive image of the brand and increasing awareness and recognition among the target audience.

Brand ambassadors play a crucial role in marketing management as they act as the face of the brand, embodying its values and ideals. They are chosen based on their credibility and influence in the industry, as well as their ability to connect with the target market.

Brand Architecture

Brand architecture refers to the hierarchical structure and relationship of a company's brands within a portfolio, with the aim of creating a cohesive and effective brand strategy. It encompasses the way in which brands are organized, presented, and connected to each other to maximize customer understanding and brand value.

In marketing management, brand architecture plays a critical role in guiding brand decisions and shaping consumer perceptions. It enables companies to manage and leverage their brand portfolio effectively by defining the relationships between different brand elements, such as sub-brands, product lines, and individual product brands.

There are different types of brand architecture models, including a monolithic or "branded house" model where all products and services are unified under one master brand, a "sub-brands" model where multiple sub-brands operate independently under a parent brand, and a "house of brands" model where each product or service has its own distinct brand identity.

The choice of brand architecture depends on various factors, including the company's business objectives, target market, and the competitive landscape. Regardless of the chosen model, an effective brand architecture facilitates brand recognition, differentiation, and customer loyalty. It helps consumers make sense of a company's wide range of offerings, builds brand equity, and enables efficient brand extensions and diversification.

In summary, brand architecture is an essential strategic tool in marketing management that provides a framework for organizing and positioning brands within a company's portfolio. It ensures clarity and consistency in brand communication, strengthens brand equity, and contributes to long-term business success.

Brand Asset Valuator (BAV)

The Brand Asset Valuator (BAV) is a marketing management tool used to measure and evaluate the strength and value of a brand. It was developed by Young & Rubicam (Y&R), a global advertising agency, and is widely used in the marketing industry.

BAV assesses brands based on four key dimensions - Differentiation, Relevance, Esteem, and Knowledge. Differentiation measures the degree to which a brand stands out from its competitors and offers unique benefits to consumers. Relevance determines how well the brand meets the needs and desires of its target audience. Esteem captures the level of consumer respect and admiration for the brand. Knowledge measures the consumer awareness and understanding of the brand.

The BAV framework utilizes a combination of quantitative and qualitative research methods to gather data on these dimensions. Surveys, interviews, and focus groups are conducted to collect information from consumers, while secondary research is used to gather market data and competitor insights.

Once the data is collected, it is analyzed and scored to generate a Brand Strength Index (BSI). The BSI provides a numerical measure of a brand's overall strength, allowing marketers to compare and rank different brands within a specific industry or market.

The BAV framework also helps identify brand positioning and growth opportunities. By understanding the strengths and weaknesses of a brand across the four dimensions, marketers can develop strategies to improve brand performance, differentiate from competitors, and create a stronger connection with consumers.

Brand Awareness Campaign

A brand awareness campaign is a strategic marketing effort aimed at increasing the recognition and recall of a brand among its target audience. It involves implementing various tactics and activities to build familiarity and credibility with consumers, ultimately leading to improved brand recognition, loyalty, and market share.

The primary goal of a brand awareness campaign is to create top-of-mind awareness, ensuring that consumers think of a particular brand when they have a need for a specific product or service. By increasing brand awareness, companies can differentiate themselves from their competitors and establish a strong presence in the market.

Businesses typically execute brand awareness campaigns through various channels, including advertising, public relations, social media, and events. The campaign may involve creating compelling brand messaging, designing eye-catching visuals, and crafting engaging content to capture the attention of the target audience.

Measurement and evaluation are crucial components of a brand awareness campaign. Companies monitor various metrics, such as brand recognition, brand recall, and brand sentiment, to assess the effectiveness of their efforts. The insights gathered from these evaluations enable marketers to make informed decisions and optimize their campaigns to achieve the desired outcomes.

Overall, a brand awareness campaign is an integral part of a company's marketing strategy, helping to enhance brand perception, increase customer engagement, and ultimately drive business growth.

Brand Awareness

Brand awareness refers to the level of familiarity that consumers have with a particular brand. It is a measure of how well a brand is known and recognized by the target market. Brand awareness is an important concept in marketing management as it directly influences consumer decision-making and brand perception.

There are two main components of brand awareness: brand recognition and brand recall. Brand recognition involves the ability of consumers to identify a brand based on its visual or verbal cues, such as a logo or a tagline. Brand recall, on the other hand, refers to the ability of consumers to retrieve and remember a brand from memory when prompted with a product or service category.

In order to build brand awareness, marketers employ various strategies and tactics. These may include advertising campaigns, sponsorships, public relations activities, social media engagement, and content marketing. By consistently exposing the target audience to the brand's messaging and visual identity, marketers aim to increase brand recognition and recall.

Brand awareness is important because it lays the foundation for brand equity and brand loyalty. When consumers are familiar with and have positive associations with a particular brand, they are more likely to choose it over competitors. Brand awareness also helps in generating word-of-mouth referrals and attracting new customers.

Brand Building

Brand building refers to the process of creating and enhancing the perceptions and associations that consumers have with a particular brand. It involves strategically shaping a brand's identity, values, and positioning in order to differentiate it from competitors and create a strong and positive brand image in the minds of consumers.

Brand building is essential for businesses as it helps to establish and maintain customer loyalty. A well-built brand provides a sense of trust, credibility, and familiarity, which encourages repeat purchases and helps to attract new customers. Additionally, a strong brand can command higher prices, as consumers are willing to pay a premium for products or services associated with a reputable and desirable brand.

Brand Collateral Design

Brand Collateral Design refers to the process of creating marketing materials and assets that are used to promote a brand and communicate its value to the target audience. It involves the design and development of various visual and non-visual elements such as logos, business cards, brochures, letterheads, templates, and promotional merchandise.

When designing brand collateral, marketers consider the brand's visual identity, messaging, and overall marketing strategy. The objective is to create a cohesive and consistent brand image across all touchpoints and communication channels. Brand collateral design plays a vital role in building brand awareness, establishing brand credibility, and fostering brand loyalty.

Brand Collateral

Brand collateral refers to the collection of visual and written assets that are used to promote and represent a brand. These assets are designed to communicate the brand's identity, values, and key messages to its target audience. Brand collateral plays a crucial role in marketing management as it helps to build brand recognition and loyalty.

Visual assets in brand collateral typically include the brand logo, colors, typography, and imagery. These elements are used consistently across various marketing materials such as websites, advertisements, packaging, and social media posts. A cohesive visual identity helps consumers to visually recognize and associate these materials with the brand, reinforcing brand awareness and recall.

Written assets in brand collateral include slogans, taglines, brand stories, and key messages. These written elements are carefully crafted to convey the brand's unique selling propositions, values, and positioning. By using consistent language and tone across different channels, brands can create a coherent and memorable brand voice that resonates with their target audience.

Effective brand collateral is essential for building brand equity and maintaining a consistent brand image in the minds of consumers. It helps to differentiate the brand from its competitors, build trust and credibility, and establish an emotional connection with consumers. Marketing managers are responsible for developing and managing brand collateral to ensure consistency and alignment with the brand's overall marketing strategy.

Brand Community

A brand community is a group of people who are connected by their shared experiences, interests, and values related to a particular brand. It is a community that forms around a specific brand and is centered on the brand's products, services, and overall brand image.

In the context of marketing management, brand communities play a crucial role in building brand loyalty and creating a strong brand identity. They provide a platform for customers to engage with the brand and with other like-minded individuals who share a similar passion or interest in the brand.

27

Brand communities serve as a means for customers to connect with the brand on a deeper level. They allow customers to feel a sense of belonging and to actively participate in the brand's activities and events. This active participation helps to create a sense of ownership and attachment to the brand, leading to increased loyalty and advocacy.

Moreover, brand communities also provide valuable insights and feedback for the brand. Through discussions and interactions within the community, customers can express their opinions, share their experiences, and provide suggestions for improvement. This feedback helps the brand management team to understand customer needs and preferences better and enables them to make informed decisions regarding product development, marketing strategies, and customer engagement initiatives.

In summary, a brand community is a group of individuals connected by their shared interest in a particular brand. It fosters brand loyalty, creates a strong brand identity, and provides valuable insights for the brand management team. By cultivating and nurturing brand communities, marketers can effectively engage with their customers and build long-lasting relationships.

Brand Consistency Monitoring

Brand Consistency Monitoring refers to the process of ensuring that a brand's messaging, visuals, and overall appearance remain consistent across various marketing channels and touchpoints. It involves regularly reviewing and evaluating the brand's marketing materials, advertisements, social media content, website, packaging, and any other customer-facing assets to maintain a standardized brand image.

In the context of Marketing Management, brand consistency monitoring is essential for building and maintaining brand equity. It helps organizations protect their brand reputation, establish brand recognition, and foster brand loyalty among customers. By ensuring consistent brand messaging and visuals, companies can effectively communicate their value proposition, differentiate themselves from competitors, and create a cohesive brand experience for consumers.

Brand Consistency

Brand consistency refers to the uniformity and coherence of a brand's messaging, imagery, and overall identity across all marketing and communication channels. It is a crucial aspect of marketing management that aims to create a strong and recognizable brand presence in the minds of consumers.

The consistent use of brand elements, such as logos, colors, typography, and tone of voice, helps to establish a sense of familiarity and trust among consumers. When a brand is consistent in its messaging and visual identity, it becomes more memorable and distinguishes itself from competitors. This consistency also helps to reinforce the brand's values, personality, and positioning in the market.

Brand Differentiation Tactics

Brand differentiation tactics are marketing strategies employed by companies to establish their brand as unique and distinct from their competitors in the marketplace. In the field of marketing management, brand differentiation is a critical concept that can significantly impact a company's success.

These tactics involve creating and promoting unique selling propositions (USPs) that set a brand apart from its competitors. USPs are specific attributes or characteristics that make a brand unique and provide value to its target customers. They can include factors such as product features, quality, price, customer service, or even the brand's ethical values.

Companies utilize various techniques to implement brand differentiation. These tactics can include innovation and product development to create new and unique offerings that competitors do not offer. They can also involve branding and positioning strategies that communicate the distinctiveness and value of the brand to consumers. Effective communication and marketing campaigns play a crucial role in establishing and reinforcing brand differentiation.

Brand differentiation tactics are essential for companies to stand out in crowded markets and capture the attention and loyalty of consumers. They enable brands to carve out a distinct identity and position themselves in a way that resonates with their target audience. By highlighting their unique attributes and advantages, companies can create a competitive advantage that sets them apart from their competitors.

In summary, brand differentiation tactics are marketing strategies aimed at establishing a brand as unique and distinct from its competitors. They encompass various techniques, including creating unique selling propositions, innovation, branding, positioning, and effective communication. These tactics are essential for companies to differentiate themselves and attract customers in competitive markets.

Brand Differentiation

Brand Differentiation refers to the process of establishing a unique and distinguishable brand image or identity in the minds of consumers in order to stand out from competitors in the marketplace. It is a strategic marketing approach that focuses on creating a clear and compelling perception of a brand's offerings, values, and advantages.

Brand differentiation encompasses various marketing efforts that aim to highlight the unique attributes, features, and benefits of a brand that make it distinct from others. This can include product features, design elements, pricing strategies, communication style, customer experience, and overall brand positioning. By effectively differentiating their brand, companies can create a competitive advantage and gain a stronger foothold in the market.

Brand Equity Analysis

Brand equity analysis refers to the evaluation of the value and strength of a brand in the marketing management discipline. It involves assessing and measuring the perception and recognition of a brand among consumers, as well as the financial value and market share it holds in its industry. This analysis aids marketers in understanding the effectiveness of their branding strategies and the overall performance of the brand.

Brand equity analysis encompasses various dimensions, such as brand awareness, brand associations, brand loyalty, and perceived quality. By examining these dimensions, marketers can determine the overall strength of a brand in relation to its competitors. Brand awareness measures the extent to which consumers are familiar with and recognize a particular brand. Brand associations assess the positive or negative associations consumers have with the brand, such as its reputation, personality, or values. Brand loyalty measures the extent to which consumers are committed to purchasing products or services from a specific brand, while perceived quality evaluates consumers' perception of the brand's product or service quality.

Brand Equity Building

Brand equity building refers to the process of enhancing the value and reputation of a brand in the eyes of consumers and stakeholders. It is a strategic marketing approach that aims to create a strong and positive perception of the brand, leading to increased customer loyalty, market share, and profitability.

This process involves various activities and strategies, such as consistent brand messaging, effective advertising and promotion, quality product and service delivery, superior customer experiences, and building strong relationships with customers and other stakeholders.

Brand Equity Measurement

Brand Equity Measurement refers to the process of evaluating and quantifying the value and strength of a brand in the market. It involves assessing various dimensions such as brand awareness, brand perception, brand loyalty, and brand associations to determine the overall impact and worth of a brand.

Marketing Management, as a discipline, is concerned with analyzing and managing the various aspects of marketing within an organization. It aims to create, communicate, deliver, and exchange offerings that have value for customers, clients, partners, and society at large. Brand equity measurement is a crucial component of marketing management as it helps in understanding the effectiveness and competitiveness of a brand.

Brand Equity

Brand Equity refers to the perceived value that a consumer attaches to a brand. It is a measure of brand loyalty and recognition, as well as the overall positive or negative associations that consumers have with a particular brand.

In marketing management, brand equity is a crucial concept as it directly impacts a company's profitability and market success. A strong brand equity allows a company to differentiate its products or services from competitors, gain customer loyalty, charge premium prices, and expand into new markets. On the other hand, a weak brand equity can result in low customer trust, reduced market share, and decreased profitability.

Brand equity is built over time through various marketing strategies and efforts, such as advertising, product quality, customer service, and brand positioning. It is influenced by factors like brand awareness, brand associations, perceived quality, brand loyalty, and brand personality.

Measuring brand equity involves evaluating consumer perception and behavior towards a brand. This can be done through market research surveys, brand tracking studies, and analysis of financial performance metrics. By understanding the level of brand equity, companies can make informed decisions on marketing investments and strategies to enhance or protect their brand's value.

Brand Experience Design

Brand Experience Design is a strategic process that combines marketing and design principles to create a holistic and engaging brand experience for customers. It is a discipline within Marketing Management that focuses on designing every touchpoint of a brand's interaction with its target audience, with the aim of creating positive emotions and perceptions that align with the brand's values and goals.

Through Brand Experience Design, marketing managers seek to develop a cohesive and consistent brand identity that resonates with consumers at every point of contact, whether it be through advertisements, packaging, website design, social media presence, or in-store experiences. By carefully crafting each element of the customer journey, from initial brand awareness to post-purchase loyalty, marketers can enhance customer satisfaction, build brand equity, and ultimately drive business growth.

Brand Experience

A brand experience refers to the overall perception and impression that a consumer has of a particular brand based on their interactions with the brand across various touchpoints.

In the context of marketing management, brand experience plays a crucial role in shaping consumer behavior and influencing purchase decisions. It encompasses all the tangible and intangible elements associated with a brand, such as its products, services, employees, marketing communications, and physical or digital environments.

Effective brand experiences are designed to engage consumers, evoke emotions, build trust, and foster long-term loyalty. By creating positive and memorable experiences, brands can differentiate themselves from competitors and establish a strong brand identity in the minds of consumers.

Brand experiences can be influenced by a range of marketing strategies and tactics, including advertising, public relations, product design, customer service, and digital marketing. These strategies aim to create a cohesive and consistent brand image that resonates with the target audience.

Furthermore, brand experiences are not limited to individual interactions but extend to the overall customer journey. Brands need to ensure that each touchpoint, from initial awareness to post-purchase support, aligns with their intended brand positioning and messaging.

Ultimately, a positive brand experience can result in increased customer satisfaction, repeat purchases, brand advocacy, and ultimately contribute to the long-term success and profitability of a brand.

Brand Extension

A brand extension is a marketing strategy that involves using an established brand name to introduce a new product or enter a new market. It is a way for companies to leverage the equity and recognition associated with their existing brand to extend their reach and capture additional market share.

Brand extensions are typically done when a company believes it has developed a strong and positive brand image that can be easily transferred to a new product or market. The goal is to capitalize on the existing brand's reputation, customer loyalty, and brand equity to drive sales and create a competitive advantage in the new market.

There are two main types of brand extensions: line extensions and category extensions. A line extension involves introducing new products within the same product category under an existing brand. For example, a company that produces toothpaste may introduce a new flavor or whitening variant under their established brand name.

A category extension, on the other hand, involves using an existing brand to enter a different product category or market segment. For example, a clothing brand may expand into accessories or footwear. Category extensions can be riskier because they require the brand to be relevant and credible in a new context.

Brand Guidelines Compliance

Brand Guidelines Compliance refers to the adherence of a company's branding guidelines and standards across all marketing efforts and communication channels. It is a crucial aspect of the Marketing Management discipline as it ensures that the brand image and messaging remain consistent, coherent, and aligned with the company's overall strategic goals.

Brand guidelines typically include specifications on the logo usage, color palette, typography, imagery, tone of voice, and other visual and verbal elements that collectively represent the brand's identity. These guidelines serve as a set of rules and standards that all marketing materials, campaigns, and communications must follow.

Compliance with brand guidelines is important for several reasons. Firstly, it helps establish and maintain a strong brand identity and recognition in the market. Consistency in branding ensures that customers can easily identify and associate certain attributes and qualities with the brand, which in turn builds trust and loyalty.

Secondly, brand guidelines compliance ensures that all marketing efforts and communication channels convey a cohesive and unified message. This promotes clarity and avoids confusion among the target audience, as well as helps in delivering a consistent brand experience across different touchpoints.

Thirdly, compliance with brand guidelines helps protect the brand's integrity and reputation. By adhering to the established guidelines, companies can prevent any misrepresentation or dilution of their brand, ultimately preserving its value and uniqueness in the market.

Brand Guidelines Enforcement

Brand Guidelines Enforcement refers to the process of ensuring that the prescribed rules and standards outlined in a brand's style guide are consistently applied and adhered to across all marketing materials and touchpoints.

These guidelines serve as a set of rules that define how a company's brand identity should be communicated visually and verbally, including elements such as logo usage, color palettes, typography, tone of voice, and overall design aesthetic. By enforcing these guidelines, companies strive to maintain a consistent, cohesive brand image that resonates with their target audience and fosters brand recognition and loyalty.

Brand Guidelines

Brand guidelines are a set of rules and specifications that define how a brand should be visually and verbally portrayed in order to ensure consistency and cohesion in its communication and marketing materials. These guidelines are developed by the marketing management team and serve as a reference document for internal and external stakeholders, including designers, writers, vendors, and employees, to maintain a unified and differentiated brand image.

The purpose of brand guidelines is to establish and reinforce the visual and verbal identity of a brand, helping to create a strong and recognizable presence in the market. These guidelines typically include information on logo usage, typography, color palette, photography style, tone of voice, and overall design principles. By adhering to these guidelines, a brand can effectively communicate its values, personality, and offerings to its target audience, while setting itself apart from competitors.

Brand Health Assessment

A brand health assessment is a systematic evaluation of a brand's overall performance and perception in the market. It is a crucial tool in marketing management that helps analyze a brand's strengths, weaknesses, opportunities, and threats, allowing companies to make informed decisions and devise effective strategies.

The assessment involves various metrics and indicators to gauge the brand's health and identify areas of improvement. These metrics may include brand awareness, brand equity, customer loyalty, market share, customer satisfaction, and brand reputation. By measuring these factors, marketing managers can assess the brand's current standing and benchmark it with competitors.

The purpose of conducting a brand health assessment is to diagnose the brand's performance, determine its market position, and uncover potential areas for growth and improvement. It provides insights into how well the brand is resonating with its target audience and whether it is meeting their needs and expectations.

By understanding the brand's health, marketing managers can make informed decisions regarding brand positioning, messaging, product development, pricing, distribution, and promotional activities. They can identify gaps in the market, address customer pain points, and capitalize on trends and opportunities.

In conclusion, a brand health assessment is a valuable tool for marketing managers to evaluate and improve a brand's performance in the market. It helps identify areas of strength and weakness, enables competitive benchmarking, and provides insights for strategic decision-making.

Brand Health

Brand health refers to the overall perception and reputation of a brand in the marketplace. It is a measure of how well a brand is performing and how it is perceived by its target audience, customers, and stakeholders. Brand health is a critical aspect of marketing management as it directly impacts a brand's ability to attract and retain customers, drive sales, and achieve long-term success.

Brand health is determined by various factors, including brand awareness, brand image, brand loyalty, and brand equity. A brand with a positive brand health score is typically recognized by its target audience and is associated with desirable qualities, such as trustworthiness, quality, and innovation. On the other hand, a brand with low brand health may struggle to differentiate itself from competitors and may face challenges in attracting and retaining customers.

Measuring brand health is essential for marketing managers as it provides insights into the effectiveness of marketing strategies and allows for the identification of areas for improvement. It involves conducting market research, such as customer surveys and brand tracking studies, to gather data on brand awareness, perception, and customer satisfaction. The collected data is then analyzed to assess the overall health of the brand and identify specific areas that require attention or enhancement.

In summary, brand health is a crucial metric in marketing management that assesses a brand's reputation and perception in the marketplace. It helps marketing managers understand how well a brand is performing and enables them to make data-driven decisions to improve brand awareness, image, and customer loyalty.

Brand Identity Management

Brand Identity Management refers to the strategic and consistent management of all elements associated with a brand in order to create a positive and distinct perception in the minds of consumers. It encompasses the coordination and control of various branding elements, such as the brand name, logo, slogan, color palette, typography, packaging, and overall brand messaging.

As a critical aspect of Marketing Management, Brand Identity Management aims to establish and maintain a strong and unique brand identity that resonates with the target market and differentiates the brand from its competitors. This involves defining and articulating the brand's positioning, values, personality, and promise, and ensuring that they are consistently communicated across all marketing channels and touchpoints.

Brand Identity

A brand identity refers to the set of visual, verbal, and sensory elements that convey the unique characteristics, values, and personality of a brand to its target audience. It is a strategic tool used by organizations to differentiate themselves from competitors and create a lasting impression on consumers.

The visual aspect of brand identity includes elements such as logo, color palette, typography, and imagery. These elements are carefully chosen to reflect the brand's essence and create a consistent and recognizable visual representation across different marketing channels and touchpoints. The verbal aspect involves the brand's name, tagline, key messages, and tone of voice, which are used to communicate the brand's values, positioning, and key attributes in a compelling way.

The sensory aspect of brand identity focuses on creating a holistic brand experience that engages the senses and strengthens the emotional connection with consumers. This can include elements such as sound, smell, taste, and touch, which are used to create memorable and immersive brand interactions.

By establishing a clear and consistent brand identity, organizations can effectively communicate their unique value proposition, build brand awareness and recognition, develop customer loyalty, and ultimately drive business success. It allows consumers to associate certain attributes and emotions with a brand, making it easier for them to make purchasing decisions and fostering trust and loyalty in the long term.

Brand Image Enhancement Techniques

Brand image enhancement techniques refer to a set of strategies and methods implemented by a company or organization to improve the perception and reputation of their brand in the minds of their target market. These techniques are employed in the field of Marketing Management to shape the way consumers perceive and interact with a brand, thus influencing their purchasing decisions and building brand loyalty.

Various techniques can be used to enhance brand image, including:

The first technique involves conducting market research and analysis to understand consumer preferences, needs, and brand perceptions. This helps in identifying the gaps and areas of improvement in the brand image.

Secondly, companies can focus on improving their product quality and design, ensuring that it aligns with the values and expectations of their target market. By consistently delivering high-quality products, brands earn trust and credibility among consumers.

Thirdly, effective communication and branding strategies play a crucial role in enhancing brand image. This includes developing a unique brand identity, consistent messaging, visual elements like logos and taglines, and leveraging digital platforms to reach and engage with the target audience.

Furthermore, brands can enhance their image by actively engaging in corporate social responsibility initiatives. By supporting causes and demonstrating a commitment to social and environmental issues, brands build a positive image and connect emotionally with their customers.

Lastly, building strong relationships with customers through personalized experiences, exceptional customer service, and loyalty programs can contribute to enhancing brand image. Satisfied customers not only become brand advocates but also influence others' perceptions of the brand.

Brand Image Enhancement

Brand image enhancement refers to the strategic activities and efforts undertaken by an organization to improve and shape the perception, reputation, and overall image of its brand among its target audience and stakeholders. It is a key aspect of marketing management discipline as it directly impacts consumer behavior, brand loyalty, and long-term business success.

Organizations strive to enhance their brand image to differentiate themselves from competitors, build a strong and positive brand identity, and establish a favorable and trustworthy reputation in the market. This involves various marketing strategies and techniques, such as advertising, public relations, corporate communications, product positioning, brand messaging, and brand experience design.

Brand Image

A brand image refers to the perception and reputation that a particular brand holds in the minds of consumers. It is the overall impression and associations that consumers have about a brand, which influences their purchasing decisions and loyalty towards the brand.

Brand image is a critical aspect of marketing management as it helps shape how consumers perceive and interact with a brand. It is built through various marketing strategies and efforts, including advertising, public relations, packaging, and customer experiences.

A strong brand image is essential for a company as it helps differentiate their products or services from competitors and establishes a unique identity in the marketplace. It also enhances brand loyalty, enables premium pricing, and drives customer preference and advocacy.

Building and managing a brand image requires consistent messaging and communication that aligns with the brand's values, positioning, and target audience. It involves creating a positive and favorable perception of the brand through storytelling, visual elements, customer testimonials, and social proof.

However, a brand image can be influenced by both internal and external factors. Negative experiences, poor product quality, or unethical behavior can harm a brand's image and lead to a loss of trust and credibility among consumers. It is, therefore, crucial for companies to monitor and manage their brand image proactively to ensure it remains positive and relevant in the dynamic marketplace.

Brand Licensing Agreements

A brand licensing agreement is a formal contractual agreement between a brand owner and a licensee that grants the licensee the right to use the brand's intellectual property, such as trademarks, logos, and copyrights, in exchange for a fee or royalty. This agreement allows the licensee to manufacture and/or distribute products or services under the brand name, leveraging the brand's existing reputation and equity to enhance their own business.

The licensing agreement typically outlines the specific terms and conditions surrounding the brand's usage, including the scope of the license, the territories or markets in which the licensee is authorized to operate, the duration of the agreement, and any limitations or restrictions imposed by the brand owner.

This form of brand extension strategy offers several benefits for both the brand owner and the licensee. For the brand owner, licensing agreements can generate additional revenue streams and expand the brand's reach into new markets, without the need for significant investment or operational involvement. It also allows the brand to capitalize on the licensee's expertise and resources, potentially increasing brand exposure and consumer awareness.

For the licensee, acquiring the rights to use an established brand can provide instant recognition and credibility, reducing the time and costs associated with building a brand from scratch. It also allows the licensee to tap into the brand's loyal customer base and benefit from its established marketing channels, enhancing their chances of success in the market.

Brand Licensing

Brand licensing is a marketing strategy that involves granting permission to a third party to use a brand's intellectual property, such as logos, trademarks, or copyrighted material, in exchange for a fee or royalty. This licensing arrangement allows the licensee to manufacture, distribute, or promote products or services using the brand's identity, while the licensor retains ownership and control over the brand.

By licensing its brand, a company can extend its reach and generate additional revenue streams without having to invest in manufacturing or distribution. It can leverage the popularity and equity of its brand to enter new markets or product categories, tapping into the licensee's expertise and resources. This can be particularly beneficial in industries where the brand holds a strong position and has a loyal customer base.

This marketing strategy offers several advantages for both the licensor and the licensee. For the licensor, brand licensing can increase brand visibility and exposure, enhance brand loyalty, and create brand extensions or co-branded opportunities. It can also provide a steady stream of income through licensing fees or royalties. On the other hand, the licensee benefits from using a well-known brand to attract customers, enter new markets, and differentiate its products or services from competitors.

However, brand licensing also poses certain risks and challenges. The licensor must carefully select licensees that align with its brand image and values to maintain consistent branding and avoid diluting the brand's equity. Additionally, the licensee must ensure compliance with the terms of the licensing agreement to avoid legal issues or negative impacts on the brand's reputation.

Brand Loyalty Program Implementation

A brand loyalty program implementation refers to the strategic process of planning, designing, and executing a program aimed at cultivating and maintaining loyal customers for a particular brand. It involves the development and implementation of various strategies and tactics to incentivize customers to repeatedly choose and purchase products or services from a specific brand over its competitors.

Marketing management professionals play a crucial role in the successful implementation of brand loyalty programs. They are responsible for analyzing customer behavior and preferences, identifying target segments, and creating relevant value propositions to attract and retain customers. These professionals collaborate with other departments, such as sales, operations, and finance, to ensure seamless integration and execution of the loyalty program.

Key components of brand loyalty program implementation include:

1. Program Design: This involves defining the program's objectives, determining the target audience, and selecting appropriate program features and rewards that align with customer preferences and brand values.

2. Communication and Promotion: Effective communication and promotion are vital to create awareness and engagement among customers. Marketing managers use various channels, such as social media, email marketing, and in-store signage, to communicate program benefits and motivate customer participation.

3. Customer Data Analysis: Marketing managers leverage customer data to gain insights into individual preferences and purchase behavior. This information helps in personalizing program offers and creating targeted marketing campaigns to enhance customer satisfaction and loyalty.

4. Measurement and Evaluation: Regular monitoring and evaluation are critical to assess the program's effectiveness and identify areas for improvement. Marketing managers use key performance indicators (KPIs) and customer feedback to measure program success and make necessary adjustments.

In summary, brand loyalty program implementation entails the strategic development and execution of initiatives aimed at fostering long-term customer loyalty and ultimately increasing brand profitability. Marketing management professionals play a crucial role in planning, executing, and evaluating these programs to ensure their success.

Brand Loyalty Program

A brand loyalty program is a strategic marketing initiative implemented by a company to encourage repeat customer purchases and create a sense of loyalty towards the brand. It is a structured system that rewards customers, typically in the form of incentives, discounts, or exclusive benefits, for consistently choosing and supporting a particular brand over its competitors.

The primary objective of a brand loyalty program is to build and maintain long-term relationships with customers, ultimately increasing customer retention and fostering brand loyalty. By offering rewards and incentives, companies aim to create a sense of value and appreciation for their customers, motivating them to continue purchasing from the brand rather than switching to a competitor.

Brand loyalty programs can take various forms, such as point systems, membership clubs, tiered programs, or personalized offers. These programs often utilize technology, such as customer databases or mobile apps, to track and manage customer participation and rewards.

Effective brand loyalty programs not only drive repeat sales but also contribute to brand advocacy, as satisfied customers are more likely to recommend the brand to others. Furthermore, these programs provide valuable data and insights into customer behavior and preferences, helping companies refine their marketing strategies and tailor their offerings to better meet customer needs.

Brand Loyalty

Brand loyalty is a concept within the discipline of Marketing Management that refers to a customer's preference for a particular brand over other alternatives based on a deep emotional and psychological connection. It is a measure of the extent to which a customer consistently chooses a specific brand and continues buying its products or services, even in the face of competing offers or market changes.

Brand loyalty is built through various factors, such as positive brand experiences, satisfaction with product or service performance, trust in the brand's reliability and quality, and identification with the brand's values and image. It involves developing strong customer relationships, fostering brand trust, and creating a sense of belonging and attachment to the brand.

Companies aim to cultivate brand loyalty because it leads to several advantages. Loyal customers are more likely to repurchase, thereby contributing to a stable revenue stream and increased market share. They are also less sensitive to price changes and are more willing to pay a premium for their preferred brand. Additionally, loyal customers tend to engage in positive word-of-mouth referrals, bringing in new customers and enhancing brand reputation.

To maintain and enhance brand loyalty, companies employ various marketing strategies. These include implementing loyalty programs, offering personalized experiences and rewards, providing exceptional customer service, and nurturing ongoing communication and engagement with customers through social media and other channels.

Brand Management Software

A brand management software refers to a technological tool that helps organizations effectively manage and control their brand identity, messaging, and overall brand experience in the marketplace. It facilitates the centralization and automation of various brand management activities, ensuring consistency, coherence, and compliance across all marketing channels and touchpoints.

By leveraging a brand management software, marketing teams can streamline and optimize their brand management processes, enabling them to efficiently create, update, and distribute brand assets such as logos, fonts, images, and brand guidelines. This software also provides a centralized platform for managing and maintaining brand collateral, allowing stakeholders from different departments, locations, or external agencies to easily access and collaborate on brand-related materials.

Furthermore, a brand management software offers functionalities for tracking and monitoring brand performance, including brand sentiment analysis, social media monitoring, and competitor analysis. It enables organizations to gather valuable insights into their brand perception, identify potential risks or opportunities, and make data-driven decisions to strengthen and enhance their brand positioning.

In summary, a brand management software serves as a comprehensive solution for managing all aspects of a brand, from visual identity to brand communication, ensuring consistency, efficiency, and strategic alignment in the ever-evolving marketing landscape.

Brand Management

Brand management is a marketing management discipline that involves analyzing, planning, and controlling all aspects of a brand in order to maximize its value and equity. It is the practice of ensuring that a brand's promise is consistently delivered to customers, employees, and stakeholders, while also aligning the brand with the organization's goals and objectives.

The process of brand management begins with understanding the brand's target market and positioning, conducting research and analysis to assess the brand's current reputation and perception, and developing a strategic plan to improve or maintain the brand's image. This includes identifying the brand's unique selling proposition, defining its core values and personality, and creating a compelling brand promise that resonates with consumers.

Once the brand strategy is in place, brand managers are responsible for implementing and executing marketing programs and activities that support the brand's objectives. This may involve developing and managing advertising campaigns, creating and distributing branded content, monitoring and responding to customer feedback and reviews, and coordinating with other departments within the organization to ensure consistency and alignment across all touchpoints.

Brand management also involves monitoring and measuring the brand's performance and health, using key metrics such as brand awareness, brand loyalty, and brand equity. By measuring the effectiveness of branding efforts, brand managers can identify areas for improvement and make data-driven decisions to enhance the brand's overall value and reputation.

Brand Performance Metrics

Brand performance metrics refer to a set of measurable indicators used to assess the effectiveness and success of a brand's marketing efforts. These metrics are essential for marketing managers to evaluate the performance of their brand and make data-driven decisions to improve marketing strategies.

Marketing managers track and analyze various brand performance metrics to gauge the brand's overall health, market position, and consumer perceptions. These metrics help assess the brand's ability to deliver value, build awareness, and maintain customer loyalty. They provide insights into how well the brand is meeting its marketing objectives and help identify areas for improvement.

Common brand performance metrics include brand equity, brand awareness, brand preference, brand loyalty, and brand perception. Brand equity measures the overall value and strength of a brand, including its reputation, customer loyalty, and market share. Brand awareness assesses the brand's visibility and recognition among the target audience. Brand preference determines the extent to which customers prefer a particular brand over competitors. Brand loyalty measures the level of customer commitment and repeat purchases. Brand perception focuses on customers' perceptions, associations, and feelings toward the brand.

By analyzing these metrics, marketing managers can gain insights into the effectiveness of their marketing strategies, identify strengths and weaknesses in the brand's positioning, and make informed decisions to enhance brand performance. The goal is to continuously improve the brand's market position and create strong brand equity, leading to increased customer loyalty, market share, and profitability.

Brand Personality Development

A brand personality is the set of human characteristics and traits that are attributed to a brand. It is an important concept in marketing management as it helps create a unique identity for a brand and establish an emotional connection with customers.

In the marketing context, brand personality development involves creating and shaping the personality of a brand to reflect its desired image and appeal to its target audience. This process involves defining the brand's personality traits, such as sincerity, excitement, competence, sophistication, ruggedness, and so on.

These traits are carefully chosen based on the brand's positioning and the characteristics that would resonate with the target market. Once the traits are identified, they are then integrated into various marketing strategies and communication channels to consistently convey the brand's personality to consumers.

For example, a brand aiming to project an image of sophistication and elegance may incorporate these traits into its packaging design, advertising campaigns, and customer service interactions. On the other hand, a brand targeting adventure-seeking individuals may incorporate traits like excitement and ruggedness in its visual branding and messaging.

A well-developed brand personality helps differentiate a brand from its competitors and creates a lasting impression in the minds of consumers. It not only influences consumer perceptions and purchase decisions but also creates strong brand loyalty and advocacy. Therefore, it is a crucial aspect of marketing management and requires careful consideration and strategic planning to ensure alignment with the brand's values, positioning, and target market.

Brand Personality

The brand personality is a concept in marketing management that refers to the set of human characteristics, traits, and qualities associated with a particular brand. It helps to establish a brand's unique identity and differentiate it from competitors in the market.

Similar to how each individual has their own personality, brands also possess a distinct personality that influences how they are perceived by consumers. This personality is the result of various factors such as brand positioning, brand messaging, visual identity, and overall brand experience.

Brand personality plays a crucial role in building brand equity and developing strong emotional connections with consumers. By defining and consistently portraying a specific personality, brands can attract and retain loyal customers who resonate with their values and traits.

There are several dimensions or archetypes commonly used to describe brand personalities, such as sincerity, excitement, competence, sophistication, and ruggedness. These dimensions help marketers create brand positioning strategies that align with the desired personality traits and resonate with the target audience.

In conclusion, the concept of brand personality in marketing management refers to the set of traits, characteristics, and qualities that define how a brand is perceived by consumers. It helps to differentiate the brand from competitors and build strong emotional connections with consumers, ultimately contributing to brand equity and loyalty.

Brand Positioning Strategies

Brand positioning strategies are the strategic actions and decisions taken by a company to create a unique and distinctive place for its brand in the minds of consumers. It involves identifying and defining the brand's target market, understanding the needs and preferences of the target audience, and establishing a unique value proposition that differentiates the brand from its competitors.

The brand positioning strategy aims to position the brand in a way that it stands out and resonates with the target market. This is achieved by carefully crafting the brand's messaging, imagery, and associations to evoke specific emotions, perceptions, and beliefs in the minds of consumers.

Brand Positioning

Brand positioning refers to the strategic process of establishing a distinct and favorable position for a brand in the minds of target consumers within a specific market. It involves crafting a unique identity and perception for the brand that differentiates it from competitors and resonates with the desired target audience.

The goal of brand positioning is to create a strong and memorable brand image that makes the product or service stand out from the competition and appeals to the target market. This is achieved by carefully selecting and communicating unique selling propositions (USPs) and key messages that highlight the brand's strengths, benefits, and value proposition.

Effective brand positioning requires a deep understanding of the target audience, market dynamics, and competitor landscape. It involves conducting thorough market research and analysis to identify opportunities, consumer needs, and competitor weaknesses. This information is then used to develop a positioning strategy that aligns with the brand's objectives and strengths.

The positioning strategy is typically expressed through various marketing elements such as brand messaging, taglines, logos, visual identity, and brand personality. These elements help to shape the brand's image and communicate its positioning to the target audience through advertising, promotional campaigns, product packaging, and other marketing channels.

Ultimately, successful brand positioning enables the brand to occupy a unique and advantageous position in the minds of consumers, thereby driving preference, loyalty, and purchase decisions. It is an ongoing process that requires continuous monitoring, adaptation, and evolution to remain relevant and competitive in the ever-changing marketplace.

Brand Recall Techniques

Brand recall techniques are strategies and methods used by marketers to enhance and maintain the recognition and remembrance of their brand among consumers. These techniques aim to ensure that the brand remains at the forefront of the consumer's mind when making purchasing decisions in the relevant product category.

The primary goal of brand recall techniques is to create a strong association between the brand and its key attributes or unique selling points. This is accomplished through various marketing activities such as advertising, public relations, and promotional campaigns. By consistently presenting the brand message and visually representing the brand identity across different channels and mediums, marketers aim to establish a lasting impression in the minds of consumers.

Some common brand recall techniques include:

- Repetition: Continuously exposing consumers to the brand's name, logo, tagline, and other brand elements through advertising and other communication channels.

- Association: Creating associations between the brand and positive emotions, experiences, or influential figures to generate favorable brand impressions and recall.

- Visual cues: Utilizing distinctive visual elements such as packaging, color schemes, and brand symbols that facilitate quick recognition and recall.

- Engaging storytelling: Using compelling narratives and storytelling techniques to captivate consumers' attention and connect emotionally with the brand.

- Consistency: Ensuring the brand message, tone, and visual identity remain consistent across all marketing touchpoints, reinforcing brand recall.

By implementing effective brand recall techniques, marketers can increase brand awareness, loyalty, and the likelihood of consumers choosing their brand over competitors when making purchase decisions within the product category.

Brand Recall

Brand recall is a marketing management concept that refers to the ability of consumers to correctly retrieve a brand in their memory when given a prompt. It is a measure of how well a brand is recognized and remembered by consumers.

In order to measure brand recall, marketers often use surveys or experiments to assess how easily consumers can remember a brand when given a specific cue. A common method is through aided recall, where respondents are presented with a list of brands and asked to identify those that they have heard of or seen before. Another method is through unaided recall, where consumers are asked to recall brands from memory without any prompts.

Brand recall is crucial for building brand awareness and establishing a strong brand presence in the marketplace. A brand that has high recall is more likely to be considered by consumers when making purchasing decisions and may have a competitive advantage over other brands that are not as well-remembered.

To enhance brand recall, marketers employ various strategies such as consistent and memorable branding elements (e.g., logos, taglines), effective advertising campaigns, and creating positive associations with the brand through positive experiences or emotional connections.

Brand Recognition

Brand recognition is a key concept within the field of marketing management. It refers to the degree to which a target audience can identify a particular brand by its attributes or characteristics, such as its logo, name, slogans, or overall visual identity. In essence, brand recognition measures the level of familiarity and recognition that consumers have with a specific brand.

Brand recognition is crucial for businesses as it plays a significant role in shaping customer perceptions and preferences. When consumers are familiar with a brand and can easily identify it, they are more likely to choose that brand over competitors, especially in a cluttered marketplace. A strong brand recognition also enhances brand loyalty, as customers tend to trust and prefer brands they are familiar with.

Brand Reputation Management

Brand Reputation Management refers to the strategic efforts undertaken by a company to manage, maintain, and enhance the perception and reputation of its brand among its stakeholders, including consumers, employees, investors, and the general public. It involves the ongoing monitoring, evaluation, and control of the different factors that shape the brand's image, such as customer reviews, social media presence, media coverage, and public opinion.

The primary goal of brand reputation management is to build a positive and credible brand image in the minds of consumers, which can lead to increased trust, loyalty, and preference for the brand. It involves various activities such as brand positioning, brand messaging, crisis management, and brand communication. By effectively managing its reputation, a brand can not only protect itself from negative publicity or crises but also capitalize on opportunities to reinforce its positive attributes and values.

Effective brand reputation management requires a combination of proactive and reactive strategies. Proactively, a company can focus on building a strong brand identity, delivering quality products or services, engaging with its audience through social media and other channels, and consistently delivering on its brand promises. Reactively, it involves promptly addressing any negative feedback or issues, resolving customer complaints, and managing public relations crises in a transparent and authentic manner.

Overall, brand reputation management plays a crucial role in shaping how a brand is perceived in the market. It is a continuous process that requires careful monitoring, analysis, and adaptation to ensure that the brand's image remains aligned with its intended positioning and resonates positively with its target audience.

Brand Reputation Monitoring

Brand Reputation Monitoring refers to the process of tracking and evaluating the perception and reputation of a brand or organization in the eyes of customers, stakeholders, and the general public. It involves monitoring and analyzing various sources of information, including social media platforms, online reviews, press coverage, and customer feedback, to gain insights into how the brand is perceived and regarded.

Marketing management professionals use brand reputation monitoring as a vital tool to assess the effectiveness of their marketing efforts and strategies. By closely monitoring the reputation of their brand, they can identify any negative perceptions or issues that may arise and take proactive steps to address them, thereby protecting the brand's image and ensuring its long-term success.

Brand Reputation Repair

Brand Reputation Repair refers to the strategic management process implemented by organizations to rebuild and enhance their damaged or tarnished brand image in the eyes of their target audience or stakeholders. It is a crucial aspect of Marketing Management that involves various activities and strategies aimed at restoring the positive perception and trust of the brand by addressing and rectifying the issues leading to a damaged reputation.

Effective brand reputation repair involves a comprehensive understanding of the factors influencing the negative perception and reputation damage, such as customer complaints, negative reviews, public scandals, or product failures. Organizations must conduct thorough research and analysis to identify the root causes of the damaged reputation and develop a well-defined strategy to address and resolve these issues.

Once the underlying issues are identified, organizations need to implement various tactics to repair their brand reputation. This may include improving product quality, customer service, communication strategies, and corporate social responsibility initiatives. Utilizing public relations, social media, and advertising channels can also help in rebuilding a positive brand image.

In addition to rectifying the damage, it is essential for organizations to establish effective brand monitoring systems to identify and address any potential reputation risks in the future. By consistently delivering on promises and maintaining transparent and ethical business practices, organizations can rebuild their brand reputation and regain the trust and loyalty of their customers and stakeholders.

Brand Reputation

Brand reputation refers to the perception, opinions, and overall image of a brand or organization in the eyes of stakeholders, including customers, employees, investors, and the general public. It is a fundamental aspect of marketing management, as it directly influences customer loyalty, purchase decisions, and brand equity.

A strong brand reputation is built on various factors, including brand awareness, quality, consistency, and trustworthiness. It is the result of effective branding strategies, product/service delivery, customer experiences, and public relations efforts. Moreover, it is shaped by feedback, reviews, and word-of-mouth communication shared by customers and other stakeholders.

Brand reputation plays a crucial role in the success of a brand or organization. It can drive customer loyalty, repeat purchases, and positive brand associations. A favorable reputation can also attract new customers, enhance market positioning, and create competitive advantage.

On the other hand, a negative brand reputation can lead to decreased customer trust, loss of market share, and financial implications. It can damage brand equity, hinder growth opportunities, and erode customer loyalty.

Therefore, managing and maintaining a positive brand reputation is essential for marketing managers. They must actively monitor and respond to customer feedback, address any negative issues promptly, and consistently deliver on brand promises. This involves creating strong relationships with customers, employees, and other stakeholders, as well as implementing effective brand communication and crisis management strategies.

Brand Storytelling Frameworks

Brand storytelling frameworks are strategic approaches used in marketing management to create and deliver compelling narratives that capture the essence of a brand and resonate with its target audience. These frameworks involve the use of storytelling techniques to communicate a brand's values, purpose, and unique selling proposition in a way that connects emotionally with consumers.

One widely recognized brand storytelling framework is the Hero's Journey, which was popularized by Joseph Campbell. This framework follows a narrative arc that involves a hero (the brand) embarking on a transformative journey, facing challenges, and ultimately emerging victorious. By aligning the brand's story with the stages of the Hero's Journey, marketers can create a captivating narrative that engages and inspires consumers.

Brand Storytelling Techniques

Brand storytelling techniques encompass the strategies and methods used by marketers to effectively communicate the brand's narrative and engage with consumers. It involves leveraging storytelling elements such as plot, characters, and emotions to create a compelling and cohesive brand message.

This technique emphasizes the power of storytelling to establish a deeper connection between the brand and its target audience. By presenting the brand's story in a coherent and engaging manner, marketers can shape the perception of the brand, differentiate it from competitors, and create a lasting impression in the minds of consumers.

Brand Storytelling

Brand storytelling is a strategic marketing approach that focuses on creating a narrative or storyline around a brand to engage and connect with consumers on an emotional level. It involves using various storytelling techniques, such as character development, plot development, and conflict resolution, to communicate the brand's values, personality, and purpose in a compelling and memorable way.

Brand storytelling revolves around the idea that consumers are more likely to connect with and remember stories rather than facts or data. By crafting an authentic and relatable brand story, marketers can tap into the power of emotions and human experiences to build a stronger connection with their target audience.

Brand Strategy

A brand strategy is a comprehensive plan that outlines the long-term goals, objectives, and approach to create a unique and consistent brand identity in order to achieve a competitive advantage in the market.

It involves a careful analysis of the target market, understanding consumer needs and preferences, evaluating competitors, and aligning the brand's values and positioning accordingly. The strategy encompasses various elements such as brand positioning, brand messaging, brand differentiation, and brand architecture.

The brand positioning defines how the brand wants to be perceived by its target audience in comparison to competitors. It aims to create a distinct place for the brand in consumers' minds and highlight its key attributes, benefits, and strengths. Brand messaging refers to the communication efforts used to convey the brand's value proposition and key messages to the target market.

Brand differentiation focuses on identifying and emphasizing unique brand attributes that set it apart from competitors. It helps to create a competitive advantage by highlighting the brand's distinctive features and benefits. Brand architecture refers to the organization and structure of a brand portfolio. It determines how various sub-brands, products, or services are organized and interconnected.

Overall, a brand strategy is a critical aspect of marketing management as it provides a roadmap for building and managing a successful brand. It helps to guide all brand-related decisions and actions, ensuring consistency and effectiveness in brand communication, customer experiences, and overall brand performance in the market.

Brand Value

Brand value refers to the perceived worth of a brand in the eyes of consumers and the market. It represents the financial value and intangible assets associated with a brand, such as brand equity, brand loyalty, brand recognition, and brand reputation. Brand value is a crucial concept in marketing management as it directly affects a company's competitive advantage, market share, and overall profitability.

The value of a brand is determined by various factors, including the brand's market position, its target audience, the quality and performance of its products or services, its marketing strategies, and the overall perception of the brand by consumers. A strong brand value can drive customer preference and loyalty, resulting in increased sales and market share for the company.

Measuring brand value is essential for marketers to make informed decisions about brand management, pricing strategies, advertising campaigns, and brand extensions. It helps businesses assess the effectiveness of their branding efforts and identify areas for improvement. Brand value can be quantified through financial metrics, such as brand equity, brand valuation, brand valuation multiples, and customer-based brand equity models.

Overall, brand value is a critical asset in marketing management that plays a significant role in shaping a company's market performance and success. It represents the culmination of a company's branding efforts and the intangible qualities that make a brand unique and valuable to consumers.

Brand Voice

Brand voice refers to the unique personality and tone of a brand's communication that reflects its values, culture, and target audience. It is an essential element of marketing management that helps to differentiate a brand from its competitors and create a consistent and memorable identity.

A brand voice encompasses various aspects such as the language, vocabulary, sentence structure, and emotions used in marketing messages across different channels, including advertising, social media, websites, and customer interactions. It should align with the brand's positioning and resonate with the target market, strengthening brand recognition and affinity.

When developing a brand voice, marketers consider factors like the brand's core values, the desired perception in the market, the characteristics of the target audience, and the competitive landscape. It should be authentic, genuine, and unique to create a lasting impression and build trust with consumers.

A well-defined brand voice helps to maintain consistency and coherence in the brand's communication, regardless of the platform or medium used. It guides the creation of content, messaging, and visuals, ensuring that they are cohesive and in line with the brand's personality and values.

In summary, brand voice plays a crucial role in marketing management by shaping a brand's identity, establishing its position in the market, and connecting with customers on an emotional level. It is an integral part of the overall brand strategy and contributes to building brand loyalty and advocacy.

Business Intelligence (BI)

Business Intelligence (BI) in the context of Marketing Management discipline refers to the process of collecting, analyzing, and interpreting data to gain deeper insights into market trends, customer behavior, and overall performance metrics. It involves utilizing various tools, technologies, and methodologies to gather and transform raw data into meaningful information that can inform strategic decision-making in marketing.

BI enables marketing professionals to identify patterns, discover correlations, and uncover hidden opportunities and threats in the marketplace. It allows them to track the effectiveness of marketing campaigns, measure customer satisfaction, and identify areas where performance can be improved. By leveraging BI, marketing managers can make data-driven decisions, optimize marketing efforts, and allocate resources more effectively.

Business-To-Government (B2G) Marketing

Business-to-Government (B2G) marketing refers to the marketing activities and strategies that businesses employ to promote their products and services to governmental entities. It involves the exchange of goods, services, or information between a business organization and a government agency at various levels, including local, regional, national, and international.

In the context of marketing management, B2G marketing involves understanding the unique needs, structures, and processes of government entities as customers. It requires businesses to tailor their marketing efforts and value propositions to meet the specific requirements and regulations set by the government. B2G marketing often involves longer sales cycles, complex procurement processes, and extensive legal and regulatory compliance.

The main objective of B2G marketing is to establish and maintain favorable relationships with government agencies to secure contracts, partnerships, or other business opportunities. This can be achieved through targeted marketing campaigns, building strong government networks and relationships, and providing customized solutions that address the government's specific needs and priorities.

Successful B2G marketing requires businesses to have a deep understanding of the political, social, economic, and legal factors that influence government decisions. It also involves effective communication and negotiation skills to navigate the bureaucratic nature of government procurement processes.

Buyer Persona

A buyer persona, in the context of Marketing Management, refers to a semi-fictional representation of an ideal customer based on market research and real data. It is designed to help marketers understand and empathize with their target audience by creating a detailed profile that outlines the demographics, behaviors, and goals of their potential customers.

A buyer persona goes beyond basic demographics to capture the essence of a specific target market segment. It takes into consideration factors such as age, gender, location, income, education, occupation, and family status. Additionally, it delves into the psychographic characteristics like personality traits, values, attitudes, interests, and lifestyle choices that influence the purchasing decisions of the target audience.

The development of buyer personas involves thorough research, data collection, and analysis. Marketers utilize a combination of methods including surveys, interviews, focus groups, and market analysis to gather the necessary data. The ultimate goal is to create a detailed profile that includes the buyer's pain points, challenges, motivations, preferences, and buying behavior patterns. This information is then used to tailor marketing strategies, messaging, and product offerings to effectively engage and convert the target audience.

In summary, a buyer persona is a strategic tool that enables marketers to understand and connect with their ideal customers. By developing a comprehensive profile based on research and data, marketers can create targeted marketing campaigns that resonate with their target audience and drive business growth.

Buyer's Journey

The Buyer's Journey refers to the process that a potential customer goes through when making a purchasing decision. It is a fundamental concept in marketing management as it helps businesses understand and cater to the needs and preferences of their target audience.

The journey can be divided into three main stages: awareness, consideration, and decision. During the awareness stage, customers become aware of a problem or a need that they have. They start researching and gathering information to understand more about the issue and potential solutions. Marketers can utilize this stage to create brand awareness and provide valuable content to educate and engage with their target audience.

In the consideration stage, customers have identified and defined their problem or need. They now evaluate different options and compare them to find the best possible solution. Marketers should focus on building relationships, providing relevant information, and showcasing the unique benefits of their products or services. This can be achieved through targeted advertising, personalized messaging, and testimonials or case studies.

Finally, during the decision stage, customers make a purchasing decision based on their evaluation of the available options. Marketers should make it easy for customers to complete the purchase by offering a seamless buying experience, clear pricing, and convenient payment options. Additionally, post-purchase follow-up and customer support are crucial in maintaining customer satisfaction and potentially generating repeat business or referrals.

Buzz Marketing

Buzz Marketing is a marketing management approach that focuses on creating a sense of excitement, interest, and anticipation around a product or brand by generating conversations, word-of-mouth referrals, and social media engagement.

Unlike traditional advertising methods, which rely on mass media to reach a broad audience, buzz marketing aims to create a "buzz" or a viral effect by targeting influential individuals or opinion leaders who can spread the message organically through personal recommendations and social interactions.

This form of marketing leverages the power of social networks, online platforms, and offline events to generate word-of-mouth publicity and capture the attention of consumers. By creating a buzz, companies aim to tap into consumers' curiosity, stimulate their interest, and generate a sense of exclusivity or urgency to drive sales and brand awareness.

Buzz marketing campaigns often rely on innovative and unconventional strategies to captivate the target audience. This may include creating unique and shareable content, organizing experiential marketing events, partnering with influencers, or leveraging user-generated content.

One of the key advantages of buzz marketing is its potential to amplify reach and engagement rapidly. When executed effectively, a buzz marketing campaign can spread like wildfire, reaching a wide audience without heavy reliance on advertising budgets.

In conclusion, buzz marketing is a strategic approach that aims to generate excitement and interest in a product or brand through targeted word-of-mouth referrals and social media engagement. By leveraging the power of social networks and influential individuals, companies can create a buzz that captivates consumers and drives brand awareness and sales.

Buzz Monitoring Tools

Buzz monitoring tools are software applications or platforms used by marketing managers to track and analyze online conversations, mentions, and discussions about their brand, products, or services. These tools scan various online sources such as social media platforms, blogs, forums, news sites, and review websites to collect data on brand mentions, sentiment, and overall perception.

By monitoring buzz, marketing managers are able to gain valuable insights into how their brand is being perceived and talked about online. These tools provide real-time data analysis and reporting, allowing managers to identify emerging trends, track the effectiveness of marketing campaigns, and measure the impact of their brand's online presence.

Buzz Monitoring

Buzz monitoring in the context of marketing management refers to the systematic process of tracking and analyzing conversations, discussions, and mentions about a brand, product, or company on various online platforms and social media channels.

It involves monitoring and analyzing user-generated content, such as online reviews, comments, tweets, blog posts, news articles, and forum discussions, to gain insights into consumer sentiment, brand perception, and overall online buzz surrounding a product or brand.

Buzzword Marketing

Buzzword marketing refers to the practice of using trendy or popular terms and phrases in marketing campaigns or strategies. These buzzwords are often used to create a sense of excitement or novelty around a product or service, and to appeal to the current interests and preferences of consumers.

In the context of marketing management, buzzword marketing can be seen as a tool or tactic used by companies to grab attention and generate buzz around their products or brand. By incorporating popular buzzwords into their marketing messaging, companies hope to make their offerings appear more relevant and appealing to their target audience.

The use of buzzwords in marketing can be effective in attracting attention and generating interest, especially in today's fast-paced and highly competitive business environment. However, it is important for marketing managers to use buzzwords strategically and authentically, as consumers can quickly see through gimmicks or insincere attempts to appear trendy.

While buzzword marketing can help create initial excitement and generate buzz, it is ultimately the value and quality of the product or service that will determine its success in the market. Marketing managers should focus on delivering on the promises made in their buzzword-driven campaigns and ensure that the product or service lives up to the expectations they have created.

Buzzword Strategy

Buzzword Strategy refers to the use of buzzwords or trendy terms in marketing management to attract attention and create a perception of innovation or relevance. This strategy aims to leverage popular or emerging buzzwords to make a brand, product, or service appear more appealing or cutting-edge.

Marketing managers may adopt a buzzword strategy to align their brand with current trends or to differentiate themselves from competitors. By incorporating buzzwords into their marketing messages, they hope to generate brand buzz, capture audience attention, and position their offerings as must-haves in the industry.

CVR Improvement Techniques

CVR Improvement Techniques refer to the strategies and tactics implemented by organizations in the field of Marketing Management to enhance their Conversion Rate (CVR). CVR is a crucial metric that measures the percentage of website visitors who take a desired action, such as making a purchase, signing up for a newsletter, or filling out a contact form.

The goal of CVR Improvement Techniques is to optimize the conversion process and increase the likelihood of visitors completing the desired action. This is achieved through various methods, including:

1. A/B Testing: This technique involves creating two or more versions of a webpage or advertisement and testing them against each other to determine which one performs better in terms of conversion. By experimenting with different elements, such as headlines, layouts, colors, and calls-to-action, marketers can identify the most effective combination to drive conversions.

2. User Experience (UX) Design: Enhancing the overall user experience is crucial for boosting CVR. This includes optimizing website navigation, improving site speed, ensuring mobile responsiveness, and simplifying the checkout process. By providing a seamless and intuitive user experience, companies can reduce friction and increase the likelihood of conversions.

3. Personalization: Tailoring the marketing message and content to individual customers can significantly impact CVR. By leveraging data and segmentation, marketers can deliver personalized recommendations, offers, and messages that resonate with customers' specific needs and preferences, thereby increasing the chances of conversion.

4. Clear and Compelling Call-to-Actions (CTAs): Effective CTAs play a vital role in driving conversions. Marketers need to create concise, action-oriented messages that clearly communicate the value proposition and prompt users to take the desired action. By using persuasive language and prominent placement, CTAs can effectively guide visitors towards conversion.

Call Center

A call center is a dedicated department or unit within an organization that handles a large volume of incoming and outgoing calls from customers, potential customers, or other individuals. It is an integral part of marketing management as it serves as a communication hub between the company and its target audience, providing support, information, and resolving queries or concerns.

The main function of a call center is to manage customer interactions efficiently and effectively. This includes answering inquiries about products or services, processing orders, providing technical support, handling complaints or disputes, and conducting market research or surveys. Through these interactions, call center agents play a vital role in building and maintaining customer relationships, which is crucial for marketing success.

A call center typically utilizes various technologies, such as customer relationship management (CRM) systems and automatic call distribution (ACD) systems, to streamline operations and enhance customer service. These systems help in routing incoming calls to the appropriate agent, maintaining customer records, tracking customer interactions, and generating reports for analysis and improvement.

Furthermore, call centers may employ different types of communication channels, including telephone calls, emails, live chats, and social media platforms, to connect with customers. This multi-channel approach allows for flexibility and convenience in customer interactions, meeting their preferences and needs.

Overall, call centers are a key component of marketing management, as they serve as a direct line of communication between the company and its customers. By providing personalized and efficient customer service, call centers contribute to customer satisfaction, loyalty, and ultimately, the success of the organization's marketing efforts.

Call Tracking

Call Tracking in the context of Marketing Management is a process that aims to track and record phone calls generated by marketing activities, campaigns, or channels. It involves the use of specialized software and tools to capture relevant data, such as the caller's phone number, call duration, call recordings, and other crucial information.

Call tracking provides marketers with valuable insights into the effectiveness and ROI of their marketing efforts, particularly in relation to phone call conversions. By assigning unique phone numbers to different marketing campaigns or channels, marketers can identify which campaigns or channels are driving the most calls and conversions. This allows them to allocate their marketing budget more efficiently and optimize their campaigns based on accurate data and analysis.

Call To Action (CTA)

A Call to Action (CTA) is a marketing term that refers to prompts or statements designed to encourage immediate responses or actions from target audiences. CTAs are strategic tools used to guide customers or prospects towards a desired action, such as making a purchase, subscribing to a newsletter, signing up for a free trial, or filling out a form.

CTAs are an integral part of marketing management as they help generate conversions and drive customer engagement. They typically aim to capture the attention of the target audience, create a sense of urgency, and provide clear instructions on what actions they should take.

Well-crafted CTAs are concise, persuasive, and relevant to the target audience's needs and desires. They often use action-oriented verbs or phrases that generate excitement and motivate customers to act immediately. For example, phrases like "Buy now," "Subscribe today," "Start your free trial," or "Download now" are commonly used in CTAs.

CTAs can take various forms depending on the marketing channel and objective. They can appear as clickable buttons, hyperlinks, banners, or pop-up messages on websites, emails, social media posts, advertisements, or landing pages. The design, placement, and visibility of a CTA are crucial factors that can affect its effectiveness.

Effective CTAs help marketers drive desired actions from target audiences, ultimately contributing to the achievement of marketing objectives, such as increasing sales, generating leads, or growing brand awareness. Thus, mastering the art of crafting compelling CTAs is vital for marketers seeking to maximize their marketing efforts and achieve desired outcomes.

Call-Only Ad Strategies

Call-only ad strategies are a type of advertising campaign used in the field of marketing management. They involve creating ads that are specifically designed to encourage users to make phone calls to a business rather than clicking through to a website. These ads typically appear on search engine results pages or in mobile apps, and are only displayed on devices that can make phone calls.

The main objective of call-only ad strategies is to drive phone calls to the business, as these phone calls often lead to higher conversion rates and greater customer engagement. This type of advertising can be particularly effective for businesses that rely heavily on phone-based interactions, such as service providers or local businesses. It allows them to connect directly with potential customers and provide a more personalized and immediate experience.

Call-Only Ads

Call-only ads are a type of advertisement that are specifically designed to encourage potential customers to make a phone call to the advertiser directly. These ads typically appear on search engine results pages and are differentiated from other types of ads by their call-only feature, which makes it easy for users to call the advertiser with just a single tap on their mobile device.

In the context of Marketing Management, call-only ads provide businesses with a direct and immediate way to connect with potential customers. By bypassing the need for users to visit a website or fill out a form, call-only ads streamline the conversion process and allow businesses to acquire leads more efficiently.

Call-To-Action (CTA) Optimization

A Call-to-Action (CTA) Optimization is an essential aspect of marketing management that focuses on improving the effectiveness of CTA elements in marketing campaigns. A CTA is a specific instruction or prompt that encourages and directs potential customers to take immediate action, such as making a purchase, subscribing to a newsletter, or requesting more information.

The process of CTA optimization involves various strategic techniques to enhance the visibility, attractiveness, and conversion rate of CTAs. This includes optimizing the placement, design, size, color, wording, and overall prominence of CTAs to encourage desired actions from the target audience.

Campaign Optimization Algorithms

An algorithm refers to a step-by-step procedure or set of rules that are followed in order to solve a problem or complete a task. In the context of marketing management, campaign optimization algorithms can be defined as a systematic approach to improving the effectiveness and efficiency of marketing campaigns.

These algorithms are designed to analyze, measure, and adjust various elements of a marketing campaign, such as target audience, messaging, media channels, and budget allocation, with the goal of maximizing the campaign's performance and return on investment.

Campaign Optimization

Campaign optimization refers to the continuous process of improving and refining marketing campaigns to achieve the desired outcomes and maximize the return on investment (ROI). It involves analyzing campaign performance, identifying areas for improvement, implementing changes, and monitoring the results to ensure optimal outcomes.

In the context of marketing management, campaign optimization plays a crucial role in maximizing the effectiveness and efficiency of marketing efforts. It involves applying various strategies and techniques to enhance campaign performance, such as targeting the right audience, selecting the appropriate marketing channels, optimizing messaging and creative elements, and allocating resources effectively.

Cannibalization Analysis

Cannibalization analysis is a strategic tool used in marketing management to evaluate the potential negative impact of introducing a new product or service on the sales of existing products or services within the same company. It involves measuring the extent to which the new offering could "cannibalize" or eat into the sales of established offerings.

By conducting a cannibalization analysis, marketing managers can assess the level of risk associated with introducing a new product or service. This analysis is critical as it helps in making informed decisions about product portfolio management, pricing, and overall marketing strategy.

During cannibalization analysis, various factors are considered, including the target market, customer preferences, pricing, and product differentiation. The analysis aims to identify the potential customer overlap between the new offering and the existing products, and determine whether the new product will attract new customers or merely shift sales from the existing products.

If the cannibalization analysis reveals a high risk of cannibalization, marketing managers may need to reconsider the launch of the new product or explore strategies to mitigate the negative impact. This could involve adjusting the positioning or pricing of the new offering, creating product bundles that encourage sales of both the new and existing products, or implementing targeted marketing campaigns to attract different customer segments.

Ultimately, cannibalization analysis enables marketing managers to make informed decisions about new product development and ensure that the launch of a new offering does not cannibalize the sales of existing products, thus maximizing overall profitability and market share.

Cannibalization Avoidance

Cannibalization avoidance is a strategy employed in the field of marketing management to mitigate the negative impact of introducing new products or services on existing ones within the same organization. It involves careful and deliberate planning to ensure that the launch of a new offering does not cannibalize or erode the market share, sales, or profitability of the company's existing offerings.

This strategy aims to prevent the scenario where the sales or demand for a new product comes at the expense of the sales or demand for an existing product or service. By avoiding cannibalization, organizations can protect their existing customer base, maintain revenue streams, and preserve the overall profitability of the business.

Cannibalization

Cannibalization, in the context of Marketing Management, refers to a phenomenon where the sales or market share of a company's existing product or service is negatively impacted by the introduction of a new product or service from the same company. This occurs when the new offering directly competes with and draws customers away from the company's existing offerings.

When a company introduces a new product or service, it aims to attract new customers and increase overall sales. However, in some cases, the introduction of the new offering may erode the sales of existing products or services within the same company. This is known as cannibalization.

Cannibalization can occur for various reasons. One common scenario is when the new product or service offers similar features or benefits as the existing ones. In such cases, customers may switch their preferences to the new offering, causing a decline in sales of the older products. Another scenario is when the pricing or positioning of the new offering is more attractive to customers, leading them to choose it over the existing options.

Cannibalization can have both positive and negative implications for a company. On one hand, it provides an opportunity for the company to capture a larger share of the market by offering a broader range of products or services. On the other hand, it can result in decreased revenue and profitability if the sales of existing products or services decline significantly.

To mitigate the negative effects of cannibalization, companies can employ strategies such as carefully positioning the new offering in a different market segment, setting different price points for the existing and new products, or implementing effective marketing campaigns to differentiate the offerings and highlight their unique value propositions.

Cause Marketing Campaigns

Cause Marketing Campaigns refer to marketing initiatives undertaken by companies in collaboration with non-profit or charitable organizations for the purpose of promoting their social responsibility and maximizing their positive impact on society while simultaneously achieving their marketing objectives. These campaigns involve the strategic alignment of a company's brand, products, or services with a specific cause or social issue, which is typically related to the company's industry or target market.

The main objective of cause marketing campaigns is to create mutual benefits for both the company and the partnered non-profit organization. By associating their brand with a cause, companies can enhance their public image, build brand trust, and differentiate themselves from competitors. In addition, cause marketing campaigns can effectively engage and mobilize customers, employees, and other stakeholders, thus fostering brand loyalty and increasing customer retention.

Moreover, cause marketing campaigns often involve various promotional activities aimed at raising awareness, encouraging donations or volunteerism, and driving consumer purchase behaviors. These activities may include advertising, public relations, social media campaigns, event sponsorship, product co-branding, or the creation of cause-related products or services.

Overall, cause marketing campaigns exemplify the integration of social responsibility and marketing strategies. By addressing societal issues and contributing to the community's well-being, companies can not only achieve their financial goals but also enhance their reputation and long-term sustainability.

Cause Marketing

Cause marketing is a strategic approach used by companies to form mutually beneficial partnerships with non-profit organizations or social causes, with the goal of generating positive impact for society while also enhancing their own brand image and reputation. This marketing technique relies on the alignment of a company's values and objectives with a specific cause, creating a unified message that resonates with consumers.

The primary objective of cause marketing is to create a win-win situation, where both the company and the cause benefit. Companies often contribute financial support, goods, services, or expertise to their chosen cause, helping to address social issues or promote social change. In return, the company gains exposure, increased brand awareness, and improved brand perception among consumers who value social responsibility.

Cause marketing campaigns can take various forms, such as fundraising initiatives, promotional events, product collaborations, or cause-related marketing campaigns. These campaigns are typically integrated into the company's marketing strategy and can be communicated through various channels, including advertising, public relations, social media, and corporate social responsibility initiatives.

Successful cause marketing requires careful selection of a cause that aligns with the company's values and target audience, as well as effective communication and transparency. Companies need to ensure that their support for the cause is authentic and genuine, as consumers are increasingly sensitive to corporate social responsibility. Moreover, it is essential to measure the impact of cause marketing initiatives to demonstrate the effectiveness of the partnership and maintain credibility.

Challenger Brand

A challenger brand, in the context of marketing management, refers to a relatively small or new company that competes against established market leaders, often with limited resources. These brands aim to disrupt the industry by challenging the dominant players and gaining market share

51

through innovative approaches and strategies.

Unlike market leaders, challenger brands do not have the advantage of a well-established reputation, customer loyalty, or economies of scale. Therefore, they need to adopt creative and unconventional tactics to break through the market clutter and attract consumer attention. They often focus on niche markets or segments that have been overlooked by the established players, allowing them to differentiate themselves and offer unique value propositions.

Challenger brands typically use disruptive marketing techniques, such as guerrilla marketing, viral campaigns, or social media engagement, to gain visibility and create buzz around their products or services. They emphasize creativity, storytelling, and emotional appeal to connect with consumers on a deeper level and build brand affinity.

Despite the challenges they face, challenger brands have the potential to disrupt and reshape industries, as they bring fresh perspectives, innovative solutions, and a willingness to take risks. They often act as catalysts for change, pushing the market leaders to adapt and evolve in response to their competition.

Channel Marketing

Channel marketing refers to the strategies and activities that a company employs to promote and sell its products or services through a network of intermediaries or resellers. These intermediaries can include wholesalers, retailers, distributors, and agents, among others.

The main objective of channel marketing is to create mutually beneficial relationships between the company and its channel partners. This involves developing effective communication and collaboration between all parties involved in the distribution process.

Channel marketing encompasses various activities such as market research, product development, pricing, promotion, and distribution. It involves identifying target markets, positioning products or services, and implementing marketing plans to attract and engage customers through the distribution channel.

Effective channel marketing requires a deep understanding of the target market, as well as the needs and preferences of the intermediaries. It also involves building strong partnerships and providing the necessary support and resources to help channel partners effectively market and sell the company's products or services.

By leveraging the expertise and reach of intermediaries, channel marketing can help companies expand their customer base, increase brand awareness, and drive sales. It allows companies to leverage the strengths and capabilities of channel partners to maximize their market penetration and revenue generation.

In summary, channel marketing is a vital component of marketing management that focuses on developing and managing relationships with intermediaries to effectively distribute and sell products or services. It plays a crucial role in achieving marketing objectives and driving business growth.

Channel Partner Collaboration

Channel partner collaboration refers to the strategic relationship and cooperative efforts between a company and its external partners, specifically those involved in the distribution and marketing of its products or services. It is a vital aspect of marketing management, aimed at maximizing the efficiency and effectiveness of the distribution channel.

Through channel partner collaboration, companies seek to align their goals, strategies, and resources with their partners to achieve mutually beneficial outcomes. This collaboration involves sharing information, resources, and responsibilities to optimize overall channel performance and generate higher customer value.

Channel Partner Relationship

A channel partner relationship refers to the collaboration between a company and its external business partners who play a crucial role in distributing and selling the company's products or services to end customers. These channel partners, also known as resellers or distributors, are independent entities that help expand the market reach of the company by leveraging their own networks and customer base.

In the context of Marketing Management, channel partner relationship management is a key strategic process that involves effectively managing and nurturing these relationships. This is done through various activities such as recruitment, training, motivation, and support to ensure the success of the partnership.

The primary goal of channel partner relationship management is to establish a mutually beneficial collaboration between the company and its partners. This includes aligning their objectives, developing a strong level of trust, and implementing effective communication channels to foster a smooth flow of information, feedback, and resources.

Marketing managers play a vital role in building and maintaining channel partner relationships. They are responsible for identifying potential partners, assessing their capabilities and fit with the company's strategic goals. They also design and execute marketing programs, incentives, and promotions to incentivize and motivate channel partners to perform at their best.

By actively managing channel partner relationships, marketing managers can gain numerous benefits such as increased market coverage, access to new customer segments, improved customer satisfaction, and higher sales volumes. Effective channel partner relationships can serve as a competitive advantage, enabling companies to quickly adapt to changing market dynamics and capitalize on new opportunities.

Channel Partner

A channel partner, in the context of marketing management, refers to a third-party company or individual that collaborates with a manufacturer or firm to sell and promote their products or services. They act as an extension of the manufacturer's sales force, leveraging their own customer base, expertise, and resources to reach a wider market and increase sales.

Channel partners play a crucial role in the distribution and marketing strategies of a company. By forming partnerships with channel partners, manufacturers can tap into their networks and leverage their established customer relationships to expand their market reach. This allows manufacturers to focus on their core competencies, such as product development and production, while relying on channel partners to handle the sales, distribution, and marketing aspects of their products or services.

Channel partners can take various forms, including distributors, resellers, value-added resellers (VARs), system integrators, consultants, and independent sales representatives. They often work closely with the manufacturer to understand the features, benefits, and target market of the products or services they represent. This enables them to effectively communicate and promote the offerings to their own customer base, as well as provide after-sales support and services.

Successful channel partner relationships are built on mutual trust, communication, and alignment of goals and objectives. Manufacturers should carefully select channel partners based on their expertise, reach, reputation, and market knowledge. They should also provide the necessary training, incentives, and marketing support to ensure that channel partners are equipped with the knowledge and resources to effectively sell and promote their products or services. In return, channel partners can benefit from access to a wider product portfolio, increased revenue streams, and the support of a trusted brand in their respective market segments.

Chatbot Advertising

Chatbot advertising is a marketing strategy that utilizes artificial intelligence (AI) chatbots to interact with users and advertise products or services. Chatbots are computer programs designed to simulate human conversation through text or voice-based interactions. They can be integrated into various messaging platforms, such as websites, mobile apps, or social media platforms.

With chatbot advertising, businesses can engage with their customers in a more personalized and interactive way. Chatbots can automatically answer customer inquiries, provide product information, make recommendations, and even complete sales transactions. They are capable of understanding natural language and context to deliver relevant and timely messages to users.

Chatbot advertising offers several benefits for marketers. Firstly, it allows businesses to reach a wider audience by leveraging popular messaging platforms that are used by millions of people globally. Secondly, chatbots provide 24/7 customer support, ensuring that customers' questions and concerns are addressed promptly. Additionally, chatbots can collect valuable customer data, such as preferences and purchase history, which can be used to improve targeting and personalize future marketing efforts.

In conclusion, chatbot advertising is an effective marketing tool that combines AI technology with messaging platforms to engage and interact with customers. It offers businesses the opportunity to provide personalized experiences, improve customer satisfaction, and drive sales.

Chatbot Marketing Platforms

Chatbot marketing platforms are digital tools that enable marketers to leverage the power of chatbots to automate and optimize their marketing campaigns. These platforms provide a range of features and capabilities to help marketers create, deploy, and manage chatbots that engage with customers, collect data, and drive conversions.

Through chatbot marketing platforms, marketers can design chatbot conversations that are personalized, interactive, and dynamic, allowing them to deliver targeted marketing messages, provide customer support, and facilitate transactions. These platforms often integrate with various communication channels, including websites, messaging apps, and social media platforms, enabling marketers to reach customers wherever they are and deliver seamless omnichannel experiences.

In addition to conversational design, chatbot marketing platforms typically offer analytics and reporting capabilities, empowering marketers to gain insights into customer behavior, preferences, and engagement. By analyzing chatbot interactions and performance metrics, marketers can refine their marketing strategies, optimize chatbot conversations, and improve the overall customer experience. Furthermore, these platforms may include features for A/B testing, segmentation, and integration with other marketing tools, allowing marketers to experiment with different approaches and automate workflows.

Overall, chatbot marketing platforms provide marketers with the tools they need to harness the power of artificial intelligence and machine learning in their marketing efforts. By utilizing chatbots, marketers can enhance customer engagement, streamline processes, and ultimately drive business growth in the digital age.

Chatbot Marketing

A chatbot marketing is a digital marketing strategy that utilizes chatbots – automated software applications designed to simulate human-like conversations – to engage and interact with customers. The primary goal of chatbot marketing is to provide personalized and timely assistance to customers, drive customer engagement, and ultimately, increase sales.

In the context of marketing management, chatbot marketing plays a crucial role in enhancing customer experiences and improving overall brand perception. By leveraging chatbots, marketers can deliver targeted and relevant content to customers, engage in real-time conversations to address queries or concerns, and guide customers through the sales funnel more effectively.

Chatbot marketing also offers several advantages for marketers. Firstly, chatbots can gather valuable customer data, including preferences, behavior patterns, and purchase history. This data can be used to segment customers and tailor marketing campaigns accordingly, resulting in higher conversion rates and customer satisfaction. Additionally, chatbots can provide 24/7 customer support, ensuring constant availability and prompt response times, thereby improving customer experience.

Furthermore, chatbot marketing can be integrated with other marketing channels such as social media, email, or websites to provide a seamless omnichannel experience. By automating repetitive tasks and handling routine inquiries, chatbots free up marketers' time and resources, allowing them to focus on more strategic and creative aspects of marketing campaigns.

Churn Rate

Churn Rate, in the context of Marketing Management, refers to the measure of customer attrition or the rate at which customers stop using a product or service offered by a company within a specific time period. It is a crucial metric that helps businesses assess customer dissatisfaction, overall customer retention strategies, and the overall health of the customer base.

The Churn Rate is typically calculated by dividing the number of customers who discontinued using the product or service during a given time period by the total number of customers at the beginning of the same time period. The result is expressed as a percentage, indicating the proportion of customers lost. A higher churn rate implies that a larger percentage of customers are leaving, which can have significant negative consequences for a company's profitability.

Click Fraud Detection

Click Fraud Detection in the context of Marketing Management discipline refers to the process of identifying and preventing fraudulent activities related to online advertising campaigns. It involves the use of advanced technology and algorithms to examine and analyze click patterns and behaviors to detect and mitigate fraudulent clicks.

Click fraud occurs when an individual or automated bot intentionally clicks on an online ad with the objective of generating false clicks or impressions, leading to inflated costs for advertisers and misleading campaign data. This practice is often carried out to deplete a competitor's advertising budget, increase revenues for ad publishers, or manipulate campaign performance metrics.

The detection of click fraud requires the implementation of sophisticated systems and tools that monitor various metrics, such as IP address, user agent, click time, and click patterns. By analyzing these factors, marketers can identify suspicious activities and distinguish between genuine and fraudulent clicks. Machine learning algorithms are commonly employed to analyze large volumes of data and identify patterns indicative of click fraud.

Once click fraud is detected, marketers can take appropriate measures to minimize its impact. This can include blocking suspicious IP addresses, implementing stricter verification processes, or seeking refunds from ad publishers. Regular monitoring and analysis of campaign data are crucial to stay vigilant against click fraud and maintain the integrity of online advertising efforts.

Click Fraud Prevention Measures

Click Fraud Prevention Measures are strategies and techniques employed by marketers to combat fraudulent activities related to online advertising, specifically the manipulation of pay-per-click (PPC) advertising campaigns. These measures are imperative in ensuring the effectiveness and accuracy of marketing campaigns while safeguarding advertising budgets. Click fraud refers to the act of deliberately clicking on online advertisements without genuine interest, often performed by automated programs (bots) or individuals with malicious intent. This fraudulent activity can lead to inflated click-through rates (CTR) and wastage of advertising budget, ultimately undermining the success of marketing initiatives. To mitigate the risks associated with click fraud, marketers implement specific prevention measures. Firstly, real-time monitoring and analysis of incoming clicks is imperative. By closely monitoring the source, frequency, and behavior of clicks, marketers can identify suspicious patterns and swiftly take action to prevent further fraudulent activities. Additionally, implementing sophisticated algorithms and machine learning models can help detect and flag potentially fraudulent clicks, enabling advertisers to take necessary steps to prevent their impact on campaign performance.

Moreover, utilizing IP blocking and geo-targeting techniques can be highly effective in preventing click fraud. By identifying and blocking certain IP addresses or targeting specific regions, marketers can significantly reduce the risk of fraudulent clicks originating from suspicious sources. Furthermore, employing stringent click verification processes and technologies is crucial. Implementing multi-step verification systems, such as CAPTCHA, can help differentiate genuine user engagements from automated or fraudulent clicks. These measures play a pivotal role in ensuring the accuracy and quality of clicks while eliminating fraudulent activities. In conclusion, click fraud prevention measures are vital in maintaining the integrity and effectiveness of online advertising campaigns. By employing real-time monitoring, algorithmic detection, IP blocking, geo-targeting, and click verification processes, marketers can minimize the financial impact of click fraud and optimize the success of their marketing initiatives.

Click Fraud Prevention

Click Fraud Prevention refers to the practices and strategies employed by marketers to protect their online advertising campaigns from fraudulent clicks. This phenomenon occurs when individuals or automated systems intentionally click on online ads with no intention of engaging with the advertised content, solely to generate revenue for the publisher or to deplete the budget of the advertiser.

In the context of Marketing Management, click fraud prevention plays a crucial role in ensuring the effectiveness and efficiency of digital advertising campaigns. By preventing fraudulent clicks, marketers can optimize their ad spend, improve campaign performance, and maximize their return on investment (ROI).

There are several techniques and tools used in click fraud prevention, including:

- IP filtering: Identifying and blocking suspicious IP addresses that exhibit behavior patterns indicative of click fraud.

- Device recognition: Distinguishing between legitimate and fraudulent devices to prevent multiple clicks from the same source.

- User behavior analysis: Monitoring and analyzing user behavior to identify abnormal click patterns and detect potential instances of click fraud.

- Ad monitoring: Regularly monitoring ad placements and performance to detect any irregularities or signs of suspicious activity.

Implementing click fraud prevention measures not only helps marketers maintain the integrity of their campaigns but also ensures more accurate data for campaign analysis and performance evaluation. By identifying and excluding fraudulent clicks, marketers can make informed decisions, allocate resources effectively, and optimize their overall digital advertising strategy.

Click Fraud

Click fraud is a deceptive practice employed in the field of Marketing Management, which involves intentionally clicking on online advertisements with the malicious intent of generating illegitimate clicks or impressions. This deceptive activity aims to misleadingly increase the number of clicks or impressions for an advertisement, in turn leading to higher costs for advertisers and potentially distorting campaign metrics.

Click fraud can occur through various methods, including manual clicking by individuals or the use of automated software programs known as bots. These fraudulent activities may be driven by competitors seeking to exhaust their competitors' advertising budgets or by publishers looking to boost their revenue by artificially inflating click counts.

This unethical practice poses significant challenges for marketers and advertisers. Not only does click fraud result in wasted advertising budgets and skewed performance metrics, but it also undermines the trust and integrity of online advertising platforms. Advertisers may suffer financial losses while receiving little to no return on investment, impacting the overall effectiveness of their marketing campaigns.

Marketing managers must actively monitor and guard against click fraud by implementing robust fraud detection systems and partnering with reliable advertising platforms. Employing advanced analytics and machine learning algorithms can help identify suspicious patterns and behaviors associated with click fraud, allowing for prompt intervention and mitigation.

In conclusion, click fraud is a deceptive practice involving illegitimate clicks or impressions on online advertisements, aiming to manipulate click counts and potentially defraud advertisers. Vigilance and technological measures are essential in combatting this fraudulent activity to protect advertising budgets and ensure accurate performance measurement.

Click-Through Rate (CTR) Optimization

Click-Through Rate (CTR) Optimization is a key concept in the field of Marketing Management. It refers to the process of maximizing the percentage of users who click on a particular link, advertisement, or call-to-action within a marketing campaign.

The goal of CTR Optimization is to increase the effectiveness and efficiency of a marketing campaign by improving the engagement and response rate of targeted users. This is achieved by carefully analyzing and manipulating various elements of the campaign, such as ad placement, ad design, messaging, targeting, and timing.

Click-Through Rate (CTR)

Click-Through Rate (CTR) is a metric used in the field of Marketing Management to measure the effectiveness of an online advertising campaign or a specific advertisement. It represents the ratio of the number of users who clicked on a particular link or ad to the number of total users who viewed the link or ad.

CTR is calculated by dividing the number of clicks on a link or ad by the number of impressions it received, and then multiplying the result by 100 to obtain a percentage. For example, if a link or ad receives 100 clicks and 1000 impressions, the CTR would be 10% ((100 clicks / 1000 impressions) * 100).

Clickbait

Clickbait is a marketing tactic used to attract attention and entice visitors to click on a specific piece of content, typically in the form of a headline or thumbnail image. This tactic aims to generate more traffic and increase the likelihood of engagement, such as page views, clicks, or shares.

Clickbait often employs sensational or provocative language, exaggerations, misleading statements, or incomplete information to create curiosity and intrigue. It is designed to tap into human psychology, leveraging our natural desire for novelty, entertainment, or answers to enticing questions. By tapping into these emotional triggers, clickbait attempts to lure users into clicking on the content, even if the actual content does not fulfill the promise made in the headline or image.

However, clickbait can be seen as a controversial practice as it can lead to a negative user experience. When users feel tricked or deceived by clickbait, it can damage a brand's reputation, decrease trust, and result in higher bounce rates or fewer conversions. Therefore, the ethical use of clickbait is crucial in marketing management to strike a balance between grabbing attention and delivering valuable, relevant, and truthful content.

Clickstream Analysis Tools

Clickstream Analysis Tools are software or systems used to collect, analyze, and interpret data on the online behavior of users navigating websites, providing valuable insights for marketing management strategies. These tools track and record user activities, such as the pages visited, links clicked, time spent on each page, and the order of these actions. They trace the users' digital footprints and offer a comprehensive view of their online journey.

The application of clickstream analysis tools in the context of marketing management discipline allows businesses to better understand their customers, optimize their online presence, and formulate effective marketing strategies. By analyzing clickstream data, marketers can gain insights into the preferences, interests, and behavior patterns of their target audience. They can identify the most popular pages, understand which links or products attract the most attention, and determine the drop-off points in the conversion process.

Clickstream analysis tools provide marketers with the ability to track the effectiveness of various marketing campaigns, advertisements, and website layouts. By analyzing the clickstream data, marketers can determine the success or failure of different marketing initiatives, identify the most effective channels, and optimize their marketing efforts accordingly. These tools enable businesses to make data-driven decisions, enhance their user experience, and ultimately increase their conversions and revenue.

Overall, clickstream analysis tools are powerful resources in the marketing management discipline, offering valuable insights into user behavior and driving informed decision-making. The ability to track and analyze online customer journeys helps businesses optimize their marketing strategies, improve customer satisfaction, and increase their bottom line.

Clickstream Analysis

Clickstream analysis refers to the systematic examination and interpretation of the digital footprints left by internet users as they navigate through websites and online platforms. It is a valuable tool used in the field of Marketing Management to gain insights into consumer behavior and optimize marketing strategies.

The clickstream data is collected from various sources, such as web analytics tools, tracking pixels, cookies, and server logs. These data points include information about the pages visited, the sequence of interactions, the time spent on each page, and the actions taken, such as clicking on links or making purchases. By analyzing this data, marketers can understand how users engage with their online assets and identify patterns, trends, and opportunities for improvement.

Cloaking

Cloaking

Cloaking, in the context of Marketing Management, refers to a disallowed practice where a website or webpage presents different content to search engine crawlers and users. It involves showing one version of a webpage to search engines for indexing purposes, while displaying a different version to actual users. This technique is often used to deceive search engine algorithms and manipulate search rankings.

Cloaking typically occurs when a website owner wants to appear relevant for certain keywords or phrases to improve their search engine rankings. They may use various methods to implement cloaking, such as IP-based cloaking, user-agent cloaking, or JavaScript-based cloaking. These methods allow the website to serve different versions of the webpage depending on the source of the request.

Search engines, like Google, consider cloaking a violation of their guidelines because it aims to deceive and manipulate the search results. Using cloaking techniques can result in penalties such as the website being banned from search engine results, impacting the visibility and credibility of the business or brand.

The use of cloaking promotes an unfair advantage over competitors who utilize legitimate marketing practices to achieve organic search rankings. It undermines the principle of providing users with accurate and relevant search results, diminishing the credibility of search engines.

In conclusion, cloaking is a prohibited technique in Marketing Management that involves presenting different versions of content to search engines and users. It aims to deceive search engine algorithms and manipulate search rankings, leading to penalties and a loss of credibility.

Closed-Loop Marketing

Closed-Loop Marketing is a strategic approach in marketing management that focuses on creating a continuous feedback loop between marketing activities and sales data. It involves collecting and analyzing customer data at various touchpoints throughout the marketing and sales funnel, using that data to make informed decisions, and then measuring the impact of those decisions to refine future marketing efforts.

The closed-loop marketing process starts with the collection of customer data, which can include demographic information, purchase history, website behavior, and other relevant data points. This data is then used to segment customers into different groups based on their characteristics and behaviors. With these customer segments in mind, marketers can craft personalized and targeted messages or offers that are more likely to resonate with each group.

Once the marketing activities are implemented, closed-loop marketing relies on tracking the impact of those activities by monitoring key performance indicators (KPIs) such as customer acquisition costs, conversion rates, sales revenue, and other relevant metrics. By comparing these metrics to the initial customer data and tracking trends over time, marketers can assess the effectiveness of their efforts and make data-driven decisions to optimize their marketing strategies.

The closed-loop marketing approach allows marketers to create a feedback loop that continuously feeds into their marketing efforts, enabling them to optimize and improve their campaigns based on real-time insights. By using data to inform decision-making, closed-loop marketing helps businesses better understand their customers, target their messaging, optimize their marketing spend, and ultimately drive more effective and efficient marketing campaigns.

Cluster Analysis

Cluster analysis is a statistical technique used in Marketing Management to segment a heterogeneous target market into homogenous groups based on similar characteristics or behaviors. This analysis enables marketers to identify distinct market segments with common preferences, needs, or buying behaviors, helping them develop targeted marketing strategies.

By grouping consumers into clusters, marketers can gain valuable insights into customer segmentation, targeting, and positioning. Cluster analysis allows marketers to understand the diversity within their target market and identify specific consumer groups that may respond differently to marketing efforts. This knowledge helps tailor marketing messages and tactics to each segment's unique needs, preferences, and behaviors, thereby improving the effectiveness of marketing campaigns.

Co-Branding Initiatives

Co-Branding initiatives refer to strategic collaborations between two or more brands to combine their individual strengths and resources, resulting in a mutually beneficial partnership. In the context of Marketing Management, co-branding initiatives are frequently used as a marketing strategy to increase brand awareness, expand market reach, and capitalize on complementary customer segments or product offerings.

Co-branding initiatives involve the establishment of a formal partnership agreement between brands, where both parties actively contribute their brand equity, market expertise, and distribution networks. The objective is to create a unique value proposition that leverages the combined strengths of the participating brands. This collaboration enables brands to tap into new customer segments, enhance their brand image, and create a competitive advantage in the market.

Co-Branding Strategies

Co-branding is a marketing strategy that involves the collaboration of two or more recognizable brands to create a unique product or service that appeals to their shared target market. This strategy aims to leverage the equity and influence of each brand to enhance the customer's perception of the joint offering and increase its overall appeal and market competitiveness.

The primary objective of co-branding is to create synergy between the partnering brands, thereby benefiting from each other's brand reputation, customer base, and market reach. By associating with a well-established brand, a company can enhance its credibility and gain access to a larger audience, while the established brand can tap into new market segments and extend its brand presence.

Co-Branding

Co-branding in the context of Marketing Management is a strategic marketing approach in which two or more brands form a partnership to create a unique product or service that is mutually beneficial. It involves the collaboration and integration of two or more brands in order to leverage each other's strengths and enhance their competitive advantage in the market.

The primary objective of co-branding is to create synergy between the participating brands, resulting in increased market share, customer loyalty, and profitability. Through co-branding, companies can combine their resources, knowledge, and expertise to develop innovative products or services that cater to the needs and preferences of a specific target audience.

Community Management

Community Management, within the context of Marketing Management, refers to the process of building and maintaining relationships with a community of individuals who share common interests or goals. It involves actively engaging with the community, fostering conversation and collaboration, and ensuring that the community's needs are met.

Effective community management plays a crucial role in marketing as it helps businesses establish a loyal customer base, increase brand awareness, and enhance customer satisfaction. By actively listening to community members, understanding their preferences, and addressing their concerns, businesses can build trust, strengthen their reputation, and create a positive brand image.

Community managers act as the bridge between a brand and its community, serving as the point of contact and facilitating communication. They are responsible for establishing and maintaining an online presence on various platforms, such as social media, forums, and blogs, to ensure that the community is engaged and nurtured.

Furthermore, community management involves implementing strategies to encourage user-generated content, such as reviews, testimonials, and discussions, which can significantly impact the decision-making process of potential customers. By fostering a sense of belonging and actively involving community members, businesses can tap into the power of word-of-mouth marketing and leverage their community as advocates for their brand.

In summary, community management in the context of Marketing Management involves building relationships, engaging with the community, and ensuring their needs are met. It is vital for businesses to actively listen, respond, and nurture their communities to drive brand loyalty, increase awareness, and enhance customer satisfaction.

Competitive Advantage

Competitive advantage refers to a company's unique set of resources, capabilities, or attributes that allows it to outperform its competitors and achieve superior market position and profitability. It is a key concept in marketing management, as it plays a crucial role in enabling a company to gain a competitive edge in the marketplace.

Competitive advantage can be achieved through various means, including differentiation, cost leadership, and focus strategies. Differentiation involves offering unique and superior products or services that are valued by customers and difficult for competitors to imitate. This can be achieved by leveraging technology, innovation, superior customer service, or strong brand reputation.

Cost leadership involves offering products or services at a lower cost than competitors, while maintaining comparable quality. This can be achieved through operational efficiency, economies of scale, or superior supply chain management. By offering lower prices, companies are able to attract price-sensitive customers and gain market share.

Focus strategies involve targeting a specific market segment or niche and tailoring products or services to meet the unique needs and preferences of that segment. By focusing on a smaller target market, companies can develop deep expertise and understanding, allowing them to better serve their customers and differentiate themselves from broader competitors.

In conclusion, competitive advantage is a key concept in marketing management that refers to a company's unique set of resources, capabilities, or attributes that allow it to outperform competitors and achieve superior market position and profitability. It can be achieved through differentiation, cost leadership, or focus strategies, allowing companies to gain a competitive edge in the marketplace.

Competitive Analysis

Competitive Analysis is a marketing management discipline that involves assessing and evaluating the strengths and weaknesses of competitors within a specific industry or market. It is an essential component of strategic planning as it provides crucial insights into the competitive landscape, which can then be used to develop effective marketing strategies.

The objective of competitive analysis is to gather information about the competitors, their products, pricing strategies, distribution channels, marketing tactics, and overall market position. This information helps businesses to identify opportunities and threats, benchmark their own performance against competitors, and make informed decisions to gain a competitive advantage.

Competitive Benchmarking

Competitive Benchmarking refers to the process of evaluating the performance of a company or product in relation to its competitors within the same industry or market. It involves gathering data and analyzing various key performance indicators (KPIs) to determine how well a company or product is performing compared to its competitors.

This process enables marketing managers to identify the strengths and weaknesses of their company or product and make informed decisions to improve their competitive advantage. By understanding the strategies and tactics employed by competitors, marketing managers can identify areas of improvement and develop effective marketing strategies to gain a competitive edge.

Competitive Intelligence

Competitive Intelligence is a key component of Marketing Management that involves the collection, analysis, and interpretation of information about the external business environment in order to gain a competitive advantage. It is the systematic and ethical process of monitoring, analyzing, and understanding competitors and their activities in the marketplace.

The aim of Competitive Intelligence is to provide organizations with insightful knowledge about their competitors' strategies, strengths, weaknesses, opportunities, and threats. By gathering and analyzing relevant information, Marketing Managers can make informed decisions and develop effective marketing strategies that are aligned with market trends and competitor actions.

Competitive Intelligence involves various methods such as market research, data mining, competitor analysis, and benchmarking. It requires the gathering of both primary and secondary data from various sources, including industry reports, financial statements, customer feedback, social media, and competitor websites.

Once the data is collected, it is analyzed and interpreted to identify patterns, trends, and market insights. This enables Marketing Managers to understand the competitive landscape and make informed decisions regarding product positioning, pricing, promotion, and distribution strategies.

Overall, Competitive Intelligence is a vital practice in Marketing Management as it assists organizations in understanding and responding to competitive threats and opportunities. By staying abreast of industry dynamics, organizations can navigate the market successfully, differentiate themselves from competitors, and ultimately achieve their marketing objectives.

Competitive Pricing

Competitive pricing is a pricing strategy in marketing management that involves setting the price of a product or service based on the prices charged by competitors. The goal of competitive pricing is to attract customers and gain a competitive advantage in the market.

Competitive pricing involves carefully analyzing the prices of similar products or services offered by competitors and then setting a price that is either lower or higher, depending on the company's marketing objectives. If the company wants to attract customers by offering a lower price, it may choose to set a price lower than that of its competitors. On the other hand, if the company wants to position itself as a premium brand and target a specific market segment, it may choose to set a higher price than its competitors.

Competitor Analysis

Competitor analysis in the context of Marketing Management is the process of identifying and understanding the strengths and weaknesses of competitors, and assessing their strategies, resources, and market positions. It helps businesses gain valuable insights into their competitive landscape and formulate effective marketing strategies.

Competitor analysis involves gathering and analyzing data on competitors' products, pricing, distribution channels, marketing tactics, and customer base. It helps identify direct and indirect competitors, as well as new entrants and substitute products. Through detailed analysis, businesses can determine their competitors' market share, brand reputation, customer satisfaction, and financial performance.

Consumer Behavior

Consumer behavior, within the marketing management discipline, refers to the study and understanding of the individuals, groups, or organizations' actions and behaviors when they purchase, use, or dispose of products, services, or ideas in order to satisfy their needs and desires.

Organizations rely on understanding consumer behavior to develop effective marketing strategies and tactics that align with consumers' preferences and motivations. By gaining insights into consumer behavior, marketing managers can make informed decisions on product design, positioning, pricing, promotion, and distribution, which are crucial for the successful implementation of marketing plans.

Consumer Surveys

A consumer survey is a systematic method of collecting data from a target audience in order to gain insights and understanding into their preferences, behaviors, and opinions related to a particular product, service, or brand. This research technique, commonly used in the field of marketing management, is designed to gather information directly from consumers in order to inform decision making and strategy development.

Consumer surveys typically involve the distribution of questionnaires or interviews that contain a series of structured questions that aim to capture various aspects of consumer behavior and attitudes. The questions may cover a range of topics such as product satisfaction, purchase intentions, brand perception, pricing preferences, and demographic information. The data collected from these surveys can be analyzed and interpreted to identify patterns, trends, and correlations that can guide marketing decision-making.

Content Calendar Automation

Content calendar automation refers to the process of using software or tools to automate the scheduling and organization of content for marketing purposes. This technology allows marketing teams to plan, create, and schedule their content in advance, ensuring that it is published consistently and strategically across various channels.

In the field of marketing management, content calendar automation plays a vital role in streamlining the content creation process and improving overall efficiency. It enables marketers to have a centralized view of their content strategy, allowing them to plan and coordinate their efforts more effectively.

Content Calendar Management

A content calendar is a tool used in the field of marketing management to plan, organize, and schedule the creation and distribution of content for various marketing initiatives. It serves as a centralized document that outlines the content strategy, themes, and key messaging for a specific timeframe, typically a month or a quarter.

The content calendar management process involves mapping out the marketing objectives and identifying the target audience for each initiative. It helps marketing teams align their content creation and distribution efforts with overall marketing goals, ensuring consistency and effectiveness in their messaging.

By using a content calendar, marketing managers can strategically plan and allocate resources for content creation, including creation of blog posts, social media updates, videos, and email newsletters. It allows them to outline the frequency, timing, and channels through which the content will be delivered to the target audience.

Content calendar management plays a crucial role in ensuring that the right content is delivered to the right audience at the right time. It helps marketing managers stay organized, streamline workflows, and maintain a consistent brand voice throughout their marketing initiatives. It also enables them to analyze and measure the performance of their content efforts, making data-driven decisions to optimize future content strategies.

Content Calendar

A content calendar, in the context of Marketing Management, refers to a strategic planning tool used to organize and schedule the creation and distribution of content across various marketing channels. It is a document that outlines the specific content to be created, the platforms or channels on which it will be shared, and the timeline for its distribution.

The purpose of a content calendar is to provide a roadmap for marketing teams, ensuring a consistent and coordinated approach to content creation and distribution. By having a clear plan in place, marketers can effectively manage their resources, align content with business objectives, and maintain a consistent brand voice and messaging.

Content Creation

Content creation refers to the process of generating, planning, and producing relevant and valuable materials such as written content, images, videos, and graphics to engage and attract a targeted audience for marketing purposes. It is an integral part of the Marketing Management discipline.

The creation of content involves a strategic approach, aimed at capturing the interest of potential customers and guiding them through the buyer's journey. Content can be created for various marketing channels, including websites, social media platforms, email campaigns, and offline marketing materials. The ultimate goal is to effectively communicate a brand's message, generate leads, drive conversions, and foster long-term customer relationships.

The content creation process typically begins with conducting thorough research to understand the target market, customer preferences, and industry trends. This enables marketers to develop a content strategy that aligns with the brand's objectives and resonates with the intended audience. Content is then created, leveraging different mediums and formats, to convey valuable information, entertain, educate, or solve problems for the target audience. The content must be unique, compelling, and tailored to address the needs and interests of the specific market segment.

Moreover, content creation involves the utilization of appropriate keywords and search engine optimization techniques to enhance visibility and organic search rankings. It also necessitates consistent monitoring and analysis of content performance to refine strategies and improve results. Effective content creation plays a pivotal role in driving brand awareness, building brand authority, fostering customer engagement, and ultimately influencing purchasing decisions.

Content Curation Software

Content curation software refers to a digital tool utilized in the domain of marketing management. It enables marketers to discover, gather, organize, and publish relevant content from various sources in an efficient and streamlined manner. This software is designed to assist marketers in curating high-quality content that aligns with their target audience's interests and preferences, ultimately enhancing their overall marketing strategy.

With content curation software, marketers can automate the process of content aggregation, ensuring a constant supply of engaging and valuable content to share with their audience. This software often incorporates intelligent algorithms and customization options, allowing marketers to filter and sort through a wide range of content types to find the most relevant and impactful pieces. Additionally, content curation software often integrates with social media platforms, content management systems, and other marketing tools, providing seamless distribution and publication capabilities.

Content Curation Tools

Content curation tools refer to software or platforms that allow marketing managers to curate, organize, and distribute relevant and valuable content to their target audience. With the constant influx of information on the internet, these tools are essential in helping marketing managers filter through the noise and select high-quality content that aligns with their marketing objectives.

These tools typically provide features such as content discovery, content aggregation, content editing, and content scheduling. Content discovery involves finding and selecting relevant articles, blogs, videos, or other forms of content from various sources, including social media, news websites, and industry-specific publications. Content aggregation allows marketing managers to gather the curated content in one place for easy access and organization.

Content Curation

Content curation in the context of marketing management refers to the process of finding, selecting, organizing, and sharing relevant and valuable content with a specific audience or target market. It involves the careful selection and filtering of information, resources, and content from various sources, such as articles, blogs, videos, infographics, and social media posts. The purpose of content curation is to provide meaningful and targeted information to customers or prospects, establishing a position of authority and expertise in the industry or niche.

Effective content curation requires the marketing manager to have a deep understanding of the target audience and their needs, interests, and preferences. It involves continually monitoring and scanning the web and other relevant sources for high-quality content that aligns with the brand's values and objectives. Once the content is curated, it is then organized and presented in a coherent and structured manner, making it easily accessible and digestible for the audience.

Content Distribution Channels

Content distribution channels refer to the various platforms and mediums through which marketing content is disseminated to the target audience. These channels play a crucial role in reaching and engaging with customers, as well as promoting products or services effectively in the marketplace.

In the field of marketing management, content distribution channels can include both online and offline methods. Online channels typically consist of websites, social media platforms, blogs, and email marketing. These digital platforms allow companies to share content such as articles, videos, infographics, and advertisements instantly with a wide-ranging audience. Offline channels, on the other hand, encompass traditional forms of distribution such as print media, television commercials, radio advertisements, and direct mail.

Content Distribution Platforms

Content Distribution Platforms are marketing tools that enable businesses to distribute their content to a wide range of online channels, such as social media sites, blogs, and websites, in order to reach a larger audience and increase brand visibility. These platforms provide a centralized hub where marketers can upload, organize, and distribute their content efficiently and effectively.

With content distribution platforms, marketers can easily distribute various types of content, including articles, blog posts, videos, infographics, and whitepapers. They offer features that allow businesses to target specific demographics and segments, ensuring that content reaches the right audience at the right time. This helps to enhance the overall effectiveness of content marketing strategies and increase the chances of engaging potential customers.

Content Distribution Strategy

Content distribution strategy refers to a planned approach that a company adopts to distribute its marketing content to the intended target audience through various channels and platforms. This strategy is a subset of the overall marketing strategy and focuses specifically on the distribution of content to ensure maximum reach and effectiveness.

This strategy involves identifying the most suitable channels and platforms for reaching the target audience, such as social media platforms, websites, blogs, email newsletters, and online publications. It also considers the best formats for content distribution, such as articles, videos, infographics, podcasts, and interactive content.

Content Distribution

Content distribution refers to the strategic process of disseminating and delivering marketing content to the target audience through various channels and platforms. It is a crucial aspect of marketing management as it helps ensure that the right content reaches the right people at the right time.

The goal of content distribution is to maximize the reach, visibility, and impact of marketing messages, ultimately driving customer engagement and conversions. This process involves identifying the target audience and understanding their preferences, behaviors, and habits to determine the most effective channels and platforms to use.

Content distribution strategies may include both online and offline tactics. Online distribution methods can include email marketing, social media marketing, content syndication, search engine optimization (SEO), influencer marketing, and paid advertising. Offline distribution methods may include print advertising, direct mail campaigns, events, and public relations.

When developing a content distribution strategy, marketers must consider factors such as the target audience's demographics, psychographics, online behavior, preferred channels, and their stage in the buyer's journey. By tailoring content distribution efforts to meet the needs and preferences of the target audience, marketers can increase the chances of reaching and engaging with them effectively.

In conclusion, content distribution is a strategic process that plays a vital role in marketing management. It involves the effective dissemination of marketing content to the target audience through various channels and platforms, both online and offline. By understanding the target audience and their preferences, marketers can create tailored distribution strategies that maximize reach, visibility, and impact, ultimately driving customer engagement and conversions.

Content Engagement Analytics

Content Engagement Analytics refers to the process of gathering and analyzing data related to the way audiences interact with a company's content or marketing materials. It is a key component of the Marketing Management discipline, as it provides valuable insights into the effectiveness and impact of the content being produced and shared.

By tracking and measuring various metrics such as views, clicks, likes, comments, and shares, content engagement analytics allows marketers to assess how well their content is resonating with their target audience. It provides quantitative data that can be used to evaluate the performance of different marketing campaigns and initiatives, helping to inform future decision-making and strategy development.

Content Engagement Metrics

Content Engagement Metrics refer to a set of measurement tools and methods used in the field of Marketing Management to quantify and evaluate the level of user interaction and interest in online content. These metrics are vital for marketers as they provide insights into the effectiveness and impact of their digital marketing strategies, helping them make data-driven decisions to optimize future campaigns.

Content engagement metrics encompass various key indicators that gauge the extent to which users interact with online content, such as blog posts, videos, social media updates, or website pages. These metrics include but are not limited to:

Average Time on Page: This metric measures the average time a user spends on a particular page of content. It indicates the level of user interest or engagement with the content. A longer time typically suggests higher engagement.

Pageviews: Pageviews refer to the total number of times a specific page of content is viewed by users. It provides marketers with an understanding of which content is attracting the most traffic.

Bounce Rate: Bounce rate measures the percentage of users who navigate away from a page without taking any further action. A high bounce rate indicates that users may not find the content engaging or relevant.

Click-through Rate (CTR): CTR measures the percentage of users who click on a specific link or call-to-action within a piece of content. It helps marketers assess the effectiveness of their content in driving user actions and conversions.

By analyzing these content engagement metrics, marketers can gain insights into user preferences, optimize content strategies, identify areas for improvement, and enhance overall user engagement and conversion rates.

Content Management System (CMS)

A Content Management System (CMS) is a software platform that allows marketers to create, manage, and publish digital content on their websites without the need for technical expertise. It enables marketers to have full control over the presentation, organization, and functionality of their online content.

Within the Marketing Management discipline, a CMS plays a pivotal role in effectively managing and optimizing marketing strategies. By providing a user-friendly interface, CMS platforms empower marketers to easily update and modify their website content, resulting in improved brand consistency, customer engagement, and conversion rates.

Through a CMS, marketers can effortlessly create and publish content, such as blog posts, articles, images, videos, and product descriptions, that align with their marketing objectives. This flexibility and efficiency allow marketing teams to swiftly respond to market trends, customer demands, and competitor activities. Additionally, a CMS enables marketers to tailor content to specific target audiences, maximizing its relevance and impact.

Furthermore, a CMS offers valuable features like content scheduling, version control, and multi-channel distribution, enabling marketers to coordinate and streamline their content marketing efforts. This centralized control ensures content is consistently displayed across various platforms and devices, creating a seamless and cohesive brand experience for consumers.

By simplifying and automating content management processes, a CMS eliminates the need for marketers to rely on web development teams, significantly reducing time and costs. This agility and independence promote faster response times, allowing marketers to quickly capitalize on market opportunities and ensure their content remains current and competitive.

In conclusion, a CMS is an essential tool in the Marketing Management discipline, providing marketers with the means to create, manage, and publish digital content efficiently and effectively. It empowers marketers to enhance brand visibility, customer engagement, and conversion rates through personalized and optimized content strategies.

Content Mapping Strategy

A content mapping strategy refers to the process of aligning specific content pieces with the needs and preferences of target customers at different stages of their buyer's journey. It is a crucial component of marketing management in the digital age, enabling brands to deliver relevant and valuable content that resonates with their intended audience.

The strategy involves creating a comprehensive map that outlines the types of content and information that will be most effective at each stage of the customer's decision-making process. This map, also known as a content matrix or content funnel, helps marketers understand the various touchpoints where potential customers interact with their brand and the kind of content that will be most useful in guiding them through the buying process.

The content mapping strategy aims to deliver personalized and contextual content that meets the specific needs and pain points of customers. By understanding the different stages of the buyer's journey, marketers can tailor their content to address each stage's unique challenges, questions, and motivations. This not only increases the chances of capturing and retaining the attention of potential customers but also helps in building brand loyalty and trust.

Furthermore, a well-executed content mapping strategy enables marketers to optimize their marketing efforts. By analyzing the performance of content assets at each stage of the buyer's journey, marketers can identify gaps, refine their messaging, and experiment with different types of content to enhance engagement and conversion rates. It helps in ensuring that the right content reaches the right audience at the right time, ultimately driving business growth and success.

Content Mapping Tools

Content mapping tools refer to software or platforms used in the field of marketing management to organize, prioritize, and plan the creation and distribution of content to target audiences. These tools enable marketers to create visual representations or maps of their content strategy, helping them streamline their efforts and ensure alignment with their overall marketing goals and objectives.

At a basic level, content mapping tools enable marketers to categorize and organize content according to various factors such as buyer personas, stages of the buyer's journey, and marketing channels. By mapping content to specific target audiences and their needs, marketers can ensure that the right content reaches the right people at the right time, increasing the effectiveness of their marketing campaigns.

Content Mapping

Content mapping in the context of marketing management refers to the process of strategically aligning content assets with the buyer's journey to effectively engage and convert prospects into customers. It involves understanding the target audience's needs, preferences, and behaviors at each stage of their journey and creating relevant, personalized content to address those needs.

Achieving effective content mapping requires comprehensive research and analysis of the target market, buyer personas, and customer touchpoints. By mapping out the customer journey, marketers can identify the key touchpoints or interactions where prospects are most likely to engage with content and make purchase decisions.

The content mapping process typically involves segmenting the target audience into distinct buyer personas based on their demographics, interests, pain points, and buying behaviors. Marketers then create a content inventory that matches the needs of each persona at different stages of the buyer's journey.

Content mapping helps marketers deliver the right content to the right audience at the right time. It ensures that the content assets align with each stage of the customer's decision-making process, from awareness to consideration to decision. By mapping content to the buyer's journey, marketers can provide valuable information and resources that guide prospects towards making a purchase or taking a desired action.

Overall, content mapping is a strategic approach that enables marketers to connect with their target audience on a deeper level, build trust, and drive conversions by delivering tailored and relevant content throughout the entire customer journey.

Content Marketing

Content marketing is a strategic marketing approach that focuses on creating and distributing valuable, relevant, and consistent content to attract and retain a target audience. It aims to provide customers with helpful and informative content that aligns with their needs and interests, instead of aggressively promoting a product or service.

The main goal of content marketing is to build and nurture strong customer relationships by delivering content that educates, entertains, and engages the audience. It involves developing and sharing various types of content, such as blog posts, articles, videos, infographics, podcasts, and social media posts, across different platforms and channels.

Content Personalization Platforms

Content Personalization Platforms refer to the technology and tools used by marketers to deliver personalized content to their target audience. These platforms are designed to collect and analyze data about each user's behavior, preferences, and interests, with the goal of delivering tailored content that meets their specific needs and interests.

Content personalization is an essential component of effective marketing management, as it allows marketers to create a more personalized and engaging experience for their customers. By delivering relevant and targeted content to each individual, marketers can increase user engagement, drive conversions, and ultimately improve their marketing ROI.

Content Personalization Tactics

Content personalization tactics refer to the strategies and methods employed by marketers to tailor and customize content to meet the individual preferences, needs, and expectations of a target audience segment. This approach focuses on delivering relevant, personalized content to enhance engagement, build loyalty, and drive conversions.

By using data and insights gathered through various sources such as customer demographics, behavior patterns, purchase history, and online interactions, marketers can create highly targeted and personalized content experiences. This can include customizing website content, email campaigns, product recommendations, social media messaging, and advertisements, among others.

Content Personalization

Content personalization refers to the practice of tailoring marketing content and experiences to individual consumers based on their unique preferences, needs, and behaviors. It involves utilizing data and technology to deliver relevant and targeted messages, offers, and recommendations to the right person at the right time.

Personalization is a key component of effective marketing management as it enables companies to establish deeper connections with their target audience, enhance customer engagement, and ultimately drive conversions and sales. By understanding and leveraging consumer data, marketers can deliver highly customized and relevant content that resonates with individuals on a personal level.

Content Promotion Platforms

Content promotion platforms are tools or services that help marketers enhance the visibility and reach of their content to a wider audience. In the field of marketing management, these platforms play a crucial role in the promotional aspect of the marketing mix.

By using content promotion platforms, marketers can distribute their content across various channels and formats to target specific audience segments. These platforms often offer features such as social media scheduling, email marketing integration, influencer outreach, and paid advertising options.

Content Promotion Strategies

Content promotion strategies refer to the various tactics and techniques used by marketing managers to increase the visibility, reach, and engagement of their content assets. In the context of marketing management, content promotion is a vital component of the overall marketing strategy aimed at driving brand awareness, generating leads, and driving customer conversions.

Marketing managers use a mix of online and offline channels to promote their content effectively. Online channels include social media platforms, email marketing, search engine optimization (SEO), paid advertising, influencer marketing, and content syndication. Offline channels may include traditional advertising, events, public relations, and direct mail.

Content Promotion

Content promotion, in the context of Marketing Management, refers to the strategic activities and tactics undertaken to increase the visibility, reach, and engagement of a brand's content assets with the target audience. It involves a combination of both organic and paid methods to ensure that the content is effectively distributed and shared across various channels and platforms.

The primary goal of content promotion is to generate awareness, attract the attention of potential customers, and ultimately drive conversions and sales. The process begins with the creation of high-quality, relevant, and valuable content that is aligned with the brand's marketing objectives and target audience's needs. Once the content is developed, it is essential to utilize various promotional strategies to maximize its exposure and impact.

The organic methods of content promotion include but are not limited to search engine optimization (SEO), social media sharing, email marketing, influencer partnerships, and guest blogging. These techniques help to increase the visibility of the content, improve its search engine rankings, and generate social proof through user shares and engagement.

On the other hand, paid content promotion involves leveraging paid advertising platforms such as Google Ads, social media advertising, sponsored content placements, and native advertising to amplify the reach and visibility of the content. Paid promotion allows brands to target specific audience segments, increase brand exposure, and drive targeted traffic to their content assets.

Content Relevance Algorithms

Content relevance algorithms refer to the computational methods and systems used in marketing management to determine the suitability and significance of content in relation to specific marketing goals and target audiences. These algorithms analyze various factors such as keywords, context, user behavior, and other relevant data to assess the relevance and effectiveness of marketing content.

Based on these algorithms, marketing managers can optimize their content strategies and create personalized experiences for their target customers. By understanding the preferences and needs of their audience, they can deliver tailored content that resonates with users and ultimately drives engagement and conversions.

Content Relevance Analysis

Content Relevance Analysis is an essential concept in the field of Marketing Management that focuses on evaluating and assessing the suitability and value of content in the context of marketing strategies and objectives. It is a systematic approach used by marketers to determine the alignment between the content they create and the needs, preferences, and expectations of their target audience.

Content Relevance Analysis involves examining various elements such as the message, format, tone, and delivery of content to ensure that it resonates with the intended audience and effectively communicates the desired marketing message. It also considers factors like the timing of content delivery and the platforms or channels through which it is distributed.

Content Strategy

Content strategy is a crucial aspect of marketing management that involves the planning, creation, and dissemination of valuable and relevant content to attract and engage a target audience. It encompasses a strategic approach to the development and management of content that aligns with an organization's marketing objectives and customer needs.

The primary goal of content strategy is to deliver the right content to the right people at the right time, with the intention of driving customer action and achieving specific marketing outcomes. It requires a deep understanding of the target audience's preferences, interests, and behaviors, as well as an awareness of market trends and competitive landscape.

Content Syndication

Content syndication is a marketing management strategy that involves the distribution and dissemination of content across various online platforms. It is a process in which a company or organization repurposes its content and shares it on third-party websites, social media platforms, or other digital channels to reach a wider audience and achieve broader visibility.

The main objective of content syndication is to increase brand exposure, amplify content reach, and drive traffic to the company's website or blog. By leveraging the reach and influence of established publishers or influencers, content syndication allows businesses to extend their content's visibility beyond their own website or social media profiles, ultimately generating more leads and conversions.

Through content syndication, companies can also establish themselves as thought leaders in their industry by providing valuable and informative content to a wider audience. Additionally, it allows businesses to tap into new audiences that may not be familiar with their brand, thus expanding their customer base.

However, it is important to note that content syndication requires careful planning and execution. Companies must strategically choose the platforms or publishers on which they syndicate their content, ensuring alignment with their target audience and brand values. It is also crucial to track and analyze the performance of syndicated content, monitoring metrics such as audience engagement, click-through rates, and conversion rates.

In summary, content syndication is a marketing management tactic that involves sharing and distributing content through various online channels to increase brand exposure, drive traffic, and reach new audiences. By collaborating with established publishers or influencers, businesses can leverage the influence and audience of these platforms to achieve their marketing goals.

Contextual Advertising

Contextual advertising refers to a form of targeted advertising that is based on the context or content of a specific webpage or online platform. It involves displaying relevant advertisements

70

to users based on the keywords or themes present in the content they are viewing. This type of advertising aims to deliver highly relevant and personalized ads to users, thus increasing the likelihood of engagement and conversion.

In the field of marketing management, contextual advertising plays a crucial role in effectively reaching and engaging the target audience. By analyzing the content, keywords, and user behavior, marketers can strategically place advertisements that align with the users' interests and preferences. This approach ensures that the ads are displayed at the right time and in the right context, maximizing their impact and effectiveness.

Conversion Funnel Analysis

A conversion funnel analysis is a marketing management technique that involves studying and evaluating the various stages that a potential customer goes through before completing a desired action or converting into a paying customer. It is a valuable tool used by marketers to understand and optimize the customer journey, identify areas of improvement, and increase conversion rates.

The conversion funnel is a visual representation of the customer's path from awareness to conversion and consists of several stages, which may vary depending on the business and industry. The typical stages include awareness, interest, consideration, intent, and purchase. Each stage represents a different level of engagement and commitment from the potential customer.

The analysis of the conversion funnel involves tracking and analyzing key metrics and data points at each stage, such as website traffic, click-through rates, bounce rates, time spent on pages, and conversion rates. This information provides insights into the effectiveness of marketing efforts and helps identify any bottlenecks or areas of improvement.

By understanding the conversion funnel and analyzing the data, marketers can identify strategies to optimize each stage of the customer journey. This may involve improving website design and user experience, creating targeted and engaging content, optimizing landing pages, implementing effective call-to-action buttons, and personalized marketing campaigns. The goal is to guide potential customers through the funnel smoothly and efficiently, increasing the likelihood of conversion.

Overall, conversion funnel analysis is a vital component of marketing management as it helps marketers understand customer behavior, improve conversion rates, and ultimately drive business growth.

Conversion Funnel Optimization

Conversion Funnel Optimization refers to the process of improving the efficiency and effectiveness of a marketing campaign by strategically analyzing and enhancing the customer journey from initial engagement to final conversion. It is a key aspect of Marketing Management as it focuses on driving higher conversion rates and maximizing the return on investment (ROI) for businesses.

The conversion funnel, also known as the sales funnel, represents the various stages a customer goes through before making a purchase or completing a desired action. These stages typically include awareness, interest, consideration, and purchase. Conversion funnel optimization involves identifying and addressing any barriers or inefficiencies at each stage to streamline the customer journey and increase the likelihood of conversion.

Through conversion funnel optimization, marketers can identify and prioritize areas for improvement, such as optimizing website design and user experience, enhancing content relevance and engagement, implementing effective call-to-action strategies, and streamlining the checkout or conversion process.

By continuously analyzing data and metrics, marketers can gain insights into customer behavior, preferences, and pain points, allowing them to make data-driven decisions and implement targeted improvements. This iterative process helps businesses to better understand their target audience, tailor their marketing efforts accordingly, and ultimately increase the conversion rate and generate more sales or conversions.

Conversion Funnel Tracking

A conversion funnel is a marketing concept that represents the path a potential customer takes from becoming aware of a product or service to actually making a purchase or completing a desired action. It is a visual representation of the various stages or steps a customer goes through before converting into a paying customer. Conversion funnel tracking refers to the process of measuring and analyzing the effectiveness of each stage in the funnel to identify any bottlenecks or areas for improvement.

In marketing management, conversion funnel tracking is a critical tool for understanding customer behavior and optimizing marketing strategies. By tracking the conversion funnel, marketers can identify which stages are performing well and which ones need improvement. This allows them to allocate resources and efforts more efficiently to maximize conversion rates and ultimately drive sales.

Conversion Funnel

A conversion funnel is a marketing concept used in Marketing Management discipline to describe the journey that a customer takes from their initial exposure to a product or service through to a desired conversion or action. It is a visual representation or metaphorical funnel that outlines the steps or stages a customer goes through in the buying process.

The conversion funnel typically consists of several stages, including awareness, interest, desire, and action. At each stage, the goal is to guide customers through the funnel, addressing their needs and overcoming any barriers or objections they may have.

Conversion Rate (CVR)

Conversion Rate (CVR) is a key metric in the field of Marketing Management that measures the percentage of visitors or users who take a desired action on a website or as part of a marketing campaign. This desired action is usually known as a conversion, which can be customized to align with specific marketing goals, such as making a purchase, filling out a form, subscribing to a newsletter, or downloading a document.

CVR is calculated by dividing the number of conversions by the total number of visitors or users, and is usually expressed as a percentage. For example, if a website receives 1000 visitors and generates 100 conversions, the CVR would be 10%.

The CVR metric is widely used by marketing professionals to assess the effectiveness of their campaigns and optimize their strategies. A higher CVR indicates that a larger proportion of visitors are successfully completing the desired action, which can lead to increased revenue, customer acquisition, or other key business objectives. On the other hand, a lower CVR may indicate issues with the website or campaign that need to be addressed, such as poor user experience, confusing messaging, or inadequate call-to-action.

CVR is influenced by various factors, including the attractiveness of the offer, the clarity and relevance of the marketing message, the ease of completing the desired action, and the overall user experience. By tracking and analyzing CVR data, marketing managers can identify areas for improvement, test different strategies, and make data-driven decisions to optimize their campaigns and drive higher conversion rates.

Conversion Rate Optimization (CRO) Tools

Conversion Rate Optimization (CRO) refers to the systematic process of improving the conversion rate of a website or any other marketing channel to increase its success in achieving desired marketing goals. It involves analyzing user behavior, making data-driven changes, and conducting experiments to enhance the overall user experience and encourage desired actions, such as making a purchase, filling out a form, or subscribing to a newsletter.

CRO tools play a crucial role in this process by providing marketers with valuable insights, advanced analytics, and innovative features to optimize their conversion rates effectively. These tools offer a variety of functionalities, including but not limited to:

- A/B Testing: CRO tools enable marketers to create multiple variations of a webpage or marketing campaign and test them simultaneously to identify the most effective option.

- Heatmaps and Click Tracking: These tools track and visualize user interactions on a website, allowing marketers to identify patterns, discover areas of interest, and optimize their website's layout and content placement.

- Conversion Funnels: CRO tools offer visual representations of the customer journey, providing information on the percentage of users at each stage and helping marketers identify areas of potential improvement.

- User Surveys and Feedback: These tools allow marketers to collect feedback directly from users, enabling them to understand pain points, gather insights, and identify opportunities for conversion optimization.

By utilizing CRO tools effectively, marketers can make informed decisions, implement successful strategies, and continuously improve the conversion rates of their marketing channels, ultimately driving business growth and achieving their marketing objectives.

Conversion Rate Optimization (CRO)

Conversion Rate Optimization (CRO) refers to the systematic process of improving the percentage of website visitors who take the desired action, such as making a purchase, filling out a form, or subscribing to a newsletter. This is achieved by analyzing user behavior, identifying areas of improvement, and implementing strategic changes to enhance the website's performance and ultimately increase conversions.

Within the field of Marketing Management, CRO plays a critical role in maximizing the return on investment (ROI) of marketing efforts. By focusing on optimizing the conversion rate, businesses can make the most out of their existing website traffic. Rather than solely relying on increasing website traffic, CRO empowers marketers to capitalize on the potential of their current visitors by enhancing their on-site experience and encouraging them to take action.

Conversion Rate

Conversion rate is a key metric in the field of Marketing Management that measures the percentage of visitors or users who take a desired action, such as making a purchase, completing a form, or subscribing to a newsletter. It represents the effectiveness of a marketing campaign or strategy in converting leads into paying customers or achieving other predefined objectives.

The conversion rate is calculated by dividing the number of conversions (desired actions) by the total number of visitors or users and multiplying the result by 100 to express it as a percentage. For example, if a website had 1,000 visitors and 50 of them made a purchase, the conversion rate would be 5%. A high conversion rate indicates that a marketing campaign or strategy is successful in persuading visitors to take the desired action. It implies that the marketing message, design, offer, or overall user experience of the website or landing page is effective in driving conversions. On the other hand, a low conversion rate suggests that the marketing efforts are not generating the desired results. It may indicate issues such as poor targeting, unclear messaging, an unappealing offer, or a complicated user journey. Monitoring and optimizing the conversion rate is crucial for marketing managers to evaluate the performance of their campaigns, identify areas for improvement, and make data-driven decisions to increase conversions and maximize return on investment (ROI).

Cost Per Click (CPC)

Cost per Click (CPC) refers to a pricing model used in online advertising, specifically in the context of pay-per-click (PPC) campaigns. It is a metric that measures the cost incurred by an advertiser each time a user clicks on their online ad. In other words, CPC is the amount of money an advertiser pays to the platform or publisher hosting their ad when a viewer successfully clicks on it.

CPC is an essential metric for marketers as it helps determine the effectiveness and efficiency of their online advertising campaigns. By tracking CPC, marketers can assess the return on investment (ROI) of their ad spend and make informed decisions regarding budget allocation and campaign optimization.

Several factors influence the CPC of an online ad. Competition within the industry, the popularity and relevance of keywords used in the ad, and the quality score of the ad are all significant determinants. Advertisers can bid for specific keywords or placements, and the cost of each click is determined by an auction-based model. The higher the advertiser's bid, the greater the likelihood their ad will be displayed, increasing the chances of receiving clicks.

CPC is a critical metric for marketers to track and manage, as it directly impacts the overall cost and success of their online advertising campaigns. By carefully monitoring and optimizing CPC, marketers can make data-driven decisions to maximize conversions, improve ROI, and achieve their marketing objectives.

Cost Per Impression (CPM)

Cost per Impression (CPM) is a vital metric used in the field of Marketing Management to measure the cost incurred for every thousand impressions of an advertisement. An impression refers to a single view or exposure of an advertisement by a potential target audience. CPM helps marketers track and evaluate the efficiency and cost-effectiveness of their advertising campaigns.

CPM is calculated by dividing the total cost of running an ad campaign by the number of impressions generated, and then multiplying the result by 1000. The formula can be expressed as:

CPM = (Total Cost / Number of Impressions) * 1000

CPM allows marketers to compare the relative expenses of different advertising channels and campaigns. It enables them to analyze the performance of media platforms, such as television, radio, print, or online, by measuring how much it costs to reach a thousand potential customers through each platform. By understanding the CPM of various channels, marketers can make informed decisions about their media budgets and optimize their advertising strategies.

Furthermore, CPM helps marketers estimate the potential cost of reaching a specific target audience on a particular platform by extrapolating the CPM data. This information is valuable in planning and budgeting for future campaigns.

In conclusion, CPM is an essential metric that provides marketing managers with insights into the cost efficiency and effectiveness of their advertising campaigns. By monitoring CPM, marketers can optimize their media strategies and make informed decisions to maximize the reach and impact of their advertisements.

Cross-Selling

Cross-selling is a marketing strategy aimed at increasing sales by promoting and selling complementary or related products to existing customers. It involves offering additional products or services that complement the original purchase and add value to the customer.

The primary objective of cross-selling is to enhance customer satisfaction by fulfilling their needs and providing them with a more complete solution while increasing the average transaction value. By analyzing customer buying patterns and preferences, marketers can identify potential cross-selling opportunities and tailor their offers accordingly.

Effective cross-selling requires a deep understanding of customer behavior and preferences. This can be achieved through data analysis, customer segmentation, and personalized marketing tactics. By segmenting customers based on their demographics, purchase history, and preferences, marketers can offer targeted recommendations that resonate with each customer segment.

In addition to improving customer satisfaction, cross-selling also benefits businesses by maximizing revenue and profitability. By offering complementary products, businesses can tap into the existing customer base and promote additional sales without significant marketing costs. It also helps in building long-term customer relationships and increasing customer loyalty, ultimately leading to repeat purchases and customer retention.

Crowdsourcing

Crowdsourcing in the context of Marketing Management refers to the practice of obtaining ideas, solutions, or content from a large group of individuals, typically through an open call, in order to address a specific marketing challenge or to gather insights for decision-making.

By leveraging the power of the crowd, organizations can tap into a diverse range of perspectives, expertise, and creativity that may not be available within their internal team. Crowdsourcing enables marketers to harness collective intelligence, engage with their target audience, and encourage participation and collaboration in the development of marketing strategies, campaigns, and initiatives.

Customer Acquisition Cost (CAC) Analysis Tools

Customer Acquisition Cost (CAC) analysis tools are tools used in the field of marketing management to measure and analyze the cost associated with acquiring new customers. These tools provide valuable insights into the effectiveness and efficiency of a company's marketing and sales efforts.

CAC analysis tools typically gather data from various sources, such as advertising campaigns, sales records, and customer relationship management systems. They calculate the total expenses incurred by the marketing and sales teams to acquire new customers, including costs related to advertising, promotions, sales commissions, and other marketing activities. These tools also take into account the time and resources invested in nurturing leads and converting them into paying customers.

By analyzing the CAC, marketing managers can evaluate the return on investment (ROI) of different customer acquisition strategies and campaigns. They can determine which channels or tactics are most effective in attracting new customers and allocate their marketing budgets accordingly. CAC analysis tools also help identify areas of inefficiency or wasteful spending, allowing companies to optimize their marketing and sales processes.

Through CAC analysis, marketing managers can make data-driven decisions about customer acquisition, better understand the economics of their customer acquisition efforts, and measure the overall health and growth potential of their business. These tools contribute to the development of effective marketing strategies and the continuous improvement of the customer acquisition process.

Customer Acquisition Cost (CAC) Analysis

Customer Acquisition Cost (CAC) Analysis is a vital concept in the discipline of Marketing Management. CAC refers to the total amount of money a company invests in acquiring a new customer. It is an essential metric for assessing the effectiveness and profitability of marketing campaigns and strategies.

CAC analysis involves calculating the expenses incurred across various customer acquisition channels and dividing it by the number of customers acquired within a specific time period. This helps marketers understand the average cost associated with each customer acquisition and make informed decisions related to resource allocation and marketing budget planning.

Customer Acquisition Cost (CAC) Reduction

Customer acquisition cost (CAC) reduction refers to the strategic efforts and initiatives undertaken by a company to minimize the expenses associated with acquiring new customers. It is a key metric used in the field of marketing management to evaluate the cost-effectiveness of a company's customer acquisition strategy.

CAC reduction is crucial for businesses as it directly impacts profitability and overall financial performance. By reducing the cost of acquiring new customers, companies can maximize their return on investment (ROI) and allocate resources more efficiently. This can be achieved through various methods such as improving targeting and segmentation strategies, streamlining the customer acquisition process, and optimizing marketing channels and campaigns.

Customer Acquisition Cost (CAC)

Customer Acquisition Cost (CAC) is a metric used in the field of Marketing Management to measure the cost incurred by a company in acquiring a new customer. It represents the total expenses invested in the marketing campaigns and activities necessary to convert a prospect into a paying customer. CAC can be calculated by dividing the total marketing costs by the number of new customers acquired within a specific time period.

In order to accurately calculate CAC, it is important to consider all the costs associated with customer acquisition, including advertising costs, sales team salaries, commissions, marketing software, and any other expenses directly related to acquiring new customers. These costs can vary depending on the company's marketing strategy and target market.

Customer Acquisition

Customer acquisition is a crucial aspect of marketing management, focusing on the process of attracting and converting new customers to a business or brand. It involves various strategic activities and tactics aimed at increasing the customer base and generating revenue.

The objective of customer acquisition is to identify the target audience, engage with them effectively, and ultimately convince them to make a purchase or perform a desired action. This process is vital for the growth and success of any business as it directly impacts the bottom line.

Several key elements contribute to effective customer acquisition, including market research, segmentation, and targeting. Market research allows businesses to understand their customers' needs, preferences, and behaviors, enabling them to tailor their marketing efforts accordingly and identify opportunities for growth. Segmenting the market based on specific characteristics, such as demographics or psychographics, helps businesses identify the most promising target audience to focus on.

Once the target audience is identified, businesses can deploy various marketing tactics to acquire customers, such as advertising, content marketing, social media marketing, search engine optimization, and email marketing. These tactics are aimed at increasing brand visibility, capturing attention, and driving traffic to the business's website or physical location.

Once potential customers have been attracted, businesses need to convert them into paying customers. This can be achieved through effective sales strategies, personalized offers, and a seamless customer experience. Additionally, businesses must continuously monitor their customer acquisition efforts, analyze the results, and make necessary adjustments to optimize their marketing activities.

Customer Activation

Customer Activation refers to the process of engaging and motivating customers to take specific actions that benefit a business or brand. It involves a series of strategic activities and initiatives designed to persuade customers to interact with a company, make a purchase, or adopt a desired behavior.

In the context of Marketing Management, customer activation plays a crucial role in driving customer acquisition, retention, and loyalty. It focuses on converting potential or passive customers into active and engaged ones. By effectively activating customers, businesses can increase their revenue, enhance customer satisfaction, and establish long-term relationships.

Customer Advocacy

Customer advocacy is a marketing management concept that focuses on creating loyal and satisfied customers who actively promote a brand, product, or service to others. It involves understanding and meeting customer needs and expectations and building long-term relationships based on trust and mutual benefits.

Customer advocacy aims to transform satisfied customers into brand ambassadors who willingly advocate for the company and its offerings to their peers, colleagues, and social networks. It involves creating a positive customer experience at every touchpoint by consistently delivering high-quality products or services, providing exceptional customer support, and actively listening to customer feedback.

To foster customer advocacy, marketing managers should implement strategies such as personalized communication, rewards programs, loyalty initiatives, and customer engagement activities. These initiatives help develop a strong emotional connection between the customer and the brand, increasing the likelihood of positive word-of-mouth recommendations.

Furthermore, marketing managers should prioritize customer satisfaction and loyalty by continuously monitoring and addressing customer concerns and complaints. By resolving issues promptly and effectively, companies not only retain customers but also enhance their reputation for excellent customer service.

Overall, customer advocacy is a crucial aspect of marketing management as it drives customer acquisition, retention, and brand reputation. By nurturing brand ambassadors, companies can benefit from increased visibility, positive word-of-mouth, and an expanded customer base.

Customer Analysis

Customer analysis is a key component of marketing management that involves gathering and interpreting data about customers in order to gain insights into their characteristics, behaviors, needs, and preferences. It is a systematic process that helps marketers to understand their target audience and make informed decisions regarding product development, pricing, promotion, and distribution strategies.

The primary purpose of customer analysis is to identify and segment the target market into distinct groups based on various criteria such as demographics, psychographics, and buying behavior. This segmentation allows marketers to tailor their marketing efforts and messages to different customer segments, ensuring that the right products are being offered to the right customers at the right time. Customer analysis involves the collection and analysis of both quantitative and qualitative data. Quantitative data includes information such as age, gender, income, and purchase history, which can be obtained through surveys, questionnaires, and databases. Qualitative data, on the other hand, involves gathering insights through methods such as interviews, focus groups, and observations to understand customers' attitudes, preferences, and motivations. Once customer data has been collected and analyzed, marketers can develop customer profiles or personas that represent different segments of the target market. These profiles help marketers to understand their customers' needs, desires, and preferences, which in turn allows them to create targeted marketing campaigns and develop products that are tailored to meet those needs. In conclusion, customer analysis is a fundamental aspect of marketing management that enables marketers to gain a deep understanding of their target market. By analyzing customer data, marketers can effectively segment the market, develop customer profiles, and tailor their marketing strategies to meet the needs and preferences of different customer segments.

Customer Behavior Analysis Software

Customer Behavior Analysis Software is a tool used in the field of Marketing Management to collect, analyze, and interpret data on consumer behavior. It helps marketing professionals gain insights into the actions, preferences, and motivations of customers, enabling them to make data-driven decisions and develop effective marketing strategies.

This software utilizes various data sources, such as customer surveys, purchase history, social media activity, website analytics, and demographic information, to create a holistic view of customer behavior. It applies advanced analytical techniques, such as data mining, predictive modeling, and segmentation, to identify patterns, trends, and correlations within the data.

Customer Behavior Analysis

Customer Behavior Analysis in the context of Marketing Management discipline refers to the systematic study and understanding of consumers' actions, preferences, and decision-making processes when making purchasing decisions. It involves analyzing various aspects of consumer behavior, such as their motivations, needs, beliefs, attitudes, and perceptions, in order to gain insights that can be used to develop effective marketing strategies and tactics.

The purpose of customer behavior analysis is to comprehend why people buy certain products or services, how they evaluate different options, and what influences their purchase decisions. By studying consumer behavior, marketers can identify patterns, trends, and correlations that can help them better understand their target audience and anticipate their needs and preferences.

There are several key components of customer behavior analysis, including market research, data collection and analysis, segmentation, and consumer profiling. Market research involves gathering and analyzing information about consumer demographics, psychographics, buying behaviors, and preferences through surveys, interviews, and other research methods. Data collection and analysis involve using techniques such as surveys, experiments, and observational studies to collect and analyze data on consumer behavior. Segmentation involves dividing the target market into distinct groups based on key characteristics or behaviors. Consumer profiling involves creating detailed profiles of target customers, including their demographics, psychographics, and buying behaviors.

By conducting customer behavior analysis, marketers can gain valuable insights into consumer motivations, preferences, and decision-making processes. This information can be used to tailor marketing messages, develop targeted campaigns, improve product design, and enhance the overall customer experience. Ultimately, customer behavior analysis helps marketers to better understand and meet the needs of their target audience, leading to increased customer satisfaction, loyalty, and ultimately, business success.

Customer Behavior Prediction

Customer behavior prediction in the context of marketing management is the process of using various techniques and methods to analyze and forecast the actions, preferences, and purchasing patterns of customers. It involves gathering and analyzing data related to customer behavior, such as past transaction history, website browsing patterns, social media interactions, and demographics.

The objective of customer behavior prediction is to gain insights into customer preferences, needs, and motivations in order to tailor marketing strategies and tactics accordingly. By understanding customer behavior, marketers can anticipate future actions and make more informed decisions when it comes to product development, pricing, distribution, and promotional activities.

Customer Centricity Culture

Customer Centricity Culture refers to a strategic approach adopted by organizations in the field of marketing management, wherein the focus is primarily on prioritizing the needs and preferences of the customers. It is a key principle that guides decision-making processes and shapes the overall business practices of an organization.

A customer-centric culture places the customer at the core of the business, aiming to understand their expectations, desires, and behaviors. By doing so, organizations can develop products and services that specifically cater to their customers' needs and provide them with a superior customer experience.

Customer Centricity Frameworks

Customer Centricity refers to the strategic approach of placing the customer at the center of an organization's activities and decision-making processes. It entails a deep understanding of customer needs, preferences, and behaviors, and using this knowledge to tailor products, services, and marketing efforts that meet and exceed those needs. This approach acknowledges that customers are the driving force behind a company's success, and by prioritizing their wants and desires, a company can achieve sustainable growth and competitive advantage.

There are several frameworks that can guide organizations in adopting a customer-centric approach:

1. Customer Lifetime Value (CLV): This framework calculates the net present value of the expected future profit a company can generate from a particular customer. By focusing on maximizing CLV, organizations can make strategic decisions that prioritize long-term customer satisfaction and loyalty.

2. Customer Segmentation: This framework involves dividing customers into distinct groups based on their shared characteristics and needs. By understanding the unique preferences and behaviors of different segments, organizations can tailor their marketing efforts and offerings to effectively meet the needs of each segment.

3. Customer Journey Mapping: This framework involves visualizing and analyzing the various touchpoints and interactions a customer has with a brand throughout their journey. By understanding the customer journey, organizations can identify pain points and opportunities for improvement, enabling them to enhance the overall customer experience.

These frameworks, among others, provide organizations with a systematic approach to understanding and meeting customer needs. By adopting a customer-centric approach, organizations can build strong, long-lasting relationships with customers, drive customer satisfaction and loyalty, and ultimately, achieve sustainable business growth.

Customer Centricity

Customer centricity is a key concept in the field of Marketing Management. It is an approach that puts the customer at the center of all marketing strategies and activities. It is about understanding and addressing customer needs, preferences, and desires to create value for them.

This approach requires marketers to gather and analyze customer data, such as demographics, behaviors, and preferences, to gain insights into their target customers. By understanding their customers better, marketers can develop products, services, and marketing campaigns that are tailored to their customers' specific needs and wants.

Customer centricity also involves building and maintaining strong relationships with customers. This includes providing excellent customer service, being responsive to customer feedback and complaints, and continuously engaging with customers to understand their evolving needs and expectations.

By adopting a customer-centric approach, businesses can differentiate themselves from their competitors and build long-lasting customer loyalty. It can lead to increased customer satisfaction, repeat purchases, positive word-of-mouth, and ultimately higher profitability.

Customer Churn Rate

Customer churn rate is a metric used in the field of Marketing Management to measure the percentage of customers who have stopped engaging with a company's products or services within a specific time period. It is a critical indicator of customer loyalty and satisfaction, reflecting the effectiveness of a company's customer retention strategies.

The formula for calculating customer churn rate is as follows:

Customer Churn Rate = (Number of customers lost during a given period / Total number of customers at the beginning of the period) x 100

A high customer churn rate implies that a company is losing a significant number of customers and may have underlying issues in its marketing strategies, customer experience, or product/service quality. It can be costly for a company as it not only signifies revenue loss from lost customers but also entails the need to acquire new customers to fill the gap.

Measuring customer churn rate allows marketing managers to track customer retention efforts, identify trends, and make data-driven decisions to improve customer satisfaction and loyalty. By understanding the reasons behind customer churn, companies can develop targeted strategies to mitigate customer loss and increase customer lifetime value.

Customer Churn

Customer churn, in the context of Marketing Management discipline, refers to the phenomenon of customers discontinuing their relationship with a company or brand. It is a crucial metric for businesses, as it directly impacts revenue and growth.

Customer churn can occur due to various reasons, including dissatisfaction with the product or service, better alternatives available in the market, or changes in personal circumstances. Identifying and understanding the factors that contribute to customer churn is essential for businesses to develop effective retention strategies and reduce the loss of valuable customers.

Customer Data Platform (CDP)

A Customer Data Platform (CDP) is a tool used in the field of Marketing Management to collect, organize, and analyze customer data from various sources. It serves as a centralized system that provides marketers with a comprehensive view of their customers, enabling them to create targeted and personalized marketing strategies.

A CDP is designed to handle large amounts of data from multiple sources, such as online and offline channels, social media, and customer interactions. It integrates data from these sources, cleanses and normalizes it, and then stores it in a unified customer database. This database is structured to enable marketers to segment and analyze the data based on various criteria, such as demographics, behaviors, preferences, and purchase history.

By utilizing a CDP, marketers can gain valuable insights into their customers' preferences, needs, and behaviors. This enables them to deliver highly personalized marketing messages and experiences across different channels, such as email, social media, websites, and mobile apps. The insights derived from a CDP can also be used to identify trends, predict customer behavior and future needs, and optimize marketing campaigns for better ROI.

Overall, a Customer Data Platform plays a vital role in the field of Marketing Management by providing marketers with a centralized system to collect, organize, and analyze customer data. It contributes to the development of targeted and personalized marketing strategies, ultimately leading to improved customer satisfaction, higher engagement, and increased revenue for businesses.

Customer Engagement Rate

Customer engagement rate refers to the measure used in marketing management to assess the level of interaction and involvement of customers with a brand or company. It is a metric that quantifies how well a company is able to engage its customers and build relationships with them.

This rate is calculated by tracking and analyzing various customer touchpoints such as website visits, social media interactions, purchases, and customer feedback. These touchpoints are indicators of the level of engagement customers have with the brand and its offerings.

Customer Engagement

Customer engagement is a fundamental concept in the field of marketing management. It refers to the ongoing interaction and communication between a company and its customers, with the aim of creating a long-lasting relationship and promoting customer loyalty. Engaged customers are active participants in the brand's activities, showing a high level of interest and commitment towards the company.

In order to achieve customer engagement, companies need to develop effective strategies that involve the customers in various aspects of the business. This can include personalized communication, active listening, and involving customers in the product development process, among other initiatives. The goal is to create a two-way relationship where both the company and the customers benefit.

Customer engagement is crucial for the success of a business as it has a direct impact on customer satisfaction, loyalty, and advocacy. Engaged customers are more likely to repurchase products and services, recommend the brand to others, and provide valuable feedback and ideas. Moreover, customer engagement can also lead to increased brand awareness and positive word-of-mouth, which are key drivers of business growth.

Companies can measure customer engagement through various metrics, including customer retention rates, customer satisfaction surveys, social media engagement, and customer lifetime value. By continuously monitoring and analyzing these metrics, companies can identify areas for improvement and develop targeted strategies to enhance customer engagement.

Customer Experience (CX)

Customer Experience (CX) refers to the overall perception and interaction that customers have with a brand or organization throughout their customer journey. It encompasses every touchpoint and interaction between the customer and the company, including pre-purchase interactions, the buying process, and post-purchase support.

In the context of Marketing Management discipline, CX plays a crucial role in building and maintaining customer relationships. It goes beyond just providing a product or service; it focuses on delivering a positive and seamless experience that exceeds customer expectations.

Effective CX management involves understanding customer needs, desires, and pain points and designing strategies to meet and address them. This includes creating personalized experiences that are relevant and tailored to individual customers, utilizing various channels and technologies to engage with customers, and continuously improving processes to ensure a consistent and exceptional customer experience across all touchpoints.

By prioritizing CX, businesses can differentiate themselves from competitors, increase customer loyalty, and drive long-term profitability. A positive customer experience not only leads to customer satisfaction but also boosts brand advocacy, as satisfied customers are more likely to recommend and promote the brand to others.

Ultimately, CX is a critical aspect of the overall marketing strategy, as it directly impacts customer perception, satisfaction, and ultimately, the success of the business. It requires a customer-centric mindset, a deep understanding of customer behavior and preferences, and a commitment to continuously improving the customer experience to drive positive business outcomes.

Customer Experience Design Tools

Customer Experience Design Tools are a set of strategies and techniques used in the field of Marketing Management to enhance and shape the overall customer experience. These tools are designed to improve customer satisfaction, loyalty, and advocacy by creating positive interactions and meaningful engagements with the brand.

These tools are based on the understanding that the customer experience is a crucial factor in the success of a business. They help marketers develop a deeper understanding of their target audience's needs, preferences, and behaviors, enabling them to create tailored experiences that resonate with customers.

Customer Experience Design

Customer Experience Design refers to the strategic process of creating and optimizing the overall journey and interactions that customers have with a company or brand. It is a discipline within the field of Marketing Management that focuses on designing and delivering exceptional experiences to customers at every touchpoint.

Customer experience encompasses all the emotions, perceptions, and interactions that customers have before, during, and after their purchase or engagement with a company. It encompasses various elements such as product design, user interface, customer service, marketing communications, and every other aspect that impacts the customer's experience.

The goal of customer experience design is to understand the needs, preferences, and expectations of customers and then tailor the journey and touchpoints to meet or exceed those expectations. It involves conducting research, gathering customer feedback, and using data and insights to inform the design and improvement of the customer experience.

By putting a strong emphasis on customer experience, companies can differentiate themselves from competitors, build customer loyalty, and ultimately drive growth and profitability. It requires a deep understanding of customer behavior, market trends, and the ability to align internal processes and systems to deliver a seamless and consistent experience across channels.

Overall, customer experience design is an essential component of the marketing management discipline as it enables companies to create meaningful and memorable interactions with customers, build strong relationships, and ultimately drive business success.

Customer Experience Optimization

Customer Experience Optimization, in the context of Marketing Management, refers to the systematic process of improving and enhancing the overall experience that customers have with a company or brand throughout their interactions and touchpoints. It involves analyzing customer behaviors, preferences, and feedback, and utilizing this information to make data-driven decisions aimed at delivering personalized and seamless experiences.

By optimizing the customer experience, companies aim to build strong and lasting relationships with their customers, increase customer loyalty, and drive repeat business. It requires companies to understand the customer journey, from initial awareness to post-purchase follow-up, and identify pain points or areas where improvements can be made to enhance customer satisfaction.

This process involves various strategies and tactics, such as improving website usability and navigation, streamlining the purchasing process, enhancing customer service and support, personalizing marketing communications, and providing relevant and timely content. Companies may also utilize technology and data analytics to track and measure customer interactions, identify patterns and trends, and gain insights to further enhance the customer experience.

Ultimately, Customer Experience Optimization aims to create a positive and memorable experience for customers, ensuring that each touchpoint aligns with their expectations and needs. By continuously optimizing the customer experience, companies can gain a competitive advantage, differentiate themselves from competitors, and ultimately drive customer satisfaction and business growth.

Customer Feedback

Customer feedback refers to the information, opinions, and sentiments shared by customers about their experiences with a product, service, or brand. In the context of the Marketing Management discipline, customer feedback plays a crucial role in understanding customer preferences, needs, and satisfaction levels.

This feedback can be obtained through various channels such as surveys, reviews, social media comments, and direct interactions with customers. It can provide valuable insights that help businesses make informed decisions, improve their products and services, and enhance overall customer experience.

Customer Insight Analysis

Customer Insight Analysis refers to the process of analyzing and interpreting customer data to gain a deeper understanding of customer behavior, preferences, and needs. It is an essential component of marketing management as it provides valuable insights that enable businesses to make informed decisions and develop effective marketing strategies.

By analyzing customer data obtained from various sources such as surveys, interviews, social media, and purchase history, businesses can identify patterns, trends, and correlations that help them understand their customers better. This analysis involves examining demographic information, purchasing behavior, product usage, and other relevant data points to create a comprehensive customer profile.

The goal of customer insight analysis is to uncover valuable insights that can drive marketing initiatives. These insights can help businesses identify and target their most profitable customer segments, tailor their messaging and communication strategies, develop new products or services that meet customer needs, and enhance customer satisfaction and loyalty.

Furthermore, customer insight analysis enables businesses to anticipate customer needs and preferences, identify opportunities for cross-selling or upselling, and improve overall customer experience. It provides marketing managers with actionable insights that can guide marketing campaigns, enhance customer engagement, and ultimately drive business growth and profitability.

In conclusion, customer insight analysis is a vital tool in marketing management that enables businesses to extract actionable insights from customer data. By understanding their customers better, businesses can make informed decisions and develop effective marketing strategies that enhance customer satisfaction, loyalty, and drive business success.

Customer Insight Generation Platforms

A customer insight generation platform is a software tool or platform used by marketers to gather, analyze, and interpret customer data in order to gain meaningful and actionable insights. These insights help marketers understand customer behavior, preferences, needs, and motivations, which can then be used to develop effective marketing strategies and tactics.

The platform typically integrates various data sources, such as customer demographic information, purchase history, online behavior, social media interactions, and customer feedback. It uses advanced analytics techniques, such as data mining, machine learning, and predictive modeling, to uncover patterns, trends, and correlations within the data. Through the platform, marketers can segment their customer base into distinct groups based on characteristics and behaviors, allowing for more targeted and personalized marketing campaigns. They can also identify opportunities for cross-selling and upselling, as well as potential areas for improvement in products or services. Customer insight generation platforms enable marketers to monitor and track the impact of their marketing efforts in real-time, providing valuable feedback to refine strategies and measure success. They help marketers gain a deeper understanding of their customers, enabling them to make informed decisions and drive customer-centric marketing initiatives.

Customer Insight Generation

Customer insight generation is a vital aspect of marketing management that involves the systematic collection, analysis, and interpretation of data to gain a deep understanding of customer behavior, preferences, and needs. It is a process of gathering valuable information about customers to make informed decisions, develop effective marketing strategies, and create meaningful customer experiences.

This process typically begins by gathering data from various sources such as market research, customer surveys, social media interactions, and website analytics. The collected data is then analyzed using various techniques to uncover patterns, trends, and insights. These insights are derived by examining customer demographics, psychographics, purchase history, browsing behaviors, and other relevant information.

Once the data is analyzed, marketers can identify key customer segments, understand their motivations, and tailor marketing efforts to meet their specific needs. Customer insights also help in predicting future behavior, identifying potential opportunities, and anticipating market trends.

By gaining a deeper understanding of customers, companies can develop more targeted marketing campaigns, personalized product offerings, and improved customer experiences. Customer insight generation is essential for building strong customer relationships, increasing customer satisfaction, and driving business growth.

Customer Insight

Customer Insight refers to the deep understanding and interpretation of customer behavior, needs, preferences, and expectations through the analysis of various data sources and research methods. It is a fundamental concept in Marketing Management, as it enables managers to make informed decisions and develop effective marketing strategies.

Customer Insight strives to go beyond surface-level understanding and seeks to uncover the underlying motivations and emotions that drive customer behavior. By collecting and analyzing customer data from sources such as surveys, focus groups, social media, and purchase history, marketers can gain valuable insights into what customers want, why they behave the way they do, and how they can be effectively targeted and satisfied.

Customer Insights

Customer insights, in the context of Marketing Management, refer to the deep understanding of customers gained through various research methods and data analysis. It involves collecting and analyzing relevant data to uncover customer preferences, behaviors, needs, and motivations.

Customer insights are crucial for effective marketing strategies as they provide valuable information that helps businesses make informed decisions and tailor their products, services, and marketing efforts to meet customer demands. By understanding customer insights, companies can anticipate and respond to changing market trends, develop targeted marketing campaigns, and create customer-centric experiences.

Customer Journey Analytics

Customer Journey Analytics refers to the process of collecting, analyzing, and interpreting data related to the interactions and experiences of customers throughout their entire journey with a brand or organization. It involves understanding the various touchpoints and channels through which customers engage with a company, and leveraging data to gain insights into their behaviors, preferences, and needs.

By utilizing customer journey analytics, marketers can identify patterns and trends in customer behavior, such as the actions they take, the channels they use, and the emotions they experience at different stages of their journey. This enables marketers to better understand the customer experience, identify areas for improvement, and make data-driven decisions to enhance customer satisfaction and loyalty.

Customer Journey Mapping Software

Customer Journey Mapping Software refers to a marketing management tool that visualizes and analyzes the various touchpoints or interactions a customer has with a brand throughout their journey or lifecycle. It enables marketers to gain a comprehensive understanding of the customer's experience, perceptions, emotions, and needs at each stage of the journey.

The software allows marketers to create detailed maps or diagrams that document the various touchpoints, channels, and actions that customers encounter, from the initial awareness and consideration stages to the conversion, retention, and advocacy stages. These maps help marketers identify gaps or pain points in the customer journey, enabling them to optimize and enhance each stage to deliver a seamless and personalized customer experience.

Customer Journey Mapping

A customer journey map is a strategic tool used in the field of marketing management to visualize and understand the various touchpoints a customer experiences while interacting with a business or brand. It provides a step-by-step representation of the customer's experience throughout their entire journey, from the initial awareness stage to the post-purchase stage.

The purpose of creating a customer journey map is to gain insights into the customer's perspective, emotions, and interactions at each stage. By mapping out the customer's journey, marketers can identify pain points, areas of improvement, and opportunities to enhance the overall customer experience.

The process of customer journey mapping involves collecting and analyzing data from various sources, including customer surveys, interviews, and feedback. This information is used to create a visual representation of the customer's journey, typically in the form of a timeline or flowchart.

The key components of a customer journey map include identifying customer touchpoints, understanding customer motivations and expectations, and assessing the effectiveness of existing marketing strategies and tactics. It allows marketers to align their efforts with the customer's needs and preferences, thus enabling them to deliver personalized and engaging experiences.

Customer Journey Orchestration

A customer journey orchestration is a strategic marketing management approach that focuses on creating and delivering personalized and seamless experiences to customers across various touchpoints and channels throughout their entire journey with a brand. It involves designing a structured and optimized customer experience that effectively engages, guides, and nurtures individuals from the initial interaction with a brand to the final conversion and beyond.

This discipline emphasizes the importance of understanding and mapping the customer journey, which involves identifying key touchpoints, interactions, and decision-making moments that customers go through during their interactions with a brand. By analyzing and gaining insights into these touchpoints, marketers can identify opportunities to enhance customer experiences and drive desired outcomes.

Customer Journey

A customer journey is a strategic framework that maps out the entire experience a customer has with a company or brand across all touchpoints and interactions. It is a representation of the customer's path from initial awareness to post-purchase satisfaction and loyalty.

The customer journey is a crucial concept in marketing management as it helps businesses understand and optimize each stage of the customer's experience. By gaining a deep understanding of the customer journey, marketers can identify pain points, opportunities, and areas for improvement.

The customer journey typically includes several stages, such as awareness, consideration, purchase, and post-purchase. Each of these stages involves specific touchpoints where the customer interacts with the brand, such as advertisements, websites, social media, customer service, and product usage.

By analyzing the customer journey, marketers can identify key moments of influence and engagement throughout the customer's experience. This allows them to tailor their marketing strategies and initiatives to better meet the needs and preferences of their customers.

Ultimately, the goal of understanding the customer journey is to enhance customer satisfaction, increase brand loyalty, and drive business growth. By providing a seamless and personalized experience at each touchpoint, companies can build stronger relationships with their customers and differentiate themselves from competitors.

Customer Lifetime Value (CLV)

Customer Lifetime Value (CLV) is a metric used in Marketing Management discipline to estimate the total monetary value a customer would generate over their entire relationship with a company. It helps businesses understand the profitability and long-term value associated with acquiring and retaining customers.

CLV explicitly acknowledges that customers have varying purchasing behaviors, and therefore, assigns a comprehensive value to each customer beyond just the initial purchase. By considering factors such as repeat purchases, average purchase value, and customer retention, CLV allows marketers to make informed decisions regarding customer acquisition, retention, and loyalty strategies.

Customer Onboarding

Customer onboarding in the context of Marketing Management refers to the process of welcoming and familiarizing new customers with a brand, product, or service. It is an essential step in building a strong and lasting relationship with customers, as it sets the foundation for their journey as a customer and helps them understand the value proposition of the brand.

The customer onboarding process involves various activities and touchpoints that aim to ensure a smooth and positive experience for the new customers. This includes providing them with all the necessary information and resources to understand the product or service, guiding them through the initial setup or implementation process, and addressing any questions or concerns they may have.

The goals of customer onboarding are to create a sense of trust, establish clear expectations, and maximize the value and satisfaction the customer derives from the brand. It is also an opportunity for the brand to gather customer feedback, assess the customer's needs and preferences, and identify opportunities for upselling or cross-selling.

Effective customer onboarding can significantly impact customer retention and loyalty, as it helps customers feel valued and supported from the very beginning of their relationship with the brand. It serves as a foundation for building long-term relationships and increasing customer lifetime value.

Customer Persona

A customer persona, in the context of Marketing Management, refers to a fictional representation or archetype of a target customer or market segment. It is created based on research, data analysis, and insights gathered through market research, surveys, customer feedback, and other sources of information.

The purpose of developing customer personas is to gain a deeper understanding of the customers' needs, preferences, behaviors, and motivations. By creating these personas, marketers can effectively tailor their marketing strategies, messaging, and product offerings to meet the specific requirements and expectations of their target audience.

Customer Profiling Solutions

Customer profiling solutions refer to the process of gathering and analyzing data to create detailed profiles of customers. In the context of Marketing Management discipline, customer profiling solutions help businesses in understanding their customers better by identifying their preferences, behaviors, and characteristics. These solutions enable marketing managers to segment their customer base and create personalized marketing strategies that cater to the unique needs and preferences of different customer groups.

By utilizing customer profiling solutions, marketing managers can effectively target their marketing efforts and allocate resources in a way that maximizes the return on investment. These solutions often leverage advanced analytics techniques to extract insights from customer data, such as demographic information, purchase history, online behavior, and social media interactions. Through the analysis of this data, businesses can identify trends and patterns, uncover hidden relationships, and gain a deeper understanding of their target audience.

Customer Profiling Tools

Customer profiling tools in the context of Marketing Management refer to a set of techniques and strategies used to gather, analyze, and interpret data about current and potential customers. These tools help marketers gain insights into consumer behavior, preferences, and characteristics, which enables them to create more effective marketing campaigns and tailor their products or services to the specific needs and wants of their target audience.

Customer profiling tools use both quantitative and qualitative data sources to build a comprehensive understanding of customers. Quantitative data includes demographic information such as age, gender, income level, and geographic location, as well as behavioral data like purchasing history and online browsing patterns. Qualitative data, on the other hand, delves into the motivations, attitudes, and lifestyle choices of customers through methods like surveys, interviews, or focus groups.

Customer Profiling

Customer profiling is a marketing management practice that involves the creation and analysis of detailed descriptions and classifications of target customers or market segments. It is a strategic tool used to better understand consumers and tailor marketing efforts to meet their needs and preferences.

By examining various demographic, psychographic, and behavioral characteristics of customers, businesses can gain valuable insights into their target audience. This information allows organizations to create more effective marketing strategies, develop targeted advertising campaigns, and personalize product offerings.

Customer Relationship Management (CRM)

Customer Relationship Management (CRM) is a marketing management discipline that focuses on building and maintaining strong relationships with customers. It involves the use of strategies, techniques, and technologies to manage interactions and engagements with customers throughout their lifecycle. CRM aims to enhance customer satisfaction, loyalty, and retention by providing personalized and tailored experiences.

CRM encompasses various activities, such as capturing customer data, analyzing customer behavior, and developing targeted marketing campaigns. It helps organizations understand their customers' needs, preferences, and buying patterns to deliver relevant and timely offerings. By leveraging CRM, companies can gather valuable insights to segment their customer base, identify high-value customers, and develop effective customer acquisition and retention strategies.

CRM systems are designed to centralize customer data, allowing businesses to track and manage customer interactions across multiple touchpoints, such as sales, marketing, and customer service. These systems enable organizations to provide personalized and efficient customer support, resolve issues promptly, and deliver consistent experiences across channels.

CRM helps businesses streamline their marketing efforts by enabling targeted customer segmentation and personalized messaging. By understanding customer needs and preferences, organizations can develop tailored marketing campaigns that resonate with their audience, leading to higher conversion rates and customer engagement.

In summary, CRM is a marketing management discipline that focuses on building and maintaining strong customer relationships. It involves the use of strategies, techniques, and technologies to manage interactions and engagements throughout the customer lifecycle, aiming to enhance customer satisfaction, loyalty, and retention.

Customer Relationship Marketing (CRM)

Customer Relationship Marketing (CRM) is a marketing management discipline that focuses on building and maintaining strong relationships with customers. It emphasizes the importance of understanding and meeting the unique needs and preferences of individual customers.

CRM involves the use of various strategies, techniques, and technologies to collect, analyze, and use customer data effectively. This data includes information about customers' demographics, behaviors, purchasing patterns, and interactions with the company. By analyzing this data, companies can gain insights into customer preferences, identify opportunities for cross-selling or upselling, and personalize their marketing efforts accordingly.

Customer Relationship

A customer relationship in the context of Marketing Management refers to the interaction and connection between a company and its customers throughout the entire customer lifecycle. It involves developing, nurturing, and maintaining strong, long-lasting relationships with customers to build loyalty, trust, and repeat business.

Effective customer relationship management (CRM) is crucial for businesses as it helps create a positive customer experience and enhances customer satisfaction. It involves understanding and meeting customer needs and expectations, and continuously engaging with them to build strong relationships.

Customer Retention Platforms

A customer retention platform in the context of marketing management is a technological tool or software solution that is used to analyze and enhance customer relationships and loyalty. It serves as a central hub for managing various customer retention strategies and activities. Customer retention is a critical aspect of marketing management, as it focuses on preserving and maximizing the value of existing customers. Studies have shown that it can cost up to five times more to acquire a new customer than to retain an existing one. Therefore, businesses have a vested interest in implementing effective customer retention strategies. A customer retention platform typically offers features and functionalities that enable marketers to track and analyze customer behavior, preferences, and purchases. This data can then be used to identify patterns, trends, and opportunities for improving customer satisfaction and loyalty. These platforms often provide tools for personalized marketing, such as targeted email campaigns, social media integration, and customer segmentation. They may also offer capabilities for managing loyalty programs, reward systems, and customer feedback. One of the main advantages of using a customer retention platform is the ability to centralize customer data and insights. This allows marketers to have a holistic view of each customer and their interactions with the business, enabling them to tailor their marketing efforts and communication accordingly. In conclusion, a customer retention platform acts as a valuable asset for marketing management by providing the tools and capabilities to analyze, optimize, and enhance customer relationships and loyalty. Its holistic approach and integration of various features make it an essential tool for businesses aiming to retain their customer base and increase customer lifetime value.

Customer Retention Rate

The customer retention rate is a metric used in the field of marketing management to measure the ability of a company to retain its existing customers over a specific period of time. It is a crucial indicator of a company's customer loyalty and satisfaction levels, as well as its overall performance in the market.

The customer retention rate is calculated by dividing the number of customers at the end of a period by the number of customers at the beginning of that period, and then multiplying the result by 100. The formula can be expressed as follows:

Customer Retention Rate = ((Number of Customers at End of Period / Number of Customers at Beginning of Period) * 100)

A high customer retention rate indicates that a company has been successful in building strong relationships with its customers, providing excellent products or services, and meeting their needs and expectations. It is generally more cost-effective for companies to retain existing customers than to acquire new ones, as retaining customers reduces marketing costs and increases the chances of generating repeat business.

On the other hand, a low customer retention rate could indicate issues such as poor customer service, product quality, or competitive offerings. It may also suggest that customers are not satisfied with their overall experience with the company, leading them to switch to competitors or discontinue using the company's products or services.

Customer Retention Strategies

Customer retention strategies refer to the various tactics and techniques used by a company to retain their existing customers and encourage repeat purchases or continued loyalty. In the context of marketing management, customer retention is a crucial aspect as it costs less to retain an existing customer compared to acquiring a new one. These strategies aim to build strong relationships with customers, providing them with value, satisfaction, and reasons to continue choosing the company's products or services over competitors.

Effective customer retention strategies involve understanding customer needs, preferences, and behaviors, and tailoring the company's offerings and communication accordingly. This may include personalized marketing campaigns, loyalty programs, excellent customer service, regular engagement and communication, and anticipating and addressing customer concerns or issues promptly and effectively.

The objective of implementing customer retention strategies is not only to maintain current revenue streams but also to increase customer lifetime value. Loyal customers tend to spend more, provide positive referrals or recommendations, and are less likely to switch to competitors. By focusing on customer retention, companies can improve customer satisfaction, reduce customer churn, increase profitability, and gain a competitive advantage in the market.

Customer Retention Tactics

Customer retention tactics refer to the strategies and actions implemented by marketers to retain existing customers and increase their loyalty towards a brand or company. These tactics are aimed at reducing customer churn, which is the rate at which customers stop doing business with a brand or switch to competitors.

One common customer retention tactic is providing excellent customer service. This involves ensuring that customers have a positive experience with the brand at every touchpoint, addressing their concerns and resolving any issues in a timely manner. By delivering exceptional customer service, brands can build stronger relationships with their customers and increase the likelihood of repeat purchases and long-term loyalty.

Customer Retention

Customer retention refers to the strategies and activities implemented by a company to maintain and enhance the relationships it has with its existing customers. It involves creating and nurturing long-term relationships with customers in order to encourage repeat business and loyalty.

In the field of marketing management, customer retention is a crucial aspect as it is much more cost-effective to retain existing customers than to acquire new ones. By focusing on retaining customers, companies can reduce their marketing and acquisition costs, increase revenue, and ultimately improve profitability.

Customer Satisfaction Index (CSI)

The Customer Satisfaction Index (CSI) is a metric used in the field of Marketing Management to assess and measure the satisfaction of customers with a particular product or service. It is a quantitative measure that helps organizations understand how well they are meeting the needs and expectations of their customers.

The CSI is typically calculated by surveying customers and asking them to rate their satisfaction on a scale, which can range from very satisfied to very dissatisfied. These ratings are then used to calculate an average score, which represents the overall satisfaction level of customers. This score can be used to compare the satisfaction levels of different products or services, as well as to track changes in satisfaction over time.

Customer Satisfaction

Customer satisfaction refers to the extent to which customers are pleased or happy with the products, services, or experiences they receive from a company or brand. It is a key concept in the field of marketing management as it directly impacts a company's profitability, customer loyalty, and brand reputation.

A high level of customer satisfaction is crucial for business success as it leads to repeat purchases, positive word-of-mouth recommendations, and higher customer loyalty. Satisfied customers are more likely to become loyal customers who continue to purchase from the same company and are less likely to switch to competitors.

Marketing managers play a vital role in achieving customer satisfaction by understanding and meeting customer expectations. They need to conduct market research to gather valuable insights into customer needs, preferences, and perceptions. Based on this information, they develop marketing strategies and implement tactics to deliver products or services that exceed customer expectations.

Effective communication, personalized customer service, and timely problem resolution are also essential components of customer satisfaction. Companies need to ensure that their employees are trained to provide excellent customer service and have the necessary tools to address customer concerns in a timely manner.

Regularly measuring customer satisfaction through surveys, feedback, and other metrics is another important aspect of marketing management. This allows companies to identify areas for improvement and take necessary actions to enhance customer satisfaction levels.

Customer Segmentation Analysis

Customer segmentation analysis is a strategic marketing management process that involves dividing a company's customer base into distinct groups or segments based on various characteristics and attributes. This analysis enables marketers to gain meaningful insights into the different needs, preferences, and behaviors of their customers, allowing them to tailor their marketing strategies and tactics more effectively.

The purpose of customer segmentation analysis is to identify and understand the diverse groups within a company's customer base so that marketing efforts can be targeted and focused. By segmenting customers, marketers can create customized marketing campaigns, messages, and offers that resonate with each segment, resulting in higher customer satisfaction, increased brand loyalty, and ultimately, improved profitability.

Customer Segmentation Software

Customer segmentation software refers to a marketing management tool that analyzes and categorizes customers into distinct groups or segments based on specific criteria or characteristics. It is designed to help businesses understand their customer base better and develop targeted marketing strategies tailored to meet the unique needs and preferences of each segment.

With the help of customer segmentation software, marketing teams can segment their customer base using various variables such as demographic information, purchase behavior, psychographic attributes, and geographic location. This software leverages data analytics techniques to identify patterns, trends, and similarities among customers, allowing companies to create more personalized marketing messages and campaigns.

Customer Segmentation Tools

Customer segmentation tools in the context of Marketing Management discipline refer to the techniques and technologies used to divide a target market into distinct groups or segments based on various criteria such as demographics, psychographics, and behaviors. These tools allow marketers to identify and understand the different characteristics, needs, and preferences of their customers, enabling them to create more targeted and personalized marketing strategies.

One of the primary goals of customer segmentation is to maximize the effectiveness of marketing efforts by tailoring messages and offerings to specific segments that are most likely to respond positively. This approach helps in optimizing resource allocation and improving overall customer satisfaction and loyalty.

Customer Segmentation

Customer segmentation refers to the process of dividing a market into distinct groups of individuals who share similar characteristics, behaviors, needs, or preferences. These groups, known as customer segments, are then targeted with tailored marketing strategies in order to maximize the effectiveness of marketing efforts.

Marketers use various criteria to segment customers, such as demographics (age, gender, income), psychographics (values, attitudes, lifestyles), geographic location, and behavioral patterns (past purchasing behavior, usage rate, brand loyalty). By understanding the unique needs, desires, and motivations of different customer segments, marketers can customize their marketing messages, products, pricing, and distribution channels to increase customer satisfaction and drive sales.

Customer Sentiment Analysis Tools

Customer Sentiment Analysis Tools in the context of Marketing Management refer to software or tools that are designed to analyze and interpret the sentiment or emotions expressed by customers towards a particular product, brand, or company. These tools use natural language processing (NLP) and machine learning techniques to analyze and extract insights from customer feedback, reviews, social media posts, and other sources of customer-generated content.

Customer sentiment analysis tools play a crucial role in helping marketing managers understand the overall perception of their brand in the market and identify areas of improvement or opportunities for growth. By analyzing sentiment, these tools categorize customer opinions as positive, negative, or neutral, allowing marketing managers to gauge customer satisfaction and identify potential issues that need to be addressed.

Some common features offered by customer sentiment analysis tools include sentiment scoring, trend analysis, topic clustering, and data visualization. Sentiment scoring assigns a sentiment value (usually a numerical score) to each customer feedback or review, indicating the overall sentiment expressed. Trend analysis helps identify patterns and changes in sentiment over time, allowing marketing managers to track the impact of their marketing strategies or product launches on customer sentiment.

Topic clustering helps group customer feedback based on common topics or themes, enabling marketing managers to identify the key areas of concern or interest among customers. Data visualization presents sentiment analysis results in graphical or visual formats, making it easier for marketing managers to interpret and communicate the findings to stakeholders.

Customer Sentiment Analysis

Customer Sentiment Analysis is a market research technique used in the field of Marketing Management to assess and understand the emotions, opinions, attitudes, and overall satisfaction of customers towards a product, brand, or company. It involves analyzing customer feedback, reviews, social media posts, and other forms of customer-generated content to gather insights about their perceptions and experiences.

Through Customer Sentiment Analysis, marketers can gain a deeper understanding of how customers feel about their offerings, identify strengths and weaknesses, and make data-driven decisions to improve their products, services, and overall customer experience. By analyzing the sentiment expressed in customer feedback, marketers can detect patterns and trends, allowing them to identify areas of improvement, address potential issues, and tailor their marketing strategies to better meet customer needs.

Customer Testimonial

A customer testimonial refers to a written or spoken statement from a customer expressing their satisfaction with a product or service. These testimonials serve as a valuable marketing tool for businesses, as they help build trust and credibility among prospective customers.

Within the discipline of Marketing Management, customer testimonials are used strategically to promote products or services to target customers. They are often incorporated into various marketing channels such as advertisements, websites, social media, and sales presentations.

Customer testimonials have several key benefits in the field of Marketing Management. Firstly, they provide social proof by showcasing the positive experiences and opinions of real customers. This reassures potential customers that the product or service has been positively received by others, increasing their confidence in making a purchase decision.

Secondly, customer testimonials help to establish trust. When potential customers see that others have had a positive experience with a particular product or service, they are more likely to trust the brand and feel more comfortable engaging with it.

Lastly, customer testimonials can also help in overcoming objections or hesitations that potential customers may have. Through sharing their positive experiences, customers address common concerns and provide reassurance, increasing the likelihood of a purchase.

Customer Touchpoint Analysis

Customer Touchpoint Analysis is a strategic approach adopted by marketing management professionals to evaluate and optimize customer interactions with a company or brand at various touchpoints throughout the customer journey. It involves identifying and assessing all the touchpoints where a customer comes into contact with a company, its products, or its services, and analyzing the effectiveness of these touchpoints in influencing customer perception and behavior.

The goal of Customer Touchpoint Analysis is to gain a holistic understanding of the customer experience and identify opportunities for improvement. By analyzing each touchpoint, marketers can uncover potential pain points, inconsistencies, or gaps in communication and identify areas for enhancement. This analysis helps in aligning marketing efforts with customer expectations, enhancing customer satisfaction, and driving customer loyalty.

Customer Touchpoint Enhancement

Customer touchpoint enhancement is a strategic approach used by marketing management to improve and optimize the interactions between a business and its customers at various touchpoints throughout the customer journey. Touchpoints refer to the moments when a customer comes into contact with a brand, whether it be through a website, social media, email, physical store, or customer service.

The goal of customer touchpoint enhancement is to create consistent and positive experiences for customers across all touchpoints, ultimately leading to increased customer satisfaction, loyalty, and advocacy. To achieve this, marketing managers must identify and analyze all touchpoints, understand customer expectations and preferences, and strive to consistently exceed those expectations.

By enhancing customer touchpoints, marketing managers can improve customer engagement, drive conversions, and strengthen brand affinity. This can be done by personalizing interactions, providing relevant and valuable content, streamlining processes, and optimizing the usability and functionality of touchpoints. Additionally, customer touchpoint enhancement involves aligning brand messaging and visuals across all touchpoints to ensure a cohesive and memorable customer experience.

Furthermore, customer touchpoint enhancement is an ongoing process that requires continuous evaluation and adjustment. Marketing managers must constantly monitor and measure the effectiveness of each touchpoint, gather customer feedback, and make data-driven decisions to address areas of opportunity and eliminate pain points.

Customer Touchpoint Mapping

Customer touchpoint mapping is a strategic process used in marketing management to identify and analyze the various interactions between a customer and a brand throughout the customer journey. It involves mapping out all the touchpoints or contact points that a customer has with a brand, from the initial awareness stage to the post-purchase stage.

The purpose of customer touchpoint mapping is to gain a deeper understanding of the customer experience and to identify areas where improvements can be made to enhance customer satisfaction and build stronger relationships with customers. By mapping out the touchpoints, marketers can pinpoint specific moments of interaction and evaluate the effectiveness and impact of each touchpoint on the customer's overall perception of the brand.

Customer Touchpoints

Customer Touchpoints refer to the various points of interaction that a customer has with a brand or company throughout their entire customer journey. These touchpoints can include both offline and online channels, such as social media, customer service, website, email, physical stores, and advertising.

The purpose of identifying and understanding customer touchpoints is to map out and manage the customer's experience, ensuring that each touchpoint delivers a consistent and positive brand message. By analyzing and optimizing these touchpoints, marketers can enhance customer satisfaction, build loyalty, and ultimately drive business growth.

Customer Value Analysis Software

Customer Value Analysis Software is a strategic tool used in the field of marketing management to assess and measure the perceived value of a product or service from the customer's perspective. It provides marketers with valuable insights into how customers perceive the value they receive from a business and helps in developing effective marketing strategies to enhance customer satisfaction and loyalty.

This software typically utilizes customer feedback and data gathered from various sources, such as surveys, interviews, and online reviews, to analyze and evaluate the key drivers of customer value. It identifies the factors that contribute to customer satisfaction and loyalty, such as product quality, price, customer service, convenience, and brand reputation.

Customer Value Analysis

Customer Value Analysis is a marketing management concept that involves investigating and evaluating the perceived value that customers derive from a product or service. It focuses on understanding the factors that influence customers' perception of value and how this perception drives their purchase decisions.

This analysis helps marketers gain insights into what customers truly value in a product or service, and how it compares to the offerings of competitors. By understanding customer value, companies can then develop strategies to enhance their value proposition and better meet customer needs and expectations, ultimately driving customer satisfaction and loyalty.

Customer Value Proposition (CVP) Analysis

A Customer Value Proposition (CVP) Analysis in the context of Marketing Management discipline refers to a strategic tool used by companies to determine and articulate the unique value they offer to their customers. It involves identifying and understanding the specific needs, desires, and preferences of the target audience, and then developing a compelling value proposition that addresses those needs.

A CVP Analysis typically begins with a thorough analysis of the target market segment, including an examination of the key market trends, competitive landscape, and customer behavior. This information is used to identify the specific needs and pain points of the target audience, and to identify any unmet or underserved needs in the market.

Based on this analysis, the company then develops a value proposition that clearly communicates the unique benefits and value that its product or service provides to customers. This value proposition should be distinctive and memorable, and should clearly differentiate the company from its competitors.

The value proposition should also be based on a deep understanding of the company's own capabilities, resources, and competitive advantage. It should leverage the company's strengths and unique selling points, and should be supported by strong evidence and proof points.

The ultimate goal of a CVP Analysis is to create a compelling value proposition that resonates with the target audience and motivates them to choose the company's product or service over those of its competitors. It should communicate the unique benefits and value the company offers, and should address the specific needs and desires of the target market segment. By developing a strong and differentiated value proposition, companies can position themselves as a preferred choice in the minds of their customers, and drive growth and profitability in the market.

Customer Value Proposition (CVP)

A Customer Value Proposition (CVP) is a statement or promise made by a company to its customers, which outlines why they should choose to buy a particular product or service. It is a strategic marketing tool that highlights the unique value and benefits that a company can provide to its target customers.

The CVP focuses on the key factors that differentiate a company's offering from those of its competitors, and emphasizes the value that customers will receive by choosing the company's product or service. It addresses the needs and wants of the target market segment and underscores how the company's offering can satisfy those needs better than any alternative options available in the market.

The CVP typically includes a combination of functional, emotional, and financial benefits that the company's product or service delivers. Functional benefits refer to the specific features and performance of the product, such as its quality, reliability, convenience, or ease of use. Emotional benefits address the feelings and experiences that the customer will derive from using the product, such as enjoyment, pride, or peace of mind. Financial benefits highlight the cost savings, return on investment, or overall value for money that the customer can expect from purchasing the product or service.

By effectively communicating its CVP, a company can attract and retain customers by convincing them of the value that it can deliver. The CVP helps companies differentiate themselves in a crowded marketplace, build a strong brand reputation, and ultimately drive sales and revenue growth.

Customer-Centric Design

Customer-Centric Design refers to a strategic approach in the field of Marketing Management that focuses on creating products and services based on the specific needs and desires of the target customers. It places the customers at the center of the design process, ensuring that their preferences, feedback, and satisfaction are taken into consideration throughout the entire product development journey.

This design approach involves gathering deep insights into the customers' wants, preferences, and pain points through extensive market research, surveys, customer feedback, and direct interaction. These insights are then used to inform the design and development of products and services that align with the target customers' expectations, resulting in enhanced customer experiences and increased customer loyalty.

Customer-Centric

Customer-centric refers to a marketing approach that prioritizes and tailors all business activities, strategies, and decisions around the needs, preferences, and expectations of the customers. It involves understanding the target audience, identifying their desires and pain points, and then developing and delivering personalized products, services, and experiences that cater to these specific customer demands.

In the context of marketing management, customer-centricity is crucial for building long-term customer relationships and generating customer loyalty. It requires a deep understanding of customer behavior, demographics, psychographics, and preferences, gained through extensive market research and data analysis. By gathering customer insights and constantly monitoring customer satisfaction, marketing managers can create effective marketing strategies that focus on delivering value and meeting customer expectations.

Customer-centric marketing management involves various practices, such as developing customer personas, conducting customer segmentation, implementing customer relationship management (CRM) systems, and utilizing data-driven marketing techniques. It emphasizes building meaningful connections with customers, fostering engagement, and promoting customer advocacy.

By adopting a customer-centric approach, businesses can gain a competitive advantage in the market. It allows companies to deliver superior customer experiences and tailor their offerings to meet the ever-changing customer needs. Moreover, customer-centric marketing enables companies to anticipate customer demands and proactively address customer concerns, leading to increased customer satisfaction, retention, and ultimately, business growth.

Customer-Centricity

Customer-Centricity refers to a business approach that focuses on creating and delivering superior value to customers. It is the notion of placing the customer at the center of all business activities and decision-making processes. Customer-centric companies prioritize the needs, desires, and preferences of their customers throughout every stage of the marketing management process.

In a customer-centric organization, marketing strategies and tactics are designed and executed based on a deep understanding of the target customers' behaviors, motivations, and expectations. This understanding is gained through comprehensive market research, customer insights, and data analysis. By leveraging this knowledge, businesses can tailor their products, services, and marketing campaigns to meet the specific needs and desires of their customer segments.

Customer-centricity involves building strong relationships with customers by providing exceptional customer experiences and personalized interactions. It requires developing customer-centric marketing strategies, such as targeted promotions, personalized offers, and relevant messaging, to engage and retain customers. Additionally, customer-centric companies actively seek customer feedback and use it to continuously improve their offerings and meet changing customer needs.

Implementing a customer-centric approach requires a company-wide commitment to customer satisfaction and placing the customer at the core of decision-making. This means aligning all functional areas, including marketing, sales, operations, and customer service, to work collaboratively towards delivering superior customer value. By adopting a customer-centric mindset, businesses can differentiate themselves from competitors and build long-term customer loyalty and advocacy.

Customer-Generated Content (CGC)

Customer-Generated Content (CGC) refers to any form of content created and shared by customers about a brand or product. It is a type of user-generated content that spans across various media platforms, including social media, blogs, forums, and review sites. In the context of Marketing Management, CGC plays a crucial role in shaping brand perception, increasing customer engagement, and influencing purchasing decisions.

CGC is an authentic and unbiased representation of the customer's perspective, opinions, and experiences with a brand. Unlike traditional advertising or promotional campaigns, CGC is not controlled or produced by the brand itself. Instead, it is voluntarily created and shared by customers who act as brand advocates or critics.

CGC can take various forms, such as customer reviews, ratings, testimonials, social media posts, videos, images, and blog posts. The content can range from positive endorsements to negative feedback, providing a comprehensive view of the brand's strengths and weaknesses.

In Marketing Management, leveraging CGC is essential for building trust, credibility, and brand loyalty. By showcasing real customer experiences, brands can establish a genuine connection with their target audience. CGC also encourages customer engagement, as it allows customers to actively participate in brand storytelling and product conversations.

Furthermore, CGC can significantly impact purchase decisions. Potential customers often rely on CGC as a reliable source of information before making a purchase. Positive CGC can influence the perception of quality and value, while negative CGC can deter potential customers from choosing a particular brand or product.

Customer-Led Innovation

Customer-led innovation refers to the process of creating new products, services, or solutions based on the insights, needs, and feedback of customers. It involves engaging customers as active participants in the innovation process, seeking their input, ideas, and preferences to drive the development of new offerings.

This approach to innovation recognizes that customers are a valuable source of knowledge and understanding about their own needs, preferences, and challenges. By involving customers in the innovation process, organizations can gain a deeper understanding of their target market and create solutions that are more relevant, valuable, and effective.

Customer-Lifetime-Value (CLV)

Customer Lifetime Value (CLV) is a metric used in the field of Marketing Management that measures the predicted net profit a company can expect to gain from a customer over the entire duration of their relationship. It is an important tool for businesses to evaluate the long-term monetary value of acquiring and retaining customers.

CLV takes into account various factors such as customer acquisition costs, customer retention rates, and average purchase value to calculate the potential profitability of each customer over their lifetime. By understanding the CLV of different customer segments, companies can make strategic decisions on resource allocation, marketing strategies, and customer relationship management.

Dark Social Monitoring Tools

Dark social monitoring tools refer to software or platforms used by marketers to track and analyze the sharing and engagement of content that occurs through channels that cannot be easily traced, such as private messaging apps, email, and secure websites.

In the context of marketing management, dark social refers to the sharing and distribution of content that happens outside of public social media channels. It encompasses the sharing of links, articles, videos, or any other type of content through private channels that do not leave a digital footprint that can be tracked by traditional analytics tools.

Dark social monitoring tools allow marketers to gain insights into this hidden world of content sharing and understand how their campaigns are being shared and engaged with. These tools provide metrics and data on the volume of dark social referrals, the types of content being shared, and the platforms or channels through which the sharing is taking place.

By monitoring dark social activity, marketers can identify influential users, understand their audience's preferences, optimize content for specific channels, and ultimately improve their marketing strategies. Dark social monitoring tools also help marketers measure the effectiveness of their campaigns across various channels and track the impact of dark social on website traffic, conversions, and overall brand awareness.

Dark Social Tracking

Dark Social Tracking refers to the process of monitoring and analyzing user interactions and referrals that occur through private channels such as email, instant messaging, and secure messaging apps, where the referral source is not easily trackable through traditional web analytics tools.

In the realm of marketing management, dark social tracking is crucial for understanding consumer behavior and measuring the effectiveness of marketing campaigns. It provides insight into the channels through which users are sharing content and allows marketers to accurately attribute traffic and conversions to specific marketing initiatives.

By tracking dark social, marketers can gain a deeper understanding of their audience's interests, preferences, and engagement patterns. This knowledge can inform targeted marketing strategies and enable brands to optimize their content for better shareability and engagement. For example, if a marketer discovers that a significant portion of their website traffic is coming from dark social referrals, they may choose to invest more resources in creating content that resonates with their audience's offline conversations and sharing habits.

Furthermore, dark social tracking can help marketers assess the impact of influencer marketing and other word-of-mouth initiatives. By identifying the specific individuals or groups responsible for driving dark social referrals, marketers can evaluate the effectiveness of their influencer partnerships and tailor their strategies accordingly.

Dark Social

Dark social refers to the traffic that is directed to a website or webpage through private channels such as email, instant messaging, and private social networks, making it difficult for marketers to track and measure. Unlike traffic from public social media platforms and search engines which can be easily tracked using analytics tools, dark social traffic does not contain referral information and appears as direct traffic in analytics reports.

Dark social is a significant challenge for marketers as it hinders their ability to accurately understand customer behavior, measure the effectiveness of marketing campaigns, and allocate resources effectively. Without proper tracking, marketers may misinterpret the sources of their website traffic, mistakenly attributing it to direct navigation or organic search rather than realizing it originated from private conversations. This can lead to incorrect assumptions about consumer preferences and interests, resulting in wasteful marketing efforts and missed opportunities.

Data Analytics

Data analytics, in the context of Marketing Management discipline, refers to the method of collecting, analyzing, and interpreting data to make informed decisions and improve marketing strategies. It involves gathering relevant data from various sources, including customer interactions, market research, and sales figures, to gain insights into consumer behavior, market trends, and the effectiveness of marketing campaigns.

The process of data analytics in marketing management begins with data collection, where information is collected through surveys, interviews, website analytics, social media monitoring, and other data sources. Once the data is collected, it is organized and cleaned to ensure its accuracy and reliability.

Next, the collected data is analyzed using statistical techniques and data mining algorithms to identify patterns, trends, and correlations. This analysis helps marketers understand customer preferences, buying behavior, and market dynamics, enabling them to make data-driven decisions and tailor marketing strategies accordingly.

Furthermore, data analytics in marketing management plays a crucial role in measuring marketing performance and evaluating the success of marketing campaigns. By analyzing key performance indicators (KPIs) such as customer acquisition, conversion rates, customer lifetime value, and return on investment (ROI), marketers can assess the effectiveness of their marketing efforts and make necessary adjustments to improve results.

In conclusion, data analytics in the context of Marketing Management discipline enables marketers to leverage data for strategic decision-making, optimization of marketing activities, and gaining a competitive edge in the market. By utilizing data analytics, marketers can better understand their audience, identify new opportunities, and develop targeted marketing campaigns that resonate with consumers, ultimately driving business growth and success.

Data Enrichment

Data enrichment refers to the process of enhancing existing data with additional information to make it more valuable and meaningful for marketing management. It involves collecting, analyzing, and integrating various data sources to fill in gaps, correct errors, and provide a comprehensive view of customers, prospects, and market trends. The main objective of data enrichment is to improve the accuracy, completeness, and relevance of marketing data. By adding new data points and attributes, marketers gain richer insights into their target audience, enabling them to create more personalized and targeted marketing campaigns. There are several methods and techniques used for data enrichment, including data appending, data cleansing, and data integration. Data appending involves adding new data elements, such as demographic information, email addresses, or purchase history, to existing customer records. Data cleansing focuses on identifying and correcting errors, inconsistencies, and duplications in the data. Data integration aims to combine data from different sources, such as web analytics, social media, and customer relationship management systems, to create a unified and holistic view of the customers. Data enrichment plays a crucial role in effective marketing management. It helps marketers gain a deeper understanding of their customers' preferences, behaviors, and needs, enabling them to develop more targeted and personalized marketing strategies. By using enriched data, marketers can segment their audience more effectively, identify potential leads, optimize campaign performance, and deliver relevant content across multiple channels. In conclusion, data enrichment is a vital process in marketing management that involves enhancing existing data with additional information to improve its value and relevance. It enables marketers to gain deeper insights into their target audience, personalize their marketing efforts, and make data-driven decisions for better campaign performance.

Data Mining

Data Mining, in the context of Marketing Management, refers to the process of extracting patterns and relevant information from large datasets to gain useful insights and make data-driven decisions in marketing strategies. It involves the use of various statistical and exploratory techniques to identify hidden patterns, correlations, and trends in the data.

By applying data mining techniques, marketers can uncover valuable insights about customer behavior, preferences, and buying patterns. This enables them to segment their target audience, personalize marketing messages, and develop effective strategies to acquire, retain, and satisfy customers. Data mining can also help in predicting customer churn and identifying potential upselling or cross-selling opportunities.

Data Privacy Compliance Solutions

Data privacy compliance solutions refer to the strategies, practices, and technologies implemented by organizations in the field of marketing management to ensure that they comply with regulations and standards regarding data privacy.

These solutions are designed to protect and secure the personal information of individuals collected and processed by marketing teams. They aim to ensure that this data is collected and used in a lawful and ethical manner, minimizing the risk of unauthorized access, data breaches, or misuse.

Some key elements of data privacy compliance solutions include:

1. Privacy policy and transparency: Organizations need to have a clear and easily accessible privacy policy that outlines how they collect, use, store, and protect personal data. This policy should be transparent about the purposes for which data is collected and provide individuals with control over their data.

2. Consent management: Organizations must obtain valid consent from individuals before collecting and using their personal data. This includes ensuring that consent is freely given, specific, informed, and unambiguous. Consent should be obtained through clear and affirmative actions, such as checkboxes or opt-in forms.

3. Data governance and security: Organizations need to implement robust data governance and security measures to safeguard personal information. This includes encryption, access controls, regular data backups, and monitoring for potential security breaches. Adequate safeguards must be in place to protect data throughout its lifecycle, from collection to deletion.

4. Data subject rights: Individuals have various rights concerning their personal data, such as the right to access, rectify, erase, or restrict the processing of their data. Organizations need to have processes and systems in place to respond to these requests in a timely and accurate manner.

By implementing data privacy compliance solutions, organizations can build trust and credibility with their customers by demonstrating their commitment to protecting personal data. This, in turn, can help to enhance the effectiveness of marketing initiatives and improve overall customer satisfaction and loyalty.

Data Privacy Compliance

Data privacy compliance in the context of marketing management refers to the adherence and compliance with laws, regulations, and industry standards pertaining to the protection and handling of personal information collected and processed in marketing activities.

Marketing activities involve collecting, analyzing, and using personal data to better understand consumer preferences, target specific audiences, and deliver personalized experiences. However, the increasing concern for individual privacy and data protection necessitates organizations to ensure that they are compliant with applicable data privacy laws and regulations.

Data privacy compliance includes implementing measures and practices that safeguard personal data, such as securing databases, using encryption techniques, and providing individuals with options to control the use of their data. It also encompasses obtaining consent from individuals before collecting and using their personal information and providing them with transparent information about how their data will be used.

Organizations must establish internal policies and procedures to govern the collection, storage, and processing of personal data, ensuring that these practices align with legal requirements. Compliance also involves training employees on data privacy practices and regularly auditing and monitoring data handling activities to ensure ongoing compliance.

Non-compliance with data privacy regulations can result in severe consequences, including financial penalties, reputational damage, and legal implications. Therefore, marketing managers must prioritize data privacy compliance to ensure ethical and lawful marketing practices while also building trust with their target audiences.

Data Privacy Regulations Compliance

Data Privacy Regulations Compliance refers to the adherence and implementation of laws, regulations, and guidelines that govern the collection, use, storage, and sharing of personal data in marketing management. It ensures that organizations handle customer data in a secure and responsible manner, protecting individuals' privacy and rights.

In the realm of marketing management, data privacy regulations compliance is crucial in maintaining customer trust and reputation. It encompasses various legal frameworks, such as the General Data Protection Regulation (GDPR) in the European Union, the California Consumer Privacy Act (CCPA) in the United States, and other similar legislations worldwide.

Data Segmentation

Data segmentation in the context of Marketing Management discipline refers to the process of categorizing and dividing a large set of data into smaller, more specific groups based on certain criteria or characteristics. This segmentation allows marketers to effectively target and tailor their marketing strategies to different customer segments, optimizing their marketing efforts and increasing the chances of success. Segmenting data involves analyzing various factors such as demographics, psychographics, behavior, and preferences of the target audience. By dividing the data into distinct segments, marketers can create more personalized and relevant marketing campaigns that resonate with each segment's unique needs and preferences. The main objective of data segmentation is to enhance the efficiency and effectiveness of marketing activities by identifying the most valuable customer segments. This allows marketers to allocate their resources and budget more strategically, focusing on the segments that offer the highest potential for generating revenue and achieving marketing objectives. Segmenting data also enables marketers to gain insights into the different characteristics and behaviors of their customers. Through data analysis, marketers can identify patterns, trends, and correlations within each segment, helping them understand customer preferences, purchase behavior, and decision-making processes. This information can then be used to create targeted marketing messages, offers, and promotions that are more likely to appeal to specific segments. Overall, data segmentation is a crucial tool in Marketing Management discipline as it helps marketers better understand and engage with their target audience. By dividing large sets of data into smaller, more meaningful segments, marketers can optimize their marketing efforts and deliver more personalized and relevant messages to their customers.

Data-Driven Decision Support Systems

Data-Driven Decision Support Systems (DSS) in the context of Marketing Management refer to an analytical framework that utilizes data to assist marketers in making strategic and tactical decisions. These systems leverage various data sources, such as customer demographics, purchase history, market trends, and competitor analyses, to provide insights and recommendations that guide marketing efforts.

The primary goal of Data-Driven DSS in Marketing Management is to enable marketers to make informed decisions based on empirical evidence rather than relying solely on intuition or past experiences. By leveraging data analytics and statistical models, these systems can uncover patterns, relationships, and trends that may not be readily apparent to marketers, allowing them to make more accurate assessments and predictions.

With the help of Data-Driven DSS, marketers can effectively target customer segments, optimize marketing campaigns, allocate resources efficiently, and measure the success of their marketing initiatives. By analyzing customer data, these systems can identify profitable market segments and develop personalized marketing strategies that resonate with specific groups of customers.

Furthermore, Data-Driven DSS can assist marketers in evaluating the effectiveness of various marketing channels and tactics. By measuring the impact of different marketing activities on customer behavior and business outcomes, marketers can optimize their marketing mix and allocate resources to the most effective channels and campaigns.

Data-Driven Decision Support

Data-Driven Decision Support refers to the practice of using data and analytical tools to aid in making informed decisions within the field of Marketing Management. It involves gathering and analyzing relevant data from various sources, such as customer records, market research, and digital analytics, to extract insights and guide strategic marketing decisions.

In the context of Marketing Management, data-driven decision support enables marketers to optimize their campaigns, allocate resources effectively, and enhance overall marketing performance. By leveraging data and advanced analytics techniques, marketers can gain deeper understanding of customer behavior, preferences, and market trends, which helps them identify new target segments, develop personalized marketing strategies, and improve customer engagement.

Data-driven decision support empowers marketers to make data-backed decisions, rather than relying solely on intuition or gut feelings. It provides objective insights that can validate or challenge existing assumptions, eliminate bias, and minimize risks. Through data-driven decision support, marketers can measure the effectiveness of their marketing efforts, track key performance indicators, and adjust their strategies in real-time to achieve desired outcomes.

Moreover, data-driven decision support facilitates data-driven marketing automation, allowing marketers to automate repetitive tasks, personalize customer interactions, and deliver relevant content. It also enables marketers to assess the return on investment (ROI) of their marketing initiatives, justify budget allocations, and drive accountability within the marketing organization.

Data-Driven Decision-Making

Data-Driven Decision-Making is a process in the Marketing Management discipline that involves using data and analytics to inform business strategies and actions. It is a systematic approach that relies on objective and quantifiable information to guide decision-making processes.

In the context of marketing, data-driven decision-making involves collecting and analyzing various types of data, such as customer demographics, purchase behavior, website analytics, and social media engagement. This data is then used to gain insights into consumer preferences, trends, and patterns, which can be applied to marketing strategies and tactics.

Data-Driven Marketing

Data-driven marketing is a marketing strategy that relies on the use of data and analytics to inform decision-making and drive marketing efforts. It involves collecting, analyzing, and interpreting customer data to gain insights and make informed marketing decisions.

With data-driven marketing, marketers can gather and analyze data from various sources, such as customer interactions, online activities, social media, and market research, to understand customer behavior, preferences, and needs. This data can then be used to segment customers into different groups based on similarities and target them with personalized and relevant marketing messages and offers.

Data-driven marketing helps marketers optimize their marketing campaigns by focusing on the most effective channels, messages, and offers. By using data to measure the effectiveness of marketing efforts, marketers can make timely adjustments and improvements to increase their return on investment (ROI). Additionally, data-driven marketing enables marketers to track and measure key performance indicators (KPIs) such as customer acquisition, conversion rates, customer engagement, and customer lifetime value.

Overall, data-driven marketing enables marketers to make data-backed decisions, improve customer targeting and personalization, optimize marketing campaigns, and measure marketing performance. By leveraging the power of data and analytics, marketers can enhance the effectiveness and efficiency of their marketing efforts, ultimately driving better business outcomes.

Data-Driven Personalization

Data-Driven Personalization refers to the process of tailoring marketing efforts and messages to individual customers based on the analysis and interpretation of relevant data. It involves using customer data, such as previous purchases, browsing behavior, demographics, and preferences, to create customized experiences and communications that resonate with each individual. This approach relies on data analysis, machine learning, and automation to gain insights into customer behavior and preferences, allowing marketers to deliver personalized messages, offers, and recommendations that are most likely to engage and convert customers.

By leveraging data-driven personalization, marketers can enhance customer experiences, improve customer satisfaction, and increase the effectiveness of their marketing efforts. Personalized marketing messages are more relevant and targeted, leading to higher levels of customer engagement and conversion rates. Additionally, data-driven personalization can help marketers identify and understand customer segments, enabling them to develop targeted marketing campaigns and create customized products or services that cater to specific customer needs and preferences.

Database Marketing

Database marketing refers to the practice of utilizing customer data to create targeted marketing campaigns and strategies. It involves collecting, analyzing, and managing customer information in a database system with the goal of increasing customer engagement, retention, and overall profitability.

In the field of marketing management, database marketing plays a crucial role in understanding and segmenting a company's customer base. By gathering data on customers' demographics, purchase history, preferences, and behavior, marketers can develop personalized and relevant marketing initiatives.

This approach allows marketers to tailor their messages and offerings to specific customer segments, increasing the chances of capturing their attention and driving desired actions. By personalizing communication, companies can establish stronger relationships with their customers, leading to increased brand loyalty and customer satisfaction.

Database marketing also enables marketers to track and measure the effectiveness of their marketing efforts, as well as identify areas for improvement. Through data analysis and reporting, marketers can gain insights into customer behaviors, preferences, and purchasing patterns. These insights can inform marketing strategies, product development, and overall business decision-making.

Overall, database marketing is a powerful tool in the marketing management discipline, as it allows companies to leverage customer data to optimize marketing campaigns, improve customer relationships, and drive business growth. By harnessing the power of data, marketers can make informed decisions and create impactful marketing strategies that resonate with their target audience.

Demand Forecasting

Demand forecasting is a crucial aspect of Marketing Management discipline. It refers to the process of estimating or predicting the potential demand for a product or service in the market over a specified period. This forecast serves as a valuable tool for businesses to make informed decisions regarding production, procurement, marketing, and resource planning.

The primary objective of demand forecasting is to minimize the risks associated with underestimating or overestimating the demand for a product or service. By accurately predicting the demand, companies can optimize their operations, reduce inventory costs, improve customer service, and enhance overall profitability.

Demand Generation Platforms

Demand generation platforms are tools used by marketers in the field of marketing management to generate and nurture customer interest, ultimately driving demand for products or services. These platforms utilize a combination of marketing tactics, strategies, and technology to attract, engage, and convert potential customers.

Through demand generation platforms, marketers can create targeted marketing campaigns that reach their desired audience effectively. These platforms assist in creating and executing various marketing activities such as content marketing, social media marketing, email marketing, search engine optimization, and online advertising.

One key component of demand generation platforms is lead generation. These platforms help marketers capture and collect valuable customer data through various channels such as landing pages, forms, and webinars. By doing so, marketers can then analyze this data to gain insights into customer behavior, preferences, and needs, enabling them to tailor their marketing efforts accordingly.

Additionally, demand generation platforms provide marketers with the necessary tools to engage with potential customers throughout their buying journey. These platforms often include features such as lead nurturing workflows, personalized messaging, and marketing automation, all of which aim to build relationships with potential customers and guide them towards making a purchase.

In summary, demand generation platforms play a crucial role in marketing management by enabling marketers to reach their target audience, generate leads, and effectively nurture customer interest. Through the use of these platforms, marketers can ultimately drive demand for their products or services, resulting in increased sales and business growth.

Demand Generation Strategies

Demand generation strategies are marketing techniques used by businesses to stimulate the interest and desire of potential customers in their products or services, ultimately leading to increased demand and sales. These strategies are an essential part of the marketing management discipline as they aim to create awareness, generate leads, and nurture prospects throughout the buyer's journey.

One common demand generation strategy is content marketing, which involves creating and distributing valuable, informative, and relevant content to attract and engage target audiences. By delivering valuable content, businesses can establish themselves as industry experts and build trust with potential customers, increasing the likelihood of them considering the company's products or services.

Another effective demand generation strategy is search engine optimization (SEO). By optimizing website content and structure to rank higher in search engine results, businesses can increase their organic visibility and attract more qualified leads. SEO helps potential customers find the company's website when searching for related keywords, increasing the chances of converting them into paying customers.

In addition, demand generation strategies may include targeted advertising campaigns, email marketing, social media marketing, events, and partnerships. These strategies help businesses reach their target audience, engage with prospects, and influence their purchase decisions.

Demand Generation

Demand generation, in the context of marketing management, refers to the strategies and tactics used to create awareness and interest in a company's products or services with the ultimate goal of generating demand and driving sales.

It involves a variety of marketing activities aimed at attracting and engaging potential customers, nurturing their interest, and ultimately encouraging them to make a purchase. Demand generation is an essential component of the marketing funnel, focusing on the top-of-the-funnel activities that drive brand recognition and lead generation.

Demographic Targeting

Demographic targeting in the context of marketing management refers to the strategy of narrowing down target market segments based on specific demographic characteristics. These characteristics can include factors such as age, gender, income, education level, occupation, ethnicity, and marital status.

The purpose of demographic targeting is to identify and reach out to the most relevant and potential customers for a particular product or service. By understanding the demographic makeup of their target market, marketers can design more effective marketing campaigns and tailor their messaging to resonate with these specific audiences.

Demographics

Demographics, in the context of Marketing Management, refers to the statistical data that characterizes a specific target market or population segment. It involves the collection and analysis of information such as age, gender, income, education, occupation, and other relevant factors that provide insights into the composition and behavior patterns of a particular group of consumers.

Demographic data is crucial for marketers as it enables them to better understand their target audience and design marketing strategies that will effectively reach and engage with them. By studying the demographics of a specific market segment, marketers can identify trends, preferences, and needs that can influence their product positioning, pricing, distribution, and promotional efforts.

Digital Advertising

Digital advertising refers to the practice of promoting products, services, or brands through digital channels such as websites, social media platforms, mobile apps, email, search engines, and display advertising. It is a crucial component of marketing management and plays a significant role in reaching targeted audiences, building brand awareness, driving website traffic, and generating leads and sales.

In marketing management, digital advertising involves the strategic planning, implementation, and monitoring of various digital advertising campaigns. This includes selecting the appropriate digital channels, creating compelling ad copies and creative assets, defining the target audience, setting campaign objectives and budgets, and measuring the effectiveness of the advertising efforts.

Digital advertising offers numerous advantages over traditional advertising methods. It provides the ability to reach a wider audience that is increasingly using digital devices and platforms. It allows for precise targeting and retargeting, ensuring that ads are shown to individuals who are more likely to be interested in the products or services being advertised. Additionally, digital advertising provides better tracking and measurement capabilities, which enables marketers to analyze the performance of their campaigns and make data-driven decisions for optimization.

Overall, digital advertising is an essential tool in the marketing management discipline, as it allows businesses to effectively communicate with their target audience, increase brand visibility, and drive business growth in the digital age.

Digital Ecosystem Analysis

A digital ecosystem analysis refers to the examination and evaluation of the various interconnected components, entities, and interactions within the digital realm, specifically focusing on the marketing management discipline. It involves an in-depth understanding of how digital platforms, technologies, customers, competitors, and other relevant factors contribute to the overall digital marketing landscape.

Such analysis helps marketing managers gain insights into the broader digital ecosystem and how it impacts their marketing strategies. By considering the complex network of digital channels, touchpoints, and stakeholders, marketers can assess opportunities, identify challenges, and make informed decisions about marketing investments and initiatives.

Digital Ecosystem Management

Digital Ecosystem Management is a strategic approach that focuses on managing the various digital platforms and channels used by a company to engage with its customers and stakeholders. In the context of Marketing Management, it refers to the management of the digital environment in which marketing activities take place.

It involves the coordination and integration of all digital assets, including websites, mobile apps, social media accounts, email marketing campaigns, and online advertising, to create a cohesive and consistent online presence. The goal of digital ecosystem management is to optimize the overall performance and effectiveness of the digital marketing efforts.

Digital Ecosystem

A digital ecosystem, in the context of Marketing Management, refers to a complex interconnected network of various digital platforms, channels, and technologies that enable organizations to deliver and promote their products or services in the digital space. It encompasses all the digital touchpoints and interactions that occur between a company, its customers, and other stakeholders.

In this ecosystem, organizations use a combination of websites, social media platforms, mobile apps, email marketing, online advertising, search engine optimization (SEO), content marketing, and data analytics to create and maintain a strong digital presence, attract and engage customers, drive sales, and build customer loyalty.

The digital ecosystem in marketing management involves the integration and coordination of different marketing activities across multiple digital channels to deliver a seamless and personalized customer experience. It requires understanding customer behavior and preferences in the digital landscape, leveraging technologies for effective targeting and segmentation, and utilizing data-driven insights to optimize marketing strategies.

With a well-established digital ecosystem, organizations can establish a strong online brand identity, increase brand visibility, reach wider audiences, and gain a competitive edge in the digital marketplace. It allows companies to leverage the power of digital media to connect and interact with customers in real-time, provide personalized experiences, and build long-term relationships.

In summary, a digital ecosystem in marketing management refers to the interconnected network of digital platforms, channels, and technologies used by organizations to effectively promote their products or services, engage customers, and enhance overall marketing performance in the digital space.

Digital Footprint

A digital footprint in the context of Marketing Management refers to the online trail left by an individual or organization as a result of their digital activities. It encompasses all the information and data associated with their online presence, interactions, and engagements across various digital platforms and channels.

Every time a person or a brand interacts or engages with any digital medium, they leave a trace behind. This digital trail includes their social media posts and comments, online purchases and transactions, website visits and click behaviors, search queries, email communications, and any other form of digital interaction. These footprints can be intentional or unintentional, active or passive, and can exist in various forms such as text, images, videos, or other types of digital content.

The digital footprint plays a crucial role in the field of Marketing Management as it provides valuable insights into consumer behavior, preferences, interests, and demographics. By analyzing and interpreting these footprints, marketers can gain a deeper understanding of their target audience and tailor their marketing strategies accordingly. It helps in developing personalized and targeted marketing campaigns, identifying potential leads and customers, and enhancing customer experience and satisfaction.

Furthermore, a digital footprint also affects an individual or organization's online reputation and branding. Positive digital footprints, such as engaging in meaningful conversations, sharing valuable content, and participating in industry discussions, can enhance credibility and brand image. On the other hand, negative footprints, such as engaging in controversial or inappropriate activities, can damage reputation and hinder success in the marketplace.

Digital Marketing Mix Models

A digital marketing mix model, in the context of marketing management, refers to a systematic approach used to evaluate and optimize the allocation of resources across various digital marketing channels. It involves analyzing the effectiveness of different online marketing strategies and tactics to determine the most efficient and effective way to reach target customers, increase brand awareness, drive traffic, generate leads, and ultimately achieve business objectives.

The digital marketing mix model consists of several key components, including data analytics, attribution models, and optimization techniques. It utilizes a combination of quantitative and qualitative data to measure the impact of different marketing activities on consumer behavior and business outcomes. Through statistical analysis and modeling, marketers can gain insights into the contribution of each digital marketing channel, such as search engine marketing, social media advertising, email marketing, content marketing, and display advertising.

By understanding the effectiveness of each marketing channel, businesses can make data-driven decisions to allocate resources more efficiently and effectively. The digital marketing mix model helps marketers identify which channels deliver the highest return on investment, better understand the customer journey and touchpoints, and make informed decisions about budget allocation and campaign optimization.

Overall, the digital marketing mix model serves as a valuable tool for marketing management, enabling businesses to optimize their online marketing efforts, improve customer targeting and engagement, and ultimately drive business growth in the digital era.

Digital Marketing Mix Optimization

Digital Marketing Mix Optimization refers to the strategic process of analyzing and adjusting various elements of a digital marketing campaign to improve its effectiveness and maximize return on investment. It involves evaluating the four key components of the digital marketing mix - product, price, promotion, and place - and making necessary adjustments to enhance their alignment with the desired marketing objectives.

Firstly, product optimization involves assessing the digital offerings and ensuring they are aligned with the target market's needs and preferences. This may involve refining product features, expanding the product line, or enhancing the overall user experience.

Secondly, price optimization focuses on determining the most appropriate pricing strategy to attract and retain customers. This entails evaluating competitors' pricing, considering market demand, and adjusting prices accordingly to maximize profitability while remaining competitive.

Thirdly, promotion optimization involves analyzing and refining the digital marketing communication strategies used to promote the product. This may include leveraging various digital channels, refining messaging, and implementing effective call-to-action strategies to maximize customer engagement and conversion rates.

Lastly, place optimization entails evaluating and optimizing the digital distribution channels to ensure that the product is easily accessible to the target market. This may involve expanding the digital presence, leveraging partnerships, or enhancing the online shopping experience to improve customer convenience.

Overall, digital marketing mix optimization is a dynamic and continuous process that allows marketers to analyze and adjust various elements of the marketing strategy to enhance its performance, reach the target audience effectively, and ultimately achieve marketing goals.

Digital Marketing Mix

The digital marketing mix refers to a set of tactics and strategies used by businesses to promote their products or services online. It is a combination of various digital marketing tools and channels that help businesses reach their target audience and achieve their marketing goals.

The digital marketing mix consists of several components, including search engine optimization (SEO), social media marketing, email marketing, content marketing, online advertising, and website optimization. Each component plays a crucial role in attracting and engaging customers and driving them towards making a purchase or conversion.

Search engine optimization (SEO) involves optimizing a website and its content to improve its visibility on search engine result pages. Social media marketing involves promoting products or services on social media platforms to increase brand awareness and engage with target customers. Email marketing involves sending targeted emails to prospects and customers to nurture relationships and encourage repeat business.

Content marketing involves creating and distributing valuable and relevant content to attract and retain a clearly defined audience. Online advertising involves placing paid advertisements on various digital platforms to reach a wider audience and generate leads. Website optimization involves improving the performance and user experience of a website to increase conversions.

The digital marketing mix is constantly evolving, as new technologies and platforms emerge. Businesses need to stay up-to-date with the latest trends and techniques to effectively leverage the digital marketing mix and stay ahead of the competition.

Digital Marketing

Digital marketing refers to the strategic use of various digital channels and technologies to promote a brand, product, or service and engage with target customers. It is a subset of marketing that focuses specifically on leveraging digital platforms to reach and influence potential consumers.

In today's technologically advanced and interconnected world, digital marketing has become an essential component of marketing management. With the widespread adoption of internet-enabled devices and the increasing popularity of online platforms, businesses are recognizing the need to adapt their marketing strategies to the digital landscape.

Key elements of digital marketing include search engine optimization (SEO), content marketing, social media marketing, email marketing, and online advertising. These techniques enable businesses to increase their online visibility, attract qualified traffic, and build meaningful relationships with customers.

One of the significant advantages of digital marketing is its ability to provide measurable results. Marketers can track and analyze various metrics to evaluate the efficacy of their campaigns and make data-driven decisions to optimize future marketing efforts.

Digital marketing also offers unique opportunities for personalization and targeting. By leveraging data and analytics, marketers can tailor their messages and offerings to specific customer segments, increasing the likelihood of engagement and conversion.

Furthermore, digital marketing allows for real-time communication and engagement with customers. Through social media channels, businesses can respond to customer queries promptly, provide personalized support, and foster a sense of brand loyalty.

In conclusion, digital marketing has revolutionized the field of marketing management by providing businesses with powerful tools and strategies to effectively reach, engage, and convert customers in the digital age.

Digital Presence

Digital presence refers to the online representation of a brand, company, or individual through various digital channels and platforms. It encompasses the visibility, accessibility, and reputation of an entity in the digital space, and is a crucial aspect of marketing management.

In today's technologically-driven world, establishing a strong digital presence is imperative for businesses to connect with their target audience, enhance brand awareness, and drive customer engagement. It involves the strategic use of digital marketing techniques and tools to effectively communicate and interact with stakeholders.

A robust digital presence encompasses several key elements. First and foremost, it involves maintaining a well-designed and user-friendly website that is optimized for search engines, providing a seamless online experience for visitors. Additionally, it includes utilizing social media platforms to engage with the target audience, share relevant content, and cultivate a community of brand advocates.

Furthermore, digital presence extends to online advertising and search engine optimization (SEO) efforts, ensuring the brand is visible and easily discoverable in search engine results pages. It also encompasses online reputation management, monitoring and responding to customer feedback and reviews, and maintaining a positive online brand image.

Overall, digital presence is an integral part of marketing management, as it allows businesses to connect with their audience in a digital-first world and leverage online channels for brand promotion and customer engagement.

Direct Mail Marketing

Direct mail marketing is a strategy employed in the field of marketing management that involves sending promotional materials or messages directly to a targeted audience via traditional mail delivery. This approach allows businesses to reach potential customers directly without relying on intermediaries such as advertising platforms, television or radio, and email campaigns.

The process of direct mail marketing typically begins by identifying a specific target market or audience segment based on various demographic, geographic, psychographic, or behavioral factors. Once the audience is determined, the marketer designs and creates promotional materials such as brochures, catalogs, postcards, letters, or product samples.

These materials are then sent through the postal service to the selected recipients. Direct mail campaigns can be executed on a large scale, targeting a broad audience, or on a smaller scale, focusing on a specific niche market.

Direct mail marketing offers several benefits. First, it allows marketers to personalize their messages for each recipient, resulting in a higher level of engagement compared to mass advertising. Second, it provides the opportunity to track responses and measure the effectiveness of the campaign, enabling marketers to refine their strategies for better results. Finally, direct mail marketing can complement other marketing channels, reinforcing brand awareness and generating additional leads.

In conclusion, direct mail marketing is a targeted advertising method that utilizes traditional mail delivery to send promotional materials directly to potential customers. With its ability to personalize messages, track responses, and complement other marketing efforts, direct mail marketing remains a valuable strategy in the field of marketing management.

Direct Marketing

Direct Marketing in the context of Marketing Management is a promotional strategy that involves communicating directly with individual customers or prospects in order to generate a response or transaction. It is a targeted and measurable form of marketing that aims to establish and maintain a direct relationship between the company and its customers.

Direct marketing often involves the use of various channels, such as direct mail, email, telemarketing, and digital marketing, to reach out to potential customers. The main goal of direct marketing is to deliver a personalized and relevant message to the target audience, which can result in enhanced customer loyalty, increased sales, and improved customer satisfaction.

One of the key advantages of direct marketing is its ability to provide immediate feedback and measurable results. Companies can track and analyze the responses to their marketing campaigns to determine their effectiveness and make appropriate adjustments. This allows for more efficient allocation of resources and better targeting of the intended audience.

Direct marketing also allows for customization and segmentation of the marketing messages. By collecting and analyzing customer data, companies can tailor their communications to individual preferences and needs, which increases the likelihood of a positive response.

In conclusion, direct marketing is a targeted and measurable promotional strategy that aims to establish a direct relationship with customers. It leverages various channels to deliver personalized messages, generate immediate feedback, and ultimately drive sales and customer satisfaction.

Direct Response Marketing

Direct response marketing is a promotional strategy in the field of marketing management that aims to elicit an immediate and measurable response from the target audience. It involves the use of targeted advertising and marketing techniques to prompt an immediate action, such as making a purchase, signing up for a newsletter, or requesting more information.

This form of marketing emphasizes the use of compelling and persuasive messaging to encourage the audience to take the desired action. Rather than focusing solely on building brand awareness or creating general interest, direct response marketing aims to generate a direct and quantifiable response, enabling marketers to track the effectiveness of their campaigns and measure their return on investment.

Direct Sales

Direct sales refers to a method of selling products or services directly to consumers without involving intermediaries or middlemen, such as wholesalers or retailers. It involves a direct interaction between the salesperson and the potential customer, typically through face-to-face meetings, phone calls, or online communications.

In the context of marketing management, direct sales is an important strategy that allows companies to establish a direct relationship with their customers, enabling them to better understand customer needs and preferences, build trust, and provide personalized solutions. This approach allows companies to have more control over the sales process and customer interactions, enabling them to tailor their offerings to meet individual customer needs.

Display Ad Creative Optimization

Display Ad Creative Optimization is a strategic process in the field of Marketing Management that involves enhancing the effectiveness and performance of display advertisements. This process focuses on optimizing various elements of the ad creative, including images, headlines, copy, and calls-to-action, to maximize the ad's impact and drive desired outcomes.

The goal of Display Ad Creative Optimization is to attract the target audience's attention, engage them, and motivate them to take the desired action, such as making a purchase, subscribing to a newsletter, or filling out a form. By testing and refining different versions of the ad creative, marketers can identify the most compelling and persuasive elements that resonate with the target audience and drive the highest level of conversions.

Display Ad Creative Testing

Display Ad Creative Testing is a marketing management practice that involves the systematic evaluation and comparison of different versions of advertisements displayed on digital platforms, such as websites, apps, or social media. It aims to determine which ad creative elements are most effective at engaging the target audience, driving conversions, and achieving marketing objectives.

During the display ad creative testing process, various elements of the ad, including headlines, visuals, copy, call-to-action buttons, and color schemes, are modified and tested against each other. This allows marketers to identify which specific components or combinations of elements perform best in terms of generating desired outcomes, such as click-through rates, conversions, or brand awareness.

Display Advertising

Display Advertising refers to a marketing strategy wherein promotional messages and visuals are displayed on various online platforms and websites to reach a wider audience and promote a brand or product. It involves the use of static or interactive visuals such as images, banners, videos, or rich media to capture the attention of potential customers.

This advertising method utilizes ad network platforms that facilitate the placement of advertisements on relevant websites and online platforms. Display ads can be targeted based on various parameters such as demographics, online behavior, interests, or browsing history to ensure that the ads are shown to the right audience.

Drip Email Marketing

Drip email marketing is a strategic approach used in the field of marketing management that involves sending a series of pre-written automated emails to a specific audience over a defined period of time. The goal of this marketing technique is to nurture leads and build relationships with potential customers by providing them with valuable information and relevant content.

The term "drip" refers to the systematic and gradual nature of the email campaign, where emails are sent out at regular intervals to keep the audience engaged and interested. Each email in the series is carefully designed to address a particular stage of the customer journey, focusing on different topics, offers, or calls to action.

This marketing strategy is effective because it allows businesses to automate their email sequences, saving time and effort while still maintaining a personalized touch. By delivering targeted messages to the right people at the right time, drip email marketing helps to nurture leads, increase engagement, and drive conversion rates.

With the help of advanced automation tools and customer segmentation techniques, marketers can tailor their drip email campaigns to specific audiences based on their behaviors, preferences, or demographic information. By understanding the needs and interests of their target audience, businesses can provide relevant and timely content, increasing the chances of conversion and customer retention.

Drip Marketing

Drip marketing refers to a strategy in marketing management that involves sending a series of pre-planned, automated messages or content pieces to potential customers over a specific period of time. The purpose of drip marketing is to nurture and cultivate a relationship with prospects, gradually moving them through the sales funnel until they are ready to make a purchase.

This marketing approach is called "drip" because it focuses on delivering relevant and valuable information to prospects in small, consistent doses, just like water dripping slowly and steadily over time. By delivering content in this manner, businesses can engage and educate their audience without overwhelming them or appearing too sales-oriented.

Dynamic Content Optimization

Dynamic Content Optimization is a marketing management strategy that involves the use of technology and data to deliver personalized and relevant content to target audiences. It is a process of creating, managing, and delivering content that is tailored to individual users based on their demographics, behaviors, preferences, and interactions with the brand.

The goal of Dynamic Content Optimization is to enhance the user experience by presenting content that is most likely to resonate with the audience and drive engagement and conversions. This approach recognizes that different individuals have unique needs and interests, and by customizing the content to meet those needs, businesses can improve their marketing effectiveness and achieve better results.

Dynamic Content Personalization Tools

Dynamic content personalization tools refer to software applications or platforms used in the context of marketing management to deliver customized and targeted content to individual users based on their preferences, behavior, and interests.

These tools enable marketers to create and deploy personalized campaigns across various digital channels, such as websites, emails, social media, and mobile apps, in order to enhance user engagement, increase conversions, and improve overall marketing ROI. By leveraging data and insights about each user, these tools can dynamically modify the content displayed or delivered to individuals in real-time, tailoring it to their unique needs and interests.

Dynamic Content Personalization

Dynamic Content Personalization refers to the process of customizing and tailoring marketing content and messages to individual customers based on their behavior, preferences, and demographics. This strategy aims to deliver highly relevant and personalized content to engage and resonate with each customer on an individual level, ultimately enhancing their overall experience and increasing their likelihood of conversion.

By leveraging data and advanced analytics, marketers can create and deploy dynamic content that adapts and adjusts in real time. This allows for the delivery of personalized messages, offers, and recommendations that align with each customer's unique interests and needs. Dynamic content personalization often involves the use of automation software and algorithms to segment and target specific customer groups, enabling marketers to efficiently manage and scale personalized campaigns.

Dynamic Content

Dynamic content, in the context of Marketing Management, refers to the personalized and tailored content that is delivered to individual users based on their specific characteristics, behaviors, and preferences.

With the advancement of technology and the increased availability of data, companies have the ability to collect and analyze information about their customers. This information can include demographics, past purchase history, browsing behavior, and engagement with previous marketing campaigns. By leveraging this data, marketers can create dynamic content that is relevant and engaging to each individual customer.

Dynamic content allows marketers to deliver personalized messages, offers, and recommendations to their target audience. This can be done through various marketing channels such as email, website, social media, and mobile apps. For example, an online retailer can use dynamic content to display product recommendations based on a customer's previous purchases or browsing history.

By using dynamic content, marketers can create a more personalized and targeted customer experience, which can lead to higher engagement, conversion rates, and customer satisfaction. Furthermore, dynamic content can help marketers to optimize their marketing campaigns by testing and refining different messages and offers based on customer responses.

In conclusion, dynamic content plays a crucial role in modern marketing management by allowing companies to deliver personalized and relevant content to their customers. It enables marketers to create more engaging and effective marketing campaigns, ultimately driving customer engagement, loyalty, and business growth.

Dynamic Pricing

Dynamic pricing in the context of marketing management refers to the practice of continuously adjusting the price of a product or service in response to various factors and conditions, with the goal of maximizing revenue and profitability. It is a pricing strategy that allows businesses to

111

adapt and optimize their pricing strategies based on real-time market conditions, demand elasticity, competition, and other relevant factors.

Dynamic pricing takes into account the dynamic nature of the market, recognizing that prices should not remain static but should reflect the changes in market dynamics. This pricing approach is particularly relevant in industries with high levels of competition and fluctuating demand, such as the airline industry, hospitality sector, and e-commerce.

E-Commerce Marketing

E-commerce marketing is a branch of marketing management that involves promoting and selling products or services online. It encompasses various strategies and techniques aimed at driving traffic to an e-commerce website, converting visitors into customers, and maximizing revenue.

One of the key objectives of e-commerce marketing is to increase brand awareness and visibility in the online marketplace. This includes utilizing search engine optimization (SEO) techniques to improve a website's ranking in search engine results pages (SERPs) and leveraging pay-per-click (PPC) advertising to display targeted ads to potential customers.

In addition to increasing online visibility, e-commerce marketing also focuses on customer acquisition and retention. This involves implementing effective social media marketing campaigns to engage with target audiences, running email marketing campaigns to nurture leads and build customer loyalty, and utilizing affiliate marketing programs to expand reach and generate sales through partnerships.

Another important aspect of e-commerce marketing is optimizing the user experience on the website. This includes designing a user-friendly interface, optimizing website navigation, and ensuring a seamless checkout process. By providing a positive user experience, e-commerce marketers aim to increase customer satisfaction and encourage repeat purchases.

Furthermore, e-commerce marketing also involves analyzing data and metrics to measure the success of marketing campaigns and identify areas for improvement. This includes utilizing web analytics tools to track website traffic, conversion rates, and customer behavior, and using A/B testing to evaluate the effectiveness of different marketing strategies.

E-Commerce

E-commerce refers to the buying and selling of goods and services over the internet using electronic means. It encompasses online retail platforms, online auctions, business-to-business exchanges, and other online marketplaces.

E-commerce has become a vital element of the marketing management discipline, as it provides businesses with the opportunity to expand their reach, enhance their customer base, and increase their revenue. By establishing an online presence, businesses can break barriers of distance and time, enabling them to reach a global audience and operate 24/7.

E-Mail List Segmentation Software

E-mail list segmentation software is a specialized computer program designed to organize and categorize a company's email subscriber list based on specific criteria. In the context of Marketing Management discipline, this software serves a vital role in helping businesses effectively target and personalize their email marketing campaigns.

The software uses various data points to segment the email list, such as demographic information, geographic location, purchase history, behavior patterns, and engagement levels. By dividing the subscriber base into smaller, more targeted segments, marketers can tailor their email content to meet the specific needs and interests of different customer groups.

Segmentation allows marketers to deliver more relevant and personalized messages to their audience, improving engagement rates and conversion rates. For example, an e-commerce company may segment their email list into categories such as loyal customers, first-time buyers, and abandoned cart users. Each segment would receive tailored emails that highlight relevant products, incentives, or reminders, thereby increasing the likelihood of conversions and retaining customer interest.

Effective segmentation can also help in reducing email list attrition rates and avoiding the risk of spam complaints or unsubscribers. By understanding the specific preferences, needs, and behaviors of different segments, marketers can avoid sending irrelevant and unwanted emails, leading to higher engagement and customer satisfaction.

In conclusion, e-mail list segmentation software is an essential tool for marketers in the field of Marketing Management. It allows businesses to categorize their email subscriber base into segmented groups based on specific criteria, enabling targeted and personalized email campaigns that lead to improved engagement, conversions, and customer retention.

E-Mail List Segmentation Tools

E-mail list segmentation tools refer to software or platforms used by marketing managers to divide their e-mail subscriber or customer database into smaller, more targeted segments for more personalized and relevant marketing campaigns. These tools help marketers categorize their contacts based on certain criteria or attributes, such as demographics, buying behavior, interests, or engagement levels, among others.

By segmenting their e-mail lists, marketers can tailor their communications and campaigns to specific groups of individuals who share similar characteristics or preferences. This allows for more effective marketing strategies, as messages can be customized to resonate with each segment's needs, wants, or pain points. Moreover, segmentation enables marketers to deliver the right message to the right people at the right time, improving overall response rates, engagement, and conversions.

E-Mail List Segmentation

Email list segmentation in the context of Marketing Management is the process of dividing a large email list into smaller, more targeted segments based on specific criteria. This segmentation allows marketers to tailor their email campaigns and messages to different groups of subscribers, resulting in more personalized and relevant content.

Segmenting an email list can be done using various factors such as demographics, purchase history, engagement behavior, geographic location, and interests. By analyzing these factors, marketers can create segments that share similar characteristics and preferences.

The main objective of email list segmentation is to increase the effectiveness of email marketing campaigns. By sending relevant and timely content to specific segments, marketers can improve open rates, click-through rates, and conversion rates. Segmentation enables marketers to send content that resonates with each segment, leading to higher engagement and ultimately, higher return on investment.

Furthermore, email list segmentation allows marketers to build strong relationships with their subscribers. By understanding their preferences and needs, marketers can provide value and build trust over time. This leads to improved customer loyalty and increased customer lifetime value.

In conclusion, email list segmentation is a critical strategy in Marketing Management that enables marketers to deliver personalized and relevant content to different groups of subscribers. It helps in improving campaign effectiveness, building relationships with subscribers, and ultimately driving better results for the organization.

Elevator Pitch

Marketing Management is a discipline focused on the practical application of marketing techniques and principles in order to drive organizational growth and profitability. It involves planning, organizing, directing, and controlling marketing activities to meet the needs and wants of customers, while also achieving the goals of the organization.

The discipline encompasses a broad range of activities, including market research, product development, pricing, promotion, and distribution. Market research helps identify customer needs and preferences, allowing organizations to develop products that meet these requirements. Product development involves creating and improving products to satisfy customer demands and stay ahead of competitors.

Price is a critical element in marketing management as it directly impacts consumer purchasing decisions. Organizations need to determine optimal pricing strategies that balance profitability with customer affordability. Promotion involves creating awareness and generating interest in products or services through various marketing channels such as advertising, public relations, and sales promotions.

Distribution is the final component of marketing management, ensuring that products reach customers efficiently and effectively. This includes selecting appropriate channels, managing inventory, and maintaining relationships with distribution partners.

Overall, marketing management is essential for businesses to build customer relationships, create value, and gain a competitive advantage in the marketplace. It requires a deep understanding of consumer behavior, industry trends, and market dynamics, along with effective decision-making and strategic planning skills.

Email Campaign

An email campaign in the context of Marketing Management is a targeted and strategic approach to promote a product or service through email communication. It involves sending a series of emails to a specific group of individuals with the goal of building brand awareness, generating leads, and ultimately driving conversions.

The purpose of an email campaign is to establish and maintain a relationship with the target audience by delivering relevant and personalized content. This can be achieved by segmenting the email list based on demographics, purchase history, or customer behavior. By understanding the needs and interests of the recipients, marketers can tailor their messages to resonate with them and increase the likelihood of engagement.

An effective email campaign requires careful planning and execution. Marketers need to define their objectives, determine the target audience, create compelling content, and choose the right timing and frequency for sending emails. They should also pay attention to the design and layout of the email to ensure it is visually appealing and mobile-friendly.

Email campaigns provide several benefits for marketers. They offer a cost-effective way to reach a large number of people quickly and easily. With the ability to track open rates, click-through rates, and conversions, marketers can measure the success of their campaigns and make data-driven decisions to optimize their future efforts. Additionally, email campaigns allow for direct communication with customers, fostering personalized interactions and promoting customer loyalty.

Email Marketing

Email marketing refers to the practice of sending commercial messages, typically in the form of email, to a group of individuals who have expressed interest or consented to receive such messages. It is a key component of digital marketing strategies and is used by organizations to cultivate relationships with existing and potential customers, promote products or services, and ultimately drive sales. Email marketing campaigns often involve the development and distribution of newsletters, promotional offers, event invitations, or updates on company news. These messages are tailored to the target audience and are designed to effectively communicate the desired message while adhering to legal and ethical standards. The primary goal of email marketing is to establish and maintain a strong customer base by fostering customer loyalty and engagement. It allows organizations to personalize their marketing efforts, as they have access to customer data, such as purchase history, preferences, and behaviors. This enables businesses to deliver highly relevant content and offers, increasing the chances of conversion and driving customer satisfaction. Effective email marketing requires careful planning, strategic segmentation, compelling content, and thoughtful design. It is crucial to adhere to email marketing best practices, such as obtaining consent, including an unsubscribe option, and using engaging subject lines and visually appealing templates. By leveraging the power of email marketing, organizations can reach a large and targeted audience, build brand awareness, and drive customer acquisition and retention. It is a cost-effective and measurable marketing tool that allows businesses to track open rates, click-through rates, and conversion rates, thereby enabling continuous improvement and optimization of marketing efforts.

Emotion Analytics

Emotion analytics in the context of marketing management is a methodological approach that involves the analysis and measurement of consumers' emotions towards products, brands, advertisements, and overall marketing campaigns. It aims to gain insights into consumers' emotional responses, which can be used to inform marketing strategies and decision-making processes.

The primary goal of emotion analytics in marketing management is to understand how consumers emotionally engage with marketing stimuli, such as advertising messages or product experiences. It involves the collection and analysis of data related to consumers' emotional states, including facial expressions, physiological responses, and self-reported emotions.

Emotional Intelligence (EQ) In Marketing

Emotional Intelligence (EQ) in Marketing refers to the ability of marketing professionals to recognize, understand, and manage the emotions of both themselves and their target audience in order to effectively promote and sell products or services. It involves leveraging emotional insights and cues to build strong connections, establish brand loyalty, and create high levels of customer satisfaction.

In the discipline of Marketing Management, practitioners with high EQ possess a set of skills and competencies that enable them to adapt their messaging and marketing strategies based on the emotional responses and perceptions of their target market. By utilizing emotional intelligence, marketers are able to accurately interpret consumer behavior and motivations, and subsequently tailor their marketing efforts to meet the unique needs and desires of their audience.

Emotional Marketing

Emotional marketing, within the context of Marketing Management discipline, refers to the strategic approach of appealing to customers' emotions in order to create a stronger connection between the brand and its target audience. It involves leveraging human emotions such as happiness, sadness, fear, or excitement to influence consumer behavior and drive desired outcomes.

The aim of emotional marketing is to establish an emotional bond with customers, making them feel connected, understood, and valued by the brand. This connection is based on the concept that emotions play a significant role in decision-making processes, often more so than logical reasoning alone. By evoking specific emotions through marketing messages, visuals, or experiences, companies seek to engage customers on a deeper level and generate a positive impact on brand perception and purchase behavior.

Employee Advocacy

Employee Advocacy refers to the marketing strategy where employees of a company serve as brand ambassadors and actively promote the organization's products, services, and values. It involves empowering employees to share company-related content on their personal social media accounts, thereby expanding the reach and visibility of the brand. This approach recognizes that employees are an essential asset and have a unique perspective on the company. By encouraging and enabling them to share their experiences and knowledge, employee advocacy harnesses their credibility and authenticity, which can significantly impact the organization's marketing efforts. Employee advocacy programs often provide employees with guidelines and training to ensure that their social media activities align with the brand's messaging and objectives. By sharing content such as blog posts, industry news, or promotional materials, employees can contribute to building brand reputation, increasing brand awareness, and driving customer engagement. The benefits of employee advocacy are numerous. Firstly, it can enhance the company's online presence and increase its reach, as employees have their own networks and connections. Additionally, the content shared by employees is often deemed more trustworthy and reliable by consumers, leading to higher levels of brand credibility. Moreover, employee advocacy can help to strengthen the bond between employees and the organization, fostering a sense of belonging and pride. However, it is crucial for companies to implement measures to ensure that employee advocacy activities are aligned with the organization's objectives and values. Regular monitoring and guidance are necessary to maintain consistency in messaging and prevent any potential risks or negative impact on the brand's reputation. In conclusion, employee advocacy is a marketing strategy that leverages employees' personal networks and credibility to promote the organization's brand and increase its visibility. By empowering employees to become ambassadors, companies can tap into their unique perspectives and enhance their marketing efforts.

Engagement Marketing

Engagement marketing refers to a strategic approach used by businesses to interact and build lasting relationships with their target audience or customers. It involves creating meaningful and valuable experiences that go beyond traditional advertising efforts.

The main objective of engagement marketing is to foster active participation and connection between the brand and the consumer. It focuses on encouraging conversation, eliciting emotional responses, and generating authentic engagement. This approach recognizes that engaged customers are more likely to become loyal brand advocates and repeat buyers.

Engagement marketing utilizes various communication channels such as social media, email marketing, events, and content marketing to connect with the target audience. It involves delivering relevant and personalized content that adds value to the consumer's experience. By providing valuable information, entertainment, or educational resources, businesses aim to capture the attention and interest of their audience.

The success of engagement marketing relies on the ability to create a two-way conversation. It encourages customers to actively participate, share their opinions, and contribute to the brand's story. By actively listening and responding to customer feedback and insights, businesses can enhance their products or services to better meet their customers' needs and preferences.

In conclusion, engagement marketing is a customer-centric approach that emphasizes building long-term relationships and meaningful connections with the target audience. By creating valuable experiences and leveraging various communication channels, businesses can foster engagement, loyalty, and advocacy, ultimately leading to increased brand awareness and sales.

Engagement Metrics Dashboards

An engagement metrics dashboard is a tool used in the field of marketing management to track and analyze various measures of customer engagement with a company or brand. The dashboard provides a visual representation of key metrics, allowing marketing managers to monitor and evaluate the effectiveness of their marketing efforts in terms of customer engagement.

The dashboard aggregates data from various sources, such as website analytics, social media platforms, email marketing campaigns, and customer surveys, to provide a comprehensive view of customer interactions. It presents the data in an easy-to-understand format, using charts, graphs, and tables, which enables marketing managers to quickly identify trends, patterns, and areas of improvement.

Engagement Metrics Tracking

Engagement Metrics Tracking refers to the process of monitoring and evaluating customer interactions and behaviors across multiple platforms and channels in order to measure the effectiveness of marketing initiatives and campaigns. It involves the collection, analysis, and interpretation of data related to customer engagement to gain insights that can inform marketing strategies and drive business growth.

In the field of Marketing Management, engagement metrics tracking plays a crucial role in assessing the success and impact of marketing efforts. By tracking various metrics such as click-through rates, social media interactions, time spent on websites or apps, and conversion rates, marketers can understand how effectively their campaigns are engaging target audiences and driving desired actions.

The objective of engagement metrics tracking is to quantify and gauge the level of customer engagement and interaction with marketing content, messaging, and overall brand experiences. This allows marketers to identify successful tactics and channels, optimize campaigns, and make data-driven decisions to improve customer engagement and drive desired outcomes.

Engagement metrics tracking provides valuable insights that enable marketers to understand which marketing activities resonate with their target audience, which channels are most effective in driving engagement, and which areas need improvement. By continuously monitoring and analyzing engagement metrics, marketers can adapt their strategies, messaging, and tactics to enhance customer experiences, increase customer loyalty, and ultimately drive business growth.

Engagement Metrics

Engagement Metrics, in the context of Marketing Management, are quantitative measures used to assess the level of interaction and involvement of customers or target audience with marketing campaigns, content, or initiatives. These metrics provide valuable insights into the effectiveness of engagement strategies and help marketers gauge the interest, satisfaction, and loyalty of their customers.

Engagement metrics typically encompass a wide range of data points, including but not limited to the number of likes, shares, comments, clicks, views, time spent, and conversions. These metrics can be derived from various channels such as social media platforms, websites, email campaigns, mobile apps, and offline events.

Engagement Rate

Engagement Rate is a metric used in the field of Marketing Management to measure the level of interaction and involvement that an audience has with a particular marketing campaign, content, or platform. It is an essential measure for marketers as it allows them to evaluate the effectiveness and success of their strategies and tactics, as well as to understand the level of interest and connection that their target audience has with their brand.

Engagement Rate is typically calculated by analyzing the number of interactions, such as likes, comments, shares, and clicks, that a piece of content or campaign has received, and then comparing it to the total number of individuals reached or exposed to that content. The engagement rate is usually expressed as a percentage, representing the proportion of people who have engaged with a particular marketing initiative out of the total number of people who have been exposed to it.

Ethical Marketing

Ethical marketing refers to the practice of promoting products and services in a moral and socially responsible manner, by considering the impact on various stakeholders and adhering to ethical principles. It involves conducting marketing activities that are fair, transparent, and respectful towards consumers, competitors, and the environment.

In the discipline of Marketing Management, ethical marketing plays a pivotal role in shaping the long-term success and reputation of a company. It requires marketers to make ethical decisions when developing marketing strategies, conducting market research, creating advertisements, and engaging with customers.

One key aspect of ethical marketing is ensuring that the information provided to consumers is accurate and truthful. Marketers are expected to avoid making false or exaggerated claims about the features, benefits, or performance of their products. This helps to build trust with consumers and avoids misleading them into making uninformed purchasing decisions.

Another important element is respecting consumer privacy and data protection. Marketers must ensure that they obtain consent from consumers before collecting their personal information and use it only for legitimate purposes. They should also adopt secure measures to protect this data from unauthorized access or misuse.

In addition, ethical marketing entails treating competitors fairly and respectfully. It is unethical to engage in practices such as spreading false rumors or sabotaging competitors' products to gain a competitive advantage. Instead, marketers should focus on differentiating their offerings based on legitimate factors such as quality, price, or innovation.

Furthermore, ethical marketing involves considering the environmental impact of marketing activities. Marketers should aim to minimize waste, pollution, and resource consumption throughout the product lifecycle. This can be achieved by adopting sustainable production practices, using eco-friendly packaging materials, or promoting recyclability.

In summary, ethical marketing is an essential component of marketing management that emphasizes responsible and morally sound practices. It requires marketers to prioritize transparency, honesty, consumer privacy, fair competition, and environmental sustainability in their marketing strategies and tactics.

Event Marketing

Event marketing is a strategic marketing approach that involves the creation and execution of promotional activities centered around a specific event or occasion. This marketing discipline is aimed at achieving brand exposure, driving customer engagement, and generating leads or sales through well-planned and executed events.

The purpose of event marketing is to leverage the power of in-person experiences to build and strengthen relationships between a brand and its target audience. It allows businesses to showcase their products or services, create memorable experiences, and communicate their brand message in a more impactful way than traditional advertising methods.

Event Sponsorship

Event sponsorship is a marketing strategy in which a company or organization provides financial or in-kind support to an event in exchange for brand exposure and promotional opportunities. It involves a partnership between the event organizer and the sponsor, where the sponsor helps fund the event in return for various benefits.

Event sponsorship is a common practice in the marketing field as it allows companies to reach a targeted audience and increase brand visibility. By sponsoring an event, companies can align themselves with the values and interests of the event attendees, creating a positive association with their brand. This can lead to increased brand awareness, customer loyalty, and potential business opportunities.

Event-Based Marketing Automation Platforms

Event-Based Marketing Automation Platforms are tools used within the field of Marketing Management that are designed to automate and personalize marketing activities based on specific events or triggers.

These platforms leverage customer data and real-time events to deliver targeted and timely marketing messages across multiple channels such as email, SMS, social media, and mobile push notifications. They enable marketers to create and execute automated marketing campaigns that are triggered by customer actions, such as website visits, email opens, purchases, or download completions.

Event-Based Marketing Automation

Event-Based Marketing Automation refers to the strategic use of automated technology and systems to deliver personalized marketing messages and campaigns based on specific events or triggers. It involves leveraging customer data and insights to create targeted and timely interactions that are tailored to individual customer needs and preferences.

By using event-based marketing automation, marketers can design and implement highly relevant and effective communication strategies that are triggered by specific events or actions taken by customers. These events could include website visits, email opens, product purchases, abandoned carts, or any other predefined triggers. When an event occurs, the automation system is triggered, and a tailored marketing message or campaign is automatically delivered to the customer through the appropriate marketing channels.

Event-based marketing automation enables marketers to engage with customers in real-time, providing them with the right information and offers at the right moment. It allows for personalized and contextual marketing experiences that can drive higher customer engagement, conversion rates, and overall marketing effectiveness.

Furthermore, event-based marketing automation helps marketers to streamline and optimize their marketing efforts by automating repetitive tasks and reducing manual intervention. It enables marketers to focus on strategy and creativity rather than time-consuming administrative tasks, leading to improved efficiency and productivity.

In summary, event-based marketing automation is a powerful tool in the marketing management discipline that allows marketers to deliver personalized and timely marketing messages and campaigns based on specific events or triggers. It helps to enhance customer experiences, drive engagement, and improve overall marketing effectiveness.

Event-Based Marketing

Event-based marketing refers to a strategy that revolves around creating and implementing marketing initiatives and activities based on specific events or occurrences, whether they are planned or unplanned. This approach enables businesses to take advantage of the opportunities presented by these events to engage their target audience, generate brand awareness, and drive conversions.

As part of event-based marketing, companies identify relevant events that have the potential to capture the attention and interest of their target audience. These events can include holidays, anniversaries, industry conferences, product launches, or even newsworthy events. By aligning their marketing efforts with these events, businesses can leverage the increased visibility and interest surrounding them to create impactful and memorable marketing campaigns.

This form of marketing requires careful planning and execution to ensure that businesses connect their brand with the event in a meaningful way. This might involve creating thematic campaigns, developing event-specific products or services, hosting special events or promotions, or using event-related themes in their messaging and visuals.

Event-based marketing can be highly effective in capturing the attention of consumers, as it taps into their existing mindset and emotions related to the specific event. By associating their brand with an event that holds significance to their target audience, businesses can establish a stronger connection and build brand loyalty.

Overall, event-based marketing is a strategic approach that allows businesses to seize opportunities presented by specific events to enhance their marketing efforts, engage their target audience, and ultimately drive business results.

Exit Intent

Exit Intent is a marketing management strategy that involves capturing and targeting potential customers who are about to leave a website or online platform without making a purchase or completing a desired action. This strategy is implemented by tracking the mouse movements and behavior of website visitors in order to detect when they are showing signs of exiting the site, such as moving the cursor towards the close button or back button.

Once exit intent is detected, marketers can employ various tactics to re-engage and persuade the potential customer to stay or take a desired action. Common techniques include displaying personalized pop-up messages, offering special discounts or incentives, presenting additional relevant content or products, or providing an opportunity for visitors to provide feedback or subscribe to a newsletter.

Exit Pop-Up

An exit pop-up refers to a marketing technique used to retain website visitors who are about to leave a website or abandon a shopping cart. It is a type of pop-up or overlay that appears when a user attempts to navigate away from a webpage, typically by moving their mouse cursor towards the browser's navigation bar or close button.

The primary purpose of an exit pop-up is to capture the attention of the leaving visitor and encourage them to reconsider their decision to exit. This is achieved by presenting an enticing offer, such as a discount, a free trial, or exclusive content, in exchange for the visitor's contact information or completing a desired action, such as making a purchase or signing up for a newsletter.

Exit pop-ups make use of psychological triggers, persuasive language, and attention-grabbing design elements to engage visitors and increase the chances of conversion. They are strategically timed to appear just before a user leaves the website, ensuring maximum visibility and impact.

When implemented effectively, exit pop-ups can serve as a powerful tool for capturing potential customers who would have otherwise been lost. They help businesses boost conversions, reduce cart abandonment rates, and grow their subscriber or customer base. However, it is crucial to strike the right balance between user experience and marketing goals when using exit pop-ups, as excessive or intrusive use can lead to a negative impression and hinder the effectiveness of the technique.

Exit Rate

Exit rate, within the context of Marketing Management, refers to the percentage of visitors who leave a website or a specific page without further interaction. It is a metric used to evaluate the effectiveness of a website or a webpage in retaining visitor engagement. The exit rate is calculated by dividing the number of visitors who exit a site or page by the total number of visitors who landed on it. Exit rate is an important metric for marketers as it helps identify the pages or areas of a website that fail to engage visitors effectively. High exit rates may indicate problems with the website's content, design, or usability, resulting in poor user experience. Marketers can use this insight to optimize and improve the identified pages, aiming to reduce the exit rate and increase visitor engagement. A high exit rate is not always a cause for concern, as some pages naturally have a higher likelihood of being exit points, such as "Thank You" or confirmation pages. In such cases, it is essential to analyze the context and purpose of the page to determine if the exit rate is within acceptable parameters. Monitoring and analyzing exit rates can provide valuable insights into visitor behavior and preferences. By identifying and addressing high exit rate pages, marketers can enhance user experience, optimize conversion rates, and ultimately improve overall website performance. In conclusion, exit rate is a crucial metric in Marketing Management that helps assess the effectiveness of a website or webpage in retaining visitor engagement. By analyzing and taking appropriate actions based on exit rate data, marketers can optimize user experience, increase engagement, and drive desired outcomes.

Experiential Advertising

Experiential advertising can be defined as a marketing strategy that aims to engage consumers in a meaningful and interactive way, creating memorable brand experiences. It involves designing and implementing events, activations, and immersive campaigns that allow consumers to physically interact with a brand and its products or services.

This form of advertising goes beyond traditional media channels, such as print, television, and online advertisements, by providing consumers with an opportunity to directly engage with a brand in a sensory and experiential manner. It allows consumers to see, touch, feel, and experience a brand's offerings, leading to a deeper level of connection and brand loyalty.

Experiential advertising can take various forms, including pop-up stores, product demonstrations, guerrilla marketing stunts, branded experiences, and interactive installations. These experiences are carefully crafted to align with a brand's values, target audience, and marketing objectives. The focus is on creating a unique and memorable experience that not only captures the attention of consumers but also leaves a lasting impression that encourages positive word-of-mouth and brand advocacy.

This form of advertising has gained popularity in recent years due to its ability to cut through advertising clutter and provide consumers with an immersive and personalized experience. By allowing consumers to actively engage with a brand, experiential advertising creates a stronger emotional connection, increasing the likelihood of brand recall, awareness, and purchase intent.

Experiential Marketing Campaigns

Experiential marketing campaigns can be defined as a strategic approach in the field of marketing management that aims to create immersive and memorable brand experiences for consumers. This form of marketing goes beyond traditional advertising methods by actively engaging the target audience and allowing them to interact with the brand or product in a personal and sensory way.

The main objective of experiential marketing campaigns is to forge a deep and emotional connection between consumers and the brand. By providing an interactive and hands-on experience, these campaigns seek to create positive associations and lasting impressions in the minds of consumers. This type of marketing strategy focuses on the overall customer experience rather than solely promoting the features or benefits of a product or service.

Experiential marketing campaigns can take various forms, including pop-up events, brand activations, product samplings, interactive installations, and immersive brand experiences. These campaigns often leverage technology, social media, and storytelling techniques to enhance the overall experience and generate buzz around the brand.

In today's highly competitive market, where consumers are bombarded with traditional advertising messages, experiential marketing campaigns offer a unique opportunity for brands to cut through the clutter and create meaningful connections with their target audience. By providing consumers with memorable and shareable experiences, these campaigns can increase brand awareness, drive customer engagement, and ultimately, contribute to increased brand loyalty and customer satisfaction.

Experiential Marketing Strategies

Experiential marketing strategies refer to the planning and implementation of marketing activities that focus on creating immersive and interactive brand experiences for consumers. This approach entails designing campaigns or events that enable consumers to personally engage with a brand or product, thereby forming a strong emotional connection.

By utilizing experiential marketing strategies, organizations seek to move beyond traditional marketing methods, such as advertising and promotions, by offering consumers a unique and memorable experience. This can include hosting live events, creating pop-up shops, or developing interactive online content. The goal is to provide consumers with an opportunity to interact with the brand, product, or service in a way that ignites their senses and emotions.

The primary objective of experiential marketing strategies is to enhance brand awareness and loyalty. By allowing consumers to experience and explore a brand on a personal level, organizations aim to create lasting and positive impressions that go beyond simple product knowledge. This can result in increased customer engagement, word-of-mouth marketing, and ultimately, higher sales and customer retention rates.

In addition to generating immediate consumer interest, experiential marketing strategies can also create a long-term impact on brand perception. When executed effectively, these strategies can create a sense of authenticity, authenticity, and credibility, as consumers are able to engage with the brand in a genuine and tangible way. This approach acknowledges the power of consumer experiences and leverages them as a valuable tool for building strong and meaningful relationships between brands and consumers.

Experiential Marketing

Experiential marketing, in the context of marketing management, refers to a strategic approach that focuses on creating memorable experiences for consumers in order to build brand loyalty and drive business growth. Unlike traditional marketing methods that primarily rely on one-way communication, experiential marketing aims to actively engage consumers through immersive and interactive experiences.

This form of marketing involves creating live events, brand activations, or experiences that allow consumers to directly interact with a brand's products or services. These experiences are designed to elicit specific emotions or reactions from consumers, leaving a lasting impression that goes beyond traditional advertising messages. By engaging the senses and emotions of consumers, experiential marketing seeks to establish a deeper connection and foster positive brand associations.

Through experiential marketing, brands can create unique and personalized experiences that resonate with their target audience. By allowing consumers to actively participate and engage with a brand, companies can build trust, loyalty, and advocacy among their customer base. Additionally, experiential marketing provides an opportunity for brands to gather valuable insights and feedback, as well as generate buzz and word-of-mouth marketing.

In sum, experiential marketing is a strategic approach that seeks to create memorable and interactive experiences for consumers, with the aim of building brand loyalty, fostering positive brand associations, and driving business growth.

External Marketing

External marketing, within the context of Marketing Management discipline, can be defined as the process of promoting and selling products or services to customers outside of the organization. It involves various strategies, tactics, and channels that aim to attract and engage external audiences in order to generate leads, acquire new customers, and increase sales.

External marketing activities typically include advertising, public relations, sales promotions, direct marketing, and digital marketing efforts. These activities are focused on reaching out to potential customers, raising awareness about the organization and its offerings, and persuading them to make a purchase or take a desired action.

Eye-Tracking Research Tools

Eye-tracking research tools refer to a set of techniques and technologies used in the field of marketing management to measure and analyze how individuals visually perceive and interact with marketing stimuli, such as ads, websites, packaging, or in-store displays. These tools capture and track the movements of a person's eyes, allowing researchers to gain insights into their attention, focus, and engagement levels during the exposure to marketing materials.

The implementation of eye-tracking research tools in marketing management helps businesses in understanding the effectiveness of their marketing strategies by uncovering the consumers' unconscious visual behaviors. By accurately measuring gaze patterns, fixation durations, and eye movements, marketers can deduce which elements of their marketing materials attract the most attention, which sections are frequently skipped over, and which areas provoke the highest levels of emotional response.

Eye-Tracking Research

Eye-tracking research is a quantitative research technique used in the field of Marketing Management to measure and analyze the visual attention and eye movements of individuals while they interact with various marketing stimuli, such as advertisements, websites, packaging, and displays. It provides valuable insights into consumers' visual behavior, perceptions, and preferences, which can be crucial in developing effective marketing strategies and improving the overall user experience.

Through the use of specialized eye-tracking devices, researchers can accurately monitor and record eye movements, including fixations (when the eyes focus on a specific point) and saccades (rapid eye movements between fixations). This data is then analyzed to understand how individuals process and prioritize visual information, which areas of a stimulus command the most attention, and how long an individual spends on each element of a marketing material.

Eye-tracking research helps marketing managers gain a deeper understanding of consumer behavior by answering questions such as:

- Which elements of an advertisement capture the most attention?

- How do consumers navigate through a website or online store?

- What visual cues influence purchasing decisions?

- Are consumers noticing and engaging with important product information?

By identifying patterns and trends in eye-tracking data, marketers can optimize their marketing materials to improve engagement, increase brand recall, and enhance overall customer satisfaction. For example, they can strategically position key information or design elements to attract more visual attention, ensure that important messages are being noticed, and eliminate distractions that may hinder customers' understanding or decision-making process.

Eye-Tracking Studies

Eye-Tracking Studies are a research technique used in the field of Marketing Management to study and analyze visual attention and cognitive processes of individuals. This method involves tracking the movement of the eye and measuring the gaze patterns of individuals as they interact with a particular stimulus, such as advertisements, websites, or product packaging. The primary goal of Eye-Tracking Studies in the context of Marketing Management is to understand how consumers perceive and process visual information. By studying eye movements and fixations, marketers can gain insights into which elements of a stimulus capture attention, how attention is distributed, and how cognitive processes influence decision-making. Eye-Tracking Studies provide valuable information for marketers in several ways. Firstly, they help identify which specific visual elements of marketing materials are most effective at attracting attention. This enables marketers to optimize the design and layout of advertisements or product packaging to maximize consumer engagement. Additionally, by studying visual attention patterns, marketers can understand how consumers allocate their attention across different elements of a stimulus, allowing for more strategic placement of key messages or visual cues. Furthermore, Eye-Tracking Studies can help marketers evaluate the effectiveness of marketing materials by measuring the level of attention and engagement they generate. By analyzing eye movements, marketers can determine whether consumers focus on the desired elements and understand the intended messages. This information can inform decision-making regarding the modification or optimization of marketing campaigns. In conclusion, Eye-Tracking Studies in the context of Marketing Management provide valuable insights into consumer attention and cognitive processes. By tracking eye movements and measuring gaze patterns, marketers can optimize the design of marketing materials and evaluate their effectiveness. Overall, this research technique contributes to improving marketing strategies and enhancing the overall consumer experience.

FOMO (Fear Of Missing Out)

FOMO (Fear of Missing Out) is a psychological phenomenon that affects consumers' decision-making processes in the context of marketing management. It refers to the intense feeling of anxiety or unease that individuals experience when they perceive that others are participating in compelling and desirable experiences, events, or opportunities that they are not a part of.

In the field of marketing management, FOMO plays a significant role as it influences consumer behavior and purchase decisions. Marketers often capitalize on the fear of missing out by creating a sense of urgency or exclusivity around their products or services. By highlighting limited availability, time-sensitive offers, or emphasizing the popularity of a product or event, they aim to trigger FOMO in potential customers.

FOMO can manifest in several ways in marketing management. One common strategy is the use of social proof, where marketers showcase testimonials, reviews, or endorsements from satisfied customers to create a fear of missing out on a positive experience. Influencer marketing is also a popular approach, as consumers may fear missing out on the lifestyle, trends, or experiences associated with their favorite influencers.

Furthermore, FOMO can drive impulsive buying behavior. When consumers fear missing out on a limited-time offer or a product that is in high demand, they are more likely to make hasty purchasing decisions without thoroughly considering the product's value or their own needs.

In conclusion, FOMO in the context of marketing management refers to the fear and anxiety consumers experience when they believe they are missing out on compelling experiences or opportunities. Marketers leverage this phenomenon by creating a sense of urgency, exclusivity, or by utilizing social proof to influence consumer behavior and drive purchase decisions.

Feature Adoption

Feature Adoption refers to the process of consumers integrating and utilizing new features or enhancements of a product or service into their daily routines or usage patterns. In the context of Marketing Management, feature adoption is a critical aspect of successful product or service launches and ongoing product management.

Marketing managers need to understand and facilitate feature adoption to maximize the value and satisfaction customers derive from the product or service. This process involves a series of steps, including creating awareness about the new features, communicating their benefits and value proposition, and providing support and guidance to users to encourage their adoption and usage.

Flywheel Marketing

Flywheel Marketing is a concept in Marketing Management that focuses on building a sustainable and continuous growth strategy for a business. It is based on the idea that customer satisfaction and loyalty are crucial for long-term success.

In Flywheel Marketing, the traditional marketing funnel is replaced with a flywheel, which represents the continuous cycle of attracting, engaging, delighting, and retaining customers. The goal is to create momentum and leverage the satisfied customers as brand advocates, who actively promote the business and attract new customers through word-of-mouth marketing.

This approach emphasizes the importance of providing exceptional customer experiences and building strong relationships with customers. By delighting customers at every touchpoint, businesses can generate positive reviews, referrals, and repeat purchases, thereby driving organic growth.

Flywheel Marketing requires a customer-centric mindset and a holistic view of the customer journey. It involves aligning marketing, sales, and customer service teams to work together towards the common goal of delivering outstanding customer experiences.

In order to implement Flywheel Marketing, businesses need to focus on personalization, customer segmentation, targeted messaging, and continuous improvement based on customer feedback. This approach requires ongoing data analysis and optimization to identify and address customer needs and preferences.

In summary, Flywheel Marketing is a strategic approach in Marketing Management that emphasizes customer satisfaction, loyalty, and advocacy. By focusing on creating exceptional customer experiences, businesses can drive sustainable growth and achieve long-term success.

Follower Growth Strategies

Follower growth strategies in the context of Marketing Management discipline refer to the planned and deliberate actions taken by businesses to increase the number of followers or subscribers on their social media platforms or other online channels. These strategies aim to attract, engage, and retain a larger audience, thereby expanding the brand's reach and potential customer base.

Effective follower growth strategies involve various tactics and techniques, such as:

1. Content Marketing: Creating and sharing valuable, relevant, and compelling content that resonates with the target audience. This content can take the form of blog posts, videos, infographics, or podcasts, among others. By consistently providing high-quality content, businesses can attract and retain followers who find value in the information shared.

2. Social Media Engagement: Actively engaging with the audience on social media platforms by responding to comments, asking questions, and initiating discussions. This interaction helps build relationships, foster brand loyalty, and encourage followers to share the brand's content with their own networks, thereby increasing the brand's visibility and attracting new followers.

3. Influencer Collaborations: Collaborating with influential individuals or organizations in the industry to endorse, promote, or feature the brand. This can involve partnerships with bloggers, social media influencers, or industry experts who have a large following and can introduce the brand to a wider audience.

4. Paid Advertising: Utilizing paid advertising campaigns on social media platforms or search engines to target specific demographics, interests, or locations. This enables businesses to reach a larger audience that may be interested in their products or services, thus increasing follower count and brand visibility.

By implementing these follower growth strategies, businesses can actively cultivate their social media presence, build brand awareness, and ultimately drive business results through increased followers and engagement.

Follower Growth Strategy

A follower growth strategy is a marketing management approach aimed at increasing the number of followers or subscribers engaged with a brand or organization.

This strategy involves implementing various tactics to attract and retain followers on social media platforms, email lists, and other communication channels. The ultimate goal is to expand the brand's reach, enhance customer loyalty, and drive sales or conversions.

Follower Growth Tactics

Follower growth tactics in the context of marketing management refer to a set of strategies and techniques used to increase the number of followers or subscribers on a particular platform or channel. These tactics are aimed at attracting and engaging more individuals who are interested in a brand, product, or service and converting them into loyal followers or subscribers.

The primary objective of follower growth tactics is to expand the reach and visibility of a brand or business by increasing its follower base. This can be achieved through various means, such as creating compelling and relevant content, optimizing social media profiles, implementing targeted advertising campaigns, and leveraging influencer partnerships.

Freemium Model

The freemium model is a marketing strategy in which a company offers a basic version of its product or service for free, while also providing additional premium features or functionality for a fee. This approach aims to attract a large number of users by removing the cost barrier, while monetizing the offering through upselling or cross-selling paid upgrades or additional services.

By offering a free version of the product, companies can generate widespread awareness and interest, as well as gain a significant user base. This can be particularly effective in industries where switching costs are high or where network effects play a significant role. The free version serves as a marketing tool to demonstrate the value and benefits of the product, enticing users to upgrade to the premium version to access enhanced features or advanced functionality.

Frequency Capping

Frequency capping is a marketing management strategy used to control the number of times a particular advertisement is shown to an individual within a specific time period. This practice ensures that the same ad does not overwhelm or irritate a potential customer, while also maximizing the efficiency of advertising resources. The purpose of frequency capping is to strike a balance between reaching a wide audience and avoiding ad fatigue. Ad fatigue refers to the point at which a user becomes fatigued or annoyed by repeatedly seeing the same ad. By limiting the number of times an ad is shown, marketers can maintain user interest, prevent ad blindness, and avoid wasted impressions. Frequency capping can be implemented across various advertising channels, including display ads, video ads, search engine advertising, and social media advertising. Advertisers typically have the flexibility to set limits on the number of times an ad can be shown per user, per day, week, or month. Setting appropriate frequency caps requires careful consideration of factors such as the target audience, campaign objectives, and the nature of the product or service being advertised. It involves analyzing user behavior, response rates, conversion rates, and other relevant metrics to determine an optimal limit. In conclusion, frequency capping is a crucial component of effective marketing management. By managing the exposure of ads to individuals, marketers can strike a balance between achieving reach and avoiding ad fatigue, ultimately maximizing the impact and efficiency of their advertising efforts.

Friction Points Analysis

Friction Points Analysis in the Marketing Management discipline is a systematic approach to identifying and addressing obstacles and barriers that hinder customer satisfaction and impede the smooth progression of marketing activities. It involves a detailed assessment of the points where customers may encounter difficulties or experience dissatisfaction during their interactions with a product, service, or brand.

The purpose of conducting a Friction Points Analysis is to enhance the overall customer experience by identifying pain points and rectifying them. These pain points can be related to various aspects such as the product itself, pricing, communication channels, distribution, or customer service. By analyzing different touchpoints along the customer journey, marketers can gain valuable insights into areas that require improvement or optimization.

The analysis typically involves collecting feedback and data from customers, conducting surveys, studying customer complaints and reviews, analyzing user experiences, and monitoring metrics like customer satisfaction scores and retention rates. The identified friction points can range from minor inconveniences to major roadblocks that prevent customers from completing a purchase or becoming loyal advocates of the brand.

Once friction points are identified, marketing managers can develop strategies and action plans to reduce or eliminate them. This may include streamlining processes, improving communication, enhancing product features, tweaking pricing strategies, optimizing the website or mobile app, or training customer service teams. The goal is to create a seamless and frictionless customer experience that fosters loyalty, drives repeat purchases, and generates positive word-of-mouth.

Friction Points Elimination

Friction Points Elimination refers to the process of identifying and resolving any barriers or obstacles that hinder the smooth flow of a customer's journey or experience with a brand, product, or service. It is a crucial aspect of Marketing Management, as it directly impacts customer satisfaction, retention, and loyalty.

Friction points can occur at various stages of the customer journey, including pre-purchase, purchase, and post-purchase stages. These points of friction can manifest in different forms, such as complex and confusing website navigation, lengthy and complicated checkout processes, lack of clear and relevant product information, slow customer service response times, or difficulty in obtaining refunds or resolving complaints.

The process of friction points elimination involves systematically analyzing the customer journey and identifying the specific areas where friction occurs. This analysis may involve collecting customer feedback, conducting surveys, analyzing website analytics data, or observing customer interactions with the brand.

Once the friction points are identified, Marketing Managers work towards eliminating or minimizing these barriers by implementing strategies and actions. This may involve streamlining the website navigation, simplifying the purchasing process, improving customer service response times, providing clear and accessible product information, or implementing effective refund and complaint handling procedures.

By eliminating friction points, Marketing Managers enhance the overall customer experience, leading to increased customer satisfaction and loyalty. It also helps in improving brand reputation and competitive advantage in the market.

Friction Points Identification

Friction Points Identification refers to the process of identifying and understanding the points of resistance or obstacles that customers may experience in their journey towards making a purchase or engaging with a brand. It is a crucial step in marketing management as it allows marketers to uncover potential barriers that may hinder the customer experience and impede sales or conversions.

By conducting a thorough analysis of the customer journey, marketers can identify various friction points that customers may encounter at different stages, such as during research, consideration, decision-making, or even after the purchase. These friction points can manifest in various ways, such as confusing website navigation, complex checkout processes, lack of information or transparency, poor customer service, or even negative perceptions about the brand.

The identification of friction points is important because it enables marketers to implement effective strategies to reduce or eliminate these barriers. By doing so, marketers can enhance the overall customer experience, increase customer satisfaction, build trust and loyalty, and ultimately drive sales and business growth. This process may involve making improvements to website design and usability, streamlining the purchase process, providing relevant and helpful information, ensuring prompt and efficient customer support, and addressing any negative perceptions or misconceptions about the brand.

Frictionless Sales

Frictionless Sales refers to the strategic approach in marketing management that aims to create a seamless and effortless customer experience throughout the sales process. It focuses on minimizing obstacles, hurdles, and inefficiencies that can potentially hinder a customer's journey from initial contact to final purchase.

This concept revolves around removing any friction points that may cause frustration or dissatisfaction among customers, ultimately leading to the loss of potential sales. Friction can occur at various touchpoints such as website navigation, checkout process, payment options, customer support, and post-purchase services.

The key objective of frictionless sales is to ensure a smooth and satisfactory customer journey by optimizing every step of the sales process. This involves streamlining website design and navigation, simplifying the checkout process, providing multiple payment options, offering personalized customer support, and optimizing delivery and return processes.

By implementing frictionless sales strategies, companies can enhance customer satisfaction, boost customer loyalty, and ultimately increase sales revenue. A frictionless sales approach requires continuous monitoring of customer feedback, analysis of sales data, and constant improvement of the sales process to ensure customer expectations are met and exceeded.

In conclusion, frictionless sales is a marketing management concept that focuses on minimizing obstacles and creating a seamless customer experience throughout the sales process. By removing friction points, companies can enhance customer satisfaction and loyalty, leading to increased sales revenue.

Gamification

Gamification in the context of Marketing Management refers to the strategic use of game elements and mechanics in order to enhance customer engagement and promote desired behaviors. It involves applying gaming principles such as competition, rewards, and challenges to non-game environments, such as marketing campaigns and customer experiences, to motivate and engage consumers.

The main objective of gamification in marketing is to create a more immersive and interactive experience for customers, ultimately driving brand loyalty, customer acquisition, and increased sales. By tapping into human psychology and the innate desire for competition, achievement, and rewards, marketers can leverage gamification to capture and maintain the attention of a target audience, encourage active participation, and foster a sense of accomplishment.

This approach can be implemented through various tactics, such as loyalty programs, leaderboards, badges, and virtual currencies. For example, a brand may reward customers with points or badges for completing certain actions, such as making a purchase, sharing a product on social media, or referring a friend. These rewards can then be redeemed for discounts, exclusive content, or other tangible benefits, providing customers with a sense of progress and status.

However, it is important for marketers to ensure that gamification aligns with their brand values and objectives, as well as respects user privacy and preferences. An effective gamification strategy requires a deep understanding of the target audience, careful planning, and continuous monitoring and analysis to optimize the gaming mechanics and incentives.

Geo-Conquesting Campaigns

Geo-conquesting campaigns refer to targeted marketing strategies that aim to capture the attention and interest of potential customers in specific geographic areas. This form of marketing utilizes location-based data and technology to engage with consumers who are in close proximity to competitors' physical locations or events.

By leveraging mobile devices and location services, geo-conquesting campaigns enable businesses to deliver personalized, relevant marketing messages to individuals who are present in or near competitor locations. The primary objective of these campaigns is to divert customers away from competitors and towards one's own products or services by offering enticing incentives, such as discounts, promotions, or exclusive offers.

Geo-Conquesting Strategies

Geo-conquesting is a marketing strategy that involves targeting potential customers in a specific geographic location where they are likely to be visiting or spending time, in order to capture their attention and divert them towards one's own business or product. This strategy is particularly effective in capturing customers who are already engaged with a competitor in the same geographic area.

Geo-conquesting is typically implemented through location-based advertising technology that allows marketers to identify the exact location of mobile devices or IP addresses within a specified area. By using this technology, marketers can deliver targeted and personalized advertisements directly to potential customers' mobile devices, such as smartphones or tablets, when they are in close proximity to a competitor's business or a specific location of interest.

Geo-Conquesting

Geo-conquesting is a marketing strategy that involves targeting potential customers based on their physical location and proximity to competitors. This technique leverages location-based technologies to deliver customized and relevant marketing messages to individuals who are in close proximity to a competitor's location.

By using geofencing technology, businesses can establish virtual boundaries around their competitor's locations and track the movements of potential customers within these boundaries. When a potential customer enters the defined geofence, businesses can send them targeted advertisements or promotions to entice them to visit their own location instead.

Geo-Fencing

Geo-Fencing refers to a digital marketing technique used in the field of Marketing Management. It involves the creation of virtual boundaries or perimeters around specific geographical areas or target locations using global positioning systems (GPS), Wi-Fi signals, or cellular network signals. These boundaries are defined by marketers based on factors such as geographical proximity, demographics, buyer personas, or specific user behaviors.

Once the virtual boundaries are established, marketers can leverage geo-fencing to trigger specific marketing messages, offers, or advertisements to individuals who enter or exit the defined geographical areas. This technique allows businesses to deliver highly targeted and personalized content to potential customers based on their real-time location, enabling them to maximize the effectiveness and relevance of their marketing campaigns.

Geo-Targeting

Geo-targeting is a marketing management strategy that aims to target a specific audience based on their geographical location. This approach allows marketers to deliver more relevant and personalized messages to consumers by taking into consideration their location-related characteristics and preferences.

By utilizing geo-targeting, marketers can tailor their marketing efforts to specific geographic regions, such as countries, states, cities, or even neighborhoods. This strategy enables businesses to create localized campaigns and advertisements that resonate with the target audience in each location, increasing the likelihood of engagement, conversions, and sales.

Geofencing Marketing

Geofencing marketing is a strategic approach in the discipline of marketing management that involves targeting potential customers based on their geographic location using mobile devices or GPS technology. It is a location-based marketing technique that allows businesses to create virtual boundaries or geofences around a specific area, such as a retail store, event venue, or tourist attraction, and deliver targeted advertisements or promotions to mobile users within that defined area.

Geofencing marketing leverages the precise location data collected by mobile devices to deliver relevant and personalized marketing messages to potential customers when they enter or exit a designated geographic area. These messages can be in the form of push notifications, mobile ads, text messages, or emails. By utilizing this targeted approach, businesses can engage with customers in real-time and influence their purchasing decisions by delivering timely and location-specific offers or information.

Geotargeted Ad Campaign Platforms

Geotargeted Ad Campaign Platforms are digital marketing tools that allow advertisers to create and manage advertisements that are shown to users who are located in specific geographical areas, often based on their IP address or GPS coordinates. These platforms enable advertisers to target their campaigns to specific regions, cities, or even neighborhoods, ensuring that their ads are seen by the right audience in the right location.

These platforms offer various features and capabilities to help advertisers optimize their geotargeting efforts. They typically provide a user-friendly interface where advertisers can define their target location, set their desired radius or boundary, and select their audience based on demographic characteristics and interests. Advertisers can also schedule their campaigns to run at specific times or days to maximize their reach and impact.

Geotargeted Ad Campaign Platforms often integrate with other digital advertising networks and channels, such as search engines, social media platforms, and mobile apps, to deliver ads to a wider audience. They utilize advanced algorithms and data analytics to track and analyze user behavior, allowing advertisers to measure the effectiveness of their campaigns and make data-driven decisions for optimization.

In conclusion, Geotargeted Ad Campaign Platforms are invaluable tools for marketers in reaching their target audience in specific locations. By utilizing these platforms, advertisers can effectively deliver targeted ads to their desired geographic areas, improve engagement rates, and ultimately drive better conversion and ROI.

Geotargeted Ad Campaigns

Geotargeted ad campaigns refer to a marketing strategy that involves targeting specific geographic locations with tailored advertisements and promotional messages. In this approach, businesses utilize geolocation data to identify the location of their target audience and create targeted campaigns accordingly.

The objective of geotargeted ad campaigns is to serve relevant advertising content to consumers based on their physical location. By doing so, marketers aim to increase the effectiveness and impact of their promotional efforts by reaching the right audience in the right place and at the right time.

Geotargeted Ads

Geotargeted ads, in the context of Marketing Management discipline, refer to advertisements that are customized and delivered to individuals based on their geographic location. This strategy allows marketers to target specific geographical areas, such as countries, regions, cities, or even neighborhoods, and display relevant ads to the users within those locations.

Geotargeting is primarily achieved by collecting users' IP addresses or utilizing GPS and other location-based technologies to determine their physical whereabouts. Based on this information, marketers can create ad campaigns that promote products, services, or offers that are relevant and appealing to individuals in a particular location.

Google Ads

Google Ads is an online advertising service provided by Google, which allows businesses to display their ads on Google's search engine and other websites affiliated with the Google Display Network. It is a pay-per-click (PPC) advertising platform, where advertisers bid on specific keywords to have their ads appear in relevant search results or on relevant websites.

Google Ads is a popular tool for marketers in the field of Marketing Management as it offers various benefits and features to effectively promote products or services. It allows marketers to target specific audiences based on factors such as location, interests, and demographics, ensuring that their ads reach the intended target market. Additionally, it provides detailed analytics and reporting, allowing marketers to track the performance of their ads, measure the return on investment (ROI), and make data-driven decisions to optimize their advertising campaigns.

Green Marketing

Green marketing, also known as sustainable marketing or environmental marketing, is an approach to marketing management that focuses on promoting products, services, and brands that have minimal negative impacts on the environment. It involves the integration of environmental considerations into all stages of the marketing process, from product development and production to packaging, distribution, and promotion.

The goal of green marketing is to meet the needs and wants of customers while also reducing overall ecological harm. This is achieved by offering environmentally-friendly products and services that are produced using sustainable practices, such as minimizing waste, conserving energy and water, and using renewable resources. Additionally, green marketing may involve educating customers about the environmental benefits of choosing sustainable options and influencing their purchase decisions based on these considerations.

Growth Hacker

A growth hacker is a professional who uses creative and unconventional strategies to rapidly grow a company's user base, customer engagement, revenue, and overall visibility. This role is primarily focused on leveraging innovative marketing techniques, data analysis, and experimentation to achieve explosive growth within a short period of time.

Unlike traditional marketers, growth hackers adopt a data-driven approach and rely heavily on technology and analytics to identify effective growth strategies. They constantly monitor key performance indicators (KPIs) and use various tools and platforms to track user behavior, measure conversion rates, and optimize marketing campaigns.

Growth hackers often employ viral marketing, social media marketing, and search engine optimization (SEO) techniques to attract and retain customers. They also implement A/B testing and conduct in-depth market research to identify untapped opportunities and target specific niches.

The primary objective of a growth hacker is to find cost-effective ways to drive exponential growth. They are constantly looking for quick wins and scalable solutions to overcome challenges and accelerate business growth. The mindset of a growth hacker revolves around experimenting with various strategies, analyzing the results, and rapidly iterating to achieve continuous optimization.

In conclusion, a growth hacker is an integral part of a marketing team who focuses on using innovative techniques, data analysis, and experimentation to achieve rapid growth in various aspects of a business, such as user base, customer engagement, revenue, and visibility.

Growth Hacking Frameworks

Growth Hacking Frameworks refer to systematic and structured approaches employed by marketers within the realm of Marketing Management discipline to drive rapid, measurable, and sustainable growth for businesses. These frameworks are essentially a set of guidelines, strategies, and tactics that enable marketers to identify growth opportunities, attract and retain customers, and optimize marketing efforts.

The focus of growth hacking frameworks lies in leveraging innovative and unconventional methods to achieve exponential growth. Marketers utilize a combination of data analysis, experimentation, creativity, and technology to drive growth. These frameworks often involve iterative processes, allowing marketers to continuously refine and improve their strategies to maximize results.

Growth Hacking Tactics

Growth hacking tactics refer to innovative and unconventional strategies implemented by marketing managers to accelerate the growth of a business or organization. These tactics are specifically designed to quickly attract and engage a large number of users or customers, resulting in increased revenues and market share.

Marketing managers who employ growth hacking tactics often think outside the box and utilize creative and cost-effective methods to achieve their objectives. They leverage various digital channels, such as social media, search engine optimization, email marketing, and content marketing, to reach their target audience effectively. By carefully analyzing data and user behavior, they identify successful growth hacking tactics and implement them to drive rapid expansion.

Growth Hacking Techniques

Growth hacking techniques refer to unconventional and innovative strategies that are used in the field of marketing management to rapidly accelerate business growth. This approach involves a combination of creativity, data analysis, and experimentation to achieve long-term and sustainable growth goals.

Growth hacking techniques often involve leveraging digital platforms and technologies to maximize marketing efforts and reach a larger target audience. These techniques focus on identifying and capitalizing on new opportunities, while also optimizing existing marketing channels.

Growth Hacking

Growth hacking is a strategic approach to marketing management that focuses on rapid and scalable growth of a business. It is a mindset and set of tactics that prioritize experimentation, data-driven decision making, and continuous optimization to achieve significant and sustained business growth.

At its core, growth hacking challenges traditional marketing methods by utilizing unconventional and innovative strategies to quickly acquire and retain customers. It embraces a "test and learn" approach, where rapid experimentation and iteration are key to identifying the most effective tactics and strategies. Growth hacking leverages data and analytics to measure and track results, allowing marketers to make data-driven decisions and pivot quickly based on real-time insights.

Growth Marketing

Growth marketing is a marketing strategy that focuses on long-term sustainable growth by using data-driven techniques and experimentation to optimize various marketing channels. It is a holistic approach that goes beyond traditional marketing methods and encompasses a combination of analytics, product development, user experience, and marketing strategies.

The goal of growth marketing is to continuously and rapidly test different tactics and iterate on the results to achieve scalable and sustainable growth. This is done through a systematic process of setting goals, measuring metrics, executing experiments, analyzing data, and making data-driven decisions.

Growth marketers leverage various marketing channels such as social media, email marketing, content marketing, search engine optimization, paid advertising, and more. They use A/B testing, conversion rate optimization, customer segmentation, and other tactics to improve the effectiveness of these channels and drive growth.

Furthermore, growth marketing focuses on acquiring new customers, retaining existing customers, and maximizing customer lifetime value by improving customer satisfaction and increasing customer engagement. This involves understanding the customer journey, identifying pain points and opportunities, and creating personalized experiences to drive customer acquisition, conversion, and retention.

In conclusion, growth marketing is a dynamic and data-driven approach that aims to drive continuous and sustainable growth by optimizing various marketing channels and improving customer experiences.

Guerrilla Marketing Campaigns

Guerrilla Marketing Campaigns refer to unconventional and low-cost marketing strategies aimed at generating maximum impact and attention for a brand or product. These campaigns often utilize creativity, innovation, and surprise elements to engage and captivate the target audience.

Unlike traditional marketing campaigns, which usually require substantial financial resources and extensive planning, guerrilla marketing focuses on leveraging alternative methods and approaches to achieve desired outcomes. Its main objective is to create buzz, generate word-of-mouth advertising, and achieve a viral effect through unconventional means.

Characteristics of successful guerrilla marketing campaigns include targeting specific niche markets, using unconventional promotional tactics (such as flash mobs or street performances), creating memorable and shareable experiences, and capturing the interest and attention of consumers through surprise and novelty.

Overall, guerrilla marketing campaigns require a deep understanding of consumer behavior and the ability to think outside the box. They rely on creativity, imagination, and resourcefulness to develop unique and impactful tactics that can generate maximum exposure with minimal financial investment.

In conclusion, guerrilla marketing campaigns offer businesses an opportunity to break through the clutter of traditional marketing methods and create a memorable, engaging, and cost-effective alternative that can drive brand awareness, increase customer acquisition, and ultimately contribute to the overall marketing objectives of a company.

Guerrilla Marketing Innovations

Guerrilla Marketing Innovations refer to unconventional and creative marketing strategies and tactics that are cost-effective and targeted towards a specific audience. This concept was first introduced by Jay Conrad Levinson in the early 1980s in his book "Guerrilla Marketing."

Guerrilla Marketing Innovations are characterized by their ability to generate maximum impact with limited resources. These campaigns often deviate from traditional marketing methods and rely on unconventional tactics to grab the attention of consumers. They are designed to create a memorable and lasting impression, encourage word-of-mouth marketing, and ultimately drive sales and brand awareness.

Guerrilla Marketing Tactics

Guerrilla marketing tactics refer to unconventional, low-cost promotional activities that aim to create maximum impact and generate buzz for a product or brand. These tactics are characterized by their creativity, surprise factor, and ability to reach a large audience without relying on traditional advertising channels.

In the field of Marketing Management, guerrilla marketing tactics are often used by companies that have limited marketing budgets or are looking for fresh and innovative ways to stand out from their competitors. By thinking outside the box and leveraging unconventional strategies, companies can effectively capture the attention of their target audience and create memorable experiences that drive brand awareness and customer engagement.

Guerrilla marketing tactics can take various forms, such as flash mobs, viral videos, street art, unconventional partnerships, or product placements in unexpected places. These activities are designed to create a buzz and generate word-of-mouth, thus maximizing the reach and impact of the marketing campaign.

While guerrilla marketing tactics can be highly effective, they also come with risks. Since they often push the boundaries of traditional marketing practices, they may encounter legal or ethical challenges. Therefore, it is crucial for companies to carefully plan and execute these tactics, ensuring they align with their brand values and comply with relevant regulations.

Guerrilla Marketing

Guerrilla marketing refers to a marketing strategy that seeks to create maximum impact and consumer attention with minimal budgetary resources. It is an unconventional and creative approach that focuses on generating buzz and word-of-mouth for a product, service, or brand.

Guerrilla marketing campaigns often rely on surprise, humor, or shock value to engage consumers and differentiate themselves from traditional marketing efforts. They may employ unique and disruptive tactics designed to capture attention in public spaces, such as flash mobs, street art, or stunts. This strategy aims to leverage the element of surprise and create a memorable experience for consumers, thereby increasing brand awareness and generating positive brand associations.

One of the key objectives of guerrilla marketing is to create an emotional connection with consumers, evoking curiosity, excitement, or amusement. By engaging with consumers on an emotional level, guerrilla marketing aims to foster brand loyalty and increase the likelihood of consumer advocacy and viral promotion.

Moreover, guerrilla marketing often relies on integrated and cross-channel communication to amplify the impact of campaigns. It leverages various marketing channels, such as social media, influencer marketing, and traditional media, to extend the reach and visibility of the campaign. By creating engaging and shareable content, guerrilla marketing aims to encourage consumers to spread the message and generate organic buzz.

In summary, guerrilla marketing is a non-traditional and resourceful marketing strategy that aims to create buzz and generate consumer attention through unconventional and creative tactics. This approach requires creativity, risk-taking, and a deep understanding of consumer behavior to successfully cut through the cluttered marketing landscape and create a lasting impact.

Hyperlocal Marketing

Hyperlocal marketing is a marketing strategy that focuses on targeting a very specific geographic area, typically within a radius of a few kilometers or even a specific neighborhood or street. This approach aims to deliver highly targeted and relevant messages to consumers based on their location and proximity to a business or service.

Hyperlocal marketing utilizes various channels and tactics to reach and engage with the target audience in a specific locality. This can include targeted online advertising, social media promotions, search engine optimization techniques, and direct mail campaigns. The goal is to create personalized and meaningful experiences for customers by tailoring marketing messages and offers to their immediate surroundings and needs.

By leveraging hyperlocal marketing, businesses can build stronger relationships with local consumers and establish a positive brand image within a specific community. This strategy can be particularly beneficial for small businesses or those with limited geographical reach, as it allows them to compete more effectively with larger corporations and reach a highly targeted local audience.

Furthermore, hyperlocal marketing can provide businesses with valuable insights into local consumer behavior and preferences, allowing them to adjust their marketing efforts accordingly. By focusing on a specific location, businesses can effectively communicate their unique value proposition to potential customers and differentiate themselves from competitors.

Hyperlocal Targeting Solutions

Hyperlocal targeting solutions in the context of marketing management refers to the use of advanced data analytics and technology to deliver highly targeted advertising or promotional messages to an extremely specific and localized audience.

These solutions involve analyzing various data points such as demographic information, geolocation, browsing behavior, and online interactions to identify the unique preferences, needs, and behaviors of consumers within specific geographic areas. With this level of granular data, marketers can create personalized and relevant campaigns that resonate with the target audience at a hyperlocal level.

Hyperlocal Targeting

Hyperlocal targeting refers to a marketing strategy that focuses on delivering tailored and personalized messages to an audience within a specific geographic location. It involves gathering data on consumer behavior, preferences, and habits from a particular area and using this information to create highly targeted marketing campaigns.

In the discipline of Marketing Management, hyperlocal targeting enables businesses to effectively reach their desired audience in a specific location with relevant and engaging content. By honing in on a specific geographic area, marketers can understand the unique needs and preferences of consumers in that region and develop targeted campaigns that resonate with them.

In-Game Advertising Platforms

In-Game Advertising Platforms refer to digital platforms that enable marketers to display promotional content within video games. These platforms leverage the immersive environment of video games to engage with target audiences and deliver targeted advertisements seamlessly integrated into the gameplay experience.

The primary objective of in-game advertising platforms is to generate revenue for both the game developers and the advertisers by monetizing the large and engaged audience base of gamers. These platforms provide marketers with the opportunity to reach a highly engaged and diverse demographic of gamers, who spend a significant amount of time immersed in virtual worlds.

These platforms often employ sophisticated targeting techniques to deliver advertisements to specific audience segments, based on factors such as player demographics, location, behavior, and preferences. This allows marketers to tailor their messages to the interests and preferences of the target audience, increasing the effectiveness of their campaigns.

In-game advertising platforms offer various ad formats, including static or dynamic ads, product placements, sponsored in-game assets, branded skins, and even interactive experiences. The advertisements are seamlessly integrated into the game environment, ensuring that they do not disrupt the user experience or detract from the gameplay.

Additionally, these platforms provide marketers with robust analytics and tracking capabilities, allowing them to measure the performance and effectiveness of their campaigns. Marketers can track metrics such as impressions, click-through rates, views, and conversions, enabling them to optimize their advertising strategies and achieve better results.

In-Game Advertising Trends

In-Game Advertising refers to the practice of incorporating advertisements within video games to reach and engage with target audiences. This advertising strategy involves seamlessly integrating branded content into the game environment, whether through product placements, in-game billboards, sponsored in-game events, or virtual items.

As a trend in the field of Marketing Management, In-Game Advertising has gained significant traction in recent years due to the rising popularity of video games as a form of entertainment. This type of advertising offers unique advantages for marketers, allowing them to leverage the immersive and interactive nature of gaming environments to effectively capture consumers' attention and promote their products or services.

In-Game Advertising

In-Game Advertising refers to the placement of advertising content within video games, also known as advergaming or dynamic in-game advertising.

It is a marketing strategy that leverages the growing popularity of video games as a channel to reach and engage with target audiences. With the proliferation of gaming platforms and the increased amount of time spent by consumers playing video games, in-game advertising has emerged as a viable method for brands and advertisers to connect with their desired demographics.

Through in-game advertising, brands can integrate their messaging and products seamlessly into the gaming environment, either through static placements, such as billboards or logos, or through more interactive and immersive approaches. These include sponsored in-game items, product placements within the virtual world, or even full-blown branded experiences within the game itself.

This form of advertising offers several advantages for marketers. Firstly, it provides access to a highly engaged and captive audience who are actively participating in the game, allowing for increased brand exposure and potential impact. Additionally, in-game advertising allows for precise targeting based on gamer demographics, preferences, and behavioral data, enabling advertisers to deliver personalized and contextualized messages.

However, it is crucial for marketers to strike the right balance between incorporating advertisements without disrupting the gaming experience or alienating the players. Advertisements should be seamlessly integrated into the game's environment and feel natural and non-obtrusive to maintain credibility and avoid negative consumer reactions.

In-Market Audience

In-Market Audience refers to a specific group of individuals who have shown an active interest in purchasing a particular product or service. It is a marketing term used to describe consumers who are highly likely to make a purchase or conversion in the near future based on their browsing behavior, search patterns, demographic information, and online interactions.

The concept of In-Market Audience is derived from the understanding that not all consumers are the same when it comes to their readiness to make a purchase. Instead of targeting a broad and general audience, marketers can leverage In-Market Audience data to focus their efforts on individuals who are more likely to convert, thereby optimizing their marketing campaigns and improving ROI.

In-Store Marketing

In-Store Marketing is a marketing strategy that focuses on promoting products and increasing sales within a physical retail environment. It involves implementing various tactics and techniques to capture the attention of customers, influence their buying decisions, and enhance their overall shopping experience.

The primary goal of In-Store Marketing is to create a compelling and engaging environment that encourages customers to make a purchase. This strategy recognizes the importance of the physical store as a powerful marketing tool and leverages its unique advantages to drive sales and build brand loyalty.

Inbound Lead Generation

Inbound lead generation refers to the process of attracting and converting potential customers through various online marketing strategies. It is a marketing management discipline aimed at creating valuable and relevant content to attract prospects and drive them towards your business.

The main objective of inbound lead generation is to attract potential customers who have shown an active interest in your products or services. Unlike outbound lead generation, which involves reaching out to a wide audience through tactics like cold calling and email blasts, inbound lead generation focuses on building trust and establishing relationships with potential customers before they make a purchase decision.

Through inbound lead generation, marketers utilize various techniques, such as content marketing, social media marketing, search engine optimization (SEO), and email marketing, to attract organic traffic to their websites. By creating high-quality and informative content that addresses the pain points and needs of their target audience, marketers can position themselves as industry experts and build credibility.

Once prospects arrive on a website or landing page, marketers use lead capture forms and landing page optimization techniques to convert them into leads. This involves offering valuable resources, such as ebooks, whitepapers, webinars, or free trials, in exchange for the prospect's contact information.

Inbound lead generation is an effective strategy for attracting qualified leads and nurturing them through the buyer's journey. By providing valuable information and personalized experiences, businesses can build trust, establish authority, and ultimately convert leads into loyal customers.

Inbound Lead Nurturing Software

Inbound lead nurturing software is a tool used in marketing management to automate and enhance the process of nurturing leads that have shown interest in a company's product or service. This software is designed to support and guide potential customers through the marketing funnel by delivering personalized and timely content, nurturing the relationship, and ultimately converting leads into paying customers.

With inbound lead nurturing software, marketers can create customized workflows that automate the delivery of relevant and targeted content based on the prospect's behavior, interests, and preferences. This helps build trust and credibility with the leads, as they receive valuable and informative content that addresses their specific needs and pain points.

The software allows marketers to engage with leads at every stage of the buying journey, from initial awareness to consideration and decision-making. It provides tools for tracking and analyzing lead behavior, allowing marketers to understand which content resonates most with their target audience and make data-driven decisions to optimize their nurturing efforts.

Furthermore, inbound lead nurturing software integrates with other marketing tools such as CRM systems, email marketing platforms, and analytics tools, providing a centralized and streamlined approach to lead nurturing. This allows marketers to track and manage leads efficiently, ensure consistent and coordinated communication across channels, and measure the effectiveness of their nurturing campaigns.

Inbound Lead Nurturing

Inbound lead nurturing is a strategic marketing approach that focuses on building relationships with potential customers who have shown interest in a company's products or services. This process involves engaging and nurturing leads through various communication channels, such as email, social media, and content marketing.

The primary goal of inbound lead nurturing is to guide leads through the marketing funnel and ultimately convert them into paying customers. This is achieved by providing relevant and valuable information to leads at each stage of their buyer's journey. The key to successful lead nurturing is to personalize and tailor the content and communication to the specific needs and interests of each lead.

Inbound Marketing

Inbound marketing is a customer-centric approach to marketing that focuses on attracting and engaging potential customers through relevant and valuable content. It is a strategy that aims to establish a strong online presence, build credibility, and establish trust with the target audience.

The main goal of inbound marketing is to attract visitors, convert them into leads, and ultimately, into loyal customers. It involves creating and sharing content such as blog posts, videos, whitepapers, and social media updates that are tailored to the needs and interests of the target audience. By providing valuable information and resources, businesses can attract potential customers and establish themselves as industry experts.

Inbound marketing is a contrast to traditional outbound marketing strategies such as cold calling, direct mail, and television advertisements. Instead of interrupting potential customers with aggressive sales pitches, inbound marketing aims to attract customers organically by providing them with valuable and helpful content that addresses their pain points and needs.

This customer-centric approach aligns with the changing behaviors and preferences of today's consumers, who are increasingly turning to the internet and social media for information and solutions. By focusing on building relationships and engaging with customers, inbound marketing allows businesses to connect with their target audience in a more personalized and meaningful way, ultimately driving long-term customer loyalty and business growth.

Inbound Sales Funnel

An inbound sales funnel is a marketing strategy that focuses on attracting potential customers through various inbound marketing tactics such as content creation, search engine optimization (SEO), social media engagement, and email marketing. It is designed to guide prospects through each stage of the buying process, from awareness to consideration to decision-making.

The inbound sales funnel consists of four main stages: attraction, conversion, closing, and delight.

The first stage, attraction, involves using compelling content and marketing tactics to attract the attention of potential customers. This can be done by creating informative blog posts, engaging social media posts, and optimizing website content for search engines to increase organic traffic. The goal is to create awareness and establish a relationship with the prospect.

Once the prospect is attracted, the next stage is conversion. This involves converting a visitor into a lead by capturing their contact information through lead generation tactics such as landing pages, forms, and calls-to-action. The goal is to gather enough information about the lead to qualify them as a potential customer.

The third stage, closing, is where the qualified leads are nurtured and guided towards making a purchase decision. This involves personalized communication, targeted email marketing, and sales interactions to address any concerns or objections the prospect may have. The goal is to convert the lead into a paying customer.

The final stage, delight, focuses on providing exceptional customer service and creating a positive customer experience. This is done through ongoing communication, follow-ups, and support to ensure customer satisfaction and loyalty. The goal is to turn customers into brand advocates who will promote the product or service to others.

Inbound Sales

Inbound sales is a marketing strategy used by businesses to attract and engage potential customers. It focuses on creating valuable content and experiences that drive qualified leads to the company. Inbound sales involves nurturing and building relationships with prospects, guiding them through the customer journey, and ultimately closing deals.

The goal of inbound sales is to provide helpful and relevant information to potential customers, addressing their pain points and offering solutions. This approach aims to earn the trust and loyalty of prospects, rather than using traditional sales tactics such as cold calling or aggressive pitching.

Influencer Marketing Analytics

Influencer marketing analytics refers to the process of using data and metrics to measure the effectiveness and impact of influencer marketing campaigns. It involves collecting, analyzing, and interpreting data related to influencer marketing efforts in order to gain insights into the performance and return on investment (ROI) of these campaigns.

These analytics allow marketers to track and measure various key performance indicators (KPIs) such as reach, engagement, conversion rates, and social mentions. By monitoring these metrics, marketers can assess the success of their influencer marketing campaigns and make data-driven decisions to optimize their strategies and achieve desired outcomes.

Influencer Marketing Campaign Metrics

In marketing management, influencer marketing campaign metrics refer to the specific measurements used to evaluate the effectiveness and success of an influencer marketing campaign. These metrics provide valuable insights into the impact and reach of the campaign, allowing marketing managers to assess its performance and make informed decisions for future campaigns.

The primary objective of influencer marketing campaigns is to leverage the influence and popularity of key individuals or organizations to promote a brand, product, or service to a specific target audience. To determine the effectiveness of such campaigns, various metrics are employed to measure key performance indicators (KPIs).

Common influencer marketing campaign metrics include:

- Reach: the total number of unique individuals who have been exposed to the campaign and its messaging.

- Engagement: the level of interaction and involvement generated by the campaign, such as likes, comments, shares, or click-through rates.

- Conversion: the number of individuals who have taken a desired action as a result of the campaign, such as making a purchase or signing up for a newsletter.

- Brand sentiment: the overall perception and sentiment towards the brand that can be influenced by the campaign.

- Return on investment (ROI): the financial return generated by the campaign compared to the investment made.

By analyzing these metrics, marketing managers can determine the effectiveness of their influencer marketing campaigns, identify areas for improvement, and make data-driven decisions for future campaigns. Moreover, these metrics provide insights into the alignment between the campaign objectives and the actual outcomes achieved.

Influencer Marketing Platform

An influencer marketing platform is a technology solution that enables marketers to identify, connect and collaborate with social media influencers to create and manage influencer marketing campaigns.

Influencer marketing has gained significant popularity and importance in recent years, as consumers increasingly trust recommendations from influencers over traditional advertising methods. However, managing influencer campaigns can be complex and time-consuming, especially for marketers who are not familiar with the influencer landscape.

An influencer marketing platform simplifies the process by providing a centralized hub where marketers can search for relevant influencers, analyze their performance metrics, negotiate and manage collaborations, track campaign results, and measure return on investment (ROI). This platform acts as an intermediary between brands and influencers, facilitating the entire campaign workflow from start to finish.

The key features of an influencer marketing platform typically include influencer discovery and vetting, campaign management and monitoring, content creation and approval, contract and payment management, and performance analytics. The platform also provides tools for influencer relationship management, enabling marketers to build and maintain long-term partnerships with influencers.

By using an influencer marketing platform, marketers can streamline their influencer marketing efforts, improve campaign efficiency, and ensure maximum reach and impact. The platform's data and analytics capabilities allow for better decision-making and optimization of influencer partnerships, resulting in more targeted and effective campaigns.

Influencer Marketing ROI Calculators

In the field of Marketing Management, Influencer Marketing ROI Calculators refer to tools or methods used to measure the return on investment (ROI) of influencer marketing campaigns. Influencer marketing is a marketing strategy that involves partnering with influential individuals or personalities, known as influencers, to promote a brand, product, or service to their audience.

ROI calculators specifically designed for influencer marketing help marketers determine the effectiveness and profitability of their campaigns. These calculators take into account various metrics and factors to provide insights into the ROI generated by influencer collaborations.

Influencer Marketing ROI Tracking

Influencer Marketing ROI Tracking refers to the process of measuring and evaluating the return on investment (ROI) generated from influencer marketing campaigns. It involves analyzing and tracking the effectiveness and success of these campaigns in terms of financial outcomes.

In the context of the Marketing Management discipline, influencer marketing has become an increasingly popular strategy for brands to promote their products or services through influential individuals or personalities in order to reach a wider audience. It allows brands to leverage the influence and credibility of these individuals to increase brand awareness, enhance brand image, and ultimately drive sales. ROI tracking in influencer marketing is crucial for marketers to justify the allocation of resources and assess the profitability of their campaigns. It involves not only measuring the financial impact of the campaign, but also considering other key performance indicators (KPIs) such as engagement metrics, reach, and brand sentiment. By analyzing these metrics, marketers can evaluate the effectiveness of their influencer partnerships and make data-driven decisions to optimize their strategies. To track influencer marketing ROI effectively, marketers employ various methods like unique tracking links, promo codes, and trackable hashtags. These techniques enable marketers to attribute sales or conversions directly to specific influencers or campaigns. Additionally, social listening and sentiment analysis tools are used to gauge the overall sentiment and perception of the brand among consumers. In conclusion, influencer marketing ROI tracking is a vital practice within the Marketing Management discipline. It enables marketers to assess the financial impact and effectiveness of their influencer marketing campaigns, aiding in decision making and optimizing future strategies.

Influencer Marketing ROI

Influencer Marketing ROI refers to the measurement of the return on investment generated through influencer marketing campaigns. It is a metric used in the field of Marketing Management to assess the effectiveness and profitability of influencer marketing initiatives.

Influencer marketing involves collaborating with influential individuals who have a significant online presence and a large following on social media platforms. These individuals, known as influencers, have the ability to impact the purchasing decisions of their audience by promoting products or services.

The goal of influencer marketing ROI is to determine the financial outcomes of influencer marketing efforts in relation to the resources invested. It involves analyzing the revenue generated, cost efficiency, and overall impact on the brand's performance and reputation.

To calculate influencer marketing ROI, various metrics and key performance indicators (KPIs) are considered. These may include the increase in sales, brand visibility and reach, engagement metrics such as likes, shares, and comments, and customer acquisition costs.

Understanding influencer marketing ROI allows marketing managers to make informed decisions regarding budget allocation, campaign optimization, and resource allocation. By examining the ROI, marketing managers can identify which influencers and campaigns are most effective in achieving their marketing goals, and which may require adjustments or discontinuation.

Overall, influencer marketing ROI provides valuable insights into the effectiveness and profitability of influencer marketing strategies, helping marketing managers optimize their campaigns and drive better business results.

Influencer Marketing Strategies

Influencer Marketing Strategies can be defined as a set of strategic activities implemented by businesses or brands to leverage the popularity, credibility, and influential power of individuals or entities (known as influencers) in their respective industries or target markets. These strategies are aimed at using influencers as a means to create and promote brand awareness, enhance brand reputation, and ultimately increase sales and customer engagement.

Influencer Marketing Strategies typically involve identifying and selecting suitable influencers based on their relevance, reach, and resonance with the brand's target audience. This selection process involves thorough research and analysis to ensure alignment with the brand's values, goals, and target market demographics.

Once the influencers are identified, the next step in Influencer Marketing Strategies is to establish mutually beneficial partnerships or collaborations. This may involve compensating influencers through various means, such as monetary payment, free products or services, personalized experiences, or exclusive access to brand events and offerings.

The core objective of Influencer Marketing Strategies is to leverage the influencers' established credibility and trust among their followers by creating authentic and persuasive content. This content can take the form of product reviews, endorsements, testimonials, sponsored posts, giveaways, or guest blogs, among others.

By strategically incorporating influencers into their marketing efforts, brands can tap into the influencers' networks and effectively reach and engage with their target audience in a more organic and relatable manner. Additionally, Influencer Marketing Strategies can also provide brands with valuable user-generated content, enhanced social proof, and an opportunity to tap into new markets or niches.

In summary, Influencer Marketing Strategies encompass the planning, selection, collaboration, and creation of authentic content with influencers as a means to amplify brand visibility, credibility, and customer engagement.

Influencer Marketing

Influencer marketing is a marketing strategy that involves collaborating with influential individuals or groups to promote a brand's products or services. It aims to leverage the credibility and reach of these influencers to increase brand awareness, engage target audiences, and ultimately drive sales and business growth.

This form of marketing relies on the power of word-of-mouth recommendations and social proof. Influencers, who are typically experts or enthusiasts in a particular niche, establish trust and authority with their followers through their expertise, authenticity, and engaging content. By partnering with influencers, brands can tap into their dedicated and loyal fanbase, gaining access to a wider audience and potentially converting their followers into customers.

Influencer Outreach Automation

Influencer Outreach Automation refers to the process of using automated tools and technologies to streamline and simplify the management and communication with influencers in a marketing campaign. It involves leveraging software and platforms to identify, contact, and engage with relevant influencers, with the aim of expanding brand reach and increasing brand awareness.

With influencer marketing becoming increasingly popular and important in the marketing landscape, brands have recognized the need to efficiently manage influencer relationships. Influencer Outreach Automation enables marketers to identify and connect with influencers who align with their brand values and target audience, offering a more targeted and effective approach.

Through automation, marketers can use software to search for influencers based on specific criteria such as industry, location, follower count, engagement rate, and content type. This helps to identify the most relevant influencers for their brand and campaign objectives. The automation tools also streamline the communication process by providing templates and automated email sending, saving marketers time and effort.

Furthermore, Influencer Outreach Automation allows for effective tracking and measurement of influencer campaigns. Marketers can monitor key metrics such as reach, engagement, and conversions to evaluate the success of their influencer partnerships and make data-driven decisions for future campaigns.

Influencer Outreach Campaign

In the context of Marketing Management, an influencer outreach campaign refers to a strategic approach used by brands and marketers to leverage the influence and reach of popular individuals or social media personalities, known as influencers, in order to promote their products or services to a wider audience.

By identifying and partnering with influencers who have a significant following and a strong connection with their audience, brands can tap into their credibility and trust to raise awareness, generate buzz, and ultimately drive consumer engagement and sales. The purpose of an influencer outreach campaign is to harness the power of word-of-mouth marketing in the digital age, where influencers act as advocates and spokespersons for a brand.

Influencer Outreach Strategies

In the context of Marketing Management, influencer outreach strategies refer to the planned and systematic approach used by businesses to establish and maintain relationships with influential individuals or entities in order to promote their brand, products, or services.

These strategies involve identifying and reaching out to influencers who have a significant following and influence over a target audience. The goal is to leverage their credibility, expertise, and social media presence to create brand awareness, increase visibility, and ultimately drive customer engagement and conversions.

Influencer Outreach

Influencer Outreach refers to a marketing strategy that involves identifying and engaging with individuals or groups who have a significant influence on a target audience. These influencers have the ability to sway the opinions, behaviors, and purchasing decisions of their followers or fans.

The process of influencer outreach typically begins with extensive research and analysis to identify the most relevant influencers for a particular brand or product. This involves looking at their social media profiles, blogs, and websites to determine their reach, engagement, and credibility within the target market.

The next step is to establish a connection with the influencers through direct communication. This can be done through various means such as email, social media direct messages, or networking events. The goal is to build a relationship based on mutual trust and understanding, as well as to educate the influencers about the brand and its products.

Once a relationship is established, the brand can leverage the influencers' reach and influence to promote its products or services. This can be done through sponsored content, product reviews, giveaways, or collaborations. The influencers act as brand ambassadors, sharing their positive experiences with their followers and encouraging them to try the brand's offerings.

Influencer outreach is an effective marketing strategy because it allows brands to tap into the trust and loyalty that influencers have built with their followers. Consumers tend to trust recommendations from influencers more than traditional advertising, as they perceive influencers as authentic and relatable individuals.

Influencer Partnerships Management

Influencer Partnerships Management refers to the strategic planning, execution, and analysis of collaborations between a brand and influential individuals or social media personalities. This practice is an essential component of Marketing Management, as it allows companies to leverage the credibility and reach of these influencers to promote their products or services.

The aim of Influencer Partnerships Management is to create mutually beneficial relationships that generate brand awareness, engagement, and ultimately, sales. This process involves several key stages: identification and selection of relevant influencers, negotiation of terms and compensation, campaign planning and execution, and evaluation of results.

Influencer Partnerships

Influencer partnerships are a marketing strategy employed by companies to leverage the popularity and reach of social media influencers to promote their products or services. This approach involves establishing collaborative relationships with influencers who have a significant following and influence over their audience.

The main objective of influencer partnerships is to tap into the influencer's credibility, expertise, and fan base to enhance brand visibility, generate brand awareness, and drive consumer engagement. By partnering with influencers, companies can effectively target their desired audience and leverage the trust and loyalty that these influencers have built with their followers.

Influencer partnerships typically require negotiable agreements between the company and the influencer, which outline the scope of the partnership, deliverables, compensation, and guidelines for content creation and promotion. These agreements ensure that both parties are aligned in terms of goals, objectives, and expectations.

When executed effectively, influencer partnerships can yield a range of benefits for companies. These include increased brand recognition, expanded reach to new audiences, improved brand perception, higher engagement rates, and potential sales growth. In addition, influencer partnerships can also offer opportunities for co-creation and content collaboration, enabling companies to tap into the creativity and unique perspectives of the influencers.

However, it is essential for companies to carefully select influencers who align with their brand values, target audience, and marketing objectives. Thorough research and due diligence are crucial to ensure that the influencers have genuine followers, an authentic online presence, and a track record of successfully promoting brands in a transparent and ethical manner.

Innovator's Dilemma

The Innovator's Dilemma, in the context of Marketing Management, refers to the challenge faced by organizations when introducing innovative products or adopting new technologies. This concept, first introduced by Harvard Business School professor Clayton Christensen, highlights the tension between sustaining and disruptive innovations.

Sustaining innovations are incremental improvements to existing products or services, aimed at satisfying the needs of existing customers. These innovations are driven by customer feedback and market demands, and they typically help organizations maintain their market share and profitability. However, sustaining innovations may not be revolutionary enough to address changing market dynamics or customer preferences.

On the other hand, disruptive innovations are breakthrough technologies or products that create entirely new markets or significantly disrupt existing ones. These innovations often cater to unmet needs, lower costs, or introduce new business models. However, disruptive innovations may initially serve smaller, niche markets and may not appeal to existing customers or meet their current requirements.

The Innovator's Dilemma arises when organizations focus too heavily on sustaining innovations while neglecting the potential of disruptive innovations. Companies that solely rely on sustaining innovations may experience a decline in their market position or even face extinction when disruptive technologies emerge and reshape the industry. Therefore, marketing managers must carefully navigate this dilemma by balancing investments in sustaining and disruptive innovations, ensuring the long-term survival and success of their organizations.

Integrated Marketing Communications (IMC) Planning

Integrated Marketing Communications (IMC) Planning is a strategic approach used in the field of

Marketing Management to effectively coordinate and integrate various marketing communication channels and activities in order to deliver a consistent and persuasive message to target audiences.

IMC Planning aims to create a unified and cohesive brand image, enhance brand awareness, and ultimately drive customer engagement and loyalty. It involves analyzing the target market, identifying key marketing objectives, and developing a comprehensive communication plan that utilizes a mix of communication tools such as advertising, public relations, sales promotion, direct marketing, and digital marketing.

The process of IMC Planning begins with conducting in-depth research and analysis to understand the target audience, their needs, preferences, and behavior. This helps in developing a deep understanding of the market and allows marketers to tailor messages that resonate with the target audience. The next step involves setting clear marketing objectives that align with the overall business goals and developing a messaging strategy that conveys a consistent brand message across different communication channels.

The IMC Planning process also entails selecting the most appropriate communication tools and media channels based on the target audience's media consumption habits and communication preferences. It involves crafting compelling and creative messages and visuals that effectively communicate the brand's value proposition and differentiate it from competitors. Additionally, IMC Planning includes establishing a timeline for executing the communication plan, monitoring and evaluating the effectiveness of the campaigns, and making necessary adjustments to optimize results.

Integrated Marketing Communications (IMC) Tools

Integrated Marketing Communications (IMC) refers to the strategic approach used by organizations to align and coordinate their various marketing communication tools and messages in a consistent and unified manner. It aims to deliver a clear and compelling message to the target audience by utilizing a combination of traditional and digital marketing channels.

IMC tools encompass a range of communication methods and tactics that are used to reach and engage with customers. These tools include advertising, public relations, sales promotions, personal selling, direct marketing, digital marketing, social media, and other forms of communication. Each tool has its unique strengths and characteristics, and when integrated effectively, they reinforce and enhance the overall impact of the marketing message.

The key objective of employing IMC tools is to achieve synergy and maximize the effectiveness of marketing communication efforts. By integrating different tools, organizations can create a seamless and consistent brand experience for consumers across various touchpoints. This approach ensures that the target audience receives a cohesive message, increasing brand awareness, trust, and recall.

Additionally, IMC tools enable organizations to tailor their communication strategies to different customer segments. By utilizing a mix of tools, marketers can reach customers through their preferred channels, increasing the likelihood of capturing their attention and influencing their purchase decisions.

In summary, IMC tools are an essential component of effective marketing management. By integrating various communication methods, organizations can create a unified and impactful message that resonates with their target audience, leading to increased brand awareness, customer engagement, and ultimately, business success.

Integrated Marketing Communications (IMC)

Integrated Marketing Communications (IMC) is a strategic approach used by organizations in the field of marketing management to combine and coordinate various communication activities in order to deliver a consistent and persuasive message to target audiences. IMC aims to create a synergy between different marketing communication tools and channels, including advertising, public relations, sales promotion, direct marketing, personal selling, and digital marketing.

IMC focuses on the development of a comprehensive and integrated marketing communication plan that aligns with the overall marketing objectives of the organization. The plan involves determining the target market, understanding consumer behavior, and selecting the most appropriate communication tools and channels to reach the target audience effectively. By integrating various communication activities, IMC ensures that the organization presents a unified and coherent message to its customers, creating a stronger impact and increasing the effectiveness of marketing efforts.

Integrated Marketing

Integrated Marketing is a strategic approach in marketing management that focuses on delivering consistent and seamless brand experiences to target audiences across multiple channels. It involves combining and coordinating various promotional methods, such as advertising, public relations, direct marketing, social media marketing, and sales promotion, to create a unified and synchronized marketing campaign.

The main objective of integrated marketing is to ensure that all marketing communications and touchpoints work together to convey a cohesive brand message and enhance brand recall and recognition. It emphasizes the importance of a holistic and integrated marketing strategy rather than implementing isolated marketing activities. By aligning all marketing efforts, integrated marketing aims to maximize reach, engagement, and conversion rates by delivering a consistent and impactful brand experience.

Interactive Content Marketing

Interactive Content Marketing is a strategic approach to marketing that involves the creation and distribution of engaging, interactive content with the goal of attracting and engaging a target audience, driving brand awareness, and ultimately, influencing consumer behavior. This form of marketing relies on interactive elements such as quizzes, calculators, assessments, polls, surveys, games, and other interactive tools to provide an immersive and engaging experience to the audience.

Interactive content marketing goes beyond traditional passive content consumption by encouraging active participation and personalization. It enables companies to capture valuable data and insights about their target audience, their preferences, and their needs. This data can then be used to tailor marketing strategies, improve customer targeting, and enhance overall customer experience.

Internal Marketing

Internal marketing is a strategic approach to marketing management that focuses on delivering effective marketing practices within an organization to enhance employee satisfaction, commitment, and performance. It involves promoting the organization's vision, mission, products, and services to internal stakeholders, such as employees, managers, and other departments.

The primary goal of internal marketing is to align and integrate the internal systems, processes, and culture of the organization with the marketing strategies and objectives. It recognizes that employees are key stakeholders who directly or indirectly contribute to the success of a marketing campaign or strategy. Thus, internal marketing aims to create an environment where employees feel valued, motivated, and engaged, and are willing to go above and beyond their responsibilities to deliver exceptional customer experiences.

Joint Venture (JV) Marketing

A Joint Venture (JV) Marketing refers to a mutually beneficial collaboration between two or more companies in the marketing domain. Under this arrangement, the participating companies pool their resources, expertise, and networks to develop and execute marketing strategies aimed at achieving a common objective.

In the context of marketing management, a JV marketing initiative typically involves the partnering companies leveraging each other's strengths and capabilities to enhance their brand visibility, expand their market reach, and access new customer segments. This collaborative approach allows the companies to combine their marketing efforts and resources, resulting in shared costs and higher efficiency.

JV marketing can take various forms, including co-branding, co-marketing, and strategic alliances. For example, two companies may create a co-branded product or service by merging their brand identities and sharing marketing activities. Alternatively, companies can engage in co-marketing campaigns where they collaborate to promote each other's products or services to their respective customer bases. In some cases, companies form strategic alliances to jointly develop and market new products or enter new markets.

By forming a joint venture, companies can leverage each other's customer base, distribution channels, and marketing knowledge to gain a competitive advantage. This collaborative approach allows the companies to tap into new markets, achieve economies of scale, and enhance their brand credibility through association with a trusted partner.

In summary, a joint venture marketing in the context of marketing management is a collaborative initiative where two or more companies join forces to develop and execute marketing strategies to achieve common marketing objectives. This arrangement allows companies to harness each other's resources and expertise, resulting in shared costs, expanded market reach, and increased brand visibility.

KPI (Key Performance Indicator)

A Key Performance Indicator (KPI) is a quantifiable metric that helps marketers measure the success of their marketing efforts in achieving specific goals and objectives. KPIs are essential performance benchmarks that provide valuable insights into the effectiveness of marketing campaigns and strategies.

In the field of Marketing Management, KPIs play a crucial role in evaluating and tracking the performance of marketing initiatives. They enable marketers to monitor progress, identify areas of improvement, and make data-driven decisions for future campaigns.

Typically, KPIs in marketing focus on various aspects such as customer acquisition, conversion rates, customer retention, brand awareness, and overall revenue generation. These indicators provide a comprehensive overview of the marketing team's performance in different areas, helping them assess whether specific objectives are being met.

For example, a common KPI in marketing is the Conversion Rate, which measures the percentage of website visitors who take a desired action, such as making a purchase or submitting a contact form. This metric helps marketers assess the effectiveness of their website design, messaging, and call-to-action strategies.

Another important KPI in marketing is Customer Lifetime Value (CLTV), which determines the total revenue a customer is expected to generate over their entire relationship with a company. Tracking CLTV enables marketers to evaluate the profitability of different customer segments and optimize their strategies accordingly.

Overall, KPIs are essential tools in marketing management, providing objective benchmarks to assess performance, guide decision-making, and drive continuous improvement in marketing strategies and tactics.

Keyword Density Analysis

Keyword density analysis is a technique used in marketing management to evaluate the relevance and importance of keywords in a piece of content. It is a quantitative measure that helps marketers understand the frequency and distribution of specific keywords within a text, webpage, or website.

The keyword density analysis is crucial for search engine optimization (SEO) because search engines rely on keywords to understand the context and relevance of a webpage. By analyzing the keyword density, marketers can ensure that their content is optimized for search engines

146

and increases the likelihood of ranking higher in search results.

Keyword Density Optimization Software

Keyword density optimization software is a tool used in the field of marketing management to analyze and improve the keyword density of a website or online content. Keyword density refers to the percentage of times a keyword or phrase appears in relation to the total number of words on a webpage or within a piece of content.

This software is designed to assist marketing managers in optimizing their websites and content for search engines. By analyzing the keyword density, the software helps managers determine whether they are using keywords effectively or overusing them, which can negatively impact search engine rankings.

Keyword Density Optimization

Keyword density optimization is a technique used in marketing management to improve the visibility and ranking of a website or webpage in search engine results. It involves strategically incorporating relevant keywords throughout the content of a webpage to increase its relevance and organic traffic from search engines.

The goal of keyword density optimization is to find the right balance between using keywords enough times to signal search engines about the topic of the webpage, without overdoing it and risking being flagged for keyword stuffing. By including keywords strategically within the content, headings, meta tags, and URLs, marketers can help search engines understand what the webpage is about and index it accordingly.

However, it is important to note that keyword density optimization should be done in a natural and user-friendly way. The content should always be written for the audience, rather than solely for search engine algorithms. Keyword stuffing, or excessively and unnaturally incorporating keywords in the content, can negatively impact the user experience and the webpage's ranking.

Moreover, search engines now prioritize relevance, user experience, and quality content over keyword density alone. Marketers should focus on creating valuable and engaging content that aligns with the search intent of their target audience, rather than solely on keyword optimization.

Keyword Difficulty

Keyword Difficulty refers to the level of challenging it is to rank a specific keyword on search engine results pages (SERPs). In the context of Marketing Management, keyword difficulty is a crucial factor that marketers consider while conducting keyword research and creating SEO strategies.

When marketers aim to optimize their website's visibility on search engines, they often target specific keywords that are relevant to their products or services. However, not all keywords have the same level of difficulty in terms of ranking. Some keywords may have high competition, making it more challenging to rank them on the first page of search results.

Keyword difficulty is determined by various factors, including the number of websites already targeting the keyword, the quality and authority of those websites, and the overall competitiveness of the search engine market. Analyzing keyword difficulty helps marketers understand the effort and resources required to rank for a particular keyword.

By assessing keyword difficulty, marketers can prioritize their SEO efforts by targeting keywords with higher chances of ranking. This analysis allows them to allocate resources effectively, focusing on keywords where the competition is relatively low and the potential for organic visibility is higher.

Consequently, marketers can make informed decisions about their overall SEO strategy, content creation, and website optimization. By selecting keywords with the right balance of relevance and difficulty, they can improve their website's search visibility, drive targeted organic traffic, and ultimately enhance brand exposure and conversion rates.

Keyword Intent Analysis Tools

Keyword intent analysis tools refer to software or platforms used in marketing management that assist in understanding the intention or purpose behind the keywords used by users in search queries or online content. These tools analyze and categorize keywords based on the underlying meaning or intent behind them, allowing marketers to gain insights into consumer behavior and optimize their marketing strategies accordingly.

Keyword intent analysis tools help marketers identify the various types of intent that users have when conducting online searches. This includes informational intent, navigational intent, transactional intent, and commercial investigational intent. By analyzing keywords and their intent, marketers can tailor their content, advertisements, and overall marketing approach to match the specific needs and expectations of their target audience.

Keyword Intent Analysis

Keyword intent analysis is a valuable technique used in the field of marketing management to understand the underlying intentions or motives behind the keywords or search terms used by consumers when conducting online searches. This analysis enables marketers to gain insights into consumer behavior, preferences, or needs, allowing them to optimize their marketing strategies accordingly.

By analyzing keyword intent, marketers can determine whether a user's search query is informational, navigational, or transactional. Informational intent refers to users seeking information or answers to their questions. Navigational intent reflects users looking for specific websites or online resources. Transactional intent signifies users intending to make a purchase or engage in a specific action.

Keyword Intent Identification

Keyword Intent Identification in the context of Marketing Management refers to the process of determining the underlying purpose or objective behind a specific keyword or search query made by users in relation to marketing-related topics. It involves analyzing the intent behind the keywords used by users to gain insights into their needs, motivations, and preferences in order to develop effective marketing strategies.

By identifying the intent behind keywords, marketers can optimize their marketing efforts to better align with customer expectations and deliver more relevant content. There are generally three main types of keyword intent:

1. Informational Intent: This type of intent is focused on seeking information, such as product reviews, industry research, or how-to guides. Understanding informational intent keywords helps marketers create informative and educational content that addresses users' queries.

2. Navigational Intent: Navigational intent refers to users searching for specific brands, websites, or online platforms. Marketers can use this intent to optimize their web presence and ensure their brand or website appears prominently in search results.

3. Transactional Intent: Transactional intent is associated with users who are ready to make a purchase or engage in a specific action. Marketers can leverage transactional intent keywords to create targeted campaigns and optimize landing pages for conversions.

By identifying the intent behind keywords, marketers can gain valuable insights into consumer behavior, preferences, and purchase intent. This helps them tailor their marketing strategies, such as content creation, SEO, paid advertising, and website optimization, to effectively target and engage their audience.

Keyword Research

Keyword research in the context of Marketing Management is the process of identifying and analyzing the words and phrases that potential customers are using to search for products or services related to a specific business. This research helps marketers understand the language

148

and terms that their target audience is using, allowing them to optimize their marketing campaigns, website content, and online presence to maximize visibility and reach.

Effective keyword research involves using various techniques and tools to uncover relevant keywords with high search volume and low competition. This process enables marketers to develop targeted and customized strategies to attract organic search traffic and improve their website's ranking in search engine results pages (SERPs).

Keyword Stuffing

Keyword stuffing is a black hat SEO technique that involves excessively using specific keywords or phrases in a website's content in order to manipulate search engine rankings. This tactic aims to trick search engines into thinking that the website is more relevant to a particular keyword than it actually is.

In the context of marketing management, keyword stuffing is considered unethical and harmful to a brand's overall online presence. While it may have temporarily boosted search engine rankings in the past, major search engines like Google have become incredibly sophisticated in recognizing and penalizing websites that engage in this practice.

Landing Page A/B Testing Platforms

A/B testing platforms are tools used in Marketing Management to conduct experiments and gather data on the performance of different variations of a landing page. A landing page is a specific web page created for the purpose of converting visitors into leads or customers. By employing A/B testing platforms, marketers can create multiple versions of a landing page, varying elements such as headlines, images, call-to-action buttons, and layout.

These platforms allow marketers to randomly divide their website traffic into two or more groups, with each group being shown a different version of the landing page. By analyzing the data from these experiments, marketers can determine which version of the landing page performs better in terms of conversion rates, click-through rates, or other key performance indicators.

Landing Page A/B Testing Tools

A/B testing is a method used in the field of Marketing Management to compare two versions of a landing page to determine which one performs better in achieving a specific goal or objective. It is a technique that allows marketers to make data-driven decisions and optimize their website or landing page for improved conversion rates.

With A/B testing, marketers create two different versions of a landing page (A and B) and randomly divide their website traffic between the two versions. The purpose is to understand which version is more effective in terms of engaging visitors, reducing bounce rates, increasing click-through rates, or ultimately driving more conversions.

Landing Page A/B Testing

Landing page A/B testing is a marketing management technique used to evaluate and compare the effectiveness of different versions of a landing page. It involves creating two or more variations of a landing page and directing a portion of website traffic to each version. The purpose of this testing is to analyze which landing page design, content, or element layout generates better user engagement and conversions.

Through A/B testing, marketers can gather data and insights to make informed decisions and optimize their landing pages for improved performance. It allows them to measure and compare metrics such as click-through rates, bounce rates, conversion rates, and time spent on the page. This method helps identify the most successful elements and combinations of elements that resonate with the target audience and drive desired actions.

Landing Page Optimization (LPO)

Landing Page Optimization (LPO) refers to the process of improving a website's landing page to increase its effectiveness in converting visitors into customers or achieving another desired action. It is a key component of marketing management, as it focuses on improving the landing page's performance and maximizing its impact on the overall marketing strategy.

The main goal of LPO is to enhance the user experience and optimize the landing page's design, content, and functionality to attract and engage visitors. This involves conducting thorough analysis and testing to identify areas for improvement and implement changes that will drive higher conversions.

Landing pages are the initial entry points for visitors, often used for specific marketing campaigns or promotions. They are designed to provide relevant information and persuade visitors to take a desired action, such as making a purchase, signing up for a newsletter, or filling out a form. Therefore, it is crucial for these pages to be optimized to maximize conversion rates and achieve marketing goals.

LPO employs various techniques and strategies, including A/B testing, multivariate testing, and user feedback analysis, to refine and optimize the landing page's elements. These elements may include headlines, call-to-action buttons, forms, images, and overall layout and design. By continuously testing and improving these elements, marketers can ensure that the landing page is compelling, user-friendly, and aligned with the target audience's preferences and expectations.

Landing Page Optimization

Landing Page Optimization is a strategic approach used in Marketing Management to enhance the performance and effectiveness of landing pages in websites. A landing page refers to the specific webpage where users arrive after clicking on a marketing campaign or advertisement. The optimization process involves making systematic changes and improvements to the design, layout, content, and overall user experience of the landing page with the aim of maximizing conversions and achieving specific marketing objectives.

The primary goal of landing page optimization is to increase the conversion rate, which is the percentage of visitors who take a desired action on the website, such as making a purchase, filling out a form, or subscribing to a newsletter. By optimizing the landing page, marketers can improve the relevance, clarity, and persuasiveness of the content, as well as streamline the user journey and eliminate any potential obstacles or distractions that may hinder conversion.

Landing Page

A landing page is a single webpage that is specifically designed to capture the attention and convert visitors into leads or customers. It is an essential tool in the field of marketing management as it serves as a focused destination for potential customers to land on after clicking on a specific advertisement, search result, or marketing campaign.

The primary objective of a landing page is to generate leads or sales by encouraging visitors to take a specific action, such as signing up for a newsletter, downloading a whitepaper, purchasing a product, or filling out a contact form. Unlike a homepage or other pages on a website, a landing page is designed with a singular purpose in mind and is devoid of distractions that may lead visitors away from the intended conversion goal.

A successful landing page is created with careful attention to various elements such as the headline, copy, visuals, call-to-action, and form. The headline should be attention-grabbing and clearly communicate the value proposition or offer. The copy should be concise, persuasive, and highlight the benefits of the product or service. Visuals, if used, should be relevant and visually appealing, complementing the overall message.

The call-to-action is a crucial element that guides visitors towards taking the desired action. It should be prominently displayed, clearly state what the visitor should do, and create a sense of urgency or value. Additionally, the form on the landing page should have minimal fields to reduce friction and make it easy for visitors to complete the action.

Lateral Marketing

Lateral marketing refers to a marketing strategy that focuses on finding innovative and unconventional ways to promote and sell products or services. It involves thinking outside of traditional marketing channels and finding new avenues to reach and engage with customers.

This approach often entails leveraging unexpected partnerships, exploring non-traditional distribution methods, and utilizing creative promotional tactics. Lateral marketing aims to disrupt traditional marketing practices and capture consumers' attention by offering unique and unexpected experiences.

Lead Attribution

Lead attribution in the context of Marketing Management refers to the process of determining and assigning credit to the marketing activities and touchpoints that contributed to the generation of a lead or conversion. It allows marketers to understand which marketing channels, campaigns, or tactics are most effective in driving customer engagement and conversions, and helps them optimize their marketing strategies and allocate resources effectively.

The goal of lead attribution is to track and analyze the customer journey across various touchpoints, both online and offline, to identify the interactions and marketing efforts that played a role in influencing a lead to take a desired action. This can include interactions such as clicking on an advertisement, visiting a website, engaging with social media content, or attending an event.

There are different models and approaches to lead attribution, including first-touch attribution, last-touch attribution, linear attribution, time decay attribution, and algorithmic attribution. Each model attributes credit to marketing touchpoints differently, based on factors such as the order of touchpoints, the time elapsed between touchpoints, or a predetermined set of rules.

Lead attribution is essential for marketers to make informed decisions about their marketing strategies and investments. By understanding which channels and efforts are driving the most valuable leads or conversions, marketers can optimize their campaigns, allocate resources more effectively, and maximize their return on investment.

Lead Funnel Management

Lead funnel management refers to the systematic process of managing and tracking potential customers throughout their journey from being a lead to becoming a paying customer. It is a critical component of marketing management that focuses on maximizing the conversion rate of leads into customers.

The lead funnel, also known as the sales funnel or customer journey, represents the stages that a lead goes through before making a purchase. These stages typically include awareness, interest, consideration, and decision. Lead funnel management involves implementing strategies and tactics to move leads smoothly through these stages and ultimately convert them into customers.

Lead Funnel Optimization

Lead funnel optimization is a marketing management strategy aimed at improving and maximizing the efficiency of the lead generation and conversion process. It involves analyzing and optimizing each stage of the lead funnel, from initial awareness to final sale, in order to increase the number of qualified leads and ultimately drive more revenue for the business.

The lead funnel refers to the journey that potential customers take from the moment they become aware of a product or service, to the point where they make a purchase decision. It typically consists of several stages, including awareness, interest, consideration, and action. The goal of lead funnel optimization is to identify and remove any obstacles or inefficiencies that may be preventing potential leads from progressing through the funnel smoothly.

This process typically involves data analysis, testing, and continuous improvement. Marketing teams use various tactics and strategies to optimize each stage of the lead funnel, such as creating targeted content, improving the website user experience, optimizing landing pages, implementing lead nurturing campaigns, and using marketing automation tools.

By optimizing the lead funnel, businesses can increase their conversion rates, reduce customer acquisition costs, and ultimately, drive more revenue. It allows marketing teams to focus their efforts on the most effective strategies and tactics, ensuring that the right message is delivered to the right audience at the right time.

Lead Funnel

A lead funnel is a strategic marketing management concept used in the sales process to describe the journey that potential customers take from being initially aware of a product or service to becoming a paying customer. The lead funnel is designed to guide potential customers through a series of steps or stages with the ultimate goal of converting them into sales.

At the top of the lead funnel, potential customers enter as leads. This could be through various channels such as social media, online advertisements, or referrals. The objective at this stage is to create awareness and generate interest in the product or service. Marketers use various tactics to attract leads, such as content marketing, search engine optimization, and targeted advertising.

As potential customers move down the lead funnel, they enter the middle stage, where they are considered qualified leads. This is where marketers focus on nurturing the leads and building a relationship with them. Tactics at this stage may include email marketing, personalized messaging, and offering valuable resources or information to further educate and engage the leads.

The final stage of the lead funnel is the conversion stage, where qualified leads become paying customers. Here, marketers employ strategies to encourage leads to take action, such as offering discounts, limited-time offers, or free trials. The goal is to remove any remaining barriers and provide an incentive for leads to complete the purchase.

Lead Generation

Lead generation in the context of marketing management refers to the process of identifying and attracting potential customers or leads for a business's products or services. It involves implementing strategies and tactics to capture the interest and contact information of individuals who are likely to have an interest in what the business offers.

The goal of lead generation is to create a pool of potential customers who can be nurtured and eventually converted into paying customers. This is achieved through various marketing activities such as content marketing, social media marketing, search engine optimization, email marketing, and paid advertising.

Lead Nurturing

Lead nurturing is a key aspect of marketing management that involves building and maintaining relationships with potential customers. It is the process of systematically guiding leads through the sales funnel and educating them about a company's products or services in order to increase their likelihood of making a purchase.

The goal of lead nurturing is to move leads from initial interest to becoming loyal customers. This is achieved by providing relevant and valuable information that addresses their needs and pain points. By consistently delivering valuable content, businesses can establish themselves as trusted advisors and increase their chances of converting leads into customers.

Lead Scoring Models Implementation

Lead scoring models implementation refers to the process of applying predictive analytics and statistical techniques to evaluate the quality and potential value of leads generated through marketing efforts. It is a key component of marketing management in order to prioritize and rank leads based on their likelihood to convert into customers.

Lead scoring models typically assign a numerical value or score to each lead based on a combination of demographic, behavioral, and firmographic data. This data can include parameters such as industry, job title, company size, website interactions, email engagement, and social media activity. The models use this data to predict the probability that a lead will become a paying customer.

Lead Scoring Models

Lead scoring models are a crucial component of marketing management in order to effectively prioritize and qualify potential leads. These models utilize data-driven techniques to assign a numerical value or score to each lead based on their likelihood to make a purchase or become a customer.

The purpose of lead scoring is to optimize the marketing and sales efforts by focusing resources on leads that have a higher probability of converting, thus increasing the overall efficiency and effectiveness of the marketing campaigns. The model takes into consideration various factors such as demographic information, online behavior, engagement level with marketing materials, and interaction with the company's website or social media channels.

Lead Scoring

Lead Scoring, in the context of Marketing Management, refers to the systematic process of evaluating and ranking potential sales leads based on their perceived value and likelihood of conversion. It allows businesses to prioritize and focus their sales and marketing efforts on leads that are more likely to result in successful conversions and sales.

The goal of lead scoring is to identify leads that demonstrate the highest potential for becoming paying customers. This is achieved by assigning scores or ratings to individual leads based on various factors such as their demographic information, behavior, level of engagement, and interactions with the marketing materials and channels.

Lead scoring involves analyzing and tracking specific lead attributes and activities to determine their relative importance in predicting conversion. It takes into account both explicit data, such as job title, industry, company size, and implicit data, including website visits, content downloads, email opens, and social media interactions.

By implementing lead scoring, marketing teams can prioritize leads with higher scores and allocate appropriate resources to nurture and engage with those leads. By focusing efforts on leads that are more likely to convert, businesses can streamline their sales processes, improve efficiency, and increase the overall success rate of their marketing campaigns.

Lifecycle Marketing

Lifecycle marketing is a strategic approach in marketing management that focuses on developing long-term relationships with customers by understanding and catering to their needs and preferences throughout the various stages of the customer lifecycle.

The customer lifecycle consists of several stages, including awareness, consideration, purchase, retention, and advocacy. In each stage, the goal of lifecycle marketing is to engage, nurture, and deliver value to customers in order to increase customer loyalty and maximize the lifetime value of customers.

At the awareness stage, the focus is on building brand awareness and generating leads. This can be achieved through targeted advertising, content marketing, social media, and other marketing channels.

During the consideration stage, the emphasis is on providing potential customers with relevant information and resources to help them make an informed decision. This may include offering product demonstrations, case studies, testimonials, and comparison guides.

Once a customer makes a purchase, the focus shifts to retention. This involves providing excellent customer service, personalized communication, and ongoing support to ensure customer satisfaction and loyalty. Repeat purchases and upselling opportunities are also pursued during this stage.

The final stage of the customer lifecycle is advocacy, where satisfied customers become brand advocates and refer new customers. This can be encouraged through referral programs, loyalty rewards, and social proof, such as testimonials and online reviews.

Overall, lifecycle marketing aims to create a positive customer experience at every touchpoint, from initial awareness to post-purchase support. By understanding and effectively managing the customer lifecycle, businesses can build strong relationships, drive customer loyalty, and ultimately, achieve long-term business success.

Lifetime Customer Value (LCV)

Lifetime Customer Value (LCV) refers to the total projected revenue that a customer will generate for a company over their entire relationship with that company. It is a key metric used in marketing management to assess the financial value of acquiring and retaining customers.

LCV takes into account not only the initial purchase made by a customer, but also the potential for repeat purchases and the overall long-term value they bring to the company. By understanding the LCV of different customer segments, companies can make more informed decisions about marketing strategies, resource allocation, and customer retention efforts.

Local SEO Best Practices

Local SEO, or local search engine optimization, refers to the strategic process of optimizing a website or online presence to improve its visibility for locally-based searches. It involves implementing various on-page and off-page tactics to enhance a business's organic search rankings within its specific geographic area.

One of the primary goals of local SEO is to increase a business's online visibility among users who are searching for products or services within a particular location. This is especially important for brick-and-mortar businesses that rely on attracting customers from their local area. By optimizing their website and online profiles, businesses can improve their chances of appearing in the top results of search engine result pages (SERPs) when users search for relevant keywords tied to their geographic location.

Local SEO best practices revolve around optimizing a business's website with local keyword targeting, ensuring consistency in online business listings across various platforms, encouraging online reviews and testimonials from satisfied customers, and utilizing structured data to provide search engines with accurate information about the business's location and offerings. Additionally, businesses should focus on developing high-quality, locally-focused content that is relevant to their target audience.

By implementing these best practices, businesses can improve their chances of ranking higher in local search results, attracting more targeted organic traffic, and ultimately boosting their online visibility and revenue in their specific geographical area.

Local SEO Optimization Tools

Local SEO optimization tools are software applications or online platforms used by marketing management professionals to improve the visibility and search ranking of local businesses in search engine results pages (SERPs).

These tools are specifically designed to help businesses enhance their online presence within a specific geographical area. They provide various features and functionalities that assist in the management and optimization of the business's local search engine optimization (SEO) efforts.

Local SEO optimization tools typically offer functionalities such as keyword research, citation management, local listing monitoring, competitor analysis, and review management. With keyword research, marketers can identify the most relevant and popular search terms used by users in their target market, enabling them to optimize website content and meta tags accordingly.

Citation management features help businesses ensure accuracy and consistency of their local business information across various online directories, improving the chances of appearing in local search results. Local listing monitoring capabilities allow marketers to track the performance of their business listings across multiple platforms and make necessary adjustments to improve visibility.

Competitor analysis features enable marketing professionals to analyze the digital marketing strategies of their competitors, identify areas of opportunity, and make improvements to their local SEO tactics. Review management functionalities help businesses monitor and respond to customer reviews, enhancing their reputation and credibility in the local market.

Local SEO Strategies

Local SEO strategies refer to the specific techniques and practices used by businesses to improve their visibility and rankings in local search engine results pages (SERPs). This form of online marketing focuses on optimizing a company's online presence to attract more relevant traffic from local search queries.

Local SEO involves various elements, including on-page optimization, off-page optimization, and technical optimization. On-page optimization involves optimizing the website's structure, content, and metadata to make it more search-engine-friendly and relevant to local searches. This may include optimizing keywords, creating location-specific pages, and ensuring consistent NAP (name, address, phone number) information across various platforms.

Off-page optimization strategies aim to increase a company's online reputation and authority within the local community. This may involve building high-quality backlinks from local directories, obtaining customer reviews and testimonials, and engaging with the local community through social media or local events.

Technical optimization focuses on improving the website's performance and accessibility to search engines and users. This may include optimizing site speed, implementing structured data markup, ensuring mobile-friendliness, and improving overall user experience.

By implementing effective local SEO strategies, businesses can enhance their online visibility, attract more targeted traffic, and increase the chances of converting local prospects into customers. Moreover, this marketing approach can particularly benefit businesses that rely on local customers, such as brick-and-mortar stores, restaurants, and service-based businesses operating in specific geographical areas.

Local SEO

Local SEO, also known as local search engine optimization, is a marketing strategy focused on improving the online visibility and search engine rankings of local businesses or physical stores. It is a subcategory of SEO that aims to target specific geographical areas and attract local customers.

Local SEO involves optimizing a website, its content, and its online presence to appear in search results when users search for businesses or services in their local area. This strategy aims to connect local businesses with potential customers by increasing their visibility, relevance, and prominence in local search engine rankings.

In order to improve local SEO, marketers employ various tactics such as optimizing website content with local keywords, creating and optimizing Google My Business listings, obtaining positive online reviews, managing local directories and citations, and ensuring consistency in NAP (name, address, phone number) information across all online platforms.

Local SEO is essential for businesses that rely on local customers or have physical locations. It helps businesses increase their online presence in specific local markets, attract more foot traffic to physical stores, and compete with other local businesses. By targeting local customers, businesses can also improve their overall website traffic, generate leads, and increase

155

conversions.

Overall, local SEO is a crucial aspect of marketing management as it enables businesses to optimize their online presence and effectively target and engage with potential customers in specific geographical areas.

Long-Tail Keywords

Long-tail keywords, in the context of Marketing Management, refer to specific and highly targeted keyword phrases that are longer and more specific than generic keywords. They are called "long-tail" because when represented on a graph, these keyword phrases create a long tail-like shape.

These keywords are essential for online marketing strategies as they allow businesses to reach and target niche audiences more precisely. Long-tail keywords are typically less competitive than broader, more generic keywords, which means that the chances of ranking higher in search engine results for these specific phrases are greater. By incorporating long-tail keywords into their marketing campaigns, businesses can attract more relevant and qualified traffic to their websites.

Loyalty Marketing

Loyalty marketing is a strategic marketing approach that focuses on building and maintaining strong relationships with customers to enhance their level of loyalty and encourage repeated purchases. It involves developing and implementing targeted marketing strategies and initiatives to retain existing customers and increase their lifetime value to the business.

Loyalty marketing is based on the principle that it is more cost-effective and profitable to retain and nurture existing customers rather than constantly acquiring new ones. By strengthening the bond between the brand and the customer, loyalty marketing aims to create a sense of trust, satisfaction, and commitment, leading to increased customer loyalty and advocacy.

Key components of loyalty marketing include:

1. Customer retention: Loyalty marketing focuses on reducing customer churn and keeping existing customers engaged and satisfied.

2. Rewards and incentives: Loyalty programs are often used to provide customers with personalized rewards, offers, and discounts, creating a sense of exclusivity and promoting continued patronage.

3. Customer segmentation: Loyalty marketing strategies involve segmenting customers based on their behavior, preferences, and purchasing patterns, in order to deliver targeted communications and offers that resonate with their specific needs.

4. Personalization: By leveraging customer data, loyalty marketing enables businesses to personalize their marketing communications, products, and experiences, creating a more personalized and relevant relationship with customers.

Overall, loyalty marketing is an essential aspect of marketing management, as it contributes to the long-term success and growth of a business by fostering loyal and profitable customer relationships.

Loyalty Program

A loyalty program is a strategic marketing initiative designed to encourage and reward customer loyalty. It involves the use of various incentives and rewards to encourage customers to continue purchasing products or services from a specific brand or company. The primary objective of a loyalty program is to build and maintain a strong and ongoing relationship between the brand and its customers.

Loyalty programs typically work by offering customers points, rewards, or discounts based on their purchase behavior. These rewards can be redeemed for future purchases or other benefits, such as exclusive access to special events or personalized offers. By providing these incentives, loyalty programs aim to increase customer retention, encourage repeat purchases, and ultimately, drive long-term customer loyalty.

Machine Learning Applications In Marketing

Machine Learning Applications in Marketing refer to the utilization of machine learning algorithms and techniques to analyze and interpret large volumes of marketing data for the purpose of making informed decisions and achieving marketing objectives. The discipline of Marketing Management involves planning, implementing, and controlling marketing activities to satisfy customer needs and achieve organizational goals. In this context, machine learning applications play a crucial role in helping marketing managers make data-driven decisions and execute targeted marketing strategies.

Machine learning algorithms can be used to gain insights from various marketing data sources, such as customer demographics, purchase history, online behavior, social media interactions, and market trends. By analyzing these data sets, machine learning models can identify patterns, trends, and correlations that may not be apparent to human marketers. These insights can then be used to segment customers, predict their behaviors and preferences, personalize marketing messages, optimize pricing strategies, forecast demand, identify cross-selling and upselling opportunities, and improve campaign effectiveness.

Machine Learning In Marketing Solutions

Machine Learning in Marketing Solutions refers to the application of artificial intelligence and statistical algorithms to analyze large amounts of data in order to make predictions, optimize marketing campaigns, and improve decision-making in marketing management.

Machine learning algorithms are trained to automatically learn patterns and insights from data, allowing marketers to gain a better understanding of customer behavior, preferences, and needs. By leveraging machine learning techniques, marketing professionals can make more informed decisions and tailor their marketing strategies to target specific customer segments and achieve higher levels of personalization and engagement.

Machine Learning In Marketing

Machine learning is a subfield of artificial intelligence that is applied in marketing management to discover and analyze patterns within large sets of data. It involves the use of algorithms and statistical models to enable computer systems to learn from and make predictions or decisions without being explicitly programmed. In the context of marketing, machine learning algorithms can be used to analyze customer behavior, segment markets, identify customer preferences, and predict future trends.

The application of machine learning in marketing management helps companies gain insights into their customers and improve their marketing strategies. By analyzing large amounts of customer data, machine learning algorithms can identify patterns, correlations, and hidden relationships that would be difficult or time-consuming for humans to uncover. These insights enable companies to better understand their customers' needs, preferences, and behaviors, allowing them to tailor their marketing messages and campaigns to specific target audiences.

Market Basket Analysis Software

Market Basket Analysis Software is a tool used in the field of Marketing Management to analyze customer purchasing patterns and identify associations or relationships between different products. This software employs data mining techniques to examine transactional data and identify co-purchased items or products frequently bought together by customers.

The primary purpose of Market Basket Analysis Software is to help marketers understand customer behavior and optimize product placement, cross-selling, and promotional strategies. By analyzing the association or co-occurrence of products in the same purchase transactions, marketers can identify patterns, trends, and correlations that can guide decision-making.

157

Market Basket Analysis Tools

Market Basket Analysis Tools are techniques used in the field of Marketing Management to identify the relationships between products that are frequently purchased together by customers. This analysis helps businesses gain insights into consumer behavior and preferences, which can be utilized to improve various aspects of marketing strategies such as product placement, cross-selling, and customer segmentation.

Market basket analysis is primarily based on the concept of association rules, which are derived from transactional data. It involves the examination of customer transaction records to uncover patterns and correlations between different products or product categories. These tools utilize advanced algorithms to calculate various statistical measures such as support, confidence, and lift to identify significant associations between items in a customer's shopping basket.

The insights derived from market basket analysis tools can be used to optimize the arrangement of products in physical stores or on e-commerce platforms. By strategically placing related products near each other or suggesting related items during the online purchasing process, businesses can increase the likelihood of customers buying additional items, thereby improving sales and profitability.

Market basket analysis tools also enable businesses to develop targeted marketing campaigns and personalized recommendations based on customers' purchasing patterns. By segmenting customers into groups with similar buying preferences, marketers can create tailored promotions or product bundles to increase customer satisfaction and loyalty.

Market Basket Analysis

Market Basket Analysis is a statistical analysis technique used in the field of Marketing Management to understand the patterns and associations between different products or items that are purchased together by consumers. It is based on the concept of "affinity," which refers to the likelihood of certain items being bought together.

By analyzing transaction data, such as sales receipts or online shopping carts, Market Basket Analysis aims to identify the relationships between products and uncover associations that can be used to optimize marketing strategies. This analysis helps marketers understand customer behavior, improve product placement, optimize pricing strategies, and implement effective cross-selling and upselling techniques.

Market Development

Market development is a strategic approach in marketing management that aims to expand the customer base for a company's existing products or services in new market segments or geographies. It involves identifying and capitalizing on untapped market opportunities to generate additional revenue streams and maximize the potential of a business.

This strategy entails thorough research and analysis of potential markets to determine their size, growth potential, and compatibility with the company's offerings. It also requires a deep understanding of the target audience's needs, preferences, and purchasing behavior to tailor marketing efforts effectively. Market development often involves adapting existing products or services to meet the specific demands of a new market while maintaining their core value proposition.

The implementation of market development strategies requires comprehensive planning and resource allocation. It may involve establishing new distribution channels, entering partnerships or alliances, conducting promotional activities, and building strong relationships with customers and stakeholders. Effective market development initiatives focus on creating awareness, generating interest, and stimulating demand for the company's offerings in previously untapped markets.

Market development can provide several benefits for a company. By diversifying its customer base and revenue sources, a business can reduce its dependence on a single market segment or geography, mitigating risks associated with changing market conditions. It can also enhance competitiveness by capturing market share from competitors or establishing a leadership position in new markets. Furthermore, market development enables a company to leverage its existing resources and capabilities to unlock incremental growth opportunities without significant investment in new product development.

Market Entry Strategy

A market entry strategy refers to the plan and tactics a company adopts to enter a new market or expand its presence in an existing market. It is a crucial aspect of marketing management as it involves identifying and evaluating potential markets, understanding the competitive landscape, and determining the best approach to enter or expand within a market.

Market entry strategies are developed based on thorough market research and analysis, taking into account factors such as consumer behavior, market size, competition, and regulatory environment. The objective of a market entry strategy is to achieve sustainable growth and profitability by effectively positioning the company and its products in the target market.

Market Expansion Approaches

Market expansion approaches refer to the strategies and tactics employed by companies to enter and gain market share in new geographic areas, expand their reach into existing markets, or target new customer segments.

There are several market expansion approaches that companies can utilize, including:

1. Geographic Expansion: This approach involves entering new geographic regions or countries where the company does not currently operate. It can be achieved through establishing new physical locations, partnering with local distributors or retailers, or entering into strategic alliances with local businesses.

2. Market Development: Market development focuses on targeting new customer segments within existing markets. This approach involves identifying untapped customer segments and tailoring marketing strategies and product offerings to meet their specific needs. Examples of market development strategies include introducing new product variations or packaging, targeting different age groups or demographics, or entering new distribution channels.

3. Product Diversification: Product diversification involves expanding the company's product portfolio to enter new markets. This approach aims to leverage the company's existing resources, expertise, and brand equity to introduce new products or services in unrelated markets. Companies can either develop new products internally or acquire existing companies to gain access to new product categories.

4. Innovation and Technology Adoption: Innovation and technology adoption are key drivers of market expansion. Companies can invest in research and development to create innovative products or technologies that disrupt existing markets or create entirely new industries. By embracing technological advancements, companies can also improve their operational efficiency, enhance customer experience, and gain a competitive edge in new markets.

Market Expansion Grid

The Market Expansion Grid, also known as the Ansoff Matrix, is a strategic marketing tool that helps organizations identify growth opportunities by evaluating their existing products and the market in which they operate. The matrix provides four possible growth strategies, each with a different level of risk and potential reward.

The first strategy is market penetration, which involves increasing market share by selling more of the current products to existing customers. This can be achieved through tactics such as aggressive advertising, price promotions, and improved distribution channels.

The second strategy is market development, which focuses on entering new markets with the existing products. This may involve expanding geographically, targeting new customer segments, or entering different distribution channels. Market development carries a moderate level of risk, as it requires organizations to understand the needs and preferences of new customers.

The third strategy is product development, which involves creating new products for existing markets. This can be achieved through innovation, research and development, or strategic partnerships. Product development carries a higher level of risk, as it requires organizations to invest in new product development and face potential resistance from existing customers.

The fourth strategy is diversification, which involves entering new markets with new products. This is the riskiest growth strategy, as it requires organizations to venture into unfamiliar territory. Diversification can be achieved through mergers and acquisitions, strategic alliances, or internal development of new products and markets.

Market Expansion Planning

Market Expansion Planning refers to the strategic process of identifying and evaluating new opportunities for a company to grow its market share and increase its customer base. It involves assessing the potential of new markets, understanding customer needs and preferences, and developing effective strategies to enter and penetrate those markets.

This planning process begins with conducting comprehensive market research to identify potential target markets that align with the company's goals and objectives. This research includes analyzing market trends, competitive landscape, consumer behavior, and potential demand for the company's products or services.

After identifying potential markets, the next step is to evaluate the feasibility and profitability of entering those markets. This involves analyzing various factors such as market size, growth potential, competitive intensity, regulatory environment, and potential barriers to entry. The company must also consider its own capabilities and resources to determine if it has the necessary expertise, infrastructure, and financial resources to successfully expand into the new markets.

Based on the evaluation, the company develops a market entry strategy, which includes determining the appropriate market entry mode (e.g., exporting, licensing, joint venture, etc.), pricing strategy, distribution channels, promotional activities, and product adaptations if necessary. The strategy also takes into account the cultural, social, and economic factors of the target market to ensure effective market penetration.

Overall, Market Expansion Planning is a critical aspect of marketing management as it enables companies to identify growth opportunities and develop strategies to expand their market presence. Through effective planning and execution, companies can capitalize on new market opportunities and achieve sustainable growth in an increasingly competitive business environment.

Market Expansion Strategies

Market expansion strategies are a set of tactics and approaches implemented by businesses to enter and penetrate new markets in order to increase their customer base and generate additional revenue. These strategies involve the identification and selection of potential markets that align with the company's products or services, and the development and implementation of plans to successfully enter and establish a presence in these markets.

The primary objective of market expansion strategies is to extend the reach of a company's products or services beyond its existing customer base and geographical boundaries. This can be achieved through various methods, such as market research, targeting new customer segments, developing new distribution channels, entering new geographic regions or countries, or introducing new product or service offerings.

Market expansion strategies typically involve a comprehensive assessment of market potential and competitive landscape to determine the viability and feasibility of entering a new market. This may include analyzing market size, growth rates, customer demographics, purchasing behaviors, competition, regulatory factors, and cultural nuances.

Once a potential market is identified, the company needs to develop an effective market entry strategy. This involves evaluating different entry modes, such as direct exporting, licensing, franchising, joint ventures, or establishing wholly-owned subsidiaries. The chosen entry mode should align with the company's resources, capabilities, and risk appetite.

Furthermore, market expansion strategies necessitate the formulation of strategic marketing plans to attract and retain customers in the new market. This may involve adapting the company's products or services to meet local preferences or needs, developing localized marketing campaigns, pricing strategies, distribution networks, and customer support systems.

Market Expansion

Market expansion refers to the strategic initiative taken by a company or organization to increase its presence in new market segments or geographic areas. It involves targeting previously untapped customer groups or regions with the aim of gaining market share and increasing sales revenue.

This marketing approach is driven by the need to sustain business growth and maximize profitability. Market expansion typically involves conducting extensive market research to identify new opportunities and understand the specific needs and preferences of the target audience. Companies may use various strategies to enter and expand into new markets, such as market penetration, market development, product diversification, or market extension.

Market Niche

A market niche is a focused segment of a larger market that a company targets with a distinct product or service offering. It allows companies to differentiate themselves from competitors by catering to the unique needs and preferences of a specific group of customers.

Identifying a market niche involves conducting thorough market research to understand the underlying factors that drive customer behavior and purchasing decisions. This research helps companies identify gaps or unmet needs in the market that can be addressed with a specialized product or service.

Once a market niche is identified, companies can develop a marketing strategy that is tailored to effectively reach and engage the target audience. This strategy may include specific messaging, pricing, distribution channels, and promotional efforts that resonate with the niche market.

By focusing on a narrow segment of the market, companies can position themselves as experts or leaders within that niche. This can lead to stronger customer loyalty, increased brand recognition, and higher profit margins.

However, it is important for companies to carefully evaluate the sustainability and growth potential of a market niche. A niche market may be limited in size, and companies must ensure that there is enough demand and profitability to justify their investment.

In summary, a market niche is a specialized segment within a larger market that companies target with unique products or services. It allows companies to differentiate themselves and cater to the specific needs of a particular group of customers, resulting in increased customer loyalty and profitability.

Market Penetration

Market penetration is a marketing strategy in which a company focuses on increasing its market share for an existing product or service within its current target market. This strategy involves attracting new customers or convincing existing customers to purchase more of the product or service offered.

The goal of market penetration is to increase the company's sales volume and overall revenue by leveraging its existing customer base and market presence. This strategy is often employed when a company believes that there is still untapped potential within its current market segment.

Market Position

Market position refers to the perception or reputation of a brand, product, or company in the minds of the target market. It is a strategic concept that relates to how a company differentiates itself from competitors and how it is perceived by customers.

Market position is influenced by a combination of factors, including the brand image, product features and quality, pricing, customer service, and marketing and advertising efforts. A strong market position is important as it allows a company to stand out from competitors and attract customers.

Market Positioning

Market positioning refers to the process of defining a product or brand's identity and image in relation to its competitors within a given market. It is a key strategic activity in marketing management that aims to establish a distinctive position for a product or brand in the minds of target customers.

Effective market positioning involves understanding the needs, preferences, and buying behaviors of the target customers, as well as assessing the strengths and weaknesses of competitors. In order to create a unique and favorable position, companies must differentiate their offerings from those of competitors by emphasizing specific attributes, benefits, or values that are important to customers.

Market Research Analysis Software

Market Research Analysis Software refers to a digital tool used by marketers to gather, process, and analyze data related to the market and consumer behavior. It plays a significant role in the field of Marketing Management by providing valuable insights that help in making informed decisions and formulating effective marketing strategies.

This software enables marketers to collect data from various sources, such as surveys, social media platforms, and customer databases. It then processes and organizes the data to identify patterns, trends, and correlations. Through statistical analysis, it helps marketers understand customer preferences, needs, and buying behaviors.

Market Research Analysis Software also offers visualization tools that enable marketers to present data in a clear and comprehensible manner. This allows them to easily interpret and communicate the findings to stakeholders, such as senior management and clients.

Moreover, this software often includes features like segmentation analysis, which helps marketers divide the target market into distinct groups based on characteristics such as demographics, psychographics, and purchase history. This segmentation enables marketers to tailor marketing campaigns and messages to different consumer segments, thus increasing the effectiveness of their efforts.

In summary, Market Research Analysis Software is a crucial tool for marketers in the field of Marketing Management. It helps in collecting, processing, and analyzing market data, providing valuable insights for making informed decisions and formulating effective marketing strategies.

Market Research Analysis Tools

Market research analysis tools refer to the various techniques and methodologies used in the field of Marketing Management to collect, interpret, and analyze data related to the market, customers, and competitors. These tools help marketers make informed business decisions and develop effective marketing strategies.

Market research analysis tools encompass a wide range of quantitative and qualitative methods. Quantitative tools include statistical analysis, data mining, and modeling techniques that help in measuring and quantifying market trends, consumer behavior, and market potential. Qualitative tools, on the other hand, focus on understanding consumer opinions, attitudes, and perceptions through techniques like focus groups, interviews, and observations.

162

The primary purpose of market research analysis tools is to provide insights into market dynamics, identify customer needs and preferences, evaluate competitor strategies, and assess potential opportunities and risks. By applying these tools, marketers can gather data from various sources, such as market surveys, social media platforms, and customer feedback, and analyze it to derive meaningful and actionable insights.

Market research analysis tools also support decision-making in marketing management by enabling marketers to segment the market, target specific customer groups, and position their products or services effectively. These tools assist in evaluating the effectiveness of marketing campaigns, optimizing pricing and distribution strategies, and monitoring market performance.

Market Research Analysis

Market research analysis is a crucial component of the marketing management discipline, as it involves the systematic gathering, interpretation, and evaluation of information related to a specific market. This process is aimed at identifying market opportunities, understanding consumer behavior, and predicting future trends and developments. By conducting thorough market research analysis, marketing managers are able to make informed decisions and develop effective strategies to meet the needs and preferences of their target audience.

The first step in market research analysis is data collection, which involves gathering both primary and secondary data. Primary data is obtained directly from the target market through surveys, interviews, or observations, while secondary data is collected from existing sources such as government publications, industry reports, or competitor analysis. Once the data is collected, it needs to be carefully analyzed to identify patterns, trends, and key insights.

During the analysis phase, marketing managers use various statistical techniques, such as regression analysis, factor analysis, or cluster analysis, to uncover relationships between different variables and identify important market segments. They also use qualitative analysis methods, such as content analysis or thematic analysis, to interpret and make sense of qualitative data, such as customer feedback or social media comments.

The final step in market research analysis is the interpretation and evaluation of the findings. Marketing managers need to make sense of the data and draw meaningful conclusions that can guide their decision-making process. This involves comparing the findings with industry benchmarks, historical data, or internal goals, and determining the implications for the marketing strategy.

Market Research

Market research is a systematic process of collecting, analyzing, and interpreting data about a specific target market or industry, in order to gain insights and make informed decisions in marketing management. It involves gathering both primary and secondary data to understand customer behaviors, preferences, and opinions, as well as evaluating market trends, competitors, and economic factors.

The primary goal of market research is to identify and assess opportunities and risks in the market, understand consumer needs and wants, and guide the development of effective marketing strategies. The process typically begins with defining research objectives and formulating research questions, followed by designing appropriate data collection methods, such as surveys, interviews, observations, or experiments. The collected data is then organized and analyzed using statistical techniques, to generate meaningful findings and actionable recommendations.

Market research plays a crucial role in marketing management, as it helps organizations make informed decisions on product development, pricing, distribution channels, promotion, and positioning. It enables businesses to evaluate the potential demand for new products or services, identify target segments, and tailor marketing activities to meet customer expectations. Moreover, market research helps companies monitor changes in the market and consumer behavior, allowing them to adapt their strategies accordingly and stay competitive in dynamic business environments.

In conclusion, market research is an essential tool for marketing management, as it provides valuable insights into the market landscape and consumer preferences, enabling organizations to make informed decisions and develop effective marketing strategies.

Market Segmentation

Market segmentation refers to the process of dividing a broad market into distinct and homogeneous groups of consumers who have similar needs, preferences, and behaviors. It involves identifying and categorizing customers based on various factors such as demographics, psychographics, geographic location, and behavior patterns. The goal of market segmentation is to enable marketers to understand their target market more effectively and to tailor their marketing efforts to meet the specific needs and wants of each segment.

This segmentation allows marketers to focus their resources and marketing strategies on the most profitable and receptive group of consumers. By dividing the market into smaller segments, marketers can better understand the unique characteristics and motivations of each segment, which helps them develop targeted marketing campaigns and offerings that are more likely to resonate with the specific needs and preferences of each segment.

Market Share Analysis

Market Share Analysis is a key concept in the discipline of Marketing Management. It refers to the process of evaluating a company's sales performance relative to the total market in which it operates. Market share is the percentage of total sales or revenue that a company generates within a specific industry or market.

Marketing managers often use market share analysis as a strategic tool to assess their company's competitive position and identify opportunities for growth. By comparing their company's market share to that of their competitors, managers can identify potential areas for improvement or expansion. Market share analysis involves several key steps. First, managers must determine the relevant market or industry for their company's products or services. This can be done by considering factors such as customer demographics, geographic location, and purchase behavior. Once the market is identified, managers can calculate their company's market share by dividing their company's sales revenue by the total sales revenue of the entire market. This calculation provides a percentage that represents the company's share of the market. After calculating market share, managers can compare their company's performance to that of its competitors. This comparison allows managers to assess their company's competitive position and identify strengths and weaknesses. Market share analysis is a valuable tool for marketing managers because it provides insight into a company's position within its market. It helps managers make data-driven decisions about product development, pricing strategy, and market expansion. In conclusion, market share analysis is a key concept in marketing management that involves evaluating a company's sales performance relative to the total market. It provides valuable insights for strategic decision-making and growth opportunities.

Market Share

Market share refers to the percentage of total sales or revenues a company or brand captures within a specific industry or market. It is a measure of a company's competitive position and success in relation to its competitors.

Market share is calculated by dividing the company's sales or revenues by the total sales or revenues of the industry or market. It provides insights into how well a company is performing compared to its rivals and how effectively it is able to attract and retain customers.

Market Trends

Market trends refer to the general direction in which a market or industry is moving. These trends are influenced by various factors such as consumer behavior, economic indicators, technological advancements, and competitive dynamics. Understanding market trends is crucial for marketing managers as it helps them make informed decisions, develop effective marketing strategies, and stay ahead of the competition.

Monitoring market trends involves conducting extensive market research and analysis to identify patterns, shifts, and emerging opportunities in the market. This process may include analyzing sales data, surveying customers, monitoring social media, studying industry reports, and keeping track of competitors. By staying updated on current market trends, marketing managers are able to identify new target segments, adjust product offerings, tailor marketing campaigns, and allocate resources strategically.

Marketing AI Platforms

Marketing AI platforms are software tools or systems that use artificial intelligence (AI) technology to assist marketing management professionals in analyzing, planning, executing, and evaluating marketing strategies and campaigns.

These platforms leverage advanced AI algorithms and machine learning techniques to process and interpret vast amounts of marketing data, such as customer demographics, behavior, preferences, and market trends. By analyzing this data, marketing AI platforms can generate valuable insights and recommendations that help marketers make data-driven decisions.

Marketing AI platforms offer numerous features and functionalities that benefit marketing management professionals. These include predictive analytics, which enable marketers to forecast future trends and outcomes, and optimize marketing campaigns accordingly. Additionally, these platforms provide personalized recommendations and prompts, ensuring that marketers are guided by AI-driven insights while designing marketing strategies and tactics.

Furthermore, marketing AI platforms automate various marketing processes to enhance efficiency and productivity. They can automate tasks such as customer segmentation, targeting, and personalized messaging, enabling marketers to reach the right audience with tailored messages at the right time. By automating these processes, marketing AI platforms streamline operations and enable marketing management professionals to focus on strategic decision-making.

Marketing AI Tools

Marketing AI tools are software applications or systems that leverage artificial intelligence (AI) technology to help marketing professionals automate and optimize various aspects of their marketing campaigns and strategies. These tools are designed to analyze large volumes of data, uncover patterns and insights, and provide actionable recommendations to enhance marketing performance and decision-making.

Marketing AI tools can be applied across different marketing areas, including customer segmentation, targeting, content creation, advertising, and campaign management. By utilizing machine learning algorithms, natural language processing, and predictive analytics, these tools enable marketers to streamline their processes, improve targeting accuracy, and deliver personalized experiences to their target audiences.

Within customer segmentation and targeting, marketing AI tools can analyze customer data and behavior to identify specific segments and create targeted campaigns for each segment. They can also help optimize the allocation of marketing resources by determining the most effective channels and tactics for reaching different customer segments.

In content creation, AI tools can generate automated content based on predefined templates and guidelines, reducing the time and effort required for marketers to create and publish engaging content. They can also provide recommendations for optimizing content based on historical performance and audience preferences.

Additionally, marketing AI tools can assist in advertising by automating the process of ad creation, targeting, and optimization. They can analyze ad performance in real-time and adjust targeting parameters to maximize campaign success.

In campaign management, these tools can provide insights and recommendations to optimize campaign performance, such as identifying the best timing and frequency for sending marketing messages or determining the optimal budget allocation across different channels.

165

Marketing AI And Automation Platforms

Marketing AI and Automation Platforms refer to software or tools that utilize artificial intelligence (AI) and automation techniques to assist in various marketing management activities. These platforms aim to streamline and enhance marketing processes by automating repetitive tasks, analyzing large datasets, and providing valuable insights to make data-driven marketing decisions.

Marketing AI and Automation Platforms typically offer a range of functionalities such as data collection and analysis, customer segmentation, campaign management, content creation, lead generation, and personalized marketing. These platforms leverage AI algorithms and machine learning to gather and process data from multiple sources, including customer interactions, social media, and website analytics. By analyzing this data, these platforms can identify patterns, trends, and customer behaviors and facilitate more targeted and effective marketing strategies.

Furthermore, Marketing AI and Automation Platforms enable marketers to automate routine tasks such as email marketing, social media scheduling, ad placements, and customer support. This automation frees up time and resources, allowing marketers to focus on more strategic initiatives. Additionally, these platforms often provide real-time reporting and analytics, allowing marketers to monitor campaign performance, optimize efforts, and measure return on investment.

In summary, Marketing AI and Automation Platforms are powerful tools that leverage AI and automation to enhance marketing management. They help marketers gather and analyze data, automate repetitive tasks, and improve efficiencies. By using these platforms, businesses can make data-driven marketing decisions, reach customers more effectively, and ultimately achieve their marketing goals.

Marketing Analytics

Marketing analytics is a crucial component of the marketing management discipline, providing valuable insights for decision-making and strategy development. It involves the systematic collection, analysis, interpretation, and presentation of data related to marketing activities and their impact on business performance.

Through marketing analytics, organizations can extract meaningful patterns and trends from data sets, enabling them to make informed decisions and allocate resources effectively. It encompasses various techniques, such as statistical analysis, data mining, predictive modeling, and segmentation, to uncover relationships and correlations between marketing initiatives and outcomes.

Marketing Attribution Modeling Techniques

Marketing attribution modeling refers to the process of assigning credit or value to various marketing touchpoints or channels based on their influence and contribution to a desired outcome or conversion. It helps marketing managers understand the effectiveness of their marketing efforts and make data-driven decisions to optimize their marketing strategies and budgets.

The goal of marketing attribution modeling is to identify and quantify the impact of each marketing touchpoint throughout the customer journey, from the initial awareness stage to the final conversion or sale. By analyzing data from different channels such as digital advertising, social media, email marketing, and offline campaigns, marketers can determine which channels are driving the most engagement, conversions, and revenue.

Marketing Attribution Modeling

Marketing attribution modeling is a method used in the field of marketing management to analyze and evaluate the impact of various marketing channels and touchpoints on the customer's decision-making process. It involves tracking and assigning credits to different marketing activities or channels that contribute to the overall conversion or sales goal.

The purpose of marketing attribution modeling is to determine which marketing channels or touchpoints are most effective in driving customer engagement, conversion, and ultimately, revenue. By understanding the effectiveness of different marketing efforts, marketers can make data-driven decisions regarding budget allocation, campaign optimization, and resource allocation.

Marketing Attribution Models Software

A marketing attribution model is a software tool or system used in the field of marketing management to accurately assign credit to various marketing channels and touchpoints for driving conversions or sales. It helps marketers understand which channels or campaigns are most effective in generating results and optimizing their marketing strategies.

Attribution models enable marketers to analyze and evaluate the impact and contribution of different marketing activities to customer conversions. These models take into account various factors such as the order in which touchpoints are encountered, the time between touchpoints, and the influence of each touchpoint on the customer journey.

Marketing Attribution Models

A marketing attribution model is a framework used in marketing management to track and evaluate the effectiveness and impact of various marketing channels and campaigns in driving conversions or desired outcomes. It helps businesses identify and understand the touchpoints and interactions that lead to a consumer's decision to make a purchase or take a specific action.

These models assign credit or value to each marketing touchpoint based on its contribution to a conversion event. They enable marketers to determine which channels, ads, keywords, or campaigns are most influential in driving conversions and allocate marketing budgets accordingly.

Marketing Attribution

Marketing attribution is a term used in the field of marketing management to describe the process of identifying and assigning credit to marketing activities that contribute to a desired outcome or conversion. It is a way of measuring the impact and effectiveness of various marketing efforts.

The goal of marketing attribution is to understand how different marketing channels, campaigns, and touchpoints contribute to driving customer acquisition, sales, or other desired actions. It involves analyzing and tracking customer interactions across different channels and touchpoints, such as online ads, social media, email campaigns, and offline activities.

By attributing credit to specific marketing activities, organizations can gain insights into which channels and tactics are most effective in driving results. This information can help marketing managers make informed decisions about resource allocation, budget planning, and campaign optimization.

Marketing attribution models are used to determine how credit is assigned to different touchpoints along the customer journey. These models can be based on various rules and algorithms, such as first touch, last touch, linear, time decay, or data-driven approaches.

Overall, marketing attribution plays a crucial role in understanding the return on investment (ROI) of marketing activities and optimizing marketing strategies. It enables organizations to better allocate resources, improve targeting and messaging, and ultimately maximize the impact of their marketing efforts.

Marketing Audit

A marketing audit is a systematic and comprehensive examination of a company's entire marketing environment, strategies, and activities. It is an essential tool used in the field of marketing management to assess the effectiveness and efficiency of a firm's marketing efforts.

167

The purpose of conducting a marketing audit is to evaluate the company's marketing performance, identify areas of improvement, and develop strategies for future success. It involves a thorough analysis of various marketing components such as the marketing objectives, target markets, marketing mix, market research, competitive analysis, and marketing budget.

The marketing audit helps companies gain valuable insights into their current marketing practices and identify any gaps or inconsistencies in their marketing strategies. By examining the external market forces, including the social, economic, and technological factors, the audit enables companies to understand the market trends and adjust their marketing strategies accordingly.

During a marketing audit, companies evaluate their marketing activities to determine their effectiveness in achieving their stated marketing objectives. This evaluation includes an analysis of the company's branding, product development, pricing strategies, distribution channels, and promotional activities.

In conclusion, a marketing audit serves as a diagnostic tool that provides companies with a comprehensive overview of their marketing efforts. It helps companies identify areas of improvement, develop strategies to capitalize on market opportunities, and ensure long-term success in a competitive market.

Marketing Automation

Marketing Automation refers to the use of technology and software to streamline and automate tasks and processes related to marketing. It involves the implementation of a system that allows marketers to manage and execute marketing campaigns, analyze data, and track customer interactions and behavior.

Marketing Automation aims to improve efficiency and effectiveness in marketing activities by reducing manual labor and human error. It enables marketers to segment their target audience, create personalized and targeted messaging, and deliver it at the right time through the most appropriate channel.

With Marketing Automation, marketers can automate repetitive tasks such as sending emails, scheduling social media posts, and managing advertising campaigns. By setting up rules and triggers, they can automatically execute actions or send messages based on specific events or customer behavior, such as website visits, form submissions, or email opens.

Marketing Automation also incorporates lead generation and nurturing capabilities, allowing marketers to capture leads, monitor their journey through the sales funnel, and nurture them with relevant content. This helps in building and maintaining better relationships with prospects and customers.

Furthermore, Marketing Automation provides marketers with valuable insights and analytics to measure and optimize their marketing efforts. It allows them to track key metrics such as conversion rates, click-through rates, and campaign performance, providing data-driven insights to make informed decisions and improve marketing strategies.

Overall, Marketing Automation plays a crucial role in modern marketing management by enabling marketers to automate repetitive tasks, personalize customer interactions, and gain valuable insights. It helps businesses to streamline their marketing processes, increase efficiency, and drive better results.

Marketing Budget Allocation

Marketing Budget Allocation refers to the process of determining how financial resources will be distributed and allocated to various marketing activities and initiatives within an organization. It involves identifying and prioritizing marketing objectives, setting clear and measurable goals, and allocating funds accordingly to achieve these objectives.

The allocation of marketing budget is a critical decision-making process that requires careful analysis, research, and evaluation. It is based on various factors such as the overall marketing strategy, target market, competitive landscape, previous marketing performance, and available resources.

Effective budget allocation is essential for optimizing marketing efforts and achieving desired outcomes. It helps in maximizing the return on investment (ROI) and improving the overall marketing effectiveness and efficiency. By allocating funds strategically, organizations can prioritize and invest in the most impactful marketing channels, tactics, and campaigns.

Marketing budget allocation typically involves dividing resources among various marketing functions, such as advertising, promotion, public relations, market research, digital marketing, and sales support. The allocation decisions may also take into account factors like seasonality, market trends, and customer behavior.

In summary, marketing budget allocation is a crucial aspect of marketing management that involves dividing financial resources to support marketing objectives and activities. It plays a vital role in determining the success of marketing efforts and ensuring optimal utilization of available resources.

Marketing Budget

A marketing budget is a financial plan that outlines the anticipated costs and expenses associated with implementing marketing strategies and initiatives. It is an essential component of marketing management, as it helps organizations allocate resources effectively and achieve their marketing objectives.

The marketing budget typically includes various categories, such as advertising, promotions, public relations, market research, and social media marketing. Each category is assigned a specific amount of money, which is based on factors such as the organization's overall marketing goals, target audience, competitive landscape, and available resources.

Creating a marketing budget involves a systematic approach that begins with setting specific marketing goals and objectives. Once the objectives are defined, marketing managers estimate the costs associated with different activities and allocate resources accordingly. This process requires careful analysis of previous marketing initiatives, market trends, and competitor activities to ensure an accurate and realistic budget.

A well-structured marketing budget helps marketing managers make informed decisions about how to allocate resources among different marketing channels and tactics. It enables them to prioritize their efforts, monitor the performance of various activities, and make adjustments as needed. The budget also serves as a benchmark for evaluating the return on investment (ROI) of marketing initiatives and justifying the allocation of funds to key stakeholders.

Marketing Campaign Analytics Platforms

A Marketing Campaign Analytics platform is a software tool that helps marketers measure and analyze the performance of their marketing campaigns. It provides insights into various aspects of the campaign, such as customer behavior, campaign reach, engagement, conversion rates, and return on investment (ROI).

These platforms collect data from multiple sources, such as website analytics, social media platforms, email marketing software, and customer relationship management (CRM) systems. They then aggregate and analyze this data to provide marketers with actionable insights and reports.

Marketing Campaign Analytics Tools

A Marketing Campaign Analytics Tool is a software or platform that helps marketing teams measure, analyze, and optimize the effectiveness of their marketing campaigns. It provides valuable insights into the performance of various marketing channels, such as email marketing, social media marketing, paid advertising, and more.

These tools typically track and aggregate data from multiple sources, such as website analytics, customer relationship management (CRM) systems, ad platforms, and email marketing platforms. They then present this data in a centralized dashboard, allowing marketers to easily analyze and interpret the results.

Marketing Campaign Analytics Tools enable marketers to measure key metrics and KPIs (Key Performance Indicators) related to their campaigns, such as click-through rates, conversion rates, engagement rates, return on investment (ROI), and more. By monitoring these metrics, marketers can identify which campaigns are yielding the best results and make data-driven decisions to improve future campaigns.

Additionally, these tools often provide advanced features such as segmentation and targeting, A/B testing, campaign automation, and performance benchmarking. They allow marketers to segment their audience based on various criteria, create personalized messaging, test different campaign variations, automate repetitive tasks, and compare their campaign performance against industry benchmarks.

Overall, Marketing Campaign Analytics Tools play a crucial role in helping marketing teams measure the effectiveness of their campaigns and optimize their marketing efforts to drive better results.

Marketing Campaign Analytics

Marketing Campaign Analytics refers to the practice of analyzing and evaluating the effectiveness and impact of marketing campaigns using data and metrics. It involves the collection, measurement, and interpretation of data to gain insights into the performance of marketing initiatives, identify areas of improvement, and optimize future campaigns.

By leveraging various analytical techniques and tools, marketers can assess the success and ROI of their marketing efforts. Marketing Campaign Analytics typically involves tracking and measuring key performance indicators (KPIs) such as conversion rates, customer acquisition cost, customer lifetime value, ROI, and revenue generated. These metrics help marketers understand which campaigns are delivering the desired results and which ones need to be adjusted or discontinued.

Marketing Campaign Analytics empowers marketers to make data-driven decisions, continuously refine their strategies, and allocate resources effectively. By understanding the impact of different marketing channels, audience segments, and messaging on customer behavior and conversions, marketers can optimize their marketing mix and allocate budgets more efficiently.

Furthermore, Marketing Campaign Analytics can provide valuable insights into consumer preferences, behavior, and engagement patterns. Marketers can use this information to tailor their messaging, target specific audience segments, and design more personalized and relevant campaigns. It also enables marketers to identify trends, patterns, and opportunities in the market, allowing them to stay ahead of competitors and seize new market opportunities.

Marketing Campaign

A marketing campaign is a coordinated set of activities designed to promote a specific product, service, or brand to a target audience. It is a strategic approach that combines various marketing tactics to achieve specific business goals, such as increasing sales, raising brand awareness, or generating leads.

In marketing management, a campaign typically involves detailed planning and execution across multiple channels, including advertising, public relations, direct marketing, digital marketing, and social media. It involves the identification of the target audience, the development of key messages and creative content, and the selection of appropriate marketing channels and tactics to reach the target audience effectively.

Marketing Channel Optimization Strategies

Marketing Channel Optimization Strategies refers to the various techniques and approaches used in marketing management to enhance the effectiveness and efficiency of the distribution channels used to deliver products or services to the target market. It involves the analysis, planning, implementation, and control of marketing activities aimed at improving the overall performance of the distribution channels.

The main objective of marketing channel optimization strategies is to maximize customer satisfaction and ensure that products or services reach the right customers at the right time, in the right place, and at the right price. This involves selecting the most appropriate distribution channels, managing channel relationships, designing effective channel structures, and implementing strategies to improve channel performance.

Marketing Channel Optimization Tools

Marketing Channel Optimization Tools refer to the various software applications and analytical techniques used by marketing professionals to evaluate and enhance the effectiveness of their marketing channels. Marketing channels are the different pathways through which goods or services are distributed from the producer to the end consumer.

These tools help marketing managers identify how their products or services move through the different channels, such as wholesalers, retailers, online marketplaces, or direct sales. By analyzing various metrics, such as channel profitability, customer satisfaction, and sales performance, these tools provide valuable insights into the performance of each marketing channel.

Marketing Channel Optimization Tools offer several benefits. Firstly, they allow marketing professionals to identify the most profitable channels and invest more resources in them. By understanding the strengths and weaknesses of each channel, marketers can optimize their marketing strategies accordingly. Secondly, these tools help to identify inefficiencies or bottlenecks in the distribution process, enabling marketers to address them and improve overall channel performance. Additionally, these tools aid in identifying the most effective marketing tactics and messages for each channel, enabling marketers to tailor their communication accordingly.

In conclusion, Marketing Channel Optimization Tools are essential for marketing managers to maximize the efficiency and profitability of their marketing channels. By leveraging data and analytics, these tools provide insights that help optimize channel performance, enhance customer satisfaction, and ultimately drive business growth.

Marketing Channel Optimization

Marketing Channel Optimization refers to the process of maximizing the efficiency and effectiveness of marketing channels in order to reach the target audience, deliver value, and achieve marketing objectives. It involves analyzing, selecting, and managing the various channels through which businesses communicate, promote, and distribute their products or services to customers.

By optimizing marketing channels, businesses can improve their overall marketing performance, increase customer reach and engagement, and enhance profitability. This process begins with understanding the target market and their preferences, behaviors, and needs. It then involves identifying and evaluating different marketing channels, such as traditional advertising, digital platforms, social media, direct marketing, and public relations, to determine the most suitable ones to use for reaching the target audience effectively.

Once the channels are selected, businesses need to allocate resources, budget, and efforts accordingly. This includes developing marketing strategies, creating compelling and consistent brand messages, designing engaging content, implementing promotional activities, and monitoring channel performance. The optimization process also entails regularly reviewing and analyzing the effectiveness and efficiency of the chosen marketing channels, measuring key performance indicators, and making adjustments as necessary.

In conclusion, Marketing Channel Optimization is a critical component of marketing management that involves strategically managing and improving the utilization of marketing channels to maximize brand exposure, customer engagement, and business performance. By optimizing marketing channels, businesses can effectively and efficiently deliver their products or services to the target market, ultimately leading to increased sales and profitability.

Marketing Channel

A marketing channel refers to a set of interdependent organizations that collaborate in order to make a product or service available for consumption by customers or end-users. These organizations work together to efficiently and effectively move goods from the point of production to the point of consumption.

Marketing channels are an essential component of marketing management as they facilitate the distribution of products and services. They involve various entities such as manufacturers, wholesalers, retailers, and intermediaries, all working towards delivering value to the end customer through the exchange process.

Marketing Channels

A marketing channel refers to the set of intermediaries and activities involved in the process of making a product or service available to the target customers. It is a key component of marketing management, as it allows companies to effectively reach and communicate with their customers.

The main purpose of marketing channels is to bridge the gap between the production of goods or services and their final consumption. These channels serve as the distribution network through which products move from the manufacturer to the end user. They encompass all the activities necessary for the efficient flow of goods, such as sourcing raw materials, manufacturing, warehousing, transportation, and retailing.

In marketing management, there are two main types of marketing channels: direct and indirect. Direct channels involve selling products or services directly to the end user without the involvement of intermediaries. This can be done through company-owned stores, online platforms, or direct sales representatives. Indirect channels, on the other hand, involve the use of intermediaries to reach the target customers, such as wholesalers, distributors, retailers, and agents. These intermediaries play a crucial role in distributing the products to the final consumers, as they have access to a wider customer base and possess specialized knowledge of the local market.

Overall, effective management of marketing channels is essential for companies to ensure that their products or services are available in the right place, at the right time, and in the right quantity. It requires careful planning, coordination, and collaboration with the intermediaries involved to optimize the flow of goods and meet the needs of the customers.

Marketing Cloud Platforms

A marketing cloud platform is a digital software solution that enables marketing teams to manage and execute various marketing activities effectively. It is designed to automate and streamline marketing tasks, allowing marketers to create, plan, execute, and analyze marketing campaigns across multiple channels.

Marketing cloud platforms integrate various marketing tools and technologies into a single unified platform. These tools typically include customer relationship management (CRM), email marketing, social media marketing, content management systems (CMS), digital advertising, and analytics.

The platform offers a centralized hub where marketers can gather and analyze customer data, enabling them to create highly targeted and personalized marketing campaigns. It provides a comprehensive view of customer interactions and engagement across different channels and touchpoints, helping marketers understand customer behavior and preferences.

By leveraging marketing cloud platforms, marketers can automate repetitive tasks, such as

172

email campaign scheduling, social media posting, and ad campaign management. This automation frees up time for marketers to focus on more strategic initiatives and creative aspects of marketing.

In addition, marketing cloud platforms enable marketers to track and measure the effectiveness of their marketing efforts. They provide real-time analytics and reporting capabilities, allowing marketers to monitor campaign performance, identify trends, and make data-driven decisions to optimize their marketing strategies.

Marketing Cloud Solutions

A marketing cloud solution is a comprehensive software platform designed to streamline and optimize various aspects of marketing management. It enables marketers to automate and integrate their marketing efforts across multiple channels, such as email, social media, and mobile, allowing them to create targeted and personalized campaigns.

By utilizing a marketing cloud solution, marketers can centrally manage and analyze their marketing data, including customer profiles, demographics, and behavioral data. This data-driven approach allows marketers to gain valuable insights, identify trends, and make informed decisions, ultimately helping them improve their marketing strategies and achieve better results.

Marketing Cloud

Marketing Cloud refers to a software platform that enables businesses to manage and automate their marketing efforts across different channels and touchpoints. It allows marketers to create, execute, and analyze integrated marketing campaigns that span email, social media, mobile, web, and other digital channels.

With Marketing Cloud, marketers can personalize and target their messaging to specific customer segments in order to deliver relevant and engaging content. They can also automate repetitive tasks such as sending email campaigns, managing social media posts, and tracking customer interactions, which helps to streamline and optimize marketing operations.

Additionally, Marketing Cloud provides marketers with advanced analytics and reporting capabilities, allowing them to measure the effectiveness of their marketing campaigns and make data-driven decisions. This includes tracking key performance indicators such as conversion rates, click-through rates, and customer response rates, as well as analyzing customer behavior and preferences to better understand and anticipate their needs.

In summary, Marketing Cloud is a comprehensive marketing management solution that empowers businesses to strategically plan, execute, and analyze their marketing activities across various channels, with the ultimate goal of driving customer engagement, loyalty, and revenue growth.

Marketing Collateral Design Software

Marketing collateral design software is a computer program or application specifically designed for creating marketing materials such as brochures, flyers, posters, banners, and other promotional materials. It is a valuable tool within the field of marketing management as it allows marketers to easily and efficiently design, customize, and produce visually appealing and professional-looking marketing collateral.

With marketing collateral design software, marketers can utilize pre-made templates or create their own designs from scratch. This software typically includes a wide range of tools and features that enable users to manipulate and edit text, images, graphics, and other visual elements. Users can also choose from various color schemes, fonts, and layouts to create cohesive and visually appealing marketing materials that align with the brand's identity and messaging.

Additionally, marketing collateral design software often provides the ability to incorporate company logos, branding elements, and other customized visuals to ensure consistency across various marketing materials. It also allows for easy revisions and updates, saving time and resources compared to traditional printing methods.

Overall, marketing collateral design software is an essential tool for marketing management professionals as it streamlines the process of creating visually appealing, consistent, and impactful marketing materials. By using this software, marketers can effectively communicate their brand's message, generate leads, and enhance overall marketing efforts.

Marketing Collateral Design Tools

Marketing collateral design tools refer to software or applications that assist marketing professionals in creating and developing various types of promotional materials. These tools are designed specifically for the field of marketing management and are utilized to support the creation of visually appealing and effective collateral materials.

The primary goal of marketing collateral design tools is to streamline the design process and enable marketing teams to create high-quality and consistent marketing materials. These tools typically include a wide range of features and functionalities, such as templates, graphic design tools, image editing capabilities, typography options, and color palette generators.

Marketing Collateral Design

Marketing collateral design refers to the strategic process of creating and developing various marketing materials and assets that are used to promote a brand, product, or service. These materials are designed to effectively communicate a company's value proposition and key messages to its target audience.

The goal of marketing collateral design is to create visually appealing and informative materials that attract and engage potential customers. This can include items such as brochures, flyers, posters, banners, business cards, and product packaging. These materials are carefully crafted to reflect the brand's identity and effectively communicate its unique selling points.

The design of marketing collateral takes into account various factors such as the target audience, the intended message, and the overall marketing strategy. It involves the use of graphic design and typography techniques to create visually appealing layouts and compositions. The choice of colors, fonts, and imagery is carefully considered to align with the brand's visual identity and evoke the desired emotional response from the audience.

Effective marketing collateral design plays a crucial role in establishing brand awareness, enhancing brand credibility, and driving customer engagement. Well-designed marketing materials can help differentiate a brand from its competitors, convey a sense of professionalism and quality, and convey key information in a clear and concise manner.

Marketing Collateral

Marketing collateral refers to the collection of materials and assets that are developed and used by a company to promote its products or services. These materials are designed to provide information, educate, and persuade potential customers to engage with the company's offerings. Marketing collateral is an essential component of a company's marketing strategy and plays a critical role in communicating its brand message and value proposition to its target audience.

Marketing collateral can take various forms, including brochures, product catalogs, sales presentations, case studies, white papers, advertisements, promotional materials, and digital assets such as videos, infographics, and social media posts. These materials are typically designed to be visually appealing and informative, with a consistent branding and messaging that aligns with the company's overall marketing strategy.

Marketing Communication Mix

The marketing communication mix refers to the combination of tools and strategies that a company uses to promote its products or services to the target market. It is a set of marketing tactics that helps in delivering a consistent and persuasive message to the customers, with the aim of influencing their buying decisions and enhancing brand loyalty.

The elements of the marketing communication mix include advertising, sales promotion, public relations, direct marketing, and personal selling. Advertising is the use of paid communication channels to reach a large audience and create awareness about the brand or product. Sales promotion involves activities like discounts, coupons, and contests to encourage immediate purchases. Public relations involves building positive relationships with the media and other stakeholders to enhance the company's image. Direct marketing involves direct communication with individual customers, such as through mail or email, to generate leads or make sales. Personal selling involves face-to-face interactions with potential customers to persuade them to buy the product or service.

The marketing communication mix is important in marketing management as it helps in effectively reaching the target market and communicating the value proposition of the product or service. By using a mix of different communication tools, companies can reach customers through various channels and engage them effectively. It allows companies to create awareness, influence purchase decisions, and build long-term relationships with customers. The marketing communication mix should be carefully planned and executed to ensure that the messages are consistent, persuasive, and aligned with the overall marketing objectives of the company.

Marketing Communications

Marketing communications refers to the various strategies and tactics used by businesses to promote their products or services to their target audience. It is a critical component of the marketing management discipline as it involves communicating with customers and potential customers to raise awareness, generate interest, and ultimately drive sales.

Effective marketing communications involve several key elements, including advertising, public relations, sales promotion, direct marketing, and personal selling. These elements work together to create a cohesive and impactful message that resonates with the target audience.

Marketing Competitive Analysis Techniques

Marketing competitive analysis techniques refer to the methods and tools used by marketing managers to evaluate and understand the competitive landscape in which their business operates. It involves gathering and analyzing information about competitors, their products, marketing strategies, and various external factors that impact their performance. By conducting a competitive analysis, marketing managers can identify potential threats and opportunities, make informed decisions, and develop effective marketing strategies to gain a competitive advantage.

There are several key techniques used in marketing competitive analysis. The first technique is analyzing competitor products and services. This involves researching and evaluating the features, benefits, pricing, and positioning of competing products or services to identify any key advantages they may have over your own offerings. Another technique is analyzing competitor marketing strategies, such as their advertising, promotions, and distribution channels. This helps identify their target market, positioning strategy, and any potential gaps or weaknesses that can be capitalized on.

Marketing Competitive Analysis Tools

A marketing competitive analysis tool is a framework or method used by marketing managers to assess and analyze the strengths and weaknesses of their own company and its competitors. It helps marketing managers understand the competitive landscape in which their company operates and identify opportunities and threats in the market.

These tools typically involve gathering and analyzing data on various aspects of competitors' marketing strategies, such as their product offerings, pricing, distribution channels, advertising and promotion activities, and customer insights. They may also consider macro-environmental factors such as economic conditions, technological advancements, and regulatory factors that may impact the competitive landscape.

Marketing Competitive Analysis

A marketing competitive analysis is a strategic evaluation and comparison of a company's products, services, and marketing strategies against its competitors in the marketplace. It involves assessing various factors such as pricing, product quality, target audience, distribution channels, brand image, and promotional activities to determine how a company stacks up against its rivals.

The goal of a marketing competitive analysis is to gain a thorough understanding of the competitive landscape and identify areas of opportunity and vulnerability. By closely examining the strengths and weaknesses of competitors, a company can better position itself to exploit market gaps and gain a competitive advantage.

Marketing Content Calendar Apps

A marketing content calendar app is a digital tool used by marketing teams to plan and organize their content marketing activities. It allows them to schedule and track the creation, publication, and promotion of their marketing content across various channels and platforms.

Marketing content calendar apps offer features such as a centralized calendar view where marketers can visualize and manage all their content activities. They enable marketers to plan and allocate resources effectively, ensuring that content creation and publication align with marketing goals and objectives.

These apps also typically provide collaboration and communication features, allowing team members to coordinate and share information. They may offer task management capabilities, enabling marketers to assign responsibilities, set deadlines, and monitor progress. Integration with other marketing tools, such as social media management platforms and email marketing software, is often available to streamline workflows.

The main benefits of using a marketing content calendar app include improved organization and efficiency, increased team collaboration and coordination, better alignment with marketing strategies, and enhanced visibility into content performance and results. By having a centralized and structured system in place, marketers can ensure a consistent and timely delivery of their content, resulting in a more effective and successful content marketing strategy.

Marketing Content Calendar Software

A marketing content calendar software is a tool used in the field of marketing management that helps plan and organize the creation, scheduling, and distribution of marketing content across various channels and platforms.

Marketing content calendars are typically used to maintain a centralized view of all marketing activities and ensure that content is created and published in a timely and coordinated manner. These tools enable marketing teams to effectively plan and execute their content strategies, ensuring that messages are delivered consistently and aligned with overall marketing objectives.

Marketing Content Calendar

A Marketing Content Calendar is a strategic tool used in the field of Marketing Management to plan, organize, and schedule marketing content activities across various channels and platforms. It serves as a centralized document that outlines the specific content to be created and distributed within a designated timeframe. The main purpose of a Marketing Content Calendar is to provide marketers with a structured framework for managing their content marketing efforts. It helps teams to align their content creation and distribution activities with overall marketing objectives and business goals. By mapping out content ideas, themes, formats, and publishing dates in advance, marketers can ensure a consistent flow of high-quality content that resonates with their target audience. The Marketing Content Calendar typically includes crucial information such as topic ideas, target audience, keywords, content types, channels, authors, and deadlines. It acts as a visual representation of the content marketing strategy, allowing marketers to easily track progress and ensure that all tasks are completed on time. Furthermore, the Marketing Content Calendar serves as a communication tool for cross-functional teams, enabling collaboration and coordination among content creators, designers, social media managers, and other stakeholders. It promotes efficiency and productivity by avoiding duplicative efforts, ensuring that resources are allocated appropriately and content is distributed evenly across channels. Overall, a well-structured Marketing Content Calendar is an essential component of strategic marketing planning. It helps organizations streamline their content creation and distribution processes, maintain consistency, and maximize the impact of their marketing efforts.

Marketing Content Management

Marketing Content Management is a strategic and holistic approach to creating, organizing, and managing marketing content assets effectively and efficiently across various channels and platforms. It encompasses the processes, technologies, and workflows used to plan, create, distribute, and measure the impact of marketing content throughout its lifecycle.

In the context of the Marketing Management discipline, Marketing Content Management focuses specifically on the management of content assets related to marketing activities. This includes content used for advertising, promotions, branding, public relations, social media, email marketing, and other marketing initiatives.

The primary goal of Marketing Content Management is to ensure that the right content is delivered to the right audience at the right time, in a consistent and engaging manner. It involves the development of a content strategy, including content planning, creation, curation, and optimization. It also involves the identification and implementation of content management systems and tools to streamline content workflows, facilitate collaboration, and improve content reuse and distribution.

By effectively managing marketing content, organizations can enhance brand consistency, improve customer engagement, and drive desired marketing outcomes. Marketing Content Management also enables marketers to track and analyze content performance to measure its impact on marketing goals and objectives.

In summary, Marketing Content Management is a strategic approach to managing marketing content assets across various channels and platforms. It encompasses content planning, creation, distribution, and measurement to ensure the right content is delivered to the right audience at the right time, driving desired marketing outcomes.

Marketing Copy

Marketing management is a discipline that focuses on analyzing, planning, implementing, and controlling marketing strategies and activities. It involves understanding customer needs and wants, formulating marketing objectives and strategies, devising marketing plans, and overseeing the execution of marketing programs to achieve organizational goals.

The primary goal of marketing management is to create and maintain mutually beneficial relationships between an organization and its customers. This involves identifying target markets, conducting market research to understand consumer behavior, and developing value propositions that meet customers' needs and preferences.

Marketing management encompasses a wide range of activities, including product development, pricing, distribution, and promotion. It involves designing products and services that offer unique benefits and stand out from competitors, setting prices that capture customer value while maintaining profitability, establishing distribution channels to reach target customers efficiently, and developing and implementing promotional campaigns to communicate value and persuade customers to purchase.

In addition, marketing management involves monitoring and evaluating marketing performance, measuring the effectiveness of marketing initiatives, and making adjustments to improve results. It requires analyzing sales data, tracking market trends, and gathering customer feedback to assess the success of marketing strategies and make informed decisions for future marketing efforts.

Marketing Dashboard

A marketing dashboard is a centralized tool used by marketing managers to monitor and measure key performance indicators (KPIs) and track the success of marketing activities and campaigns. It provides a visual representation of various marketing metrics and data, allowing managers to gain real-time insights into the effectiveness and impact of their marketing efforts.

The marketing dashboard typically displays a variety of KPIs that are relevant to the marketing department, such as website traffic, conversion rates, customer acquisition costs, social media engagement, email open rates, and campaign ROI. This data is organized and presented in a clear and intuitive way, using charts, graphs, and other visual elements.

By regularly monitoring the marketing dashboard, managers can quickly identify trends, patterns, and areas of improvement. They can easily spot performance gaps, compare results against targets and benchmarks, and make data-driven decisions to optimize their marketing strategies and tactics.

The dashboard often integrates with various marketing tools and platforms, pulling data from different sources and presenting it in a unified view. This allows managers to have a holistic understanding of their marketing activities, eliminating the need to manually gather and analyze data from multiple systems.

Marketing Data Visualization Platforms

A marketing data visualization platform is a tool or software that enables marketers to transform raw marketing data into visually appealing and informative charts, graphs, and other visual representations. It allows marketers to interpret and analyze complex marketing data more easily, making it a valuable asset in the field of marketing management.

By using a marketing data visualization platform, marketers can present data in a graphical format that is easy to understand and interpret. This helps them to spot patterns, trends, and correlations that may not be apparent when looking at raw data alone. The visual representations provided by these platforms enable marketers to make data-driven decisions more effectively, leading to improved marketing strategies and outcomes.

Marketing Data Visualization Tools

Marketing Data Visualization Tools refer to software or platforms used by marketing professionals to visually represent and analyze marketing data. These tools enable marketers to transform complex and large datasets into easily understandable charts, graphs, and other visual representations, which can help identify trends, patterns, and insights.

These visualization tools are specifically designed for marketing management purposes, allowing marketers to make data-driven decisions, track campaign performance, and optimize marketing strategies. They can handle various types of marketing data, including customer demographics, sales figures, website traffic, social media engagement, and more.

Marketing Data Visualization

Data visualization in the context of Marketing Management is the representation of marketing data in a visual format to aid in understanding patterns, trends, and insights for effective decision-making. It involves the use of various visual elements such as charts, graphs, and maps to present complex marketing data in a simplified and easily digestible manner.

The primary goal of marketing data visualization is to enhance the comprehension and analysis of data, enabling marketing managers to identify valuable information and make well-informed strategic decisions. By visually representing data, it is easier to identify patterns, correlations, and anomalies that might not be apparent when examining raw data alone. It allows marketers to extract actionable insights and discover new opportunities for growth or optimization.

Data visualization enhances communication and collaboration within marketing teams, enabling effective reporting and presentations. By presenting data visually, marketers can communicate complex information more efficiently, ensuring that key findings are easily understood by all stakeholders.

This practice is particularly valuable in marketing management as it helps marketers measure and evaluate the success of marketing campaigns, track customer behavior, analyze market trends, and monitor key performance indicators (KPIs). It allows marketers to quickly identify areas of improvement or areas where marketing efforts are performing exceptionally well.

In conclusion, data visualization plays a crucial role in marketing management by transforming complex marketing data into visual representations that facilitate decision-making, communication, and performance evaluation. It empowers marketing managers to gain deeper insights from data, make data-driven decisions, and drive marketing success.

Marketing Data

Marketing data refers to the information and statistics that are collected and analyzed to gain insights into customer behavior, market trends, and the effectiveness of marketing strategies. It plays a crucial role in marketing management by helping businesses make informed decisions and improve their marketing efforts.

Marketing data can be categorized into two types: primary data and secondary data. Primary data is collected directly from customers through surveys, interviews, focus groups, and other research methods. It provides firsthand information about customers' preferences, buying patterns, and perceptions. Secondary data, on the other hand, is collected from various sources such as industry reports, government publications, and competitor analysis. It helps businesses understand the broader market context and identify opportunities and threats.

The analysis of marketing data involves various techniques and tools to extract meaningful insights. These include statistical analysis, data mining, predictive modeling, and market segmentation. By analyzing marketing data, businesses can identify their target market, tailor their marketing messages, and allocate resources effectively.

Marketing data is a valuable asset for businesses as it enables them to make data-driven decisions and measure the success of their marketing campaigns. It helps businesses track key performance indicators (KPIs) such as customer acquisition, conversion rates, and return on investment (ROI). By continuously monitoring and analyzing marketing data, businesses can identify areas of improvement and optimize their marketing strategies for better results.

Marketing Decision Support Systems (MDSS) Solutions

Marketing Decision Support Systems (MDSS) Solutions are tools and technology-based platforms that assist marketing managers in making strategic decisions by providing them with relevant and timely information. These systems combine data analysis, modeling, and simulation techniques to support marketing decision-making processes.

MDSS solutions integrate various sources of data, including customer demographics, market trends, competitor analysis, sales data, and marketing research findings. They help marketing managers organize and interpret this data, providing them with the insights necessary to effectively analyze market opportunities and threats, develop marketing strategies, and track the performance of marketing campaigns.

By leveraging MDSS solutions, marketing managers can access real-time and historical data, which enables them to monitor and evaluate the effectiveness of their marketing strategies. The systems also facilitate performance measurement and tracking, allowing managers to identify areas of improvement and adjust their marketing tactics accordingly.

Moreover, MDSS solutions play a crucial role in marketing resource allocation and optimization. They assist marketing managers in allocating budgets across different marketing channels, such as advertising, digital marketing, and promotions, by analyzing the return on investment (ROI) of each channel. By optimizing resource allocation, MDSS solutions help maximize the impact of marketing activities on the target market.

Marketing Decision Support Systems (MDSS)

A Marketing Decision Support System (MDSS) is a computer-based tool or software used by marketing managers to analyze and evaluate marketing data, facilitate decision-making, and support the development and implementation of marketing strategies. It is designed to provide relevant and timely information to assist marketing managers in making well-informed decisions and improve the overall effectiveness of marketing activities.

The primary purpose of an MDSS is to collect, integrate, and analyze data from different sources, such as market research, customer databases, sales data, and external data sources. It provides marketers with comprehensive and up-to-date information about the market, customers, competitors, and other relevant factors that can impact marketing decisions. By utilizing advanced analytical techniques, the MDSS enables marketing managers to identify patterns, trends, and relationships in the data, and derive meaningful insights and recommendations.

The features and capabilities of an MDSS may vary depending on the specific software or tool being used. However, common functionalities include data visualization, forecasting, segmentation, targeting, and campaign management. These functionalities allow marketing managers to monitor key performance indicators (KPIs), track marketing campaigns, evaluate the effectiveness of various marketing activities, identify market segments to target, and allocate resources accordingly.

Overall, an MDSS empowers marketing managers to make data-driven decisions, enhance marketing planning and execution, optimize resource allocation, and improve the overall performance and profitability of marketing activities. It has become an essential tool in modern marketing management, enabling marketers to stay ahead in the dynamic and competitive marketplace.

Marketing Decisions

Marketing decisions refer to the choices and actions taken by marketing managers and executives to achieve the objectives of an organization's marketing plan. These decisions are based on careful analysis of market research, consumer behavior, and competitive analysis.

The process of making marketing decisions involves a systematic approach and requires a deep understanding of various marketing concepts and frameworks. Marketing managers need to consider factors such as product development, pricing strategies, distribution channels, and promotional activities to make informed decisions that align with the overall marketing strategy of the company.

Marketing Effectiveness Measurement Solutions

Marketing Effectiveness Measurement Solutions refer to the tools and techniques used by marketing managers to assess and evaluate the success and impact of their marketing strategies, campaigns, and activities. These solutions aim to examine the efficiency and effectiveness of marketing efforts in achieving the desired objectives and goals.

Marketing effectiveness measurement solutions involve the collection, analysis, and interpretation of various data and metrics related to marketing performance. This may include a range of quantitative and qualitative measures, such as sales revenue, market share, customer satisfaction, brand awareness, and customer retention. By measuring and analyzing these indicators, marketing managers can gain insights into the overall effectiveness of their marketing initiatives.

The primary objective of marketing effectiveness measurement is to provide marketing managers with actionable intelligence and insights that can inform decision-making and improve marketing strategies. By understanding which activities are generating the desired outcomes and which are not, managers can allocate resources more effectively, optimize marketing budgets, and adjust strategies accordingly. Additionally, these solutions can help identify areas of improvement and opportunities for innovation in marketing activities.

In summary, marketing effectiveness measurement solutions enable marketing managers to assess the impact and success of their marketing efforts. By utilizing various data and performance metrics, they can gain valuable insights into the overall effectiveness of their initiatives, make informed decisions, and enhance marketing strategies to drive business growth.

Marketing Effectiveness Measurement Tools

A marketing effectiveness measurement tool is a method or framework used by marketing managers to evaluate the success and impact of marketing activities and campaigns. It aims to assess the extent to which these activities have met their intended objectives and generated value for the organization.

These measurement tools typically involve the collection and analysis of various types of data, such as sales figures, market research findings, customer feedback, website traffic, and social media engagement. The data is used to identify key performance indicators (KPIs) that help quantify the effectiveness of marketing efforts.

Marketing effectiveness measurement tools provide insights into the return on investment (ROI) of marketing activities, helping managers make informed decisions about resource allocation and future marketing strategies. They enable organizations to track the performance of different marketing channels and tactics, identify areas of improvement, and optimize the allocation of marketing budgets.

By using these tools, marketing managers can measure the impact of campaigns on brand awareness, customer acquisition, customer loyalty, and overall sales. They can also identify which marketing activities are the most effective in reaching target audiences and generating desired outcomes.

Overall, marketing effectiveness measurement tools play a crucial role in the marketing management discipline, providing data-driven insights that inform decision-making and optimization of marketing strategies.

Marketing Effectiveness Metrics

Marketing effectiveness metrics refer to the quantitative or qualitative measures used to evaluate the success and impact of marketing activities and strategies. These metrics provide valuable insights into the efficiency and profitability of marketing efforts, helping organizations make informed decisions and optimize their marketing performance.

In the context of the Marketing Management discipline, marketing effectiveness metrics play a crucial role in assessing the overall effectiveness and efficiency of marketing campaigns, initiatives, and resources. These metrics can be used to determine the return on investment (ROI) of marketing activities, measure customer acquisition and retention rates, evaluate brand equity, and assess customer satisfaction and loyalty.

Marketing Effectiveness

Marketing effectiveness refers to the ability of a company to achieve its marketing objectives and goals. It is a measure of how successful a company's marketing efforts are in terms of generating customer interest, creating brand awareness, and ultimately driving sales.

In the field of marketing management, marketing effectiveness is a critical metric that is used to evaluate the impact and value of various marketing strategies and tactics. It involves assessing the efficiency of the marketing activities in relation to the resources invested, as well as the overall return on investment (ROI) achieved.

The evaluation of marketing effectiveness typically includes the analysis of key performance indicators (KPIs) such as market share, customer acquisition and retention rates, customer satisfaction, brand equity, and profitability. These metrics provide insights into the effectiveness of different marketing initiatives, allowing companies to gauge the success of their marketing campaigns and make informed decisions regarding resource allocation and strategy refinement.

Marketing effectiveness is influenced by a variety of factors, including market conditions, competitive landscape, target audience preferences, and the alignment of marketing activities with overall business objectives. By continuously monitoring and measuring marketing effectiveness, companies can identify areas of improvement, optimize their marketing efforts, and enhance their competitive advantage in the marketplace.

Marketing Ethics Compliance

Marketing ethics compliance refers to the adherence and implementation of ethical principles and guidelines in marketing activities, as outlined by regulatory bodies and industry standards. It involves conducting marketing initiatives in a responsible and morally upright manner, ensuring that all practices and strategies are aligned with ethical standards.

The primary objective of marketing ethics compliance is to maintain the integrity and credibility of marketing efforts while simultaneously prioritizing the well-being of consumers and society as a whole. This entails avoiding deceptive practices, misleading advertising, and unethical tactics that may harm consumers or violate their rights.

By adhering to marketing ethics compliance, organizations demonstrate their commitment to transparency, honesty, and accountability. This includes providing accurate information about products and services, respecting consumer privacy, and refraining from unfair competitive practices. It also involves upholding the principles of fairness, social responsibility, and environmental sustainability in marketing activities.

Marketing ethics compliance plays a crucial role in building and maintaining trust between organizations and their target audiences. By acting ethically, companies can establish a positive brand image and enhance their reputation, which ultimately contributes to long-term business success. Moreover, compliance with ethical standards helps organizations mitigate legal risks and avoid potential penalties or reputational damage.

In conclusion, marketing ethics compliance ensures that organizations engage in ethical marketing practices that align with societal expectations and legal requirements. By prioritizing consumer welfare and maintaining transparency, organizations can uphold ethical values, build trust with their target audiences, and contribute to the overall betterment of society.

Marketing Ethics Guidelines Compliance Tools

Marketing Ethics Guidelines Compliance Tools are tools utilized by businesses to ensure they are adhering to ethical practices and guidelines in their marketing efforts. These tools provide a structured framework that helps businesses assess, identify, and address any ethical concerns or issues that may arise in their marketing campaigns.

These tools typically include a set of policies, procedures, and best practices that businesses can incorporate into their marketing strategies. They are designed to promote transparency, honesty, and fairness in marketing communications, as well as protect consumers from any deceptive or misleading practices.

Marketing Ethics Guidelines

Marketing ethics guidelines refer to the principles and standards that guide the ethical behavior of marketers in the field of marketing management. These guidelines help marketers make morally responsible decisions and conduct their activities in a manner that is fair, honest, and respectful to all stakeholders involved.

Marketing ethics guidelines are important in ensuring that marketing practices are conducted with integrity and adhere to ethical standards. They provide a framework for marketers to evaluate their actions and make choices that are consistent with ethical principles. By following these guidelines, marketers can build a positive reputation for their brands, establish trust with customers, and contribute to the overall well-being of society.

Marketing Ethics

Marketing ethics refers to the moral principles and values that guide the actions and decisions of marketers in the field of marketing management. It encompasses the ethical considerations and responsibilities that marketers have towards their customers, competitors, society, and the environment.

Marketers, as the key players in promoting and selling products and services, are expected to adhere to ethical standards to ensure fairness, honesty, and transparency in their marketing practices. This includes refraining from engaging in deceptive advertising, false or misleading product claims, and manipulative sales techniques.

Marketing ethics involves the ethical treatment of customers, taking into account their needs, preferences, and overall well-being. It requires marketers to provide accurate and truthful information about their products, without exaggerations or omissions, allowing customers to make informed choices. Marketers should also respect consumer privacy and ensure the secure handling of customer data.

Furthermore, marketing ethics extends to fair competition practices, where marketers must refrain from engaging in unfair competitive strategies such as price fixing, collusion, or misleading comparisons. Marketers should strive to create a level playing field and uphold the principles of free and fair competition.

Moreover, marketing ethics encompasses the responsibility towards society and the environment. Marketers should consider the social and environmental impact of their marketing initiatives and strive to minimize any negative effects. This includes practicing sustainable marketing, supporting socially responsible initiatives, and avoiding any forms of exploitation or harm to individuals or communities.

Marketing Forecasting

Marketing forecasting is a vital practice in the field of Marketing Management that involves the systematic and data-driven estimation of future marketing outcomes and trends. It serves as a crucial tool for marketing strategists and decision-makers, enabling them to make well-informed decisions and plans.

The main objective of marketing forecasting is to predict future market conditions and consumer behaviors based on historical data, market research, and industry analysis. By analyzing past trends and patterns, marketers can anticipate changes, risks, and opportunities that may impact their marketing initiatives.

Marketing Funnel Stage Optimization Platforms

A marketing funnel is a visual representation of the customer journey from awareness to purchase. It is divided into various stages, each representing a different level of engagement with the brand or product. The stages typically include awareness, consideration, and conversion.

Marketing funnel stage optimization platforms are tools and technologies that help marketers optimize each stage of the marketing funnel to drive better results. These platforms provide insights, data, and automation capabilities to identify and target the right audience, deliver personalized messaging, and measure performance.

Marketing Funnel Stage Optimization

A marketing funnel is a model used in marketing management to describe the customer's journey from awareness to purchase. It is a visual representation of the different stages a prospect goes through before becoming a customer. The marketing funnel consists of several stages, each with its own specific objectives and strategies.

Stage optimization refers to the process of improving and maximizing the effectiveness of each stage in the marketing funnel. It involves analyzing the performance of each stage, identifying opportunities for improvement, and implementing strategies to enhance the conversion rate and overall efficiency of the funnel.

Marketing Funnel Stages

The marketing funnel stages refer to the various steps that a customer goes through during the purchasing process, from initial awareness to the final conversion. It is a framework used in marketing management to understand and analyze the customer journey and create effective strategies to move customers through the funnel.

The marketing funnel typically consists of four stages: awareness, interest, consideration, and conversion. In the awareness stage, the customer becomes aware of the product or service through various marketing channels such as advertisements, social media, or word of mouth. The goal of this stage is to create brand awareness and attract the attention of potential customers.

Once the customer has become aware of the product or service, they enter the interest stage. In this stage, the customer shows interest in the product and seeks more information. They may visit the company's website, read reviews, or engage with the brand's content. The goal at this stage is to provide valuable information and generate leads.

The consideration stage is where the customer evaluates the available options and compares them. They may consider factors such as price, features, and customer reviews. The goal in this stage is to convince the customer that the product or service meets their needs and is the best choice among the alternatives.

Finally, in the conversion stage, the customer makes the decision to purchase the product or service. This is where the marketing efforts pay off, and the prospect becomes a customer. The goal in this stage is to facilitate the purchase process and provide a seamless experience for the customer.

Marketing Funnel

A marketing funnel, also known as a sales funnel, is a conceptual model that represents the different stages a customer goes through when making a purchase decision. It is widely used in marketing management to understand and track the customer journey from initial awareness to the final purchase.

The marketing funnel consists of several stages, each representing a different level of customer interaction and engagement. These stages typically include awareness, consideration, conversion, and retention. At each stage, the goal is to move the customer to the next stage and ultimately convert them into a paying customer.

Marketing Information System (MIS)

A Marketing Information System (MIS) refers to the structured and continuous process of collecting, analyzing, and managing marketing data and information to support the decision-making process in the field of marketing management. This system aids in effectively identifying, assessing, and responding to marketing opportunities and challenges by providing timely and relevant information.

MIS plays a vital role in marketing management by facilitating the acquisition and dissemination of information related to various aspects of the marketing environment, including market trends, consumer behavior, competitor analysis, and product performance. It enables marketing managers to make informed and data-driven decisions, formulate effective marketing strategies, and monitor their implementation and outcomes.

Marketing Intelligence Platforms

A Marketing Intelligence Platform is a tool or system that helps marketing managers gather, analyze, and interpret data and information about various aspects of the market environment. It enables marketers to make informed decisions and develop effective marketing strategies.

Marketing intelligence platforms utilize various data sources, such as market research reports, online surveys, customer feedback, social media data, competitor data, and internal sales and customer data, to provide a comprehensive view of the market landscape. These platforms leverage advanced analytics techniques, predictive modeling, and data visualization to transform raw data into meaningful insights.

The primary goal of a marketing intelligence platform is to support marketing managers in understanding customer needs, preferences, and behaviors, as well as monitoring market trends, competitor activities, and overall industry dynamics. By accessing real-time and historical data, marketers can identify opportunities, assess market potential, and identify threats and challenges that may impact their marketing strategies.

With the help of marketing intelligence platforms, marketing managers can track the performance of their marketing campaigns, measure the effectiveness of their marketing efforts, and gauge the success of their marketing tactics. These platforms enable marketers to optimize their marketing functions, allocate resources efficiently, and achieve their marketing objectives.

Marketing Intelligence Solutions

Marketing Intelligence Solutions refers to the collection, analysis, and interpretation of data and information to support decision-making and strategic planning in the field of marketing management. It involves the use of various tools, techniques, and processes to gather relevant data on market trends, consumer behavior, competitor analysis, and other factors that can impact the success of marketing initiatives.

The primary objective of Marketing Intelligence Solutions is to provide marketers with valuable insights and actionable information that can help them make informed decisions and develop effective marketing strategies. This involves monitoring and analyzing both internal and external data sources, such as sales data, customer feedback, market research reports, social media trends, and industry news.

By leveraging Marketing Intelligence Solutions, marketers can gain a better understanding of their target market, identify emerging market trends, predict consumer preferences, and evaluate the effectiveness of marketing campaigns. It enables them to gain a competitive edge by identifying growth opportunities, optimizing marketing budgets, and enhancing customer satisfaction and loyalty.

Overall, Marketing Intelligence Solutions play a critical role in improving the effectiveness and efficiency of marketing management. By utilizing data-driven insights, marketers can make more informed decisions, minimize risks, and maximize the return on investment (ROI) of their marketing efforts.

Marketing Intelligence Tools

Marketing Intelligence Tools can be defined as technological resources and techniques utilized by organizations to collect, process, analyze, and interpret relevant market data and information. These tools serve the purpose of providing valuable insights into consumer behavior, market trends, competition analysis, and other critical aspects of the marketing environment.

The primary objective of employing marketing intelligence tools is to enable marketing managers to make well-informed decisions and develop effective marketing strategies based on accurate and up-to-date information. By utilizing these tools, organizations can gain a competitive edge by staying ahead of market trends, identifying opportunities, anticipating customer needs, and mitigating potential risks and threats.

Marketing intelligence tools encompass a wide range of software applications and systems that help gather and analyze data from various sources such as market surveys, social media platforms, customer databases, sales records, and public databases. These tools often utilize advanced technologies such as data mining, machine learning, and predictive analytics to process large amounts of data efficiently and uncover meaningful patterns and insights.

Some common examples of marketing intelligence tools include customer relationship management (CRM) systems, social listening tools, competitive intelligence platforms, web analytics software, and marketing automation software. These tools enable marketing managers to understand customer preferences, track campaign performance, monitor social media sentiment, analyze competitor strategies, and optimize marketing efforts based on real-time data.

In summary, marketing intelligence tools play a crucial role in the marketing management discipline by providing accurate and actionable insights to support decision-making and enable organizations to adapt to the dynamic marketplace. By harnessing the power of these tools, organizations can enhance their competitiveness, improve customer satisfaction, and drive business growth.

Marketing Intelligence

Marketing intelligence refers to the systematic collection, analysis, and interpretation of relevant information about the market, customers, competitors, and the general business environment. It involves gathering data through various sources such as market research, surveys, customer feedback, social media monitoring, and competitor analysis.

The purpose of marketing intelligence is to provide insights and understanding of market trends, customer preferences, competitors' strategies, and other external factors that impact the organization's marketing efforts. By analyzing and interpreting the data, marketing managers can make informed decisions and develop effective marketing strategies.

The process of marketing intelligence includes identifying relevant data sources, collecting data through surveys, interviews, or monitoring tools, organizing and analyzing the data, and finally interpreting the findings to extract meaningful insights. These insights help in identifying opportunities, understanding customer needs, evaluating market potential, and developing strategies to gain a competitive edge.

Marketing intelligence plays a crucial role in marketing management as it enables managers to make informed decisions, anticipate market changes, and identify potential threats and opportunities. It helps in identifying market gaps, understanding customer behavior, identifying market segments, evaluating the effectiveness of marketing campaigns, and tracking competitors' activities.

Overall, marketing intelligence provides valuable information and knowledge that forms the basis for strategic decision-making and planning in marketing management. It helps organizations stay ahead in a dynamic and competitive market by providing insights into consumer behavior, market trends, and competitors' actions.

Marketing KPIs

Marketing KPIs, or Key Performance Indicators, are measurable values that indicate the success or effectiveness of marketing efforts within an organization. These indicators are used by marketing managers to evaluate the performance of marketing initiatives and make data-driven decisions to achieve strategic marketing objectives.

KPIs are essential for organizations to assess and monitor their marketing performance and ensure that they are on track to achieve their marketing goals. They provide quantifiable benchmarks that can be tracked over time to gauge the effectiveness and efficiency of marketing campaigns, strategies, and tactics.

Marketing Metrics

Marketing Metrics refers to the measurable indicators or data that are used to assess the performance and effectiveness of marketing activities and initiatives. These metrics are used in the field of Marketing Management to evaluate the impact of marketing efforts, determine the return on investment (ROI), and make informed decisions for future marketing strategies.

The use of marketing metrics helps organizations to track, measure, and analyze various aspects of their marketing campaigns, channels, and tactics. These metrics provide valuable insights into critical aspects such as customer behavior, market penetration, brand awareness, customer acquisition, customer retention, and revenue generation. By quantifying and analyzing these metrics, marketers can make data-driven decisions, optimize marketing efforts, allocate resources effectively, and identify areas for improvement.

The selection of marketing metrics depends on the marketing goals and objectives of an organization. Commonly used metrics include customer lifetime value (CLV), customer acquisition cost (CAC), conversion rate, customer churn rate, click-through rate (CTR), return on ad spend (ROAS), net promoter score (NPS), and market share. These metrics can be obtained from various sources such as customer data, market research, web analytics, social media analytics, and sales data.

It is crucial for marketers to regularly monitor and analyze marketing metrics to assess the performance of their marketing efforts, identify trends and patterns, measure the success of marketing campaigns, and make necessary adjustments. By understanding the impact and effectiveness of different marketing activities, marketers can make informed decisions, allocate resources efficiently, and optimize marketing strategies to achieve desired business outcomes.

Marketing Mix (4Cs)

The Marketing Mix, also known as the 4Cs, is a concept that refers to the key elements or components that a marketer must consider when developing a marketing strategy and implementing it in the market. It represents a fundamental framework for Marketing Management, guiding marketers in their decision-making process and helping them effectively meet the needs and wants of their target customers.

The 4Cs consist of four interrelated elements: Customer, Cost, Convenience, and Communication. Each one plays a critical role in determining the success of a marketing strategy:

Customer: The customer is at the center of the Marketing Mix. Understanding the target market's needs, preferences, and behavior is essential for creating products or services that meet their demands. Marketers need to thoroughly analyze and segment their target customers to develop a deep understanding of their wants and desires in order to tailor their marketing efforts accordingly.

Cost: Cost refers to the price that customers are willing to pay for a product or service. Marketers must carefully consider the perceived value of their offering and set a price that is attractive to customers while still generating a profit for the company. This involves analyzing the pricing strategies of competitors, determining the appropriate pricing model, and considering the impact of various pricing factors on customer perception and purchasing decisions.

Convenience: Convenience refers to the accessibility and availability of a product or service to customers. Marketers need to ensure that their offering is easy to find, purchase, and use by customers. This includes considering the distribution channels, the location of physical stores, the ease of online purchasing, and the overall experience provided to customers throughout the buying process.

Communication: Communication refers to the promotional activities and messages used to inform, persuade, and remind customers about a product or service. Marketers must develop effective communication strategies to reach their target customers and create brand awareness. This involves selecting the right mix of advertising, public relations, sales promotions, and personal selling techniques to effectively communicate the value proposition of their offering.

Marketing Mix (4Ps)

The marketing mix, also known as the 4Ps, is a fundamental concept in the field of marketing management. It refers to a set of tools that businesses use to promote their products or services and effectively reach their target market. The 4Ps include product, price, place, and promotion.

Product represents the tangible or intangible goods and services that a company offers to its customers. It encompasses the features, design, packaging, and branding of the product. The product should be able to satisfy customers' needs and wants, and differentiate itself from competitors' offerings.

Price refers to the amount of money that customers are required to pay in order to acquire the product. It should be set in a way that is both affordable for customers and profitable for the company. Factors such as production costs, competition, and customer demand heavily influence pricing decisions.

Place refers to the distribution channels and locations where customers can purchase the product. It involves decisions about the selection, management, and optimization of various channels such as retailers, wholesalers, and online platforms. The goal is to ensure that customers have convenient access to the product.

Promotion encompasses the activities that businesses undertake to communicate and promote their products to customers. It includes advertising, sales promotion, public relations, and personal selling. The aim is to generate awareness, interest, and desire for the product, and ultimately drive sales.

In summary, the marketing mix (4Ps) is a strategic framework that enables businesses to effectively market their products or services. By carefully considering and managing the product, price, place, and promotion elements, companies can create a compelling offering, attract their target market, and ultimately achieve their marketing objectives.

Marketing Mix (7Ps)

The marketing mix is a strategic tool used by marketing managers to create a comprehensive plan for positioning a product or service in the market. It consists of seven key elements, known as the 7Ps: product, price, place, promotion, people, process, and physical evidence.

The first element, product, refers to the tangible or intangible goods or services offered by a company. It includes factors such as design, features, quality, and branding. Price, the second element, involves determining the cost of the product and the pricing strategy employed to maximize profits and meet customer demand.

The third element, place, focuses on the distribution channels and methods through which the product is made available to customers. This includes considerations such as retail locations, online platforms, and partnerships with distributors.

Promotion, the fourth element, involves the communication and marketing efforts used to promote and sell the product. This includes advertising, public relations, sales promotions, and personal selling techniques.

The fifth element, people, refers to the individuals involved in delivering the product or service to customers. This includes employees, sales representatives, and customer service personnel.

The sixth element, process, outlines the procedures and systems implemented to deliver the product or service. It includes factors such as order processing, customer support, and product delivery.

The final element, physical evidence, refers to the tangible aspects that support the product or service delivery. This can include elements such as packaging, store layout, and service guarantees.

Marketing Mix Analysis Models

The marketing mix analysis models are strategic tools used in the field of Marketing Management to understand and analyze the various elements that make up a company's marketing efforts. It helps marketers to make informed decisions about their product, pricing, promotion, and distribution strategies.

One of the commonly used marketing mix analysis models is the 4Ps model, which includes Product, Price, Promotion, and Place. Product refers to the goods or services that a company offers to its target market. Price is the monetary value that customers are willing to pay for the product. Promotion involves the communication and promotional activities that create awareness and persuade potential customers to purchase the product. Place refers to the distribution channels and locations where the product is made available to customers.

Marketing Mix Analysis Tools

A marketing mix analysis is a tool used in the field of marketing management to assess and evaluate various factors that contribute to the success or failure of a marketing strategy. It helps marketers understand the key elements of their marketing plan and how they can be adjusted to achieve desired outcomes.

The marketing mix consists of four fundamental components, also known as the 4Ps: product, price, place, and promotion. Each element plays a crucial role in shaping the marketing strategy and is analyzed individually to ensure optimal alignment with the target market.

The product component focuses on the actual offering being marketed. It involves examining the features, benefits, quality, and packaging of the product or service in relation to customer needs and preferences. This analysis helps marketers identify areas for improvement and innovation, ensuring their offering stands out from competitors in the market.

The price component revolves around determining the monetary value of the product or service. Here, marketers evaluate factors such as pricing strategy, pricing methods, discounts, and payment terms. By conducting a thorough analysis of pricing, businesses can determine the most effective and profitable pricing structure that resonates with their target market.

The place component refers to the distribution and availability of the product or service. Analysis in this area involves evaluating distribution channels, inventory management, logistics, and channel partners. Effective place analysis ensures that the product reaches the right customers at the right time, maximizing convenience and accessibility.

The promotion component focuses on communication and marketing efforts aimed at creating awareness and generating demand. Analyzing promotion involves assessing advertising, public relations, sales promotions, and digital marketing channels. By understanding the most effective promotional methods, marketers can develop compelling campaigns that effectively reach and engage their target audience.

Marketing Mix Analysis

The marketing mix analysis is a fundamental concept in the field of marketing management. It refers to the set of marketing tactics that a company uses to promote its products or services. The analysis helps marketers effectively plan and implement their marketing strategies by considering four key factors known as the "4 Ps" - product, price, place, and promotion.

The first element of the marketing mix is the product. This refers to the actual goods or services that a company offers to its customers. Marketers must carefully analyze the features, benefits, and quality of their products to ensure they meet the needs and desires of their target market.

The second element is price. This involves determining the right pricing strategy for the product. Marketers need to consider factors such as production costs, competition, and customer perception when setting the price. The goal is to find a balance that maximizes profitability while remaining attractive to customers.

The third element is place, also known as distribution. This involves selecting the appropriate channels of distribution to make the product available to customers. Marketers must decide whether to sell through wholesalers, retailers, or directly to consumers. They also need to consider factors such as logistics, location, and inventory management.

The final element is promotion. This involves the various marketing activities used to communicate and promote the product to the target market. Marketers must develop effective advertising, sales promotion, public relations, and personal selling strategies to create awareness, generate interest, and ultimately drive sales.

Marketing Mix Modeling (MMM)

Marketing Mix Modeling (MMM) is a strategic tool used in the field of Marketing Management to measure the impact and effectiveness of various marketing activities on the sales and profitability of a product or service. It involves the analysis of historical data to understand the relationship between marketing inputs (known as the marketing mix variables) and key business outputs (such as sales, revenue, or market share).

The marketing mix variables typically include the four Ps of marketing: Product, Price, Promotion, and Place. MMM helps marketers in optimizing these variables by providing insights into their individual and combined effects on the business outcomes. By quantifying the impact of different marketing elements, MMM enables marketers to allocate their resources effectively and make informed decisions regarding marketing investments.

To conduct a MMM analysis, marketers collect and analyze data from various sources like sales records, advertising expenditures, pricing information, and market research data. Statistical techniques are then used to establish relationships and causality between marketing inputs and business outcomes. The model allows marketers to measure the ROI of their marketing efforts, identify the most effective marketing mix strategies, and forecast the potential impact of changes to the marketing mix.

In summary, Marketing Mix Modeling is a valuable tool for marketing managers to evaluate and optimize their marketing strategies. By understanding the impact of different marketing variables on business outcomes, MMM helps marketers make data-driven decisions and allocate resources more efficiently.

Marketing Mix Modeling

Marketing Mix Modeling is a technique used in the field of Marketing Management to measure and evaluate the effectiveness of marketing strategies. It involves analyzing the impact of various marketing elements, or the "marketing mix," on key performance indicators such as sales, customer acquisition, and brand awareness.

The marketing mix refers to the combination of product, price, promotion, and place (distribution) that a company utilizes to position its products or services in the market. These elements can be adjusted and optimized to achieve specific marketing goals.

Marketing Mix Modeling helps marketers make data-driven decisions by quantifying the impact of each element of the marketing mix. By analyzing historical data and running statistical models, marketers can gain insights into the relationships between marketing activities and business outcomes. This allows them to identify the most effective marketing strategies and allocate resources more efficiently.

Through Marketing Mix Modeling, marketers can evaluate the effect of different scenarios or "what-if" situations. For example, they can assess the impact of changing the price of a product, increasing promotional activities, or targeting a different consumer segment. This enables them to make informed decisions and optimize marketing campaigns to generate higher sales and profitability.

Marketing Objectives

Marketing objectives are specific goals set by a company or organization that outline what they want to achieve through their marketing efforts. These objectives are developed as part of the overall marketing strategy and serve as a guide for decision-making and planning.

The primary purpose of marketing objectives is to drive business growth and success. They help marketers effectively utilize their resources, make informed decisions, and measure the effectiveness of their marketing initiatives. In other words, marketing objectives provide clarity and direction to marketing managers and teams.

Marketing Operations (MO)

Marketing Operations (MO) refers to the strategic planning and execution of marketing activities within an organization. It involves the management and coordination of various marketing processes, systems, and tools to enable the smooth functioning and effectiveness of marketing campaigns and initiatives.

The primary goal of Marketing Operations is to streamline marketing operations and improve the overall efficiency and productivity of marketing teams. It includes activities such as budget allocation, project management, resource planning, performance tracking, and reporting. By optimizing these processes, Marketing Operations helps organizations to achieve their marketing objectives in a cost-effective and timely manner.

Marketing Operations Management Platforms

Marketing operations management platforms refer to software applications or systems that enable marketers to streamline, automate, and manage various marketing processes and activities effectively. These platforms provide a centralized repository or workspace for planning, executing, and tracking marketing campaigns, while also facilitating collaboration and communication among team members.

By leveraging marketing operations management platforms, marketing professionals can gain better control over their workflows, enhance productivity, and improve overall marketing effectiveness. These platforms typically offer features such as project management, campaign planning, asset management, budgeting, reporting, and analytics. They also integrate with other marketing tools and technologies, ensuring seamless data flow and promoting data-driven decision-making.

Marketing Operations Management Solutions

Marketing Operations Management Solutions refers to the software, systems, and processes that support the planning, execution, and optimization of marketing activities within an organization. It encompasses the tools and techniques used to manage and streamline marketing operations, including the creation and management of marketing campaigns, budget and resource allocation, project management, performance measurement, and reporting.

Marketing Operations Management Solutions help marketing teams to effectively coordinate and manage all aspects of their work. They enable organizations to improve efficiency, increase productivity, and achieve better results by providing a centralized platform for collaboration, automation, and data analysis. These solutions typically include functionality such as campaign planning and execution, asset management, workflow management, budgeting and financial management, performance tracking and reporting, and integration with other marketing and business systems.

Marketing Operations Management

Marketing Operations Management is a critical function within the discipline of Marketing Management that focuses on the planning, execution, and analysis of marketing activities to optimize efficiency and effectiveness.

It involves overseeing the coordination and integration of various marketing processes, technologies, and resources to ensure the smooth execution of marketing strategies and campaigns. Marketing Operations Management aims to streamline marketing operations, enhance collaboration and communication, and maximize performance and return on investment.

Key responsibilities of Marketing Operations Management include developing and implementing marketing plans, managing budgets and resources, coordinating cross-functional teams, monitoring and analyzing marketing metrics, and leveraging technology and data to support decision-making and continuous improvement.

Marketing Operations Management plays a crucial role in aligning marketing activities with overall business objectives, ensuring consistency of messaging and brand image, and driving growth and profitability. It helps organizations to achieve greater marketing efficiency, reduce costs, increase productivity, and enhance customer relationships.

191

In today's rapidly evolving marketing landscape, Marketing Operations Management is increasingly important. It enables companies to adapt to changing market conditions, leverage emerging technologies, and capitalize on data-driven insights to drive marketing excellence and competitive advantage.

Marketing Performance Dashboard Software

A marketing performance dashboard software is a tool used in the field of marketing management to collect, analyze, and present data on marketing activities and their impact on business outcomes. It provides marketers with a comprehensive view of their marketing performance, allowing them to track key metrics, measure the success of marketing campaigns, and make data-driven decisions to optimize marketing strategies.

The software gathers data from various marketing channels, such as social media, email marketing, search engine optimization, and paid advertising. It then organizes and visualizes this data into easily understandable charts, graphs, and reports. Marketers can customize the dashboard to display the specific metrics and KPIs (Key Performance Indicators) that are most relevant to their marketing goals and objectives.

By having real-time access to accurate and up-to-date data, marketing teams can monitor the effectiveness of their marketing efforts, identify trends, spot opportunities, and identify areas of improvement. They can measure the ROI (Return on Investment) of different marketing campaigns, track website traffic and conversions, monitor customer engagement and satisfaction, and assess the overall impact of their marketing activities on the bottom line.

In summary, a marketing performance dashboard software empowers marketing professionals to leverage data-driven insights to improve marketing performance and achieve their business objectives. It serves as a central hub for monitoring and analyzing marketing activities, enabling marketers to make informed decisions, optimize their strategies, and drive business growth.

Marketing Performance Dashboards

Marketing performance dashboards are tools used in the field of marketing management to track, analyze, and visualize key performance indicators (KPIs) and metrics related to marketing activities and campaigns. These dashboards provide marketers with a comprehensive view of their marketing efforts and allow them to monitor and evaluate the effectiveness of their strategies and tactics.

By consolidating data from various sources such as website analytics, social media platforms, email marketing software, and customer relationship management (CRM) systems, marketing performance dashboards provide real-time insights into important marketing metrics such as lead generation, conversion rates, customer acquisition costs, return on investment (ROI), and customer lifetime value.

With the help of visualizations like charts, graphs, and tables, marketers can easily identify trends, patterns, and correlations in their marketing data, enabling them to make data-driven decisions and optimize their marketing activities for better results. These dashboards also allow marketers to set goals, track progress, and compare actual results against targets, which helps them to stay focused on their objectives and measure the success of their marketing campaigns.

In addition, marketing performance dashboards can facilitate collaboration and communication among marketing teams and other stakeholders by providing a shared platform to access and interpret marketing data. This allows for a more efficient and effective decision-making process based on accurate and up-to-date information.

Marketing Performance Measurement

Marketing Performance Measurement is the practice of quantifying and assessing the effectiveness and efficiency of marketing activities and initiatives in achieving the organization's marketing objectives. It involves the collection, analysis, and interpretation of relevant data and metrics to evaluate the performance of marketing strategies, campaigns, channels, and tactics.

By measuring marketing performance, organizations can gain valuable insights into the impact and return on investment (ROI) of their marketing efforts. This allows marketing managers to make data-driven decisions, optimize resource allocation, and improve the overall effectiveness of their marketing initiatives. It helps in identifying areas of improvement, understanding target audience behavior and preferences, and benchmarking against competitors.

Marketing performance measurement encompasses a range of metrics, including but not limited to sales revenue, market share, customer acquisition and retention rates, customer lifetime value, brand awareness, customer satisfaction, website traffic, social media engagement, and cost per lead. These metrics are tracked over time, compared with benchmarks or targets, and analyzed to identify trends, patterns, and areas requiring attention.

It is essential for marketing managers to select relevant and meaningful metrics that align with their specific marketing objectives and KPIs (Key Performance Indicators). The chosen metrics should be measurable, consistent, and linkable to financial outcomes. Marketing performance measurement provides the foundation for continuous improvement and evidence-based decision-making in marketing management.

Marketing Performance Metrics

Marketing Performance Metrics refers to the set of quantitative measures used to assess the effectiveness and efficiency of marketing activities and strategies in achieving the overall goals and objectives of an organization. These metrics provide insights into the performance of various marketing initiatives and help marketing managers make data-driven decisions to optimize their marketing efforts and improve the return on investment.

Marketing Performance Metrics encompass a wide range of indicators that evaluate different aspects of marketing performance, such as brand awareness, customer acquisition, customer retention, customer satisfaction, market share, sales revenue, marketing costs, and customer lifetime value. These metrics can be categorized into different dimensions, including financial metrics, customer metrics, operational metrics, and strategic metrics.

Marketing Plan

A marketing plan is a written document that outlines the strategies and tactics an organization will use to promote its products or services to target customers. It serves as a roadmap for the marketing team, providing direction and guidance for achieving specific marketing goals and objectives. The purpose of a marketing plan is to identify and analyze the organization's strengths, weaknesses, opportunities, and threats (SWOT analysis) in relation to the market and competitors. This analysis helps to determine the target market segments and develop a marketing strategy that will effectively reach and attract those potential customers. A marketing plan typically includes detailed information about the organization's target market, such as demographics, psychographics, and buying behavior. It also outlines the marketing mix, which consists of the four Ps: product, price, promotion, and place. These elements are strategically combined to create a compelling offering that meets the needs and wants of the target customers. Furthermore, a marketing plan establishes specific marketing objectives and sets measurable goals and targets to evaluate the success of the marketing efforts. It also includes a budget allocation and timeline for implementing the marketing activities and campaigns. Overall, a marketing plan serves as a comprehensive document that guides the marketing team in achieving the organization's marketing objectives. It provides a clear roadmap for executing marketing initiatives, ensuring that resources are utilized effectively and efficiently.

Marketing Psychology Insights Tools

Marketing psychology insights tools refer to the techniques, strategies, and methodologies used by marketers to gain a deep understanding of consumer behavior and decision-making processes. These tools enable marketers to leverage psychological principles and theories to influence consumer perceptions, attitudes, and purchasing decisions.

By applying marketing psychology insights, marketers can effectively target and position their products or services, create persuasive marketing messages, and build strong emotional connections with customers. These insights often involve analyzing consumer motivations, needs, desires, and preferences, as well as studying how individuals respond to various marketing stimuli.

The use of marketing psychology insights tools can provide valuable information for marketing management practitioners. It helps them identify consumer segments, develop effective marketing strategies, and optimize marketing campaigns. These tools may include qualitative research methods such as interviews and focus groups, as well as quantitative techniques like surveys, experiments, and data analysis.

Furthermore, marketing psychology insights tools can assist in understanding the impact of psychological factors such as perception, memory, learning, attitudes, and emotions on consumer decision-making. Marketers can use this knowledge to design marketing communications that resonate with consumers, create positive brand associations, and stimulate desired consumer responses.

In conclusion, marketing psychology insights tools are integral to the marketing management discipline as they help marketers gain a deeper understanding of consumer behavior and tailor their marketing efforts to effectively meet consumer needs and preferences.

Marketing Psychology Insights

Marketing Psychology refers to the application of psychological principles and theories in the field of marketing. It involves understanding consumer behavior, motivations, perceptions, and decision-making processes to effectively promote and sell products or services.

Marketing Psychology is essential in the discipline of Marketing Management as it helps marketers gain insights into consumer behavior, enabling them to develop targeted marketing strategies and tactics. By understanding how consumers think and make purchase decisions, marketers can create more persuasive advertising messages, design compelling product packaging, and develop engaging online experiences.

Marketing Psychology

Marketing psychology is a branch of marketing management that focuses on understanding and influencing consumer behavior. It involves the application of psychological principles and theories to marketing strategies and practices. The main objective of marketing psychology is to analyze and predict how consumers think, feel, and make decisions in relation to products and brands.

Marketing managers utilize marketing psychology to develop effective marketing campaigns, optimize product designs, and enhance customer experiences. By understanding the psychological factors that influence consumer behavior, marketers can tailor their strategies to meet the needs and desires of their target market. They study various aspects of human psychology such as perception, motivation, learning, memory, and attitude formation, and apply these insights to differentiate their products, create persuasive advertisements, and establish strong brand identities.

Marketing Qualified Lead (MQL)

Marketing Qualified Lead (MQL) refers to a prospective customer or contact who has shown a certain level of interest or engagement with a company's marketing efforts, indicating that they may be more likely to become a sales lead or opportunity. MQLs are typically identified and qualified through a combination of demographic, behavioral, and contextual criteria.

In the context of marketing management, an MQL is usually identified using various lead scoring techniques. These techniques involve assigning points to specific actions or attributes that indicate a higher likelihood of a prospect becoming a customer. For example, visiting a website, downloading a piece of content, or attending a webinar may be assigned different point values based on their relevance and importance to the company's sales process.

Once a prospect reaches a pre-determined threshold of points, they are classified as an MQL and are considered to have moved from the awareness stage to the consideration stage of the marketing and sales funnel. At this point, the marketing team may pass the MQL to the sales team for further qualification and nurturing.

The purpose of identifying and tracking MQLs is to enable marketing and sales teams to focus their efforts on leads that have a higher likelihood of becoming customers. By prioritizing MQLs, companies can optimize their resources and increase the efficiency and effectiveness of their marketing and sales processes.

Marketing ROI Analysis

Marketing ROI Analysis refers to the process of measuring and evaluating the return on investment (ROI) generated from marketing activities. This analysis helps marketing managers assess the effectiveness and efficiency of their marketing efforts by quantifying the financial outcomes and benefits achieved from these activities.

The analysis involves comparing the cost of marketing initiatives to the revenue and profit generated as a result. It takes into account various metrics such as sales revenue, customer acquisition costs, customer lifetime value, and marketing expenses. By calculating and analyzing these metrics, marketing managers can determine the profitability and success of their marketing campaigns and make data-driven decisions to optimize their future marketing strategies.

Marketing ROI Analysis provides valuable insights into the financial impact of marketing initiatives and their contribution to the overall business goals. It helps marketing managers identify the most effective marketing channels, campaigns, and tactics, allowing them to allocate resources effectively and prioritize investments in the areas that generate the highest return. By understanding the ROI of marketing activities, organizations can optimize their marketing budgets, improve their decision-making processes, and achieve better financial results.

Overall, Marketing ROI Analysis plays a crucial role in marketing management by providing a quantifiable and objective measurement of the financial outcomes and benefits of marketing efforts. It enables marketing managers to assess the effectiveness of their strategies, make informed decisions, and continuously improve their marketing performance.

Marketing ROI Calculation Methods

Marketing ROI Calculation Methods are quantitative tools or formulas used by marketing managers to determine the return on investment (ROI) of their marketing activities. ROI is a financial metric that measures the profitability and effectiveness of marketing campaigns or initiatives in relation to the resources invested. These methods help marketing managers evaluate the impact and effectiveness of their marketing efforts and make informed decisions about resource allocation and future marketing strategies.

There are several commonly used marketing ROI calculation methods, including:

1. Incremental Revenue Method: This method determines the ROI by measuring the additional revenue generated as a result of the marketing activity, minus the cost of that marketing activity.

2. Customer Lifetime Value (CLV) Method: This method calculates the ROI by estimating the future revenue and profit generated from acquiring and retaining customers over their lifetime.

3. Marketing Mix Modeling: This method uses statistical techniques to analyze historical sales and marketing data to determine the impact of different marketing variables (such as price, promotion, and advertising) on sales or market share.

4. Marketing Attribution Modeling: This method assigns credit to different marketing touchpoints or channels for driving desired customer actions or conversions, such as purchases or sign-ups.

5. Cost per Acquisition (CPA) Method: This method calculates the ROI by comparing the cost of acquiring a customer (such as advertising expenses or sales commissions) to the revenue generated from that customer.

By using these marketing ROI calculation methods, marketing managers can gain insights into the effectiveness and efficiency of their marketing strategies, optimize resource allocation, and make data-driven decisions to drive business growth and profitability.

Marketing ROI Calculation Tools

Marketing ROI calculation tools are quantitative instruments used in the field of marketing management to measure the return on investment (ROI) for marketing initiatives. ROI is a metric that evaluates the profitability and effectiveness of a marketing campaign or activity by comparing the generated revenue to the associated costs.

These tools assist marketing professionals in understanding the impact and efficiency of their marketing efforts. By employing data analytics and financial calculations, marketing ROI calculation tools provide insights into the outcomes and success of marketing strategies, enabling organizations to make data-driven decisions.

Marketing ROI Calculation

Marketing ROI calculation is a quantitative analysis that measures the effectiveness and profitability of marketing investments. It is a key performance indicator used in the field of Marketing Management to evaluate the return on investment generated from marketing activities.

The calculation involves comparing the net profit or revenue generated from marketing efforts to the costs incurred to execute those marketing activities. By analyzing the return on investment, marketing managers can assess the impact of their marketing strategies and tactics on the overall business performance.

Marketing ROI is typically calculated as a ratio or percentage, where the numerator represents the net profit or revenue generated from marketing and the denominator represents the total marketing investment. The formula for calculating marketing ROI is as follows:

Marketing ROI = (Net Profit or Revenue from Marketing / Total Marketing Investment) x 100

This calculation allows marketing managers to determine the profitability of their marketing initiatives and make informed decisions about resource allocation. It provides insights into which marketing activities are generating the highest returns, enabling managers to optimize their marketing budget and efforts.

Marketing ROI calculation is an essential tool in evaluating the effectiveness and efficiency of marketing activities, enabling marketing managers to justify the allocation of resources, demonstrate the impact of marketing on business outcomes, and align marketing strategies with overall business objectives.

Marketing ROI

Marketing ROI refers to the measurement of the return on investment generated by a marketing activity or campaign. It is a financial metric used to evaluate the effectiveness and efficiency of marketing efforts in terms of generating revenue and contributing to the overall profitability of the organization.

In marketing management, ROI serves as a key performance indicator (KPI) that helps managers and executives gauge the success and value of their marketing initiatives. By quantifying the return on marketing spend, organizations can make informed decisions and allocate resources wisely to maximize their marketing impact.

Marketing ROI is calculated by dividing the net profit generated from a marketing campaign by the total cost of that campaign, and then multiplying the result by 100 to express it as a percentage. A positive ROI indicates that the marketing campaign has generated more revenue than the amount invested, resulting in a profitable outcome for the organization.

Measuring marketing ROI is essential for effective marketing management as it provides insights into the performance of different marketing activities and helps prioritize future investments. It allows marketers to identify which campaigns are most successful and allocate resources accordingly to optimize their marketing strategy.

Additionally, marketing ROI helps justify marketing budgets to top management and stakeholders by demonstrating the financial impact and value of marketing activities. It enables organizations to align marketing efforts with business objectives and make data-driven decisions to improve marketing productivity and profitability.

Marketing Research Process

The marketing research process is a systematic approach used by marketing managers to gather, analyze, and interpret data in order to make informed marketing decisions. It involves a series of steps that are designed to identify the needs and preferences of customers, understand the competitive landscape, and assess the effectiveness of marketing strategies.

The first step in the marketing research process is to define the problem or objective. This involves clearly articulating the research question or the purpose of the study. It helps marketing managers to identify the specific information that needs to be gathered and analyzed in order to address the problem or achieve the objective.

The second step is to design the research plan. This involves determining the most appropriate research method or approach to gather the required data. It may involve conducting surveys, interviews, focus groups, or observational studies. The research plan also includes designing the survey or interview questions, and determining the sample size and target population.

The third step is to collect the data. This involves actually gathering the data using the chosen research method. It requires careful attention to detail to ensure that the data is accurate and reliable. Marketing managers may also need to consider ethical considerations and privacy concerns when collecting data from customers.

The fourth step is to analyze the data. This involves organizing and summarizing the data using statistical techniques and data visualization tools. It helps to identify patterns, trends, and relationships in the data. The analysis of the data provides valuable insights that can be used to make informed marketing decisions.

The final step is to present the findings and make recommendations. This involves creating a report or presentation that effectively communicates the results of the research. Marketing managers need to interpret the findings and provide recommendations based on the insights gained from the research. The recommendations should be actionable and relevant to the marketing objectives.

Marketing Resource Allocation Models Software

A marketing resource allocation model is a software tool used in the field of marketing management to aid in the strategic decision-making process regarding the allocation of resources. This model helps marketers determine how to allocate their limited resources, such as budget, time, and personnel, among various marketing activities to maximize their return on investment (ROI).

The purpose of a marketing resource allocation model is to provide insights and recommendations to marketers on the most effective way to distribute their resources across different marketing channels, campaigns, and initiatives. This is done by considering various factors such as the potential impact of each activity, the target audience, the competitive landscape, and the available budget. By using a marketing resource allocation model, marketers can make informed decisions about which activities to prioritize and allocate resources accordingly.

Marketing Resource Allocation Models

A marketing resource allocation model refers to a strategic framework used in the field of marketing management to determine the optimal distribution of resources such as budget, time, and personnel across various marketing activities and channels. The main goal of using such models is to maximize the overall return on investment (ROI) by efficiently allocating resources to activities that have the highest potential for generating profitable outcomes.

Typically, marketing resource allocation models involve a systematic and data-driven approach that takes into account various factors such as market conditions, customer segmentation, marketing objectives, and competitive landscape. These models often use quantitative techniques such as statistical analysis, optimization algorithms, and predictive modeling to provide insights and recommendations for resource allocation decisions.

Marketing Resource Allocation

Marketing resource allocation refers to the strategic distribution of financial and non-financial resources within an organization for the purpose of achieving marketing objectives. It is a crucial process in marketing management that involves making decisions about how to allocate resources such as budget, personnel, time, and technology across various marketing activities and initiatives.

The goal of marketing resource allocation is to optimize the use of limited resources in order to maximize return on investment (ROI) and achieve desired marketing outcomes. This involves assessing the potential impact and effectiveness of different marketing channels, campaigns, and tactics, and making informed decisions about where to allocate resources based on their expected contribution to organizational goals.

This process typically involves analyzing market trends, consumer behavior, competitive landscape, and internal capabilities to identify opportunities and prioritize marketing activities. It requires careful consideration of factors such as target audience preferences, marketing goals and objectives, resource availability, and expected outcomes. Through effective resource allocation, organizations can prioritize high-potential marketing initiatives, optimize budget allocation, minimize risk, and improve overall marketing performance.

In summary, marketing resource allocation is a strategic decision-making process that determines how an organization allocates its resources to achieve marketing objectives. By effectively managing and optimizing the use of resources, organizations can enhance their marketing effectiveness, generate higher returns, and gain a competitive advantage in the marketplace.

Marketing Resource Management (MRM)

Marketing Resource Management (MRM) refers to a set of processes and technologies used by organizations to efficiently plan, execute, and manage their marketing activities and resources. It integrates marketing strategies, financial planning, project management, and collaboration tools to optimize marketing performance and ensure effective allocation of resources.

With MRM, marketing teams can streamline their workflows, automate repetitive tasks, and gain real-time visibility into their projects and campaigns. It provides a centralized platform for storing and organizing marketing assets, such as creative materials, brand guidelines, and campaign templates, allowing teams to easily access and reuse them. This not only improves marketing efficiency but also helps maintain brand consistency across different channels and touchpoints.

MRM also facilitates collaboration among cross-functional teams, enabling them to work together seamlessly on marketing initiatives. It provides tools for assigning tasks, setting deadlines, and tracking progress, ensuring that everyone involved is aligned and accountable. By maintaining a clear and transparent communication channel, MRM helps minimize miscommunication and delays, leading to faster decision-making and more successful marketing campaigns.

Moreover, MRM enables organizations to measure and analyze the effectiveness of their marketing efforts. It offers reporting and analytics capabilities that provide valuable insights into campaign performance, customer engagement, and return on investment. By leveraging these insights, marketers can make data-driven decisions, optimize their strategies, and allocate resources more effectively to maximize their marketing ROI.

Marketing Segmentation Models Platforms

Marketing segmentation refers to the process of dividing a heterogeneous market into smaller, more homogeneous segments that share similar characteristics. This allows marketers to better understand and target specific groups of consumers with tailored marketing strategies and messages. By segmenting the market, marketers can identify the unique needs, preferences, and behaviors of different customer groups, which helps them develop more effective marketing campaigns and improve the overall performance of their marketing efforts.

There are several segmentation models and platforms available to marketers to assist them in the process of market segmentation. These models and platforms provide marketers with data-driven insights and tools to identify and analyze different segments within a market. They use various variables such as demographic, geographic, psychographic, and behavioral factors to define and characterize market segments.

Marketing Segmentation Models

Marketing segmentation models are frameworks used in marketing management to divide a heterogeneous market into smaller, more homogeneous groups or segments. These models help businesses identify and understand different customer segments, allowing them to tailor their marketing strategies and offerings to meet the specific needs and preferences of each segment.

The purpose of marketing segmentation is to increase the effectiveness and efficiency of marketing efforts by focusing resources on the most profitable segments. By dividing the market into smaller groups with common characteristics, businesses can design targeted marketing campaigns and messages that resonate with each segment. This allows them to deliver personalized experiences, identify new opportunities, and increase customer satisfaction and loyalty.

Marketing Segmentation

Marketing segmentation is the process of dividing a heterogeneous market into smaller, more homogeneous segments based on common characteristics, needs, and behaviors. It is a crucial strategy in marketing management that allows businesses to identify and target specific groups of customers more effectively.

Segmentation helps businesses better understand their target market and enables them to tailor their marketing efforts accordingly. By grouping consumers who share similar needs, preferences, and behaviors, businesses can develop more targeted marketing campaigns, products, and services. This approach allows companies to deliver messages and offerings that resonate with specific segments, increasing the likelihood of attracting and retaining customers.

Marketing Software Platforms

Marketing software platforms refer to a set of digital tools that are designed to assist marketing managers in planning, executing, analyzing, and optimizing marketing campaigns. These platforms are specifically developed to streamline marketing activities and enhance overall efficiency and effectiveness in the field of marketing management.

Marketing software platforms typically encompass a wide range of functionalities and features, including customer relationship management (CRM), campaign management, lead generation, social media management, email marketing, content management, analytics, and reporting. These platforms aim to provide a holistic solution for marketers to manage various aspects of their marketing strategy in one centralized location.

Marketing Software Solutions

Marketing software solutions refer to digital tools and platforms specifically designed to assist marketing professionals in managing and executing various marketing activities and strategies.

These solutions help streamline and automate processes, improve overall efficiency, and enhance marketing performance.

Marketing management involves planning, organizing, implementing, and controlling marketing activities to achieve predefined marketing objectives and goals. This discipline encompasses a wide range of activities, including market research, product development, pricing strategies, promotion, distribution, and customer relationship management.

Marketing software solutions provide marketers with a centralized platform where they can efficiently manage these activities. These solutions typically offer features such as customer relationship management (CRM), email marketing, social media management, content creation and management, analytics and reporting, campaign management, and lead generation. They also often integrate with other essential tools, such as customer service, sales, and project management software.

By utilizing marketing software solutions, marketing professionals can streamline their workflows, improve collaboration, and ensure consistent and effective communication across different channels. These tools also enable marketers to gather and analyze data, gain valuable insights into customer behavior, and make data-driven decisions to optimize marketing strategies. Additionally, marketing software solutions can help automate repetitive tasks, freeing up time for marketers to focus on more strategic and creative initiatives.

Marketing Software

Marketing software in the context of Marketing Management discipline refers to a set of computer programs, applications, or tools that are designed to assist marketing managers in planning, executing, and analyzing marketing activities. It is a digital solution that enables marketers to streamline their tasks, improve their efficiency, and make data-driven decisions to achieve their strategic objectives.

Marketing software offers a range of functionalities that cover various aspects of marketing, including market research, customer segmentation, campaign management, digital advertising, social media management, email marketing, lead generation, and performance analysis. It leverages technology to automate repetitive tasks, provide real-time insights, and facilitate collaboration among marketing team members.

By using marketing software, managers can efficiently collect, organize, and analyze valuable marketing data, such as customer demographics, purchase behavior, and campaign performance. This data can then be utilized to develop targeted marketing strategies, personalize customer experiences, and optimize marketing campaigns for better results.

Moreover, marketing software allows for seamless integration with other business systems, such as customer relationship management (CRM) software, sales automation tools, and analytics platforms. This integration enables marketing managers to align their efforts with other departments, efficiently manage customer relationships, and measure the impact of marketing activities on overall business growth.

Marketing Spend

Marketing spend refers to the financial resources allocated by an organization towards its marketing activities in order to promote its products or services, reach its target audience, and achieve its marketing objectives. It encompasses the various costs incurred in developing, executing, and managing marketing strategies, campaigns, and initiatives.

Marketing spend typically includes expenses related to advertising, public relations, sales promotions, market research, digital marketing, events and sponsorships, marketing personnel, marketing technology, and other marketing-related investments. It can be both a fixed cost, such as salaries of permanent marketing staff, and a variable cost, such as media buying or campaign-specific expenses.

Marketing Stack

A marketing stack refers to the collection of tools and technologies that marketers use to plan, execute, track, and analyze their marketing efforts. It encompasses a wide range of software and platforms that are specifically designed to support various aspects of marketing management and operations.

The marketing stack typically includes tools for customer relationship management (CRM), email marketing, social media management, content management, search engine optimization (SEO), data analytics, and more. These tools help marketers automate manual processes, enhance collaboration, optimize campaigns, and measure the effectiveness of their marketing activities.

By utilizing a marketing stack, marketers are able to streamline their workflow, improve productivity, and make data-driven decisions. For example, a CRM system allows marketers to manage customer data, track interactions, and personalize marketing communications. An email marketing tool enables them to create, send, and track email campaigns. A social media management platform assists in scheduling posts, monitoring engagements, and analyzing social media performance.

In addition, a marketing stack often integrates with other tools and platforms through APIs, allowing for seamless data exchange and workflow integration. This integration enables marketers to create a cohesive and consistent customer experience across multiple channels and touchpoints. It also facilitates the sharing of data between different teams and departments, such as marketing, sales, and customer support.

Marketing Strategy Alignment Software

Marketing Strategy Alignment Software refers to a digital tool or platform designed specifically for the marketing management discipline, aimed at aligning and synchronizing marketing strategies with overall organizational goals and objectives.

This software enables marketing managers to effectively plan, execute, and measure marketing initiatives in line with the broader business strategy. It helps create a cohesive framework where marketing decisions and actions are guided by a comprehensive understanding of the company's mission, vision, and target market.

Marketing Strategy Alignment Tools

A marketing strategy alignment tool is a tool used in the field of Marketing Management to align the company's marketing strategy with its overall business strategy. It helps in ensuring that the marketing activities and initiatives are in line with the overall goals and objectives of the organization.

This tool typically involves a systematic approach that includes analyzing the market, identifying target audiences, setting marketing objectives, and developing strategies and tactics to achieve these objectives. It helps in defining the key marketing messages, selecting the appropriate marketing channels, and allocating resources effectively.

Marketing Strategy Alignment

Marketing Strategy Alignment refers to the process of ensuring that an organization's marketing activities are consistent with its overall strategic goals and objectives. It involves aligning marketing strategies with the overall business strategy to maximize the impact and effectiveness of marketing efforts.

In the context of Marketing Management discipline, Marketing Strategy Alignment is a crucial component for success. It requires a deep understanding of the organization's goals, target market, and competitive landscape. By aligning marketing strategies with the overall strategy, organizations can create a coherent and integrated approach to marketing that drives business growth and achieves a competitive advantage.

Marketing Strategy

Marketing strategy refers to the overall plan and approach devised by a company or organization to achieve its marketing objectives. It is a vital component of marketing management, as it guides the allocation of resources and efforts towards specific marketing activities and initiatives. The purpose of a marketing strategy is to enable the company to connect with its target audience effectively, differentiate itself from competitors, and ultimately increase sales and achieve business goals.

A well-designed marketing strategy considers various factors such as target market analysis, competitive analysis, consumer behavior, and market trends. It involves identifying the target audience, understanding their needs and preferences, and developing products or services that fulfill those needs. The strategy also encompasses determining the most effective channels and methods to reach the target market, creating compelling marketing messages, and setting appropriate pricing and promotion strategies.

Marketing Technology (MarTech)

Marketing Technology (MarTech) refers to the tools, platforms, and solutions that marketers use to plan, execute, and measure their marketing activities. It involves the use of software, hardware, data, and analytics to automate and optimize marketing processes and campaigns.

MarTech plays a crucial role in modern marketing management by enabling marketers to streamline their operations, improve efficiency, and drive better results. It empowers marketers to gather and analyze customer data, create targeted and personalized campaigns, and deliver relevant content to the right audience at the right time. By leveraging MarTech, marketers can effectively reach their target market, build brand awareness, increase customer engagement, and ultimately drive sales.

Mass Customization

Mass customization is a marketing strategy that aims to provide individualized products or services to large numbers of customers. It involves combining the efficiency of mass production with the personalization of custom-made goods or services, thereby meeting the unique needs and preferences of each customer without sacrificing economies of scale.

Through the application of advanced technologies and flexible production systems, mass customization allows companies to offer a wide range of options and features that can be tailored to meet individual customer requirements. This customization can be achieved in various aspects of the product or service, including design, packaging, pricing, delivery, and after-sales support.

Media Buying

Media buying is a strategic process in the field of marketing management that involves the procurement of advertising space or time slots from media outlets. It is a crucial component of the overall media planning and advertising campaign execution process.

The primary objective of media buying is to reach and engage the target audience effectively and efficiently by selecting the most appropriate media channels and negotiating favorable terms for the placement of advertisements or promotional content. It involves identifying the target market, conducting market research, and analyzing consumer behavior to determine the most suitable media outlets that can maximize the campaign's reach and impact.

Media buying professionals work closely with media representatives, such as publishers, broadcasters, or digital platforms, to negotiate pricing, placement, and timing of ad placements. They leverage their knowledge of the media landscape, market trends, and audience data to secure the best possible ad inventory and reach the desired audience in the most cost-effective manner.

Throughout the media buying process, marketers analyze various factors, including target audience demographics, media reach, frequency, and cost metrics. They evaluate different media options, such as television, radio, print, outdoor, and digital platforms, to identify the optimal media mix and allocate the advertising budget effectively.

Overall, media buying plays a vital role in ensuring that marketing messages are delivered to the right people, at the right time, and through the most relevant and impactful media channels. It requires careful planning, negotiation skills, and data-driven decision-making to achieve the desired marketing objectives and maximize return on investment for advertising campaigns.

Media Planning

Media planning is a crucial aspect of marketing management that involves the strategic selection and utilization of various media channels to effectively reach and communicate with the target audience. It encompasses the process of identifying the most suitable media platforms, such as television, radio, print, outdoor advertising, and digital channels, to deliver promotional messages and advertising content.

The main goal of media planning is to optimize the allocation of marketing resources by carefully considering factors such as target demography, market trends, competitor activities, budget constraints, and campaign objectives. By conducting thorough research and analysis, media planners aim to identify the ideal combination of media channels that will deliver maximum exposure and impact.

Media planning involves several key steps, including defining campaign objectives, researching target audience demographics and media consumption habits, evaluating media options, negotiating media contracts and rates, establishing media schedules, and monitoring and evaluating campaign performance. Effective media planning requires a deep understanding of consumer behavior, market dynamics, and media landscape, as well as creative thinking and analytical skills.

In summary, media planning is a strategic process that involves identifying and utilizing the most appropriate media channels to effectively communicate promotional messages to the target audience. It plays a crucial role in enhancing brand visibility, driving consumer engagement, and ultimately achieving marketing objectives.

Meme Marketing

Meme Marketing is a novel marketing strategy that utilizes internet memes to promote a brand, product, or service. It involves creating and sharing humorous or relatable content in the form of memes to engage with the target audience and spark conversations about the brand.

This type of marketing strategy relies on the viral nature of memes, as they are often shared rapidly across social media platforms. Memes are humorous images, videos, or text that convey a specific cultural idea or reference, typically in a concise and relatable manner. By incorporating memes into their marketing campaigns, businesses aim to generate buzz and increase brand awareness.

Micro-Influencers

Micro-Influencers are individuals who have a relatively small number of followers on social media platforms, typically ranging from 1,000 to 10,000 followers. These individuals possess the ability to influence the purchasing decisions of their followers due to their expertise, authenticity, and engagement with their audience.

In the context of Marketing Management, micro-influencers play a crucial role in brand promotion and building brand awareness. Compared to macro-influencers or celebrities, micro-influencers tend to have a more niche and loyal following, resulting in higher levels of engagement and trust. They are seen as more relatable and trustworthy by their followers, which increases the effectiveness of their marketing efforts.

Micro-influencers are particularly effective for niche or specialized products, as they have a deeper knowledge and understanding of their specific target audience. They have the ability to create authentic and personalized content that resonates with their followers, making it more likely for them to take action and make a purchase.

Brands often collaborate with micro-influencers to leverage their influence and reach within their target market. These collaborations can take the form of sponsored posts, product reviews, giveaways, or endorsements. By partnering with micro-influencers, brands can tap into their dedicated and engaged audience and benefit from the increased visibility and credibility that these influencers bring.

In summary, micro-influencers are key players in marketing management, offering brands an effective way to reach and engage with a specific target market. Due to their authenticity, expertise, and niche focus, micro-influencers are highly influential in shaping the purchasing decisions of their followers.

Micro-Moments Strategy Implementation Tools

Micro-Moments Strategy Implementation Tools are a collection of techniques, approaches, and methods that are used in the field of Marketing Management to effectively execute micro-moments strategies. Micro-moments refer to the crucial instances when consumers actively search for information, make decisions, and engage with brands on digital platforms. These moments are characterized by their instantaneity, as they occur on-the-go, often on mobile devices, and shape consumers' perceptions and buying behaviors.

The primary objective of implementing micro-moments strategy is to capitalize on these critical moments by providing relevant and valuable information to consumers to influence their decision-making process. The tools used for implementing micro-moments strategies are designed to ensure that brands are present, helpful, and easily accessible during these moments.

These tools can include consumer insights and analytics platforms that provide valuable data on consumer behavior, preferences, and trends in real-time. By leveraging these insights, marketers can tailor their messaging and content to suit the specific needs and expectations of consumers during micro-moments. Additionally, technologies like location-based targeting and push notifications enable brands to deliver personalized and timely messages to consumers when they are most likely to engage.

Moreover, mobile optimization techniques and responsive design are essential tools for ensuring that brands' digital assets are accessible and user-friendly across devices. This allows brands to provide seamless experiences to consumers during micro-moments, increasing the chances of capturing their attention and driving conversions.

Micro-Moments Strategy Implementation

A micro-moments strategy refers to a marketing approach that focuses on understanding and leveraging the various consumer interactions that occur throughout the customer journey. In today's digital age, consumers have access to a wealth of information and have become more demanding, expecting real-time assistance and personalized experiences.

This strategy seeks to identify and engage consumers during specific moments when they are actively searching for information, making decisions, or taking action. These micro-moments can be categorized into four main types:

1. I-want-to-know moments: These are moments when consumers are seeking information or answers to their questions. Marketers can provide relevant content or ads that address their queries and establish themselves as a trusted source of information.

2. I-want-to-go moments: During these moments, consumers are looking for local businesses or retailers near their location. Marketers can optimize their online presence and provide location-specific information to capture these opportunities.

3. I-want-to-do moments: These are moments when consumers are seeking guidance or instructions on how to complete a task or solve a problem. Marketers can provide useful content, tutorials, or how-to guides to assist them.

4. I-want-to-buy moments: These moments occur when consumers are ready to make a purchase. Marketers can leverage relevant ads, special offers, or incentives to prompt

conversions.

By understanding and effectively targeting these micro-moments, marketers can deliver timely and relevant information, engage consumers at the right moment, and increase their chances of converting prospects into customers. This strategy requires a deep understanding of consumer behavior, effective data analysis, and the ability to create and distribute compelling content across various digital channels.

Micro-Moments Strategy

A micro-moments strategy refers to a marketing management approach that focuses on leveraging consumer's immediate and intent-driven actions in order to reach and engage with them at crucial points throughout their decision-making journey. This strategy recognizes that consumers today have access to information instantaneously through their mobile devices, and as a result, their expectations and attention spans have significantly changed.

Marketers utilizing a micro-moments strategy aim to deliver relevant and helpful content to consumers at the exact moment they are searching for it. This can be achieved through various tactics such as search engine optimization (SEO), pay-per-click (PPC) advertising, and mobile-friendly website designs. By understanding consumer behavior, intent, and context, marketers can effectively target consumers during these micro-moments to provide the right information or solution they are seeking.

Micro-Moments

Micro-Moments refers to the brief instances when consumers reflexively turn to their devices to fulfill an immediate need or desire. These moments generally occur throughout the day and can be categorized into four key types: "I want to know," "I want to go," "I want to do," and "I want to buy."

In the context of Marketing Management, Micro-Moments represent crucial opportunities for businesses to reach and engage with their target audience. By understanding consumer behavior and leveraging the power of technology, marketers can effectively connect with potential customers during these micro-moments, ultimately influencing their decision-making process.

Mobile Advertising

Mobile advertising refers to the practice of promoting products or services through mobile devices such as smartphones and tablets. It is a marketing strategy that leverages the widespread usage of mobile devices to reach and engage target audiences.

In the context of marketing management, mobile advertising plays a crucial role in the overall marketing strategy of a company. With the increasing adoption of mobile devices, marketers have recognized the importance of targeting consumers on their mobile platforms. Mobile advertising allows marketers to connect with consumers on a more personal and direct level, as mobile devices are often used on a daily basis and are constantly carried by individuals.

Mobile App Marketing Platforms

Mobile App Marketing Platforms refer to the software or online platforms that businesses use for promoting and advertising their mobile applications to reach their target audience effectively. These platforms provide a range of tools and features that help marketers manage and streamline their app marketing campaigns.

Mobile App Marketing Platforms offer various capabilities, including app store optimization, user acquisition, engagement, and retention. App store optimization involves optimizing the mobile app's metadata, keywords, and visuals to improve its visibility and ranking in the app store search results. User acquisition features enable marketers to identify and target potential users through various advertising channels, such as social media, search engines, and mobile ad networks. These platforms may also provide analytics and tracking capabilities to monitor user behavior and campaign performance.

By using Mobile App Marketing Platforms, marketers can create and optimize targeted ad campaigns to attract new users and retain existing ones. They can leverage advanced targeting options and personalized messaging to reach the right audience at the right time. These platforms often offer A/B testing functionality, allowing marketers to experiment with different marketing strategies and optimize their campaigns based on data-driven insights.

In summary, Mobile App Marketing Platforms empower marketers to effectively promote and advertise their mobile applications. With a range of tools and features, these platforms enable businesses to optimize their app store presence, acquire new users, engage and retain them, and measure the overall success of their mobile app marketing efforts.

Mobile App Marketing Strategies

Mobile app marketing strategies refer to the specific plans and tactics implemented by a marketing team to promote and advertise a mobile application to its target audience. These strategies aim to increase the visibility, downloads, and usage of the app, ultimately driving user engagement and achieving the desired business goals.

Marketing a mobile app requires a comprehensive approach that encompasses various elements such as market research, competitor analysis, pricing, positioning, and promotional activities. The goal is to create awareness among potential users, generate interest, and convince them to download and use the app regularly.

To develop effective mobile app marketing strategies, marketers need to understand the characteristics of their target audience, including their demographics, preferences, and behavior patterns. This information helps in tailoring the marketing messages and selecting appropriate communication channels to reach the intended users.

Some common mobile app marketing strategies include app store optimization (ASO), social media marketing, influencer partnerships, email marketing, content marketing, paid advertising, and public relations. These strategies are often integrated into a coherent marketing plan that outlines specific objectives, target metrics, and timelines.

In addition, continuously monitoring and analyzing the performance of the marketing efforts is crucial. This allows marketers to identify and track key performance indicators (KPIs), measure the success of their strategies, and make necessary adjustments to optimize the outcomes.

Mobile App Marketing

Mobile App Marketing refers to the process of promoting and advertising a mobile application in order to increase its visibility, downloads, and user engagement. It is a strategic approach to market a mobile app and involves various techniques and tactics across different marketing channels.

Mobile App Marketing is an essential part of marketing management as it helps app developers and businesses reach their target audience and drive app installs. It involves understanding the target audience, setting specific marketing goals, and creating marketing strategies to achieve those goals.

This discipline requires a deep understanding of mobile app analytics, user behavior, and the competitive landscape. It involves optimizing the app's visibility on app stores by optimizing keywords, descriptions, and app screenshots. Additionally, it includes leveraging other marketing channels such as social media, email marketing, influencer marketing, and digital advertising to reach potential users and encourage downloads.

Effective Mobile App Marketing also focuses on user retention and engagement. It involves implementing strategies to encourage app usage, such as personalized push notifications, in-app rewards, and user feedback collection. This helps to improve user satisfaction and retention, leading to long-term success for the app.

In conclusion, Mobile App Marketing plays a crucial role in the marketing management discipline by helping businesses effectively promote and advertise their mobile applications. It involves various techniques and strategies aimed at increasing app visibility, driving downloads, and promoting user engagement.

Mobile Marketing

Mobile marketing involves the use of mobile devices, such as smartphones and tablets, to promote products or services to consumers. It is a marketing technique that aims to reach a target audience through various mobile channels, such as mobile apps, SMS messaging, email, social media, and mobile websites. Mobile marketing is a subset of digital marketing and is becoming increasingly important in today's digital age.

The key advantage of mobile marketing is its ability to reach consumers on the go, as mobile devices are increasingly becoming an integral part of people's daily lives. With the rapid growth of mobile technology and the increasing number of smartphone users, mobile marketing offers marketers a unique opportunity to connect with their target audience anytime, anywhere.

Multichannel Attribution Analysis Solutions

Multichannel attribution analysis solutions refer to the methods and tools used by marketing managers to determine the contribution of various marketing channels in influencing consumer behavior and driving conversions.

Marketing managers rely on these solutions to gain insights into the effectiveness of their marketing initiatives across different channels, such as digital advertising, social media, email marketing, search engine optimization, and offline marketing activities. These solutions help them understand how each touchpoint along the customer journey contributes to the overall conversion and customer acquisition.

The analysis is typically conducted by analyzing data from multiple sources, such as web analytics, CRM systems, and marketing automation platforms. The data is used to calculate and attribute the conversion and revenue generated by each marketing channel, taking into account the interactions and touchpoints a consumer has before making a purchase.

By applying multichannel attribution analysis, marketing managers can make data-driven decisions, optimizing marketing budgets and resource allocation across various channels. They can identify the most influential touchpoints and channels in driving conversions, thereby improving the overall efficiency and effectiveness of their marketing strategies.

Multichannel Attribution Analysis Tools

Multichannel attribution analysis tools are a crucial component of marketing management practices. They provide marketers with the ability to analyze and evaluate the impact of various marketing channels and touchpoints on consumer behavior and conversions.

By using these tools, marketers can gain insights into the effectiveness and ROI of their marketing efforts across multiple channels, such as search engines, social media platforms, email campaigns, display advertising, and more. Multichannel attribution analysis tools use advanced statistical models and algorithms to attribute credit to different marketing touchpoints based on their contribution to the customer journey and conversion actions.

These tools enable marketers to understand which marketing channels and touchpoints are driving the most conversions and revenue. They help optimize marketing strategies by identifying the most effective channels for reaching and engaging with target audiences. Additionally, multichannel attribution analysis tools allow for a more accurate allocation of marketing budgets, as marketers can allocate resources based on the channels and touchpoints that have the highest impact on conversions.

Overall, multichannel attribution analysis tools provide marketers with actionable insights that can inform decision-making and improve the effectiveness of their marketing campaigns. By understanding the customer journey and the role of different marketing channels, marketers can optimize their marketing mix and allocate resources more effectively to maximize ROI.

Multichannel Attribution Analysis

Multichannel Attribution Analysis refers to the process of identifying and analyzing the impact and effectiveness of various marketing channels in a customer's conversion journey. In the context of the Marketing Management discipline, it is a method used to measure and allocate credit to different marketing channels based on their contributions to generating sales or conversions.

The goal of Multichannel Attribution Analysis is to gain insights into the customer journey across multiple touchpoints and understand how different marketing channels interact and influence consumer behavior. By evaluating the effectiveness of each channel, marketers can optimize their marketing strategies, allocate resources more efficiently, and improve overall campaign performance.

Multichannel Marketing

Multichannel marketing is a strategic approach in marketing management that focuses on targeting and engaging customers through multiple channels or platforms simultaneously to create a seamless and integrated customer experience. It involves utilizing various offline and online channels such as physical stores, websites, mobile apps, social media platforms, email marketing, and direct mail, among others, to reach and interact with customers.

The main objective of multichannel marketing is to reach a wider audience and provide them with a consistent message and experience across different channels. By using multiple channels, companies can increase their brand visibility, customer engagement, and ultimately drive sales and customer loyalty.

One of the key advantages of multichannel marketing is the ability to target different customer segments and meet their preferred communication and purchasing preferences. For example, some customers may prefer shopping online, while others might prefer in-store experiences. By offering multiple channels, companies can cater to different customer needs and preferences, ultimately increasing the chances of conversion.

In addition, multichannel marketing allows companies to gather valuable data and insights about their customers' behavior, preferences, and buying patterns across different channels. This data can be used to optimize marketing strategies, personalize communications, and enhance the overall customer experience.

Multisensory Marketing Solutions

Multisensory Marketing Solutions refers to the use of various sensory elements, such as sight, sound, touch, taste, and smell, in marketing strategies and campaigns. This approach aims to engage multiple senses of the target audience to create a more impactful and memorable brand experience.

In the field of Marketing Management, multisensory marketing solutions are used to create a sensory-rich environment that enhances consumer engagement and influences their buying behavior. By incorporating different sensory stimuli, marketers can effectively connect with consumers on an emotional level, leaving a lasting impression on their minds.

Multisensory Marketing Techniques

Multisensory marketing techniques refer to the strategic use of multiple sensory stimuli to engage and influence consumers in the marketing process. This approach recognizes that humans perceive and process information through multiple senses, including sight, hearing, touch, taste, and smell, and aims to create a rich and immersive sensory experience that enhances brand awareness, perception, and engagement.

In the field of marketing management, the application of multisensory techniques involves leveraging sensory inputs such as visual design, sounds, textures, flavors, and scents to carefully craft an environment or product that elicits emotional responses and stimulates sensory receptors. By engaging multiple senses simultaneously, marketers have the opportunity to create a more memorable and impactful brand experience that resonates with consumers on a deeper level.

Through multisensory strategies, marketers can tap into the power of sensory cues to leave a lasting impression, trigger associations, evoke emotions, and influence consumer behavior. For example, a brand might create a visually appealing and aesthetically pleasing store layout, utilize carefully selected background music, incorporate pleasant fragrances, or offer product samples that engage consumers' senses. The goal is to create a holistic sensory experience that aligns with the brand identity and messaging, reinforces positive emotions, and encourages a stronger connection between consumers and the brand.

Multisensory marketing techniques have proven to be effective in attracting attention, enhancing brand recall, increasing purchase intention, and fostering brand loyalty. However, it is crucial for marketers to carefully consider the target audience, brand positioning, and the congruence between sensory cues and the desired brand image to ensure that the multisensory approach aligns with consumers' expectations and preferences.

Multisensory Marketing

Multisensory marketing is a marketing strategy that aims to engage multiple senses of consumers in order to create a more immersive and memorable brand experience.

By appealing to more than just one sense, such as sight or hearing, multisensory marketing draws upon a combination of different sensory stimuli, including touch, taste, and smell, to enhance the overall brand experience. It recognizes that consumers are not solely driven by rational decisions but are also influenced by emotions and sensory experiences that can shape their perceptions and attitudes towards a brand.

Native Advertising

Native advertising refers to a form of paid advertising that seamlessly blends with the surrounding editorial content in terms of look, feel, and context. It is strategically designed to mimic the form and function of the platform on which it appears, making it less obtrusive and more efficient in capturing the attention of the target audience.

In the context of marketing management, native advertising is an effective tool for brands to promote their products or services in a way that does not disrupt the user experience or appear overtly promotional. By aligning the advertising content with the platform's native format, it can create a sense of authenticity and trust among consumers. The goal is to provide relevant and valuable content that not only grabs attention but also entertains, educates, or informs the audience.

Native ads can take various forms, including sponsored articles, videos, infographics, or social media posts. They are typically labeled or identified as "sponsored" or "promoted" to ensure transparency and maintain ethical standards. The key advantage of native advertising is its ability to deliver targeted messages to specific audiences, increasing the likelihood of engagement and conversion.

However, it is essential for marketing managers to carefully plan and execute native advertising campaigns to avoid misleading or deceiving the audience. It is crucial to maintain a balance between providing valuable content and clearly identifying it as advertising to prevent any negative impact on the brand's reputation.

Native Content

Native content refers to marketing content that seamlessly integrates with the user experience of a particular platform or medium. It is designed to resemble and blend in with the organic content of the platform in order to provide a more natural and non-disruptive advertising experience to users.

Native content often takes the form of articles, videos, or social media posts that are created and sponsored by brands. It is carefully crafted to align with the editorial style, tone, and format of the platform where it is located. The goal of native content is to engage and educate users while maintaining their trust and interest in the content.

By presenting native content in a contextually relevant and non-intrusive manner, marketers can enhance brand visibility, build brand awareness, and establish a more authentic connection with their target audience. Native content encourages users to interact and engage with the content, resulting in higher levels of brand recall and a more positive brand perception.

Native content is an effective marketing strategy as it does not disrupt the user's browsing experience or feel like a traditional advertisement. It provides value to users by offering relevant and valuable information, thus increasing the likelihood of users considering the brand or product being promoted. However, it is important for marketers to ensure transparency and disclose when content is sponsored to maintain ethical practices and consumer trust.

In conclusion, native content is a form of advertising that seamlessly integrates with a platform's user experience, providing valuable and relevant content to users without disrupting their browsing experience.

Net Promoter Score (NPS)

The Net Promoter Score (NPS) is a metric used in Marketing Management to measure customer loyalty and satisfaction. It is a simple and effective way to determine how likely customers are to recommend a company, product, or service to others.

NPS is based on a single question that asks customers to rate, on a scale of 0 to 10, how likely they are to recommend a brand to friends or colleagues. Based on their responses, customers are categorized into three groups: Promoters (score 9-10), Passives (score 7-8), and Detractors (score 0-6).

The NPS is calculated by subtracting the percentage of Detractors from the percentage of Promoters. The resulting score ranges from -100 to +100. A positive score indicates that a company has more Promoters than Detractors, which suggests strong customer loyalty and a high likelihood of positive word-of-mouth recommendations. On the other hand, a negative score signifies more Detractors than Promoters, indicating customer dissatisfaction and potential negative word-of-mouth impact.

The NPS is a valuable tool for evaluating customer satisfaction and loyalty as it is easy to understand and track over time. Additionally, it provides actionable insight into a company's customer base, allowing marketers to identify areas for improvement and strategic focus. By consistently monitoring and analyzing NPS scores, businesses can make data-driven decisions to enhance customer experience, increase customer retention, and drive growth.

Neuro-Linguistic Programming (NLP) In Marketing

Neuro-Linguistic Programming (NLP) in Marketing refers to the application of NLP techniques and principles in the field of marketing management. NLP is a psychological approach that focuses on understanding and influencing human behavior, communication, and perception. It encompasses a range of techniques and strategies that can be used to enhance marketing efforts and improve customer engagement.

In the context of marketing management, NLP can be used to analyze and understand consumer behavior, preferences, and decision-making processes. By studying language patterns, sensory perception, and communication styles, marketers can gain valuable insights into the needs, desires, and motivations of their target audience.

The application of NLP techniques in marketing management involves various strategies such as language framing, rapport building, and modeling successful patterns of communication. Marketers can use these techniques to create persuasive and impactful messages, develop strong connections with customers, and influence their buying decisions.

NLP also emphasizes the importance of aligning marketing communications with the sensory preferences of the target audience. By understanding and utilizing various sensory modalities such as visual, auditory, and kinesthetic cues, marketers can enhance the effectiveness of their marketing campaigns and create a more memorable and engaging brand experience.

Overall, NLP in marketing management provides marketers with a toolkit of techniques and strategies that can be used to better understand consumer behavior, communicate effectively, and ultimately drive successful marketing outcomes.

Neuro-Marketing Research Platforms

Neuro-Marketing Research Platforms refer to tools and technologies that utilize insights from neuroscience to understand and optimize consumer behavior and decision-making processes. In the discipline of Marketing Management, these platforms enable marketers to gain a deeper understanding of the subjective experiences, emotions, and cognitive processes that influence consumer preferences and buying behavior.

By combining techniques from neurology, psychology, and marketing research, neuro-marketing research platforms provide unique and valuable insights into consumer decision-making. These platforms utilize various tools such as brain imaging, eye-tracking, facial coding, and biometric measurements to collect data on consumer responses to marketing stimuli.

The data gathered through neuro-marketing research platforms allows marketers to evaluate the effectiveness of their marketing strategies, campaigns, and advertisements. It helps them identify the emotional and cognitive factors that drive consumer preferences, strengthen brand engagement, and influence purchasing decisions.

Furthermore, neuro-marketing research platforms provide marketers with a deeper understanding of consumer attention, memory, and emotional response to different marketing stimuli. This knowledge can be used to develop more targeted and impactful marketing strategies that resonate with the target audience on a subconscious level, thereby increasing the likelihood of influencing their behavior.

Overall, neuro-marketing research platforms are valuable tools for marketers, allowing them to gain deeper insights into consumer behavior and make data-driven decisions that enhance marketing effectiveness and drive business growth.

Neuro-Marketing Research Studies

Neuro-marketing research studies refer to the examination and analysis of consumer behavior and decision-making processes using neurological and psychological techniques. It aims to uncover the underlying brain processes and emotional responses that drive consumer preferences, buying behaviors, and brand perceptions. By combining insights from neuroscience, psychology, and marketing, neuro-marketing research provides valuable insights into the subconscious motivations and influences that shape consumer choices.

Neuro-marketing research studies employ various methodologies, including brain imaging techniques like functional magnetic resonance imaging (fMRI), electroencephalography (EEG), and eye-tracking technology. These methods help researchers measure brain activity, eye movements, and physiological responses to advertising stimuli, product packaging, pricing, and other marketing stimuli. By tracking and interpreting brain responses, neuro-marketing research aims to understand consumers' preferences, perceptions, emotions, and subconscious associations with brands and products.

Neuro-Marketing Research

Neuro-Marketing Research is a subfield of Marketing Management that studies the application of neuroscience principles and techniques to understand consumer behavior and preferences. This field combines traditional marketing research methods with neuroscientific tools, such as brain imaging and physiological measurements, to gain deeper insights into consumers' unconscious reactions and decision-making processes.

By using various non-invasive neuroimaging techniques, such as functional magnetic resonance imaging (fMRI), electroencephalography (EEG), and eye-tracking, neuro-marketers can assess consumers' brain activity, emotional responses, attention, and engagement levels during exposure to marketing stimuli. This allows them to determine how consumers perceive and respond to different marketing strategies, such as advertisements, packaging designs, logos, and pricing techniques.

The insights obtained from neuro-marketing research provide valuable information to marketers, allowing them to optimize their marketing campaigns and tactics. By understanding the neural mechanisms underlying consumer behavior, marketers can tailor their messages and advertisements to better evoke desired emotional responses and influence consumers' decision-making processes. For example, by analyzing brain activity, marketers can identify which features of a product or advertisement capture consumers' attention and elicit positive emotional responses, thus informing the design of more compelling and persuasive marketing materials.

Overall, neuro-marketing research brings a scientific perspective to marketing management, enabling marketers to go beyond traditional self-report measures and gain a deeper understanding of consumer behavior at the subconscious level. It enhances the understanding of consumer decision-making processes and offers valuable insights to create more effective marketing strategies and improve overall business performance.

Neuromarketing

Neuromarketing is a branch of marketing management that utilizes neuroscience principles and techniques to understand and influence consumer behavior and decision-making processes. It seeks to uncover the subconscious factors that drive consumer choices and preferences by studying the brain's cognitive and emotional responses to marketing stimuli.

By combining neuroscientific research methods, such as brain imaging and biometric measurements, with traditional marketing practices, neuromarketing aims to provide valuable insights into how consumers perceive and respond to various marketing strategies. It explores how the brain processes sensory information, generates emotions, and forms memories associated with brands and products.

Niche Market

A niche market is a segment of the overall market that is defined by a specific set of characteristics or preferences. It represents a smaller, more specialized group of consumers with unique needs that may not be adequately met by mainstream products or services.

In the context of marketing management, identifying and targeting a niche market is crucial for businesses to differentiate themselves from their competitors and effectively reach their target audience. By understanding the distinct preferences, behaviors, and demographics of a niche market, companies can tailor their marketing strategies and offerings to better meet the specific needs of these consumers.

Niche Marketing

Niche marketing refers to a marketing strategy that focuses on targeting a specific segment of the market with specialized products, services, or messaging. This approach aims to meet the unique needs and preferences of a small, defined group of customers, rather than trying to appeal to a broad audience.

By identifying and understanding a niche market, businesses can develop strategies to effectively serve and engage with this specific group of customers. This involves conducting thorough market research to identify the specific characteristics, preferences, behaviors, and purchasing patterns of the target niche.

A successful niche marketing strategy involves tailoring products or services to meet the specific demands of the target niche, highlighting the unique benefits and value proposition that set them apart from competitors. This could include offering specialized features, customization options, personalized customer experiences, or addressing specific pain points.

In addition to product or service customization, niche marketing often involves targeted marketing communications and messaging. This can be done through various channels, such as online advertising, social media marketing, content marketing, and public relations, to reach and engage the niche audience effectively.

Niche marketing can be highly effective in driving customer loyalty and building a strong brand in a competitive market. By focusing resources on a specific segment, businesses can build deep relationships with customers, position themselves as experts in their niche, and gain a competitive advantage. However, it is crucial for businesses to continuously monitor and analyze market trends and changes in customer preferences to ensure their niche marketing strategy remains relevant and effective.

Non-Profit Marketing

Non-profit marketing refers to the marketing activities undertaken by non-profit organizations in order to achieve their mission and objectives. It encompasses the strategies, tactics, and activities used by these organizations to promote their cause, attract donors and volunteers, and raise awareness about their programs and services.

Unlike for-profit organizations, non-profit organizations do not aim to generate profit for their own benefit. Instead, they focus on serving the needs of the community or a specific cause. Non-profit marketing, therefore, involves creating and implementing marketing strategies that will help these organizations reach their target audience effectively and efficiently.

Omnichannel Marketing Solutions

Omnichannel marketing solutions refer to comprehensive strategies and tools implemented by marketers to seamlessly integrate and coordinate various channels and touchpoints of their marketing campaigns, with the aim of delivering a consistent and personalized customer experience across all interactions.

These solutions recognize that consumers today engage with brands through multiple channels, such as websites, social media, email, physical stores, mobile apps, and more. The goal is to provide a unified and cohesive brand experience regardless of whether a customer is browsing online, visiting a store, or using a mobile device.

The key elements of omnichannel marketing solutions include:

1. Integration: The ability to synchronize and connect data, content, and campaigns across all channels to ensure a seamless customer journey.

2. Personalization: The use of customer data and insights to deliver targeted and relevant messages, offers, and experiences to individuals based on their preferences, behaviors, and past interactions.

3. Cross-channel consistency: Ensuring a consistent brand identity, messaging, and experience across all channels, enabling customers to easily recognize and understand the brand regardless of where they interact.

4. Flexibility and adaptability: The ability to adapt marketing strategies and tactics to new channels and technologies as they emerge, ensuring that the brand stays relevant and accessible to customers.

Omnichannel marketing solutions can improve customer satisfaction, engagement, and loyalty by providing a seamless and convenient experience. They also enable marketers to track and measure the effectiveness of their campaigns across different channels, optimizing their marketing efforts and maximizing ROI.

Omnichannel Marketing Strategies

Omnichannel marketing strategies refer to a comprehensive approach used by businesses to create a seamless and integrated customer experience across multiple channels and touchpoints. In the field of marketing management, this strategy involves leveraging various marketing channels, such as online platforms, social media, mobile apps, physical stores, and email, to engage with customers and provide a consistent brand message.

Under the omnichannel marketing approach, companies aim to deliver a unified and personalized customer experience irrespective of the channel or device being used. This means ensuring that customers receive consistent information, promotions, and customer service, regardless of whether they interact with the brand through a physical store, a website, or a mobile app.

The implementation of omnichannel marketing strategies requires careful integration and synchronization of various channels, customer data, and messaging. By successfully implementing this approach, businesses can enhance customer satisfaction, loyalty, and overall engagement. Moreover, omnichannel marketing enables companies to track and analyze customer behavior across different touchpoints, which can provide valuable insights for targeted marketing campaigns and personalized experiences.

In summary, omnichannel marketing strategies are vital in marketing management as they allow businesses to create a connected and holistic customer experience across multiple channels. By leveraging various platforms and ensuring consistency in messaging and service, companies can enhance customer satisfaction, build brand loyalty, and drive business growth in today's increasingly digital and interconnected world.

Omnichannel Marketing

Omnichannel marketing refers to a marketing strategy that focuses on delivering a consistent and seamless experience across multiple channels and touchpoints. It involves integrating different marketing channels, such as online and offline platforms, to provide customers with a unified and holistic experience.

In the context of marketing management, omnichannel marketing recognizes that consumers nowadays interact with brands through various channels, including social media, websites, brick-and-mortar stores, mobile apps, and more. It emphasizes the need for businesses to establish a strong presence across these channels and ensure that each interaction aligns with the brand's overall message and values.

Omnichannel Retailing

Omnichannel retailing refers to a marketing strategy that integrates various channels to provide a seamless and consistent shopping experience for consumers. It involves the coordination and integration of different marketing channels, such as physical stores, e-commerce websites, mobile apps, social media platforms, and call centers, into a unified and interconnected system.

The goal of omnichannel retailing is to enable customers to engage with a brand or retailer through multiple touchpoints and have a consistent experience across all channels. It focuses on bridging the gap between offline and online channels, allowing consumers to switch between different channels at any stage of their shopping journey without any disruption.

Online Advertising Auction Insights Tools

An online advertising auction insights tool is a marketing management tool that provides businesses with valuable information and analysis on online advertising auction activities. It helps businesses understand their competition's advertising strategies, bidding behavior, and overall performance in online advertising auctions.

Using an online advertising auction insights tool, businesses can gather insights and data about the online advertising landscape, including the number of advertisers competing for the same keywords or audience, the average position of competitors in search results, the overlap between their ads and their competitors' ads, and the impression share of each competitor.

Online Advertising Auction Insights

Online advertising auction insights refer to the analysis and evaluation of data obtained from

214

online advertising auctions to gain competitive intelligence and inform marketing strategies. In the context of marketing management, online advertising auctions are virtual marketplaces where advertisers bid for ad space or impressions on websites, search engines, or social media platforms.

The insights obtained from these auctions provide valuable information about the advertising strategies and performance of competitors. This data can include information such as the types of ads being bid on, the bid prices, ad placement positions, and the overall competitiveness of the market. Analyzing these insights helps marketers understand the advertising landscape, identify trends, and make informed decisions about their own advertising campaigns.

By examining online advertising auction insights, marketing managers can gain a deeper understanding of competitor tactics, identify opportunities to differentiate their own campaigns, and optimize their bidding strategies to achieve better results. These insights can inform various aspects of marketing management, including budget allocation, audience targeting, messaging, and channel selection.

Overall, online advertising auction insights are a vital tool for marketing managers in today's digital advertising landscape. They provide critical information about competitors' activities and industry trends, enabling marketers to make data-driven decisions that enhance their advertising effectiveness and competitive advantage.

Online Advertising Auctions

An online advertising auction is a process in which advertisers bid for the opportunity to display their ads on a publisher's website or app. It is a key component of programmatic advertising, which uses automated technology to buy and sell advertising space in real-time.

During an online advertising auction, advertisers submit their bids through a demand-side platform (DSP), which is a software platform that helps them manage their campaigns. The DSP takes into account various factors such as the targeting criteria, the bid amount, and the ad's relevance to the audience. These factors help determine the ad's rank or position in the auction.

Once all the bids are submitted, the auction takes place in milliseconds, and the winning ad is selected based on the highest bid and other factors. The winning ad is then displayed on the publisher's website or app, typically in the form of a banner, video, or native ad.

Online advertising auctions provide benefits to both advertisers and publishers. Advertisers can reach their target audience more effectively by participating in real-time auctions and gaining access to valuable ad inventory. Publishers, on the other hand, can maximize their revenue by selling their ad space to the highest bidder.

Online Community Engagement Platforms

Online community engagement platforms refer to digital tools and platforms that facilitate and enhance customer interactions in the online space. These platforms provide a virtual environment where individuals can connect, share information, and engage with each other, ultimately building a sense of community.

Within the context of marketing management, online community engagement platforms are crucial for brands to develop and maintain relationships with their target audience. These platforms enable companies to foster two-way communication with customers, strengthening brand loyalty, and increasing customer engagement. By providing a space for customers to interact with each other and with the brand, these platforms create opportunities for businesses to gather valuable insights, generate authentic user-generated content, and drive customer conversions and sales.

Online Community Engagement Strategies

Online community engagement strategies in the context of Marketing Management discipline refer to the tactics and techniques used by businesses to engage and interact with their target audience online. This involves building and nurturing an online community, which includes customers, fans, followers, and other stakeholders who are interested in the brand and its offerings.

These strategies aim to create a sense of belonging and participation within the online community by encouraging active involvement, collaboration, and sharing of ideas. Businesses leverage various digital platforms and tools such as social media, forums, blogs, and online communities to facilitate this engagement. The ultimate goal is to build strong relationships with customers, enhance brand loyalty, and drive business growth.

One key aspect of online community engagement strategies is content creation and dissemination. By producing relevant and valuable content, businesses can attract and retain the attention of their target audience. This content can take the form of blog posts, articles, videos, infographics, and other forms of multimedia.

Moreover, these strategies emphasize the importance of two-way communication between businesses and their online community. This includes responding to customer queries, addressing concerns, and acknowledging feedback in a timely manner. By actively engaging and listening to their audience, businesses gain valuable insights and can make improvements to their products, services, and overall customer experience.

Additionally, online community engagement strategies often involve organizing and promoting events such as webinars, live chats, and Q&A sessions to facilitate real-time interactions and foster a sense of community. These events provide opportunities for businesses to showcase their expertise, connect with customers, and create memorable experiences.

Overall, online community engagement strategies are essential in today's digital landscape, as they help businesses foster meaningful connections, drive customer loyalty, and cultivate a favorable brand image.

Online Community Engagement

Online Community Engagement refers to the strategic efforts taken by businesses and organizations to interact and build relationships with their target audience through online platforms. It involves the use of various online channels such as social media, forums, blogs, and online communities to connect, communicate, and engage with customers, stakeholders, and potential consumers.

In the context of Marketing Management, online community engagement plays a crucial role in enhancing brand awareness, building brand loyalty, and fostering customer relationships. It goes beyond traditional one-way marketing communication and focuses on nurturing a sense of community and shared interests among the target audience.

By participating in online communities and engaging in meaningful conversations, businesses can gain insights into customer needs, preferences, and opinions. This information can be utilized to customize marketing strategies, develop products or services that align with customer expectations, and provide relevant and personalized content to the target audience.

Furthermore, online community engagement allows companies to establish themselves as industry leaders and trusted sources of information. By actively participating and sharing valuable knowledge and expertise, businesses can solidify their position as thought leaders and influencers within their respective domains.

Overall, implementing effective online community engagement strategies can help businesses forge strong connections with their target audience, foster brand advocacy, increase customer loyalty, and ultimately drive business growth and success in the digital era.

Online Community

An online community refers to a group of individuals who come together and interact with each other through digital platforms, typically with shared interests, goals, or values. It is a valuable tool in the field of marketing management as it offers businesses the opportunity to engage with their target audience, build relationships, and enhance brand recognition.

In the context of marketing management, an online community acts as a virtual hub where customers, prospects, and brand advocates can connect and engage with a company or its products. It provides a space for users to share their opinions, experiences, and feedback, allowing businesses to gather valuable insights to improve their offerings and customer experience.

By actively participating in online communities, businesses can nurture and strengthen customer relationships. They can address customer queries, provide support, and offer personalized recommendations, fostering a sense of trust and loyalty among the community members. This not only helps in maintaining customer satisfaction but also generates positive word-of-mouth marketing, leading to potential new customers.

Furthermore, online communities can act as a platform for businesses to showcase their thought leadership and expertise. By sharing valuable content, insights, and industry trends, businesses can position themselves as authoritative figures in their field, attracting potential customers and establishing themselves as industry leaders.

Overall, an online community provides marketing management professionals with a unique opportunity to engage, connect, and build relationships with their target audience. It allows businesses to gather insights, strengthen customer relationships, and position themselves as industry leaders, ultimately contributing to the success of their marketing efforts.

Online Marketing

Online marketing, also known as digital marketing or internet marketing, refers to the strategic planning, execution, and analysis of marketing efforts using various online platforms and technologies. It is an integral part of the Marketing Management discipline, focusing specifically on online channels and tactics to promote products, services, or brands to a targeted audience.

The primary objective of online marketing is to drive traffic, generate leads, and convert prospects into customers using digital channels such as websites, search engines, email, social media, and online advertising. It encompasses a wide range of activities, including search engine optimization (SEO), pay-per-click (PPC) advertising, content marketing, social media marketing, email marketing, mobile marketing, and analytics.

Online marketing enables marketers to reach a global audience, targeting individuals based on their demographics, interests, behaviors, and preferences. It allows for personalized and tailored marketing campaigns, as well as real-time interaction and measurement of results. Through effective online marketing strategies, businesses can increase brand visibility, engage with customers, improve customer acquisition and retention, and ultimately drive revenue growth.

Successful implementation of online marketing requires a deep understanding of target markets, competitors, and industry trends. It involves developing a comprehensive digital marketing plan, identifying key performance indicators (KPIs), deploying appropriate tools and technologies, and continually monitoring, analyzing, and optimizing marketing campaigns to maximize return on investment (ROI).

Online Reputation Management (ORM)

Online Reputation Management (ORM) refers to the practice of managing and influencing the perception of a brand or an individual on the internet. It involves monitoring and addressing any content or comments that may be harmful to the reputation of the brand or individual, and proactively working to enhance and promote a positive online image.

In the context of the Marketing Management discipline, ORM plays a crucial role in building and maintaining a strong brand image. With the increasing prevalence of online platforms and social media, consumers have greater access to information and are more likely to form opinions based on what they find online. Therefore, managing and shaping the online perception of a brand or individual is of utmost importance in influencing consumer decision-making and maintaining a competitive edge.

Online Reputation

Online reputation refers to the overall perception and portrayal of a brand, organization, or individual on the internet. It is the collective impression that people develop based on their online interactions, reviews, comments, and experiences with a particular entity.

The management of online reputation in the context of marketing involves actively monitoring and influencing how a brand is perceived online in order to build and maintain a positive image. This requires implementing strategies and tactics that aim to shape public opinion, address negative feedback, and enhance the overall online presence.

Effective online reputation management involves several key elements. Firstly, it requires listening to and monitoring online conversations and feedback about the brand in order to gain insights into how it is perceived. By understanding public sentiment and identifying potential issues or concerns, marketers can proactively respond and address any negative sentiment or misinformation that may arise.

Secondly, online reputation management focuses on creating and distributing valuable and engaging content that reflects the brand's values, expertise, and offerings. This can be done through various online channels such as social media platforms, websites, blogs, and online review platforms.

Thirdly, it involves engaging with the online community by responding to comments, reviews, and inquiries in a prompt and professional manner. This demonstrates a commitment to customer satisfaction and can help mitigate any negative feedback or misunderstandings that may occur.

In conclusion, online reputation management is an essential component of marketing management. It involves actively shaping and maintaining a positive perception of a brand, organization, or individual by monitoring online conversations, creating valuable content, and engaging with the online community. By effectively managing online reputation, marketers can enhance brand perception, build trust, and ultimately drive customer loyalty and business growth.

Organic Search Results

The term "organic search results" refers to the listings of web pages that appear in a search engine's results page naturally, without any paid advertising. These results are determined by the search engine's algorithm and are ranked based on their relevance to the user's search query.

In the context of marketing management, organic search results are an essential aspect of search engine optimization (SEO) strategies. SEO aims to improve a website's visibility and ranking in organic search results, driving more traffic to the site.

Outbound Marketing

Outbound marketing is a traditional marketing approach that involves businesses reaching out and initiating contact with potential customers through various channels, such as advertising, telemarketing, direct mail, and email campaigns. Unlike inbound marketing, which focuses on attracting customers through content creation and engagement, outbound marketing relies on interrupting the audience's attention with sales messages to generate awareness, interest, and action.

This marketing strategy aims to cast a wide net and target a large audience, relying on mass media and widespread communication to reach as many potential customers as possible. It often involves paid advertising efforts, such as TV and radio commercials, print advertisements, billboards, and online banners. Additionally, outbound marketing includes direct sales efforts, such as cold calling, door-to-door sales, and trade show exhibitions.

The effectiveness of outbound marketing largely depends on the specific target audience and the message's relevancy and timing. Successful outbound marketing campaigns typically employ methods that are tailored to the audience's preferences, interests, and needs. Moreover, measuring and tracking the response and conversion rates of outbound marketing initiatives is crucial for evaluating their success and optimizing future campaigns.

In recent years, outbound marketing has faced challenges due to changing consumer behaviors and preferences. As customers have become increasingly resistant to intrusive marketing messages, businesses have shifted towards more personalized and targeted marketing tactics. However, outbound marketing can still be an effective strategy for businesses aiming to create brand awareness, reach a wide audience, and drive immediate sales or conversions.

Outbound Sales

Outbound sales, in the context of marketing management, refers to a proactive approach where sales representatives initiate contact with potential customers or leads in order to generate sales and drive revenue for an organization.

Unlike inbound sales, which involves attracting leads through various marketing initiatives and waiting for them to express interest, outbound sales involves actively reaching out to prospects through methods such as cold calling, email campaigns, social media outreach, and direct mail. The primary objective of outbound sales is to engage with potential customers, identify their needs, and persuade them to make a purchase or take a desired action.

Effective outbound sales strategies require a deep understanding of the target market, as well as the ability to personalize and tailor messages to the needs and interests of individual prospects. Sales representatives may use market research, customer segmentation, and data analysis to identify high-potential leads and develop targeted sales pitches.

Outbound sales can be highly effective in industries where proactive outreach plays a crucial role in securing sales, such as B2B (business-to-business) sales or high-value items with long sales cycles. However, it is important to note that outbound sales can be time-consuming and resource-intensive, requiring a skilled and persistent sales team to achieve desired results.

Owned Media

Owned media refers to the digital properties that a company or brand owns and has control over. In the context of marketing management, owned media encompasses the various online platforms and channels that a company uses to communicate and engage with its target audience.

This can include websites, blogs, social media profiles, mobile apps, and email marketing campaigns. These digital assets are unique to the brand and act as a direct communication channel between the company and its customers. Unlike earned or paid media, owned media allows companies to have full control over the content, messaging, and branding.

Paid Advertising

Paid advertising refers to a marketing strategy that involves paying a fee to display promotional content or messages to a specific audience or target market. This form of advertising is typically conducted through various channels such as television, radio, print media, outdoor billboards, and digital platforms.

In marketing management, paid advertising plays a crucial role in promoting products, services, or brands to a wider audience, ultimately aiming to increase sales and generate revenue. It allows businesses to reach potential customers who may not be aware of their offerings or be actively seeking their products or services.

Paid Media Campaign Optimization Tools

Paid media campaign optimization tools refer to the various software and technologies that aid marketing managers in maximizing the effectiveness and efficiency of their paid advertising campaigns. These tools provide data-driven insights and analysis to help optimize various aspects of the campaign, such as targeting, budget allocation, and messaging, in order to achieve the desired marketing objectives.

These tools offer features and functionalities that enable marketing managers to track and measure the performance of their campaigns, including key metrics such as click-through rates (CTR), conversion rates, and return on investment (ROI). They provide real-time data and analytics that allow for ongoing monitoring and optimization, as well as the ability to make informed decisions and adjustments to campaign strategies in response to changing market conditions or audience behaviors.

Paid Media Campaign Optimization

Paid media campaign optimization refers to the process of improving the effectiveness and efficiency of a marketing campaign that involves paid advertising across various media channels. It is a critical component of marketing management, as it allows businesses to maximize their return on investment (ROI) and achieve their marketing objectives.

During the optimization process, marketers analyze the performance of their paid media campaigns using key performance indicators (KPIs) such as click-through rates, conversion rates, and cost per acquisition. By closely monitoring these metrics, marketers can identify areas of improvement and implement necessary adjustments to enhance campaign performance.

Paid Media Campaigns

Paid media campaigns, in the context of marketing management, refer to advertising efforts that involve paying for the placement and distribution of promotional content across various channels. These campaigns are typically a part of a company's overall marketing strategy and are intended to reach a specific target audience, drive brand awareness, increase customer engagement, and ultimately, generate sales or other desired outcomes.

Unlike earned or owned media, which are obtained organically or through owned channels, paid media campaigns require a financial investment to ensure that the promotional content reaches a wider audience and is displayed in relevant spaces. Examples of paid media channels include search engine advertising, social media advertising, display advertising, sponsored content, influencer marketing, and email marketing.

Paid Media

Paid media refers to a marketing strategy used by organizations where they pay for advertising space or time on various platforms to promote their products or services. This method involves the creation and distribution of paid advertisements across different channels, such as television, radio, print media, online banners, search engines, and social media platforms.

The objective of using paid media is to increase brand visibility and reach a larger target audience. By investing in paid media, businesses can place their advertisements in front of potential customers who may not be aware of their products or services. This can help to generate leads, increase website traffic, and ultimately drive sales.

Paid Search Advertising

Paid search advertising, also known as Pay-per-click (PPC) advertising, is a strategic marketing technique in which businesses pay a fee to search engines or online advertisers each time their advertisement is clicked. It is a cost-effective approach that allows businesses to drive targeted traffic to their website or landing page by displaying paid ads within search engine results. The primary objective of paid search advertising is to increase brand visibility, generate leads, and drive conversions by placing ads in front of users who are actively searching for specific products or services. This form of online advertising enables businesses to directly target their potential customers based on keywords, demographics, location, and other relevant factors. Paid search ads typically appear at the top of search engine results pages (SERPs) with a small tag indicating their sponsored status. These ads are specifically designed to blend in with organic search results, seamlessly integrating into the user's search experience. The search engine's algorithm determines the positioning of paid ads based on various factors, including bid amount, ad relevance, and click-through rates. To effectively implement paid search advertising, businesses must conduct thorough keyword research to identify keywords and phrases that resonate with their target audience. By bidding on these keywords, businesses can secure ad placements, ensuring their ads are displayed when users search for related terms. The success of paid search advertising campaigns relies heavily on monitoring and optimizing performance. Marketers must continually analyze key metrics such as click-through rate (CTR), conversion rate, cost per click (CPC), and return on ad spend (ROAS) to identify areas for improvement and refine their strategies. Overall, paid search advertising is a valuable marketing tool that allows businesses to enhance their online visibility, drive targeted traffic, and achieve measurable results in terms of brand exposure, lead generation, and conversions.

Participatory Marketing

Participatory marketing, also known as engagement marketing or co-creation marketing, is a concept in the field of marketing management that focuses on involving customers and other stakeholders in the marketing process. It is based on the idea of mutual collaboration and active engagement between the company and its target audience.

In participatory marketing, companies seek to empower their customers by giving them a voice and involving them in various marketing activities. This can include soliciting feedback, encouraging customer-generated content, inviting customers to co-create products or services, and involving them in decision-making processes. By doing so, companies aim to establish a sense of community and foster a deeper level of engagement and loyalty among their customers.

Partner Marketing Program Management Software

A partner marketing program management software is a tool used in the field of marketing management that enables businesses to effectively manage and track their partner marketing initiatives. Partner marketing refers to the collaboration between a company and its external partners, such as resellers, distributors, or affiliates, to promote and sell products or services.

This software provides a centralized platform where businesses can create, monitor, and manage their partner marketing programs. It allows companies to easily onboard partners, set up promotional campaigns, and track the performance of each partner in real-time.

With partner marketing program management software, businesses can efficiently allocate marketing resources, collaborate with partners, and monitor the success of their marketing initiatives. The software typically offers features such as partner enablement tools, lead tracking and management, campaign scheduling, performance analytics, and reporting capabilities.

By using this software, businesses can streamline their partner marketing efforts and improve overall efficiency. It helps companies optimize their marketing strategies, identify successful partnerships, and make data-driven decisions to drive sales and revenue growth.

In summary, a partner marketing program management software is a valuable tool for businesses engaged in partner marketing, providing them with the necessary features and functionality to effectively manage, track, and optimize their partner marketing programs.

Partner Marketing Program Management

Partner Marketing Program Management is a crucial aspect of Marketing Management that focuses on the planning, execution, and evaluation of collaborative marketing initiatives between a company and its partners.

It involves developing and implementing strategies to establish and maintain strong relationships with strategic partners, such as distributors, retailers, resellers, and other relevant stakeholders. The primary objective of Partner Marketing Program Management is to leverage the combined strengths and resources of both parties to achieve mutual marketing and business goals.

The process starts with identifying potential partners who share similar target markets and have complementary products or services. Once partners have been identified, the Program Manager works closely with them to define the scope and objectives of the marketing program. This includes setting clear objectives, outlining the roles and responsibilities of each partner, identifying key performance indicators, and establishing a timeline for execution.

The next step involves the creation and implementation of collaborative marketing plans. These plans often include joint advertising campaigns, co-branded marketing materials, and co-hosted events, among others. Partner Marketing Program Managers are responsible for coordinating the various activities, ensuring consistent messaging and branding, and tracking the performance of each initiative.

Lastly, Program Managers evaluate the success of the partner marketing programs by analyzing key metrics such as sales revenue, customer acquisition, and brand awareness. They use this data to identify areas for improvement and make necessary adjustments for future programs.

Partner Marketing Programs

Partner Marketing Programs are strategic initiatives developed by organizations to collaborate with external partners in order to drive mutual business growth and achieve marketing objectives. These programs involve the joint efforts and resources of two or more companies, typically operating in complementary industries or markets.

The primary goal of Partner Marketing Programs is to leverage the strengths and capabilities of both organizations to create a mutually beneficial partnership that enhances brand reputation, increases customer reach, and drives revenue generation. Through these programs, companies can tap into the expertise and customer base of their partners, allowing them to expand their market presence and gain a competitive edge.

Partner Marketing Programs often involve various activities, which may include joint advertising and promotional campaigns, co-branded marketing materials, collaborative product development, shared customer data and insights, and referral partnerships. These initiatives are typically guided by a formal agreement or contract that outlines the roles, responsibilities, and expectations of each partner.

Effective management of Partner Marketing Programs requires careful planning, coordination, and ongoing communication between the partnering organizations. Success hinges on establishing clear objectives, aligning marketing strategies, and ensuring a mutually beneficial value proposition for all parties involved.

In conclusion, Partner Marketing Programs play a crucial role in marketing management by enabling organizations to leverage the strengths and resources of external partners to enhance brand reputation, expand market reach, and drive revenue. By fostering collaboration and strategic alliances, companies can achieve greater success in a competitive marketplace.

Pay-Per-Call Advertising

Pay-Per-Call advertising is a marketing strategy where advertisers pay for each phone call generated by their ad campaign. It is a form of performance-based advertising that aims to generate leads and drive sales by encouraging consumers to contact the company directly through a phone call.

In Pay-Per-Call advertising, advertisers typically create ads with a unique phone number that is associated with a specific campaign. These ads are displayed on various marketing channels such as websites, search engines, social media platforms, or mobile apps. When consumers see the ad and are interested in the product or service being promoted, they can directly call the provided phone number.

The cost of Pay-Per-Call advertising is determined based on the number of completed phone calls or the duration of the calls. Advertisers only pay when a call is completed, ensuring that they only pay for actual lead generation. The cost per call can vary depending on factors such as the target audience, the industry, and the competitiveness of the market.

Pay-Per-Call advertising offers several benefits to advertisers. It allows them to track and measure the effectiveness of their advertising campaigns in real-time. By monitoring the number of phone calls generated and analyzing the call data, advertisers can optimize their campaigns and make data-driven marketing decisions.

Overall, Pay-Per-Call advertising provides a highly targeted and measurable marketing approach that can drive high-quality leads and increase conversion rates for businesses.

Perceived Value

Perceived value refers to the subjective assessment of a product or service's worth or usefulness in the eyes of consumers. It is a key concept in marketing management that focuses on understanding how customers perceive and evaluate the benefits and costs associated with a product or service.

Perceived value is influenced by various factors, including the product's attributes, the customer's needs and preferences, and their past experiences with similar products or services. It is not solely determined by the actual features or benefits of the product itself, but rather by how customers perceive those features and benefits.

In marketing management, the goal is to create and deliver products or services that provide a high perceived value to customers. This is because customers are more likely to purchase products or services that they perceive as valuable. Additionally, a higher perceived value can also help a company differentiate itself from competitors and command premium prices.

To enhance perceived value, marketers must understand the needs and preferences of their target customers and ensure that their products or services meet or exceed those expectations. This can be achieved through various strategies, such as improving product quality, offering superior customer service, providing personalized experiences, and effectively communicating the benefits and advantages of the product or service.

Perceptual Mapping

Perceptual mapping is a strategic marketing tool used to visually represent consumers' perceptions of brands, products, or attributes. This technique helps marketers gain valuable insights into how their target audience perceives different offerings and identify positioning opportunities.

The process of perceptual mapping involves creating a visual representation of consumers' perceptions based on their ratings or evaluations of specific product attributes. These attributes can include quality, price, design, performance, and others that are relevant to the market. The mapping is typically represented as a two-dimensional graph, with each axis representing a specific attribute or dimension.

By plotting different products or brands on the map, marketers can understand how they are positioned in the minds of consumers relative to their competitors. This knowledge enables marketers to identify gaps in the market and develop effective positioning strategies to differentiate their offerings.

Perceptual mapping also helps marketers evaluate consumers' ideal or desired brand positions, enabling them to align their brand positioning strategies accordingly. It can further aid in identifying potential target segments that have specific preferences or needs, allowing for more focused targeting and tailored marketing campaigns.

Overall, perceptual mapping provides marketers with a visual representation of consumers' perceptions, allowing them to better understand their target audience and make informed marketing decisions. By uncovering positioning opportunities and gaining insights into consumers' preferences, marketers can develop effective strategies to attract and retain customers in today's competitive marketplace.

Performance Marketing

Performance marketing is a marketing approach that focuses on the measurable performance of marketing campaigns and initiatives. It is a disciplined and data-driven approach that aims to maximize the return on investment (ROI) through various marketing activities.

In performance marketing, marketers set specific and measurable objectives, such as generating leads, increasing sales, or driving website traffic. These objectives are then tracked and analyzed to evaluate the effectiveness of different marketing strategies and tactics.

Performance marketing relies on data and analytics to inform decision-making and optimize marketing efforts. Marketers use various tools and technologies to track key performance indicators (KPIs) and evaluate the success of their campaigns. By closely monitoring the performance of different marketing channels and tactics, marketers can make data-driven adjustments to improve results and achieve their marketing goals.

Performance marketing is often associated with digital marketing channels, such as search engine marketing (SEM), display advertising, social media advertising, and affiliate marketing. These channels provide opportunities for precise targeting, real-time tracking, and performance measurement.

In summary, performance marketing is a results-focused approach to marketing that emphasizes measurable outcomes and data-driven decision-making. By continuously monitoring and optimizing campaigns, marketers can maximize the effectiveness and efficiency of their marketing efforts.

Permission Marketing

Permission marketing is a marketing strategy that focuses on obtaining the consent of consumers before delivering marketing messages. It aims to build and nurture long-term relationships with customers based on trust and relevance.

In permission marketing, marketers seek permission from consumers to engage with them through various channels such as email, social media, and mobile notifications. This voluntary opt-in process allows marketers to send targeted and personalized messages to individuals who have explicitly expressed interest in their products or services. By obtaining permission, marketers ensure that their messages are welcomed and appreciated by consumers, increasing the likelihood of positive engagement.

This approach differs from traditional interruption marketing, where advertisements are pushed onto consumers without their consent or desire. Permission marketing recognizes that consumers are overwhelmed with information and provides them with the power to choose which brand communications they receive.

Implementing permission marketing requires a deep understanding of the customer's preferences and interests. Marketers must create compelling offers and incentives to entice consumers to grant permission. They must also deliver valuable and relevant content to maintain engagement and build trust over time. This approach fosters loyalty and advocacy among customers, as they feel appreciated and respected by the brand.

Persona-Based Marketing Approaches

Persona-based marketing approaches are a strategic approach to marketing management that focuses on creating and targeting specific consumer personas or profiles. These personas are fictional representations of ideal customers that are created based on data and insights about their demographics, behaviors, motivations, and goals.

By understanding the unique needs and preferences of each persona, marketers can develop personalized marketing strategies and tactics that effectively resonate with and engage their target audience. This approach allows marketers to tailor their messaging, content, and offers to better meet the needs and desires of each persona, increasing the likelihood of generating leads, driving conversions, and building customer loyalty.

Persona-Based Marketing Tools

Persona-Based Marketing Tools refer to a set of strategies and techniques used by marketing professionals to identify, understand, and target specific market segments based on consumer personas.

Consumer personas are fictional representations of target customers that are created using extensive research and analysis. These personas include demographic information, behavioral patterns, goals, needs, and pain points of the target audience. Persona-based marketing tools help marketers gather and analyze data to develop these personas.

These tools include various data collection methods, such as surveys, interviews, and analytics, to gather insights into consumer behavior and preferences. Market research and segmentation tools are used to identify distinct market segments and create personas based on common characteristics and behaviors.

Persona-based marketing tools also enable marketers to personalize their marketing campaigns based on these personas. They help in tailoring marketing messages, developing relevant content, and selecting appropriate channels to reach target customers effectively.

By using persona-based marketing tools, marketers can better understand their customers, target their marketing efforts more efficiently, and improve overall customer satisfaction. These tools aid in creating customer-centric marketing strategies, enhancing customer engagement and loyalty, and ultimately driving business growth.

Persona-Based Marketing

Persona-based marketing is a strategic approach used in the field of marketing management to understand and target specific consumer groups based on their characteristics, preferences, and behavior patterns. It involves creating fictional personas that represent different segments of a target audience in order to personalize marketing strategies and messages.

These personas are developed through data analysis, market research, and customer insights. By identifying common demographic, psychographic, and behavioral traits among customers, marketers can create detailed profiles that help them understand the needs, motivations, and pain points of different customer segments.

This approach allows marketing teams to tailor their messaging, content, and promotional activities to resonate with each persona and effectively address their unique needs and preferences. By understanding the specific challenges, preferences, and goals of different personas, marketers can develop targeted marketing campaigns that are more likely to engage and convert the desired audience.

The persona-based marketing approach also helps marketers improve customer acquisition and retention by allowing them to prioritize resources and efforts on the most valuable customer segments. By focusing on the personas that align best with their product or service offerings, marketers can optimize their marketing tactics and allocate resources efficiently.

Point-Of-Purchase (POP) Display Platforms

Point-of-Purchase (POP) Display Platforms refer to marketing tools used by businesses to attract and influence consumers at the point of purchase, typically in retail settings. These platforms are strategically designed to showcase products and promotional messages in a visually appealing manner, with the aim of increasing impulse purchases and overall sales.

POP display platforms can take various forms, such as standalone displays, shelves, racks, or signage, and are strategically positioned within the retail environment to capture the attention of shoppers. They are often placed near checkout counters, end-caps, or high traffic areas to maximize visibility and engagement. These platforms effectively communicate the value proposition of a product as well as any special offers, discounts, or incentives, ultimately influencing purchasing decisions.

Point-Of-Purchase (POP) Display Strategies

Point-of-Purchase (POP) display strategies refer to the various techniques and approaches used by marketing managers to create compelling displays at the point of sale to attract customers and increase sales. These strategies involve the careful selection, arrangement, and presentation of products within a retail environment to grab the attention of shoppers and influence their purchase decisions.

Marketing managers utilize POP display strategies to create visually appealing and impactful displays that effectively communicate the value proposition of the products being offered. These strategies involve elements such as product placement, signage, graphics, lighting, and overall store layout and design. The goal is to create a desirable shopping experience that engages customers and encourages them to make impulsive or planned purchases.

Effective POP display strategies take into consideration various factors including the target market, product characteristics, store layout, and customer behavior. They are designed to capitalize on the psychology of consumers, leveraging factors such as color, positioning, and product grouping to create a sense of urgency, exclusivity, or convenience. By strategically placing popular or high-margin products near checkout counters or entrances, for example, marketing managers can increase the likelihood of impulse buys.

Furthermore, POP display strategies often incorporate promotional elements such as discounts, offers, or samples to generate interest and incentivize immediate purchases. These displays may be themed around specific events, seasons, or holidays to enhance relevance and appeal to customers' needs and preferences.

In summary, point-of-purchase display strategies are a fundamental aspect of marketing management that involve utilizing visual merchandising techniques to create attention-grabbing displays in retail environments. These strategies aim to engage customers, increase sales, and enhance brand visibility by strategically arranging and presenting products in an enticing and persuasive manner.

Point-Of-Purchase (POP) Displays

Point-of-Purchase (POP) displays, also known as in-store displays, are marketing tools used by retailers to attract and engage customers at the place where products are being sold. These displays are strategically placed near the checkout counter or other highly trafficked areas within a store to draw attention to specific products or promotions.

POP displays are typically designed to showcase a single product or a group of related products, with the goal of increasing sales and influencing purchasing decisions. They are often eye-catching and visually appealing, utilizing various design elements such as bold colors, unique shapes, and compelling graphics to capture customers' attention. POP displays can be temporary or permanent, depending on the length of the promotional campaign or the specific product being featured.

Positioning Statement

A positioning statement is a concise statement that communicates the unique value and positioning of a product or brand in the market. It is typically used in marketing management to guide the development of marketing strategies and tactics.

The positioning statement articulates the key benefits and attributes of the product or brand, and highlights the target market segment or audience that it is intended to serve. It answers the question of "what sets us apart from competitors?" by identifying the specific characteristics and values that differentiate the product or brand. This statement also helps to align the marketing efforts across different channels and touchpoints, ensuring a consistent and cohesive message is delivered to the target audience.

The positioning statement is developed through a combination of market research, competitor analysis, and internal reflection. It requires a deep understanding of the target market, including their needs, preferences, and behaviors. It also involves evaluating the competitive landscape to identify gaps and opportunities for differentiation.

Once the positioning statement is defined, it serves as a guiding principle for the marketing team to develop and execute marketing strategies that effectively communicate the unique value proposition to the target market. It informs decisions on product design and development, pricing, distribution, and promotion.

In summary, a positioning statement is a concise statement that communicates the unique value and positioning of a product or brand in the market. It guides the development of marketing strategies and tactics, and helps differentiate the product or brand from competitors. It ensures a consistent and cohesive message is delivered to the target audience, and informs decisions on product, pricing, distribution, and promotion.

Positioning Strategy

Positioning strategy refers to the process of creating a distinct and favorable perception of a product or brand in the minds of the target market. It involves developing a unique and compelling position for a product that sets it apart from competitors and meets the needs and desires of the target customers. The goal of positioning strategy is to establish a differentiated and meaningful position in the market that resonates with the target audience and influences their purchasing decisions.

There are several key elements to consider when developing a positioning strategy. Firstly, it is important to clearly define the target market and understand their needs, preferences, and behaviors. This information forms the foundation for determining the unique value proposition that the product can offer to the target customers. Secondly, competitive analysis is crucial to identify the strengths and weaknesses of competitors and identify opportunities for differentiation.

Once the target market and competitive landscape have been analyzed, marketers can develop a positioning statement that succinctly communicates the unique and compelling position of the product. This statement should address the target market, the product category, the key points of differentiation, and the desired perception in the minds of the customers. Effective positioning statements are clear, concise, and memorable.

Positioning In Marketing

Positioning in marketing refers to the process of creating an image or perception of a product or brand in the minds of the target market. It involves establishing a unique and differentiated position for the product or brand in relation to competing offerings in the market.

The goal of positioning is to create a distinct and favorable perception of the product or brand in the minds of consumers, which sets it apart from competitors and makes it more appealing and desirable. This perception is created through a combination of marketing strategies, including the product's features and benefits, its pricing, distribution, and promotion.

Predictive Analytics In Marketing

Predictive analytics in marketing refers to the use of statistical models and algorithms to analyze and interpret data in order to predict future outcomes and trends for marketing campaigns and initiatives. It involves the application of advanced analytics techniques on historical data to gain insights and make data-driven decisions that drive marketing success.

By utilizing predictive analytics, marketing managers can leverage data from various sources such as customer demographics, past purchase behavior, online interactions, social media engagement, and more to forecast customer behavior, anticipate market changes, and optimize marketing strategies and tactics. This enables marketers to identify high-value customer segments, personalize marketing messages and offers, and allocate resources more effectively.

Predictive Analytics

Predictive analytics is a complex but highly valuable tool utilized within the realm of Marketing Management. It involves the use of advanced statistical techniques, data mining, and machine learning algorithms to analyze historical data and make predictions about future events and outcomes.

This powerful tool enables marketers to uncover meaningful patterns and trends within large datasets, allowing them to anticipate customer behavior, market trends, and the success of various marketing strategies. By employing predictive analytics, marketers can make more

227

informed decisions and develop targeted campaigns designed to maximize their return on investment.

Predictive Lead Scoring Models Software

Predictive lead scoring models software refers to a marketing management tool that uses data analytics and machine learning algorithms to predict the likelihood of a lead converting into a sales opportunity. This software evaluates a variety of factors and assigns a numeric score to each lead based on their potential to generate revenue.

The primary goal of predictive lead scoring models software is to help marketing teams prioritize leads and allocate resources effectively. By leveraging historical data and analyzing various attributes of leads, such as demographics, firmographics, online behavior, and engagement with marketing campaigns, this software identifies patterns and trends that are indicative of a lead's propensity to convert.

Typically, predictive lead scoring models software uses sophisticated statistical techniques like regression analysis, decision trees, and neural networks to build predictive models. These models are trained on historical data, and their performance is continuously evaluated and refined based on feedback from actual sales outcomes.

Once the predictive lead scoring models software has assigned scores to leads, marketing teams can prioritize their efforts and focus on the leads with the highest potential. This allows them to allocate resources efficiently, personalize marketing campaigns based on lead characteristics, and ultimately improve conversion rates and revenue generation.

Predictive Lead Scoring Models

Predictive Lead Scoring Models are statistical algorithms used in Marketing Management to determine the likelihood of a lead in converting into a sale or becoming a profitable customer. These models assist marketers in prioritizing leads and allocating resources effectively.

The models rely on historical data and machine learning algorithms to analyze various attributes of leads, including demographic information, past interactions, engagement levels, and buying behavior. By comparing these attributes with the outcomes of previously converted leads, the models assign a score or probability to each lead, indicating the likelihood of conversion.

Predictive Lead Scoring

Predictive lead scoring is a methodology used in the field of marketing management to prioritize and evaluate potential leads based on their likelihood of conversion. It leverages data-driven algorithms and machine learning techniques to analyze historical patterns and identify key characteristics and behaviors that are indicative of a lead's propensity to become a customer.

The process of predictive lead scoring involves the collection and integration of various types of data, such as demographic information, firmographics, web analytics, and customer engagement data. This data is then analyzed and transformed into a predictive model, which assigns a score or rank to each lead based on their likelihood to convert.

By implementing predictive lead scoring, marketing teams can better allocate their resources and focus on leads that are more likely to convert, increasing efficiency and maximizing return on investment. This methodology helps organizations to streamline their lead management process, enabling them to prioritize sales efforts, personalize marketing campaigns, and ultimately drive revenue growth.

Overall, predictive lead scoring is a powerful tool that enables marketing managers to make data-driven decisions, optimize lead nurturing strategies, and improve overall business performance.

Predictive Modeling

Predictive modeling, within the context of Marketing Management, refers to the use of statistical algorithms and machine learning techniques to forecast and predict future customer behavior, preferences, and trends. This approach enables marketers to make informed decisions, allocate resources effectively, and develop targeted strategies to maximize customer acquisition, retention, and loyalty.

By analyzing historical data and identifying patterns, predictive modeling helps marketers understand and anticipate customer needs and preferences. It leverages various data sources such as demographics, purchase history, browsing behavior, social media interactions, and other relevant customer data points to generate accurate predictions.

Through predictive modeling, marketers can segment their customer base, allowing them to tailor their marketing efforts to specific target groups. This personalized approach ensures that offers, promotions, and messages resonate with customers, resulting in higher conversion rates and increased customer satisfaction.

Additionally, predictive modeling enables marketers to optimize resource allocation by identifying which marketing channels and tactics are most likely to yield positive results. It facilitates effective budget planning, as marketers can determine the optimal investment for each campaign to maximize ROI.

In summary, predictive modeling in Marketing Management empowers marketers to leverage data-driven insights to proactively anticipate customer behavior, optimize marketing strategies, and enhance overall organizational performance.

Product Adoption Curve

The Product Adoption Curve refers to a marketing concept that illustrates the different stages of consumer acceptance and adoption of a new product or innovation.

According to the curve, potential customers can be categorized into five distinct groups based on their level of readiness to adopt a new product: innovators, early adopters, early majority, late majority, and laggards. Each group exhibits unique characteristics and behaviors towards the adoption process, which marketers can use to tailor their strategies.

Product Development

Product Development is the process of creating, designing, and introducing new products or improving existing products in response to consumer needs and market trends. In the field of Marketing Management, it is a vital strategic activity that helps companies stay competitive and meet customer demands.

Product Development involves various stages, including idea generation, market research, concept development, design, testing, and commercialization. Throughout these stages, companies gather insights from market research to understand consumer preferences, identify gaps in the market, and generate product ideas.

Once a viable concept is generated, companies begin the design and development process, which entails creating prototypes, conducting rigorous testing, and refining the product to meet quality standards and customer expectations. Marketing management plays a crucial role during this phase to ensure that the product aligns with market needs and company objectives.

After the product is developed and tested, companies must determine its market potential, pricing strategy, and positioning. They utilize various marketing techniques such as target market analysis, competitive analysis, and consumer behavior research to effectively position and launch the product in the market. Marketing management also plays a crucial role in developing marketing campaigns, promotional strategies, and distribution plans to reach the target market and generate sales.

In summary, product development in the context of marketing management is a strategic process of creating, designing, and introducing new or improved products that align with market demands and consumer preferences. It involves multiple stages of research, development, testing, and commercialization, and requires effective marketing strategies to ensure successful product launch and market positioning.

Product Differentiation

Product differentiation refers to the process of distinguishing a company's product or service from those of its competitors. It involves creating a distinct identity and positioning for the product in order to make it stand out in the market. This differentiation can be based on various factors such as product features, quality, design, functionality, packaging, branding, and customer service.

The main objective of product differentiation is to create a perceived value for the product that is unique and superior to alternative offerings. By highlighting the unique aspects of the product, companies aim to attract customers, build brand loyalty, and gain a competitive advantage. Product differentiation enables companies to charge higher prices, increase market share, and improve profitability.

Product Launch

A product launch refers to the process of introducing a new product to the market and making it available for purchase by consumers. This strategy is a crucial aspect of marketing management and involves various activities aimed at generating awareness, anticipation, and demand for the new product.

During a product launch, a marketing team utilizes a combination of promotional tactics, such as advertising, public relations, and digital marketing, to engage target customers and create a buzz around the product. This includes developing compelling marketing messages and branding strategies that highlight the unique features and benefits of the new product.

Product Life Cycle

Product life cycle refers to the various stages a product goes through from its introduction in the market until its decline and eventual discontinuation. It is a concept widely recognized in the field of marketing management, helping businesses understand and manage their products effectively throughout their lifespan.

The product life cycle consists of four distinct stages: introduction, growth, maturity, and decline. In the introduction stage, the product is launched into the market, and customer awareness and sales are low. Marketing efforts focus on creating product awareness and generating demand through advertising, promotions, and other marketing strategies.

In the growth stage, the product gains acceptance and sales begin to increase rapidly. Competitors may enter the market, and the company aims to expand its customer base by offering new features, enhancing product quality, or targeting different market segments.

The maturity stage is characterized by a plateau in sales growth, as the product reaches its maximum market penetration. Competition intensifies, and the company focuses on maintaining market share by enhancing customer loyalty, improving distribution channels, or introducing product extensions. Price promotions and advertising become important tools to combat competition.

The final stage of the product life cycle is decline, where sales and profits start to decline. This could be due to changing customer preferences, advancements in technology rendering the product obsolete, or the emergence of substitute products. Businesses must make strategic decisions to manage profit margins and possibly consider discontinuing the product or reinventing it to extend its life cycle.

Product Line Extension

A product line extension is a marketing strategy that involves introducing new products or variations of existing products within the same product line. This strategy aims to expand the product line and cater to different customer segments or meet specific customer needs.

The main objective of a product line extension is to leverage the brand awareness and loyalty associated with the existing product line to drive sales and increase market share. By introducing new products or variations, companies can tap into new market opportunities, reach a wider customer base, and enhance customer satisfaction.

Product Placement

Product placement is a form of advertising and promotion where brands or products are featured or integrated within various forms of media, such as movies, television shows, music videos, or video games. It involves the strategic placement of a product or brand within the content of the media, aiming to reach a large audience and create brand awareness.

The purpose of product placement is to influence and shape consumer perceptions, attitudes, and behavior towards a particular brand or product. By integrating products within popular media, marketers hope to create a subconscious association between the brand and the desirable qualities or lifestyle portrayed by the characters or celebrities associated with the media content.

Product placement can be an effective marketing strategy, as it allows brands to reach a wide audience and gain exposure in a non-intrusive way. It also provides opportunities for brands to align themselves with popular culture and influential figures.

However, product placement should be carefully executed to ensure it resonates with the target audience and does not come across as forced or overly promotional. It is important for marketers to choose the right media platforms and content that align with the brand's image and target market. Additionally, transparency and disclosure are essential to maintain trust and avoid any potential backlash from consumers.

Product Portfolio

A product portfolio refers to the collection of products offered by a company or a business unit. It represents the range of products that a company sells to meet the needs and wants of its target market. This collection of products can include both existing products as well as new product offerings.

The product portfolio of a company plays a crucial role in its marketing strategy and overall business success. It helps the company to diversify its product offerings, cater to different market segments, and capitalize on market opportunities. A well-managed product portfolio enables the company to achieve its overall business objectives and maintain a competitive advantage in the market.

Managing a product portfolio involves various tasks, including product development, launching new products, optimizing existing products, and phasing out outdated or underperforming products. It requires a comprehensive understanding of the market, customer needs, and industry trends.

In marketing management, analyzing and evaluating the performance of the product portfolio is an essential task. This involves assessing the profitability, market share, growth potential, and strategic fit of each product in the portfolio. Based on this analysis, companies can make informed decisions about investing in product development, marketing resources allocation, and portfolio optimization.

Product Recall Management

Product recall management is a critical aspect of the marketing management discipline that involves the efficient and effective handling of product recalls by organizations. A product recall refers to the process of removing and/or replacing a product from the market due to safety concerns, quality issues, or non-compliance with regulations. The primary goal of product recall management is to mitigate any potential harm or negative consequences to consumers, while also protecting the reputation and financial interests of the company.

In the context of marketing management, product recall management encompasses several key activities. Firstly, it involves establishing a robust recall plan that outlines the procedures, responsibilities, and communication channels in the event of a recall. This plan should be developed proactively to ensure that all necessary steps are in place when a recall is necessary.

Secondly, product recall management includes prompt and effective communication with stakeholders, such as consumers, retailers, distributors, and regulatory authorities. It is crucial to provide clear and transparent information about the reason for the recall, potential risks, and instructions for affected consumers. Effective communication helps build trust, demonstrate accountability, and minimize the impact on the company's reputation.

Product Recall

A product recall is a formal process in the field of Marketing Management where a manufacturer or distributor retrieves a product from the market due to safety concerns or defects identified in the product. It is a crucial decision made by a company in order to protect the customers from potential harm and maintain its reputation.

The primary objective of a product recall is to address any issues that may arise after the product has been released into the market. This may include issues related to the product's effectiveness, safety, or compliance with regulatory standards. By recalling the product, the company aims to mitigate any potential risks to the customers and prevent any further damage to the company's brand image.

Product-Market Fit

The term "Product-Market Fit" refers to the degree to which a product satisfies the needs and preferences of a specific target market. It is a measure used in marketing management to assess whether a product is well-suited to its intended market and if it is meeting the demands and expectations of customers.

An effective product-market fit means that the product is in sync with the market's requirements, resulting in high levels of customer satisfaction and demand. When a product has achieved a strong fit, it indicates that the business has successfully identified a significant customer problem and developed a solution that resonates with the target market.

Product-Market Matrix

The product-market matrix, also known as the Ansoff matrix, is a strategic tool used in marketing management to help businesses analyze their growth strategy options. It was developed by Igor Ansoff in 1957 and provides a framework for identifying and evaluating different growth opportunities for a company.

The product-market matrix consists of four growth strategies: market penetration, market development, product development, and diversification.

Market penetration involves selling more of current products or services to existing customers. This strategy focuses on increasing market share by acquiring more customers or convincing existing customers to buy more. It often involves aggressive marketing techniques such as price discounts or promotional campaigns to attract customers away from competitors.

Market development entails expanding into new market segments or geographical areas with existing products. This strategy seeks to find new customers who may have different needs or preferences than the company's current customer base. It may involve conducting market research to identify untapped markets and tailoring marketing efforts to attract these new customer segments.

Product development involves creating new products or modifying existing ones to better meet the needs of existing customers. This strategy aims to increase sales by providing enhanced or innovative products that offer a competitive advantage. It requires extensive research and development, as well as understanding customer preferences and market trends.

Diversification is the most risky and complex growth strategy, involving entering entirely new markets with new products or services. It allows companies to reduce dependence on one industry or product line, but it requires significant investment and carries higher uncertainty. Diversification can be either related (entering a new market that is similar to the existing business) or unrelated (entering a completely different market).

Programmatic Advertising Platforms

Programmatic advertising platforms are digital tools used by marketing management professionals to automate and optimize the process of buying, selling, and displaying online advertisements. These platforms rely on advanced algorithms and artificial intelligence (AI) to analyze vast amounts of data in real-time and make data-driven decisions about which ads to show to which users, at what time, and on what platforms.

With programmatic advertising platforms, marketers can target specific audiences based on various factors such as demographics, interests, browsing behavior, and previous interactions. This enables them to create personalized and highly relevant ad experiences for their target customers, increasing the chances of engagement and conversions. These platforms also allow for real-time bidding, where advertisers can bid for ad placements on websites and apps in real-time auctions, ensuring maximum reach and efficiency for their ad spend.

Programmatic Advertising

Programmatic advertising is a strategic marketing approach that utilizes automated technology and algorithms to buy and sell advertising space in real-time, with the aim of delivering highly targeted and personalized ads to the desired audience at the right time and place.

This advertising method focuses on utilizing data-driven technologies to streamline and optimize the ad buying process, replacing traditional manual negotiations and placements. Through programmatic advertising, marketers can now leverage advanced targeting capabilities, such as behavioral and demographic data, to reach specific customer segments and deliver tailored messages.

Promotion

Promotion refers to the communication activities that organizations undertake to inform, persuade, and remind target customers about their products or services. It is a critical component of the marketing mix and plays a key role in achieving the organization's marketing objectives.

The main objective of promotion is to create awareness and generate interest among the target audience. It includes various marketing communication tools such as advertising, personal selling, sales promotion, public relations, and direct marketing.

Advertising is a paid form of communication that uses mass media channels such as television, radio, print, and online platforms to reach a large audience. It aims to create brand awareness and influence purchase decisions by providing information and creating positive associations with the brand.

Personal selling involves face-to-face communication between a salesperson and a potential customer. It allows for a personalized approach and enables the salesperson to address specific customer needs and provide tailored solutions. Personal selling is particularly effective in building relationships and closing sales.

Sales promotion includes activities such as discounts, coupons, contests, and free samples. It aims to stimulate immediate buying behavior and create a sense of urgency among consumers. Sales promotion techniques are often used in combination with other promotional tools to enhance their impact.

Public relations activities focus on building a positive image of the organization and fostering goodwill with various stakeholders. This may involve media relations, sponsorship, events, and community engagement. Through public relations, organizations strive to create a favorable perception of their brand and maintain a positive reputation.

Direct marketing refers to promotional activities that are delivered directly to individual customers via channels such as email, direct mail, telemarketing, and SMS marketing. It allows for direct communication with the target audience and enables organizations to personalize their messages based on customer data and preferences.

Promotional Mix

The promotional mix is a marketing management concept that refers to the combination of different promotional tools and activities used by a company or organization to communicate and promote its products or services to the target market.

The promotional mix consists of several elements, including advertising, sales promotion, public relations, personal selling, and direct marketing. Each element plays a crucial role in effectively reaching and persuading the target audience, and they are usually used in combination to achieve the desired marketing objectives.

Psychographic Segmentation

Psychographic segmentation is a marketing management concept that involves dividing a market into different groups based on psychological and lifestyle characteristics. It takes into account individuals' attitudes, values, interests, beliefs, opinions, and behavior patterns to create distinct customer segments. This segmentation strategy goes beyond traditional demographics such as age, gender, and income, as it focuses on understanding consumers' motivations, preferences, and personality traits.

Psychographic segmentation helps marketers gain a deeper understanding of their target audience by identifying shared psychological characteristics that influence purchasing decisions. By analyzing customers based on their lifestyle choices, hobbies, and values, companies can tailor their marketing efforts and develop more targeted and impactful strategies. This approach allows businesses to deliver personalized messages and create product offerings that resonate with specific psychographic segments, ultimately increasing customer engagement and loyalty.

Psychological Pricing Strategies Tools

Psychological pricing strategies are marketing tools used by organizations to influence consumer perception and behavior through price manipulation. These strategies aim to exploit the psychological tendencies of individuals in order to maximize sales, revenue, and profit.

One commonly used psychological pricing strategy is known as the charm pricing or the left-digit effect. This strategy involves setting prices just below a whole number, such as pricing a product at $9.99 instead of $10. Research suggests that consumers tend to focus more on the leftmost digits when evaluating price, perceiving $9.99 as significantly cheaper than $10. This perception can create an illusion of affordability and maximize the likelihood of purchase.

Another psychological pricing strategy is known as the prestige pricing or the price-quality effect. This strategy involves setting higher prices for products or services to create a perception of superior quality. Consumers often associate higher prices with higher quality, assuming that a higher price tag indicates better performance, durability, or exclusivity. By using this strategy, companies can enhance their brand image, attract a specific target market, and generate higher profit margins.

Psychological Pricing Strategies

Psychological pricing strategies are marketing techniques that utilize the principles of human psychology to influence consumer behavior and perception of prices. These strategies use various pricing techniques and tactics to convey certain price perceptions and manipulate the customers' decision-making process.

One commonly used psychological pricing strategy is the concept of charm prices, which involves setting prices just below a round number (e.g., $0.99 instead of $1.00). This is based on the perception that customers perceive prices ending in 9 as significantly lower than they actually are. Another technique is the use of reference pricing, where a higher original price is presented alongside a lower promotional price to make the promotional price seem more attractive, even though customers may rarely pay the higher price. The goal of this strategy is to make customers feel like they are getting a good deal.

Additionally, psychological pricing strategies often rely on the concept of price anchoring, whereby a high-priced product or service is presented alongside a lower-priced option to make the lower-priced item seem more affordable. This strategy capitalizes on customers' tendency to base their perception of value on a reference point or anchor price. Furthermore, decoy pricing involves introducing a third option that is strategically priced to influence customers' choices between the other two options.

In conclusion, psychological pricing strategies are marketing tactics that exploit consumers' cognitive biases and emotional responses to prices. By understanding how customers perceive prices and leveraging psychological principles, marketers can shape consumer behavior and increase sales.

Public Relations (PR)

Public Relations (PR) is a strategic communication function within Marketing Management that aims to build and maintain a positive image and reputation of an organization. It involves the practice of managing information flow between a company and its various stakeholders, including customers, employees, investors, media, and the general public. The goal of PR is to effectively communicate the organization's messages, values, and objectives to its target audience, while also addressing any potential issues or challenges that may arise.

PR activities encompass a wide range of tactics and strategies, such as media relations, crisis management, content creation, event planning, community relations, and social media engagement. These activities are all aimed at shaping public perception, generating positive publicity, and fostering a favorable relationship between the organization and its stakeholders.

Publicity Stunt

A publicity stunt refers to a planned event or action performed by a company or organization with the objective of attracting media attention and generating publicity. It is a strategic marketing tactic that aims to create buzz, increase brand awareness, and ultimately, drive consumer engagement and sales.

Publicity stunts are typically characterized by their unconventional and attention-grabbing nature. They often involve highly visual or extraordinary elements that captivate the audience's attention and generate interest. These stunts can take various forms, such as publicity events, demonstrations, contests, or even provocative actions that challenge societal norms.

The success of a publicity stunt relies heavily on its ability to generate media coverage. Media outlets, including traditional media such as newspapers, magazines, television, and radio, as well as digital and social media platforms, play a crucial role in amplifying the visibility of the stunt. The stunt's capacity to generate widespread media coverage is essential in reaching a broader audience and maximizing the potential impact of the marketing message.

While publicity stunts have the potential to be extremely effective in terms of generating buzz and public awareness, they also come with risks. The success of a publicity stunt relies heavily on careful planning, execution, and timing. Poorly executed stunts or those that are seen as controversial or offensive can damage a brand's reputation and result in negative publicity.

Publicity

Publicity is a marketing management strategy used to create awareness about a product, service, or brand through various communication channels. It is a non-personal form of communication that aims to generate positive media attention and coverage, thereby influencing the target audience's perception and purchasing behavior.

Publicity involves utilizing different media platforms, such as newspapers, magazines, television, radio, and online platforms, to disseminate information about a company, its products, or its activities. It can take the form of press releases, news articles, interviews, reviews, social media posts, and other promotional content.

Publicity aims to attract attention, generate interest, and ultimately influence public opinion and behavior. When effectively implemented, publicity can enhance a company's reputation, build brand equity, increase sales and market share, and create a competitive advantage.

However, as a non-paid form of communication, publicity is subject to the control and editorial decisions of media outlets. This means that the reach and content of publicity efforts may vary, depending on the relevance and newsworthiness of the information provided. Publicity can also be influenced by external factors such as media trends, competition, and the overall business environment.

In conclusion, publicity is a strategic marketing communication tool used to create broad awareness, generate positive media coverage, and influence public opinion. It is a powerful means of building brand equity and gaining a competitive edge in the marketplace.

Pull Marketing

Pull marketing is a marketing strategy that focuses on attracting and enticing potential customers towards a product or service. This approach involves creating a strong brand presence and generating consumer interest, which leads to customers actively seeking out the product or service.

In pull marketing, the primary goal is to make the product or service highly visible to the target audience and create a desire or need for it. This is achieved through various tactics such as advertising, content marketing, social media engagement, public relations, and search engine optimization.

Unlike push marketing, which involves pushing products or services onto customers through aggressive promotional efforts, pull marketing leverages the power of attraction. By building a strong brand, offering valuable content and engaging with customers, pull marketing creates a positive perception and encourages customers to proactively seek out and purchase the product or service.

This strategy is particularly effective when the target audience has a higher level of involvement or interest in the product or service. By creating a strong brand image and providing relevant and valuable information, pull marketing ensures that customers are not only aware of the product, but also actively interested in it.

In conclusion, pull marketing is a customer-centric approach that aims to create a demand for a product or service by attracting and enticing potential customers through various promotional and engagement strategies. By focusing on creating a positive brand image and offering value, pull marketing drives customers to actively seek out and choose the product or service.

Purchase Intent

Purchase Intent refers to the likelihood or inclination of a consumer to buy a particular product or service. It is a measure or indicator of the consumer's intention to make a purchase in the near future, based on their evaluation and consideration of various factors such as need, desire, cost, availability, and alternatives.

In the context of marketing management, understanding and assessing purchase intent is crucial for companies to develop effective marketing strategies, target the right customer segments, and maximize sales and profits. By identifying consumers with high purchase intent, businesses can allocate their resources and efforts towards these individuals, increasing their chances of converting them into loyal customers.

Push Marketing

Push marketing is a marketing strategy that focuses on proactively pushing products or services towards potential customers. It involves promoting and advertising products through various channels to create demand and generate sales. In this approach, marketers actively seek to communicate with consumers, capture their attention, and persuade them to make a purchase.

In push marketing, companies often use traditional advertising methods such as television, radio, print media, and direct mail to reach a wide audience. They also employ personal selling techniques, in which salespeople directly approach and engage with consumers to introduce products and provide information. Additionally, push marketing may involve aggressive tactics such as door-to-door sales, telemarketing, and email marketing campaigns.

This strategy aims to push a product or service into the marketplace, creating brand recognition and stimulating consumer interest. It relies on the assumption that consumers may not actively seek information about a particular product or service, so it is the marketer's responsibility to find ways to ensure that the message reaches the target audience. By employing push marketing techniques, businesses can target specific demographics, increase visibility, and influence consumer behavior.

Push Strategy

A push strategy is a marketing approach that focuses on "pushing" a product or service through the distribution channel towards the final consumer. It involves the manufacturer or producer actively promoting or persuading resellers, retailers, or intermediaries to carry and sell their products to end consumers.

In a push strategy, the company's marketing efforts are primarily directed towards the intermediaries in the channel, such as wholesalers and retailers, with the aim of pushing the products through the channel to reach the target customers. This is often achieved through various promotional and sales techniques, such as personal selling, trade shows, advertising, incentives, and discounts, aimed at encouraging resellers to promote and stock the product.

The push strategy is particularly effective when the target market is unaware of the product or has a low level of involvement or interest. By focusing on the intermediaries, the company can quickly and aggressively introduce the product in the market and generate initial demand. It can also help in creating product visibility and shelf space in retail stores, ensuring wider availability and convenience for customers.

However, the push strategy is not always suitable for all products or markets. It can be less effective when the target market is highly involved and informed, as customers may have specific preferences and actively seek out products themselves. In such cases, a pull strategy, which focuses on generating demand directly from the end consumers, may be more appropriate.

Quantitative Data

Quantitative data, in the context of Marketing Management, refers to numerical information that can be measured and analyzed. This type of data is obtained through systematic and structured methods such as surveys, questionnaires, and statistical analysis. Quantitative data provides objective and reliable insights into various aspects of marketing, including customer behavior, market trends, and financial performance.

Quantitative data is essential for making informed decisions and developing effective marketing strategies. It allows marketers to identify patterns, quantify results, and spot statistically significant relationships or correlations. By analyzing quantitative data, marketing managers can gain valuable insights into consumer preferences, purchase behavior, and market potential.

Real-Time Data Analytics Platforms

Real-Time Data Analytics Platforms in the context of Marketing Management discipline refer to technological solutions that enable organizations to collect, process, analyze, and interpret data in real time to make timely and data-driven marketing decisions. These platforms leverage advanced analytics techniques, data visualization capabilities, and real-time data processing engines to provide marketers with actionable insights and facilitate effective decision-making processes.

Real-Time Data Analytics Platforms in marketing management play a crucial role in helping organizations monitor, measure, and optimize their marketing campaigns and activities by providing real-time feedback on marketing performance and consumer behavior. By integrating data from various sources such as websites, social media platforms, customer databases, and online advertisements, these platforms enable marketers to gain a comprehensive and holistic view of their target audience and marketing initiatives.

Real-Time Data Analytics Tools

Real-Time Data Analytics Tools are software or applications that enable marketers to gather, process, analyze, and interpret large volumes of data in real-time. These tools provide up-to-the-minute insights and information on various marketing activities and campaigns, allowing marketers to make data-driven decisions and optimize their strategies accordingly.

Real-Time Data Analytics Tools are essential in the field of Marketing Management as they allow marketers to monitor and track marketing efforts in real-time, rather than relying on historical or outdated data. These tools help marketers to identify trends, patterns, and consumer behavior instantly, enabling them to respond quickly and adapt their marketing strategies accordingly.

Real-Time Data Analytics

Real-Time Data Analytics in the context of Marketing Management refers to the continuous analysis and interpretation of data generated by various marketing activities in order to make informed and timely decisions. It involves the use of advanced analytical tools and techniques to process data in real-time, enabling marketers to quickly identify patterns, trends, and correlations that can be used to optimize marketing strategies and improve overall business performance.

Real-time data analytics allows marketers to monitor and analyze data as it is generated, providing immediate insights into customer behavior, market trends, and the effectiveness of marketing campaigns. This enables them to adjust their strategies in real-time, targeting the right audience with the right message at the right time. By leveraging real-time data analytics, marketers can make data-driven decisions that are based on up-to-date information, rather than relying on gut feelings or historical data.

Real-Time Data

Real-time data refers to information that is collected and analyzed instantly, allowing marketers to make quick and informed decisions for their marketing strategies. In the context of Marketing Management, real-time data is crucial for optimizing and improving marketing activities in real-time, leveraging current and accurate insights to maximize results and drive better customer engagement.

Real-time data in marketing management entails monitoring and tracking various metrics, including but not limited to website traffic, social media interactions, email open rates, sales leads, customer behavior, and campaign performance. By capturing these data points in real-time, marketers can assess the effectiveness of their marketing initiatives, identify trends, detect anomalies, and respond promptly to any emerging opportunities or challenges.

Real-Time Marketing

Real-time marketing refers to the use of up-to-date and timely information in marketing activities to provide relevant and personalized experiences to consumers. It involves the immediate response and adaptation to current events, trends, or customer behavior to create meaningful connections with the target audience.

In the context of marketing management, real-time marketing emphasizes the importance of agility, flexibility, and responsiveness in a rapidly changing digital landscape. It leverages real-time data, advanced analytics, and technology tools to monitor, analyze, and react to consumer interactions across various channels, such as social media, websites, and mobile apps.

Rebranding Strategies

Rebranding strategies refer to the planned, strategic changes made to a company's brand identity, including its name, logo, tagline, packaging, and messaging, with the objective of revitalizing or repositioning the brand in the market. It is a core component of marketing management that aims to address changing market dynamics, consumer preferences, and competitive pressures.

The process of rebranding involves a comprehensive analysis of the company's current brand image, perception, and market position. This analysis helps identify gaps, weaknesses, or opportunities for growth, which then guide the development of a rebranding strategy. The strategy may include various elements such as altering the visual and verbal identity, refining the brand's value proposition, redefining its target audience, or even expanding into new product lines or markets.

The goals of rebranding strategies can vary depending on the circumstances. Some companies may rebrand to shed negative associations or outdated perceptions, while others may aim to differentiate themselves from competitors or to target a new audience segment. The strategy should align with the broader marketing objectives of the company and be communicated consistently across all customer touchpoints.

Effective rebranding strategies require careful planning and execution. They often involve extensive market research, analysis of consumer behavior, competitive benchmarking, and a deep understanding of the brand's strengths and weaknesses. Companies must also consider the potential risks and challenges associated with rebranding, such as loss of brand equity or confusion among existing customers.

Rebranding Strategy Execution Tools

A rebranding strategy execution tool is a marketing management tool that helps businesses implement a rebranding strategy effectively. Rebranding refers to the process of changing the visual identity and/or positioning of a brand in order to better align with the company's objectives, target market, or competitive landscape.

This tool is used to streamline and coordinate the various activities and tasks associated with the rebranding process, ensuring that it is executed smoothly and efficiently. It provides a framework for planning, organizing, and tracking the progress of rebranding initiatives, allowing marketing managers to stay on top of deadlines, budgets, and resources.

Rebranding Strategy Execution

Rebranding Strategy Execution refers to the process of implementing a new brand identity and messaging to effectively communicate a company's repositioning or revitalization efforts to its target market. It involves a comprehensive and integrated approach to changing various marketing elements, such as the brand name, logo, tagline, colors, packaging, advertising, and other promotional tactics, in order to create a fresh and distinct image for the brand.

This strategy execution is a crucial step in the rebranding process as it helps in aligning the organization's internal and external stakeholders with the new brand identity. It requires effective planning, coordination, and communication to ensure that all marketing touchpoints accurately convey the desired brand image and effectively engage the target audience.

Rebranding

Rebranding refers to the process of changing a brand's identity, image, or positioning in the market. It involves updating or modifying various elements such as the brand name, logo, tagline, color scheme, packaging, and communication strategies, in order to create a new and improved brand perception among consumers.

The primary objective of rebranding is to redefine the brand's value proposition and connect with the target audience more effectively. This strategic marketing approach is often undertaken by companies to adapt to changing market trends, overcome negative brand perceptions, enter new markets, or revive a stagnant brand.

Recency, Frequency, Monetary (RFM) Analysis

Recency, Frequency, Monetary (RFM) Analysis is a marketing management technique that is used to segment customers based on their buying behavior and identify valuable customer segments for targeted marketing campaigns. It is a data-driven approach that allows marketers to gain insights into the behavior and preferences of their customers, which helps them make informed decisions to maximize revenue and customer satisfaction.

RFM Analysis evaluates customers based on three key parameters:

Recency: This parameter measures the time elapsed since a customer's last purchase. It helps identify how recently a customer has interacted with the brand and indicates their level of engagement and loyalty. Customers who have made recent purchases are considered more valuable and likely to respond positively to marketing efforts.

Frequency: This parameter measures the number of times a customer has made purchases within a specific timeframe. It helps understand how often customers engage with the brand and indicates their level of loyalty. Customers who make frequent purchases are more likely to be loyal and generate higher revenue.

Monetary: This parameter measures the total monetary value of a customer's purchases. It helps identify customers who have made high-value purchases and are likely to contribute significantly to the company's revenue. Customers with higher monetary value are considered more valuable and may be targeted with premium offers or loyalty programs.

By segmenting customers based on RFM Analysis, marketers can tailor their marketing strategies to meet the specific needs and preferences of each customer segment. This approach helps improve customer retention, increase customer lifetime value, and enhance overall marketing effectiveness.

Referral Marketing

Referral marketing is a strategic marketing approach that encourages and incentivizes individuals, typically existing customers, to recommend a product, service, or brand to others. It relies on the power of word-of-mouth communication and leverages personal relationships to generate new business and increase customer acquisition.

The primary goal of referral marketing is to tap into the existing network of satisfied customers and turn them into advocates who actively promote the product or service. By incentivizing referrals, companies can amplify their marketing efforts and benefit from the credibility and trust associated with recommendations from friends, family members, or colleagues.

This marketing strategy typically involves providing existing customers with incentives, such as discounts, rewards, or even monetary compensation, for referring others. By leveraging the personal connections and trust that already exist within these relationships, referral marketing has the potential to generate high-quality leads and conversions.

In addition to increasing customer acquisition, referral marketing can also contribute to brand awareness and reputation building. Positive recommendations can enhance the perception of a brand and increase its credibility in the market. This can lead to greater customer loyalty and repeat business, as well as attract new customers who trust the recommendations of others.

Referral Program

A referral program is a marketing strategy that encourages customers, friends, or business partners to refer potential customers to a business in exchange for incentives. It is a systematic approach adopted by companies to leverage the power of word-of-mouth marketing.

The goal of a referral program is to incentivize individuals to promote and recommend a product or service to their network of contacts. This can lead to increased brand awareness, customer acquisition, and sales for the business implementing the program.

A well-designed referral program typically involves the following steps:

1. Identification of target referrers: Businesses must identify their most loyal and satisfied customers or influential individuals who have the potential to refer customers.

2. Offering attractive incentives: To motivate referrers, businesses can provide rewards such as discounts, gift cards, or exclusive access to special offers. The incentives should be appealing enough to encourage participation.

3. Providing easy-to-use referral tools: To simplify the referral process, businesses often provide referrers with personalized referral codes, referral links, or online referral forms. These tools make it easy for referrers to share the product or service with their network.

4. Tracking and rewarding successful referrals: Businesses need to track and monitor the referrals generated through the program. Once a referral results in a new customer or sale, the referrer should be rewarded promptly.

A successful referral program can have a significant impact on a company's bottom line by harnessing the power of satisfied customers and their networks. It not only helps in acquiring new customers but also builds stronger customer relationships and enhances brand loyalty.

Remarketing Ad Campaign Platforms

Remarketing ad campaign platforms are online advertising platforms that allow marketers to target and display ads to users who have previously interacted with their website or mobile app. These platforms use cookies or other tracking technologies to track users' activities and then serve them with relevant ads across different websites and apps.

The main goal of remarketing ad campaign platforms is to re-engage users who have shown some level of interest in a brand or product but have not yet converted into a customer. By showing targeted ads to these users, remarketing platforms aim to remind them about the brand, increase brand awareness, and eventually drive conversions.

Remarketing Ad Campaigns

Remarketing ad campaigns, also known as retargeting ad campaigns, are a marketing strategy that involves targeting advertisements to individuals who have previously interacted with a brand or visited its website. This technique allows marketers to reconnect with potential customers and increase the likelihood of conversion by keeping the brand top of mind.

The process of remarketing involves using tracking cookies or pixels to identify users who have previously shown interest in the brand. Once identified, these users are targeted with customized ads that are tailored to their specific interests or actions on the brand's website. These ads can be displayed across various online platforms, including social media, websites, and mobile apps.

Remarketing campaigns leverage the power of personalized advertising to deliver relevant messages to individuals who are more likely to engage with the brand. By reminding them of their previous interactions with the brand or showcasing products or services they have shown interest in, remarketing aims to drive repeat visits, increase brand awareness, and ultimately boost conversion rates.

When executed effectively, remarketing ad campaigns can be highly effective in improving overall marketing performance. By reaching out to individuals who have already shown an interest in the brand, marketers can significantly increase their chances of converting these leads into customers, as they are already familiar with the brand and its offerings.

Overall, remarketing ad campaigns are a valuable tool in a marketer's toolbox, as they provide an opportunity to bring potential customers back into the sales funnel and increase the likelihood of conversion.

Remarketing Ads

Remarketing ads refer to a marketing strategy that involves targeting and displaying advertisements to users who have previously interacted with a brand or visited its website. It is a powerful tool in the field of marketing management that aims to re-engage potential customers and increase conversions.

The concept of remarketing ads revolves around the use of cookies, which track user behavior on websites. When a user visits a website or takes a specific action, such as adding a product to their shopping cart, a cookie is placed on their device. This cookie enables the website to recognize the user and deliver customized advertisements to them as they browse the internet.

The primary objective of using remarketing ads is to remind potential customers about a brand and its offerings, thereby increasing brand awareness and fostering brand recall. By reaching out to users who have already shown interest, remarketing ads allow marketers to target a more qualified audience and potentially boost conversion rates.

Remarketing ads can take various forms, including display banners, text ads, or even video ads. These ads can be displayed on websites that are part of the ad network where the remarketing campaign is set up. For example, if a user abandons their shopping cart, they may later see a banner ad for the exact product they left behind when visiting other websites that are part of the same ad network.

Overall, remarketing ads serve as a valuable tool in marketing management by helping brands reconnect with potential customers, increase brand visibility, and drive conversions. By strategically targeting individuals who have expressed interest in a brand, these ads can significantly enhance a company's marketing efforts and ultimately drive business growth.

Remarketing Campaign

Remarketing campaign refers to a marketing strategy that involves targeting individuals who have previously interacted with a brand or its products/services, but did not proceed with a purchase or conversion. It aims to re-engage these potential customers through tailored advertisements and personalized content, with the objective of influencing their decision to make a purchase or revisit the brand.

Remarketing campaigns rely on the use of cookies or tracking codes to identify website visitors who have shown interest in a brand or its offerings. Once identified, these individuals are included in a segmented audience that receives targeted ads across various platforms such as social media, search engines, and websites. The ads typically highlight the brand's unique selling propositions, special offers, or incentives to entice the potential customer back into the conversion funnel.

This marketing tactic leverages the power of repetition and personalized messaging to increase brand awareness, maintain top-of-mind presence, and encourage return visits or purchases. Remarketing campaigns benefit from detailed analytics and tracking capabilities, allowing marketers to measure the effectiveness of their ads, adjust targeting parameters, and refine their messaging. Through continuous optimization, remarketing campaigns can drive higher conversion rates and maximize return on investment.

In summary, a remarketing campaign is a targeted marketing strategy that aims to re-engage individuals who have previously shown interest in a brand or its offerings. By delivering personalized ads and content, marketers seek to influence these potential customers to take desired actions, ultimately increasing conversions and brand loyalty.

Remarketing Campaigns

Remarketing campaigns refer to the strategic marketing approach of targeting and engaging with individuals who have already interacted with a brand or its products/services. This discipline is an integral part of marketing management as it aims to increase brand awareness, enhance customer engagement, and drive conversions.

Remarketing campaigns typically involve tracking the online behavior of potential customers through cookies or pixels. When a user visits a website, performs a specific action, or abandons a shopping cart, their information is captured. This information allows marketers to create personalized and targeted advertisements that are displayed to these individuals as they browse the internet.

Remarketing

Remarketing is a strategic marketing approach that involves targeting and re-engaging potential customers who have previously shown interest in a product or service but did not make a purchase or take the desired action. This technique allows marketers to reconnect with their audience and increase the chances of converting them into loyal customers.

The process of remarketing typically begins with the collection and analysis of data related to visitors' behavior, preferences, and interactions with a company's website or other digital platforms. This data is then used to create personalized and highly targeted advertising campaigns that specifically cater to the interests and needs of potential customers.

By delivering relevant and compelling messaging, remarketing aims to remind and persuade individuals to revisit the website or take the desired action, such as making a purchase, subscribing to a newsletter, or filling out a form. This technique leverages various marketing channels, including display advertising, email marketing, social media, and search advertising, to reach and engage with the target audience effectively.

Remarketing can be particularly beneficial for businesses as it allows them to stay top-of-mind with potential customers, increase brand awareness, and maximize the return on investment for their marketing efforts. Moreover, it enables marketers to tailor their messaging based on the stage of the customer journey, providing more personalized and relevant content to drive conversions.

Repositioning

Repositioning, in the context of Marketing Management, refers to the strategic process of modifying the positioning of a product, brand, or company in the minds of the target market. It involves changing the perception, image, or attributes associated with the offering in order to create a new position or reinforce an existing one.

Repositioning is typically undertaken when a company identifies a need to adapt to changing market conditions, address competitive threats, capitalize on new opportunities, or better align with evolving customer preferences. This strategic realignment can be achieved by altering various elements of the marketing mix, including product features, pricing, promotional messaging, distribution channels, or even the overall brand identity.

The repositioning process typically begins with a thorough analysis of the current market positioning and the identification of the desired market position. This may involve market research, customer surveys, competitor analysis, and other strategic assessment techniques. Once the desired positioning is determined, a detailed marketing plan is developed to guide the implementation of the repositioning strategy.

Repositioning can take various forms, such as rebranding, product line extensions, entering new market segments, adjusting pricing strategies, or changing the overall marketing communication approach. Successful repositioning requires effective communication and engagement with the target market to ensure the new positioning is effectively conveyed and understood by customers.

In summary, repositioning is a strategic marketing process that involves modifying the perception, image, or attributes of a product, brand, or company to create a new position or reinforce an existing one. It is undertaken to respond to market changes, address competitive pressures, explore new opportunities, or better align with customer preferences.

Reputation Management

Reputation management, within the context of marketing management, refers to the process of controlling and influencing the perception and reputation of a company or brand among its target audience. It involves managing and monitoring the online and offline reputation, as well as the public image of a business, to maintain or enhance its overall reputation and credibility. Effective reputation management involves several key components. Firstly, it requires actively listening to and monitoring what customers, stakeholders, and the general public are saying about the company or brand. This includes monitoring social media platforms, review websites, news articles, and other sources for mentions or feedback. Secondly, reputation management involves promptly addressing any negative feedback or complaints that are received. This may require acknowledging the concern, providing a solution or explanation, and taking appropriate action to resolve the issue. Thirdly, reputation management involves proactively engaging with customers and stakeholders to build positive relationships and foster goodwill. This can include responding to positive feedback, participating in community events, supporting charitable initiatives, and communicating transparently with the target audience. Finally, reputation management also involves continuously assessing and evaluating the effectiveness of reputation-building efforts and making necessary adjustments or improvements. Overall, effective reputation management is crucial for businesses as it directly impacts the perception and trustworthiness of a company or brand. A positive reputation can attract and retain customers, boost sales, and enhance overall business success. Conversely, a negative reputation can lead to loss of customers, damage to brand image, and decreased profitability. Therefore, companies must actively manage and maintain their reputation to ensure long-term success and sustainability.

Responsive Design

Responsive design is a fundamental concept in the field of Marketing Management. It refers to the approach taken in web design and development that aims to create websites and applications that provide optimal user experience across various devices and screen sizes.

With the proliferation of smartphones, tablets, and other internet-enabled devices, consumers are accessing online content from a wide range of platforms. Responsive design ensures that websites and applications are visually appealing and functional regardless of whether they are viewed on a desktop computer, laptop, tablet, or smartphone.

Responsive Web Design For Mobile Tools

Responsive web design for mobile tools refers to the practice of creating websites that automatically adapt and optimize their layout and content to provide an optimal user experience on mobile devices, such as smartphones and tablets. It involves designing and developing websites in a way that ensures they are visually appealing, user-friendly, and fully functional on smaller screens with limited display space.

This approach to web design is crucial in today's digital landscape, where mobile usage has surpassed desktop usage and more and more consumers are accessing the internet on their smartphones. Responsive web design allows marketers to effectively reach and engage with their target audience on mobile devices, ensuring that their websites are accessible and easy to navigate regardless of the screen size or device being used.

Responsive Web Design For Mobile

Responsive Web Design for Mobile is a marketing strategy aimed at creating a seamless user experience by adapting websites to different screen sizes and devices. This approach ensures that the website's layout and content dynamically adjust to provide optimal viewing and interaction, regardless of the device used to access the site. In today's mobile-dominated world, having a responsive website is crucial for businesses to effectively reach and engage with their target audience. With the increasing use of smartphones and tablets, responsive design allows marketers to deliver a consistent brand message across various devices, enhancing user satisfaction and driving conversions. Implementing responsive web design involves the use of fluid layouts, flexible images, and media queries that determine the appropriate design and layout based on the device's screen size and resolution. By designing websites with a mobile-first approach, marketers can prioritize important content and features, optimizing the mobile user experience and ensuring that key information is readily accessible. Responsive web design also plays a critical role in search engine optimization (SEO) as search engines favor mobile-friendly websites and rank them higher in search results. With a responsive design, marketers can improve their website's visibility and generate more organic traffic, leading to increased brand exposure and potential business growth. In summary, responsive web design for mobile is a marketing management strategy that prioritizes user experience by adapting websites to different devices. By embracing this approach, businesses can effectively engage their target audience, optimize their online presence, and stay ahead in today's mobile-driven marketplace.

Retail Merchandising

Retail merchandising is a branch of marketing management that focuses on the planning, execution, and control of the activities related to presenting products in a retail environment. It involves the selection, pricing, promotion, and display of products in order to attract customers and maximize sales.

One of the primary goals of retail merchandising is to create a visually appealing and organized store layout that encourages customers to make purchases. This includes carefully arranging products on shelves and displays, using attractive signage and packaging, and utilizing effective lighting and color schemes to enhance the overall shopping experience.

In addition to creating an inviting store environment, retail merchandising also involves determining the appropriate product assortment to offer customers. This includes analyzing market trends, identifying customer preferences, and selecting products that meet the needs and wants of target customers. It also entails managing inventory levels, ensuring that the right products are available in the right quantities at the right time.

Pricing is another critical aspect of retail merchandising. Merchandisers must set prices that are competitive, yet still profitable. This requires considering factors such as production costs, competitor prices, consumer demand, and desired profit margins. Effective pricing strategies can help retailers attract customers, increase sales volume, and ultimately achieve profitability.

Furthermore, retail merchandising involves promoting products to drive customer awareness and generate sales. This can include advertising campaigns, in-store promotions, digital marketing initiatives, and other promotional activities. It requires understanding the target market, identifying the most effective channels for communication, and crafting compelling messages to capture the attention and interest of potential customers.

Retargeting

Retargeting is a marketing strategy that involves targeting individuals who have previously interacted with a brand's website or digital content in order to encourage them to take a desired action or make a purchase. It is a form of online advertising that aims to re-engage potential customers by displaying relevant ads to them across various websites and platforms.

The process of retargeting typically starts with the placement of a tracking pixel or code snippet on a website. This code tracks the behavior of visitors, such as the pages they visit, the products they view, or the actions they take. This allows marketers to create customized audiences based on specific criteria, such as people who abandoned a shopping cart or those who showed interest in a particular product.

Once these audiences are defined, retargeting ads can be shown to them as they browse the internet. These ads are designed to remind potential customers about the brand and influence their decision-making process. They may feature products or offers that the individual has previously shown interest in, or provide additional information or incentives to encourage conversion.

Retargeting can be an effective marketing tool as it allows brands to reach out to individuals who have already shown some level of interest in their products or services. By keeping the brand top-of-mind and providing personalized messaging, retargeting aims to increase brand recall, engagement, and ultimately, conversion rates.

Retention Marketing

Retention marketing is a strategic marketing approach that focuses on building and maintaining long-term relationships with existing customers. It involves implementing various techniques to encourage repeat purchases, increase customer loyalty, and minimize customer churn. Retention marketing aims to optimize customer lifetime value by ensuring that customers continue to engage with a brand or product over an extended period of time.

The primary goal of retention marketing is to retain customers rather than solely acquiring new ones. This is because it is typically more cost-effective to retain existing customers than to acquire new ones due to the high costs associated with acquiring new customers. By maintaining and strengthening the relationship with existing customers, retention marketing can lead to increased revenue, profitability, and brand loyalty.

Retention Rate

A retention rate, in the context of Marketing Management, refers to the percentage of customers or users who continue to engage with a product or service over a specific period of time. It is a key performance indicator that measures the effectiveness of a marketing strategy in customer loyalty and repeat business.

The retention rate is calculated by dividing the number of customers at the end of a period by the number of customers at the beginning of the same period, and then multiplying by 100 to express it as a percentage. A high retention rate indicates that customers are satisfied with the product or service and are likely to continue using it, which is crucial for sustaining long-term profitability and growth.

Return On Ad Spend (ROAS) Analysis Software

Return on Ad Spend (ROAS) Analysis Software is a tool used in the field of Marketing Management to analyze the effectiveness of advertising campaigns. It provides quantitative insights into the return generated from advertising investments across different channels and campaigns.

This software is designed to calculate the ratio of revenue generated to the cost of advertising. By tracking ad spend and correlating it with the corresponding sales or conversions, ROAS Analysis Software enables marketers to measure the impact of their advertising efforts and make data-driven decisions.

Return On Ad Spend (ROAS) Analysis Tools

Return on Ad Spend (ROAS) Analysis Tools are tools used in Marketing Management to measure the effectiveness and profitability of advertising campaigns. ROAS is a metric that calculates the revenue generated for every dollar spent on advertising. It helps marketers evaluate the success of their advertising efforts and make informed decisions about allocating their advertising budget.

ROAS analysis tools provide valuable insights into various aspects of advertising performance. They enable marketers to track and measure key performance indicators (KPIs) such as conversion rates, revenue generated, and return on investment (ROI). By analyzing these metrics, marketers can identify which advertising strategies and channels are driving the most valuable results and optimize their advertising campaigns accordingly.

ROAS analysis tools also play a crucial role in budget planning and forecasting. By understanding the ROAS of different advertising channels and campaigns, marketers can allocate their budget more effectively and efficiently. They can identify underperforming campaigns and reallocate funds to those that deliver higher returns. This optimization process helps maximize the overall profitability of advertising investments.

In addition to tracking and analyzing ROAS, these tools often provide advanced features such as campaign attribution modeling, customer segmentation, and ad performance benchmarking. These features enable marketers to gain deeper insights into the customer journey, understand the impact of different touchpoints, and identify opportunities for improvement.

Return On Ad Spend (ROAS) Analysis

Return on Ad Spend (ROAS) analysis is a vital performance metric used in the field of Marketing Management. It measures the profitability of a marketing campaign or an advertising investment by comparing the revenue generated to the amount of money spent on advertising.

ROAS is calculated by dividing the total revenue generated from a specific advertising campaign by the cost of that campaign. The result is expressed as a ratio or percentage, indicating the return on investment (ROI) for the advertising expenditure. A higher ROAS indicates a more profitable campaign, while a lower ROAS suggests a less effective one.

Return On Ad Spend (ROAS)

Return on Ad Spend (ROAS), in the context of Marketing Management, is a metric used to measure the effectiveness and profitability of a marketing campaign or advertisement. It quantifies the revenue generated from a campaign in relation to the amount of money spent on that campaign.

ROAS is calculated by dividing the total revenue generated from the campaign by the total cost of the campaign. The result is expressed as a ratio or a percentage. A higher ROAS indicates a more successful campaign, as it means that the revenue generated was higher than the amount spent on advertising.

Return On Investment (ROI)

Return on Investment (ROI) is a crucial metric in the field of Marketing Management. It measures the profitability of an investment by evaluating the net gain or loss generated from it in relation to the cost of the investment. ROI is used to assess the effectiveness and efficiency of marketing strategies, campaigns, and initiatives undertaken by an organization. ROI is typically expressed as a percentage or a ratio, allowing marketers to compare the returns of different marketing investments and make informed decisions. A positive ROI indicates that the investment has generated more revenue than its cost, resulting in a profit. On the other hand, a negative ROI suggests that the investment has resulted in a loss. To calculate ROI, the net profit or loss generated by the investment is divided by the cost of the investment and multiplied by 100 to obtain the percentage value. This formula allows marketers to quantify the financial impact of their marketing efforts and determine the value of their investments. By analyzing ROI, marketers can identify the most effective marketing activities and allocate resources accordingly. It helps in determining which marketing campaigns or channels are driving the highest returns and which ones need adjustments or termination. ROI analysis aids in optimizing marketing budgets, improving decision-making, and aligning marketing strategies with business goals. In summary, ROI is a key performance measure in Marketing Management that quantifies the profitability of marketing investments. It enables marketers to assess the impact of their activities, make data-driven decisions, and maximize the value generated from their marketing efforts.

Return On Marketing Investment (ROMI)

Return on Marketing Investment (ROMI) is a metric used in the field of Marketing Management to evaluate the effectiveness and efficiency of a marketing campaign or initiative. It measures the financial return that a company or organization achieves as a result of its marketing activities.

ROMI is calculated by dividing the revenue generated from a marketing campaign by the cost of the campaign. The result is expressed as a ratio or percentage, indicating the return on the investment made in the marketing efforts. A positive ROMI suggests that the revenue generated from the campaign is higher than the cost, indicating a profitable marketing initiative.

Revenue Attribution

Revenue attribution is a marketing management concept that involves tracking and assigning revenue generated from marketing activities to specific channels or touchpoints. It provides insight into the effectiveness and return on investment (ROI) of different marketing efforts and allows marketers to allocate resources more efficiently.

By analyzing and attributing revenue, marketers can understand which channels or campaigns are driving sales and which are underperforming. This enables them to optimize marketing strategies, determine which channels deserve more investment, and identify areas that need improvement. Revenue attribution helps marketers make data-driven decisions and allocate budgets based on the channels that contribute the most to revenue generation.

SWOT Analysis (Marketing)

A SWOT analysis is a strategic management tool used to evaluate the internal and external factors that can impact the success of a marketing initiative or overall marketing strategy. It is a framework that helps marketers identify and understand the organization's strengths, weaknesses, opportunities, and threats.

The strengths and weaknesses refer to the internal factors of the organization. This includes assessing the organization's resources, capabilities, and competencies. Strengths are the positive characteristics or advantages that give the organization a competitive edge. It can include things like a strong brand reputation, advanced technology, or skilled employees. Weaknesses, on the other hand, are the areas where the organization is lacking or has a disadvantage. It can include things like limited market share, outdated infrastructure, or poor customer service.

The opportunities and threats refer to the external factors that are beyond the control of the organization. Opportunities are the favorable conditions or trends in the external environment that can be leveraged to the organization's advantage. This can include things like emerging markets, changes in consumer behavior, or new technologies. Threats, on the other hand, are the unfavorable conditions or trends that pose risks to the organization. It can include things like new competitors entering the market, changes in government regulations, or economic downturns.

By conducting a SWOT analysis, marketers are able to gain a comprehensive understanding of the internal and external factors that can impact their marketing efforts. This helps them make informed decisions, develop effective marketing strategies, and allocate resources efficiently to maximize their chances of success.

SWOT Analysis In Marketing Applications

SWOT analysis is a strategic planning tool that is widely used in the field of marketing management. It is a technique that helps businesses identify and evaluate their internal strengths and weaknesses, as well as external opportunities and threats, in order to develop effective marketing strategies.

SWOT stands for strengths, weaknesses, opportunities, and threats. The strengths and weaknesses refer to the internal factors that a business possesses, such as its resources, capabilities, and competitive advantages. These factors can include a strong brand image, innovative products, skilled workforce, and efficient production processes. On the other hand, weaknesses are the aspects that the business lacks or needs improvement in, such as limited financial resources, outdated technology, or poor customer service.

Opportunities and threats, on the other hand, refer to the external factors that can impact a business. Opportunities are the favorable conditions in the market that a business can exploit to its advantage, such as emerging trends, untapped market segments, or changes in government regulations. Threats, on the other hand, are the unfavorable conditions that can pose challenges to the business, such as intense competition, changing consumer preferences, or economic downturns.

By conducting a SWOT analysis, marketing managers can gain a deeper understanding of their business's current situation and its competitive position in the market. This analysis helps them identify their unique selling points, areas for improvement, potential growth opportunities, and external threats that they need to mitigate. Marketing managers can then use this information to develop targeted marketing strategies that leverage their strengths, minimize their weaknesses, take advantage of opportunities, and overcome threats. The ultimate goal of using SWOT analysis in marketing applications is to enhance the business's competitive advantage and drive its success in the marketplace.

SWOT Analysis In Marketing

A SWOT analysis is a strategic planning tool used in the field of marketing management to evaluate the Strengths, Weaknesses, Opportunities, and Threats of a company or a product. It provides a comprehensive overview of the internal and external factors that can impact the success or failure of a marketing strategy.

The Strengths category focuses on the internal factors that give a company or product a competitive advantage. This could include a strong brand reputation, unique features, a talented workforce, or cost advantages. Identifying and leveraging these strengths can help a company differentiate itself from competitors and attract more customers.

The Weaknesses category considers the internal factors that may hinder a company's performance. These can include a lack of resources, poor product quality, ineffective marketing strategies, or a limited customer base. Recognizing and addressing these weaknesses is vital to improving the overall marketing strategy and preventing potential failures.

The Opportunities category examines external factors that can benefit a company or product. These opportunities may arise from changes in the industry or market trends, technological advancements, emerging markets, or potential partnerships. By seizing these opportunities, companies can expand their customer base and increase their market share.

The Threats category analyzes external factors that may pose risks to a company or product. This may include intense competition, changing consumer preferences, economic downturns, or regulatory changes. Understanding these threats enables companies to develop contingency plans and mitigate potential risks.

Overall, a SWOT analysis is an essential tool in marketing management as it helps companies identify their competitive advantages, address weaknesses, capitalize on opportunities, and minimize risks. It allows marketers to make informed decisions and develop effective marketing strategies that enhance a company's overall performance and profitability.

SWOT Analysis

A SWOT Analysis is a strategic planning tool used in the field of marketing management. It involves evaluating the internal Strengths and Weaknesses of an organization, as well as the external Opportunities and Threats present in the market or industry.

The Strengths and Weaknesses are internal factors within the control of the organization. A strength can be any aspect or characteristic of the organization that gives it a competitive advantage, such as a strong brand reputation or a unique product offering. On the other hand, a weakness is a limitation or deficiency that puts the organization at a disadvantage, such as poor customer service or outdated technology.

Opportunities and Threats are external factors that are not directly under the control of the organization, but they can have a significant impact on its performance. An opportunity is a favorable condition in the market that can be exploited to create a competitive advantage, such as emerging market trends or new customer segments. Conversely, a threat is a challenge or obstacle that the organization faces in the market, such as intense competition or changing regulations.

By conducting a SWOT Analysis, marketing managers can gain insights into the internal and external factors affecting the organization's marketing strategies. This analysis can help identify areas of strength that can be utilized, weaknesses that need to be addressed, opportunities to be pursued, and threats to be mitigated. The information gathered from the SWOT Analysis can guide marketing managers in developing effective marketing plans and making informed decisions to achieve the organization's marketing objectives.

Sales Enablement

Sales Enablement is a strategic approach to Marketing Management that aims to equip sales teams with the tools, resources, and knowledge necessary to effectively engage potential customers throughout the sales process. This discipline focuses on streamlining and enhancing the sales process by aligning marketing efforts with sales objectives.

Through sales enablement, marketing teams collaborate closely with sales teams to develop and deliver targeted content, training, and support materials that enable sales representatives to effectively communicate the value proposition of a product or service to prospective customers. The goal of sales enablement is to empower sales teams to be more knowledgeable, efficient, and successful in their interactions with customers.

Sales Funnel Visualization Software

Sales funnel visualization software refers to a specialized tool used in the field of Marketing Management to visually represent the different stages that a customer goes through before making a purchase. It provides a graphical representation of the sales process from the initial awareness stage to the final conversion, allowing marketers to track and analyze the progression of leads through each stage. The software enables marketers to create a visual representation of the sales funnel by mapping out the various stages and touch points that customers encounter along their buying journey. This includes capturing leads, qualifying them, nurturing relationships, and finally converting them into paying customers. The visualization often takes the form of a funnel shape, representing the decreasing number of leads as they progress through each stage. Sales funnel visualization software offers a range of features and functionalities that help marketers analyze and optimize the sales process. This may include the ability to track key metrics such as conversion rates, average deal size, and time spent at each stage. It can also provide insights into customer behavior, enabling marketers to identify optimization opportunities and refine their marketing strategies accordingly. Furthermore, the software often integrates with other marketing tools and platforms, such as CRM systems and marketing automation software, allowing for seamless data sharing and automation of tasks. This streamlines the marketing process and enhances efficiency, ultimately leading to improved sales performance. In summary, sales funnel visualization software is a critical tool for marketers in understanding and optimizing the customer journey. By providing a visual representation of the sales process, it enables marketers to identify bottlenecks, experiment with different strategies, and ultimately drive higher conversions and revenue.

Sales Funnel Visualization Solutions

Sales funnel visualization solutions are tools used in the field of marketing management to visually represent the process of converting potential customers into actual paying customers. A sales funnel refers to the journey that a customer takes, starting from the initial awareness stage, through consideration and evaluation, and finally reaching the decision to make a purchase. It is called a funnel because, at each stage, the number of potential customers decreases, similar to how a funnel narrows down. Sales funnel visualization solutions provide a graphical representation of this process, allowing marketers to track and analyze the progress and effectiveness of their marketing strategies. These solutions typically involve the use of software or digital platforms that offer features such as customizable templates, drag-and-drop functionality, and data integration. By visualizing the sales funnel, marketing managers can gain valuable insights into various aspects of their marketing campaigns. They can identify bottlenecks or areas of improvement in the customer journey, understand the conversion rates at each stage, and optimize their strategies to enhance customer engagement and drive higher sales. The visualization of the sales funnel enables marketers to view the overall customer flow, from the initial acquisition of leads to the final conversion. This allows them to identify potential areas where customers drop off or lose interest, facilitating the implementation of targeted strategies to address these issues. Overall, sales funnel visualization solutions provide marketing managers with a comprehensive and clear understanding of their customer acquisition and conversion process. By utilizing these tools effectively, marketers can optimize their marketing efforts, improve customer engagement, and ultimately drive business growth.

Sales Funnel Visualization

The sales funnel visualization is a key concept used in marketing management to understand and analyze the customer journey from the initial stage of awareness to the final stage of making a purchase. It represents a series of stages that a potential customer goes through before becoming a paying customer.

The first stage of the sales funnel is the awareness stage, where the customer becomes aware of the existence of a product or service. This is typically achieved through various marketing activities such as advertising, social media campaigns, or word-of-mouth referrals.

The next stage is the interest stage, where the customer shows interest in the product or service and seeks more information. This is often done by researching online, reading reviews, or engaging with the brand through email or chat support.

Once the customer has gathered enough information, they move on to the consideration stage. In this stage, they evaluate different options and compare features, pricing, and benefits. They may also seek advice from friends, colleagues, or experts to help them make a decision.

After the consideration stage, the customer enters the decision stage, where they make a final decision to purchase the product or service. At this point, they may negotiate pricing, sign contracts, or make a direct purchase.

The final stage of the sales funnel is the action stage, where the customer takes action and completes the purchase. This may involve making a payment, signing up for a subscription, or confirming an order.

By visualizing the sales funnel, marketing managers can identify areas of improvement, optimize the customer journey, and ultimately increase conversion rates. This helps businesses better understand their customers and align their marketing strategies accordingly.

Sales Funnel

A sales funnel is a conceptual model that represents the journey a customer takes from being aware of a product or service to making a purchase. It is a visual representation of the various stages a customer goes through and the actions they take along the way.

The sales funnel is based on the idea that not all leads will convert into customers, and it helps marketers understand and manage the customer's progression through the buying process. The funnel is divided into different stages, each representing a different level of customer engagement and commitment.

The first stage of the sales funnel is awareness, where the customer becomes aware of the product or service. This can be through various marketing channels such as advertising, social media, or word-of-mouth. The next stage is interest, where the customer shows interest in the product and starts to consider it as a potential solution to their needs.

The third stage is evaluation, where the customer conducts research, compares different options, and evaluates the features and benefits of the product. At this stage, marketers can use various tactics such as providing case studies, testimonials, or free trials to convince the customer of the product's value.

The fourth stage is decision, where the customer makes a purchase decision. This is the stage where the sales team or website plays a crucial role in closing the deal and converting the lead into a customer. Finally, the last stage is post-purchase, where the customer's experience with the product or service determines whether they become a loyal customer and advocate for the brand.

Search Engine Marketing (SEM) Tactics Tools

Search Engine Marketing (SEM) Tactics Tools refers to the various methods and tools used in the field of Marketing Management to promote and optimize websites through search engine advertising. SEM Tactics Tools are specifically designed to enhance online visibility and drive more traffic to a website by improving its ranking in search engine results pages (SERPs).

One of the key SEM tactics is keyword research, which involves identifying the most relevant and high-performing keywords or search terms that users enter into search engines. This research enables marketers to optimize their website's content and structure to align with user search intent and improve its visibility in search results. Keyword research tools such as Google Keyword Planner, SEMrush, and Moz Keyword Explorer are commonly used for this purpose.

Another important SEM tactic is paid advertising, also known as pay-per-click (PPC) advertising. This involves creating targeted ads that appear at the top or side of search engine results when users search for specific keywords. Popular platforms for PPC advertising include Google Ads (formerly Google AdWords) and Microsoft Advertising (formerly Bing Ads). These platforms provide tools for managing and optimizing PPC campaigns, such as bid management, ad scheduling, and performance tracking.

Search Engine Marketing (SEM) Tactics

Search Engine Marketing (SEM) tactics refer to the strategies and techniques used by marketing professionals to improve a website's visibility and traffic through paid advertising on search engines. It is a form of digital marketing that focuses on optimizing a company's website to increase its ranking on search engine results pages (SERPs).

SEM tactics typically involve the use of pay-per-click (PPC) advertising, where businesses pay a fee each time their ad is clicked. This allows companies to target specific keywords and phrases that are relevant to their products or services, ensuring that their ads are displayed to users who are actively searching for what they offer.

In addition to PPC advertising, SEM tactics may also include search engine optimization (SEO) techniques. SEO involves optimizing a website's content, structure, and HTML coding to improve its visibility and organic ranking on search engine results pages. By strategically incorporating relevant keywords, creating high-quality and shareable content, and optimizing meta tags and URLs, businesses can improve their chances of appearing higher in search engine results.

SEM tactics are essential for businesses looking to increase their online presence and attract more customers. By implementing effective SEM strategies, companies can reach a wider audience, increase website traffic, and ultimately improve their conversion rates and ROI. It is crucial for marketing professionals to stay updated on the latest SEM trends and best practices to ensure their campaigns are effective and successful.

Search Engine Marketing (SEM)

SEM, which stands for Search Engine Marketing, is a marketing management discipline that focuses on promoting websites and increasing their visibility through search engine results pages (SERPs). It involves various strategies and techniques that aim to optimize a website's ranking on search engine platforms, such as Google, Bing, Yahoo, and others. One of the primary goals of SEM is to attract organic (unpaid) traffic to a website by targeting specific keywords or phrases that are relevant to the business or industry. This is achieved through search engine optimization (SEO), which involves optimizing website content, meta tags, and other elements to improve its relevance and visibility in search engine results. In addition to SEO, SEM also encompasses paid advertising methods, commonly known as pay-per-click (PPC) advertising. PPC campaigns involve bidding on keywords and displaying ads in search engine results or relevant websites. Advertisers only pay when a user clicks on their ad, making it a cost-effective advertising method. Another crucial aspect of SEM is tracking and analyzing the performance of campaigns using various metrics, such as click-through rates (CTR), conversion rates, and return on investment (ROI). This data helps marketers understand the effectiveness of different strategies and make data-driven decisions to optimize their SEM efforts. Overall, SEM plays a vital role in digital marketing by helping businesses increase their online visibility and drive targeted traffic to their websites. By leveraging both organic and paid search tactics, SEM allows marketers to reach their target audience effectively and ultimately drive business growth.

SEM, or Search Engine Marketing, is a marketing management discipline that focuses on promoting websites and increasing their visibility through search engine results pages (SERPs). The goal is to attract organic traffic through search engine optimization (SEO) techniques, as well as through paid advertising methods like pay-per-click (PPC) campaigns. SEM also includes tracking and analyzing the performance of these campaigns to optimize their effectiveness.

Search Engine Optimization (SEO) Ranking

Search Engine Optimization (SEO) ranking refers to the position at which a website appears in the search engine results page (SERP) when a user performs a search using specific keywords or phrases. The goal of SEO is to improve a website's visibility and increase organic (non-paid) traffic from search engine users.

SEO ranking is crucial in marketing management as it directly impacts a website's visibility and potential to attract customers. Websites that rank higher in search results are more likely to receive clicks and visits, translating into increased brand exposure, website traffic, and potential conversions. Moreover, higher rankings often imply that a website is considered more trustworthy and relevant by search engines, improving its credibility and reputation.

Search Engine Optimization (SEO)

Search Engine Optimization (SEO) is a marketing management discipline that focuses on improving a website's visibility and ranking on search engine results pages (SERPs). It involves optimizing various aspects of a website, such as its content, structure, and HTML code, in order to make it more appealing to search engines and to increase its chances of being indexed and ranked highly.

SEO aims to enhance both the quantity and quality of organic (non-paid) traffic to a website by targeting relevant keywords and phrases that potential customers might use in their search queries. By employing SEO strategies, marketers can increase a website's visibility to users searching for products or services in their industry, ultimately leading to more website traffic, conversions, and revenue.

Effective SEO involves conducting keyword research to identify high-ranking keywords with reasonable search volume, incorporating these keywords into website content and meta tags, and optimizing the website's structure to make it easy for search engine crawlers to index and understand the content. Additionally, SEO often involves building high-quality backlinks from reputable websites, as search engines tend to see backlinks as votes of credibility and relevance.

While the exact algorithms used by search engines to determine rankings are not publicly disclosed, SEO professionals stay up-to-date with industry trends and best practices to ensure their websites remain optimized for search engine success.

Search Engine Results Page (SERP)

A Search Engine Results Page (SERP) is a webpage displayed by a search engine in response to a user's search query. It lists the websites and other content relevant to the query in a ranked order, based on their perceived relevance and quality by the search engine's algorithm.

The primary goal of a SERP in the context of marketing management is to provide users with the most relevant and useful information related to their search query. This is important for marketers as it determines the visibility and exposure of their website or content in organic search results. The higher the ranking on the SERP, the higher the chances of attracting organic traffic to their site.

Search Intent Targeting Techniques Software

Search intent targeting techniques software in the context of Marketing Management refers to a tool or platform that helps marketers identify and cater to the specific search intents of their target audience.

Search intent, also known as user intent, refers to the underlying purpose or goal behind a user's online search query. Understanding search intent is crucial for marketers as it allows them to tailor their content and advertising strategies to meet the needs and expectations of their target audience.

Search intent targeting techniques software employs various methods and algorithms to analyze search queries and determine the intent behind them. This software combines data analysis, machine learning, and natural language processing techniques to extract meaningful insights and patterns from search data.

With search intent targeting techniques software, marketers can segment their target audience based on different search intents such as informational, transactional, navigational, or commercial. By understanding the search intent of their audience, marketers can create more relevant and personalized content, optimize on-page SEO, improve ad targeting, and enhance the overall user experience.

This software provides marketers with valuable insights into consumer behavior, allowing them to identify emerging trends, optimize marketing campaigns, and make data-driven decisions. By aligning their marketing strategies with search intent, marketers can drive more qualified traffic, increase conversion rates, and ultimately achieve their business goals.

Search Intent Targeting Techniques

Search intent targeting techniques refer to the strategies and methodologies employed by marketers to optimize their online presence and advertisements based on the intent of online users during their online search activities. These techniques help in delivering relevant and personalized content to users, thereby improving the user experience and increasing the chances of conversions.

One of the key search intent targeting techniques is keyword research and analysis. Marketers identify and analyze the keywords and phrases that users frequently search for related to their products or services. This helps them create relevant content and optimize their websites for better search engine rankings.

Another technique is creating landing pages tailored to specific search intents. This involves designing and optimizing landing pages to align with the search intent of users. Marketers aim to provide accurate and valuable information that users are looking for, thus increasing the chances of conversion.

Personalization is also an important aspect of search intent targeting. By collecting user data and employing various technologies, marketers can personalize the content and advertisements shown to users based on their search intent and previous interactions. This enhances the user experience and increases the engagement and conversion rates.

Furthermore, analyzing user behavior and search patterns can provide insights into the intent behind their search queries. Marketers can utilize this data to tailor their marketing efforts and strategies accordingly, effectively reaching and engaging with the target audience.

Search Intent Targeting

Search intent targeting is a marketing strategy used in the field of marketing management to optimize search engine marketing campaigns. It involves identifying and understanding the intent behind an individual's search query and tailoring marketing efforts to effectively meet those specific needs.

By analyzing search queries, marketers can determine the intent of the searcher, whether it is informational, navigational, or transactional. Informational intent refers to searches where individuals are looking for information or answers to their questions. Navigational intent refers to searches where individuals are looking for a specific website or brand. Transactional intent refers to searches where individuals are looking to make a purchase or take a specific action.

With search intent targeting, marketers can create targeted campaigns that align with the intent of the user's search query. This involves creating relevant and optimized content, including keywords and ad copy, that directly addresses the searcher's needs and matches their intent. By delivering the right content to the right audience at the right time, marketers can improve the effectiveness and efficiency of their marketing efforts.

Furthermore, search intent targeting allows marketers to understand customer behavior and preferences, enabling them to make data-driven decisions when it comes to campaign optimization and resource allocation. By continuously monitoring and analyzing search intent data, marketers can refine their strategies and make informed marketing decisions that lead to higher conversion rates and better overall campaign performance.

Segmentation Strategies

Segmentation strategies refer to the techniques and approaches used by marketers to divide a heterogeneous market into smaller, more homogeneous groups called market segments. This process involves identifying and categorizing customers based on their shared characteristics, preferences, needs, and behaviors. The ultimate goal of segmentation strategies is to enable marketers to design and implement targeted marketing campaigns that effectively reach and engage specific segment(s) of the market.

Segmentation strategies offer several benefits for marketers. Firstly, they allow marketers to gain a deeper understanding of their target customers by identifying the unique needs, motivations, and preferences of different market segments. This understanding enables marketers to tailor their marketing efforts, products, and services to meet the specific needs and desires of each segment, thus increasing customer satisfaction and loyalty.

Secondly, segmentation strategies help marketers to optimize the allocation of resources by targeting the most profitable and responsive market segments. By focusing their efforts on segments that are most likely to be interested in and purchase their offerings, marketers can achieve higher returns on investment and improve overall marketing efficiency.

Lastly, segmentation strategies enable marketers to differentiate themselves from competitors by creating a strong positioning and competitive advantage in the marketplace. By understanding the unique needs and preferences of different segments, marketers can design and communicate customized value propositions that resonate with each segment, thereby establishing a distinctive brand image and attracting customers away from competitors.

Segmentation Variables

Segmentation variables refer to the various criteria or factors that marketers use to divide a market into distinct groups or segments. These variables help marketers to identify and understand the different needs, characteristics, behaviors, and preferences of different customer segments.

In the context of marketing management, segmentation variables serve as the foundation for market segmentation. Market segmentation is the process of dividing a market into homogeneous groups or segments based on similar attributes or characteristics. The purpose of segmenting a market is to enable marketers to develop targeted marketing strategies and initiatives that effectively address the unique needs and wants of each segment.

Sentiment Analysis

Sentiment analysis in the context of Marketing Management is a process of determining and interpreting the attitudes, opinions, and emotions expressed in customer feedback, online reviews, social media posts, and other forms of consumer communication. It involves analyzing text data to understand the sentiment or overall sentiment polarity of a particular content or brand.

By employing natural language processing and machine learning techniques, sentiment analysis enables marketers to gain actionable insights into how customers perceive their products, services, or brand image. It helps identify positive, neutral, or negative sentiments associated with specific aspects such as price, quality, customer service, features, and more.

The application of sentiment analysis in marketing management extends beyond brand monitoring. It assists in identifying customer preferences, gauging customer satisfaction, evaluating the effectiveness of marketing campaigns, and conducting competitive analysis. Marketers can use sentiment analysis to identify patterns and trends in customer sentiments, enabling them to make informed decisions and tailor their marketing strategies to target customer needs and preferences effectively.

Sentiment analysis plays a crucial role in reputation management by allowing marketers to promptly address negative sentiments and mitigate potential damage to brand reputation. It also aids in identifying brand advocates and leveraging positive sentiments for marketing purposes, such as testimonials, user-generated content, and influencer marketing campaigns.

Service Marketing

Service Marketing can be defined as a specialized branch of marketing management that focuses on promoting and selling services rather than physical products. It involves marketing strategies and techniques that are specifically tailored to address the unique characteristics and challenges associated with marketing intangible offerings.

Services are intangible, perishable, and cannot be stored like physical goods. Additionally, they are typically produced and consumed simultaneously, making the service experience a crucial factor in customer satisfaction. These characteristics necessitate a different approach to marketing compared to product marketing.

Service marketing encompasses activities such as service design, pricing, promotion, and distribution. It involves identifying the target market, understanding their needs and preferences, and developing service offerings that meet those requirements. Service marketers also focus on building strong, long-term customer relationships, as repeat business and positive word-of-mouth play a significant role in service business success.

Effective service marketing incorporates elements of traditional marketing, such as market research and segmenting, targeting, and positioning. However, it also includes specialized strategies to manage service quality, customer expectations, and service delivery. Service marketers often utilize techniques like service blueprinting, customer journey mapping, and service recovery to ensure a consistent and exceptional service experience.

In conclusion, service marketing refers to the application of marketing principles and strategies to promote intangible services. It entails understanding the unique characteristics of services, developing tailored marketing approaches, and managing service quality to create customer value and satisfaction.

Service-Dominant Logic (SDL)

Service-Dominant Logic (SDL) is a theoretical framework within the field of Marketing Management, that challenges the traditional view of marketing where the focus is on the exchange of tangible goods. Instead, SDL emphasizes the co-creation of value through the exchange of services.

This perspective recognizes that value is not solely derived from the features and benefits of products or services, but rather from the ongoing interaction between the provider and the customer. It highlights that value is co-created through a collaborative process where both parties actively engage in the creation and delivery of value.

Share Of Wallet (SOW)

Share of Wallet (SOW) is a key metric used in Marketing Management to measure the percentage of a customer's spending that a particular company captures within a specific market or industry. It provides insights into the company's market share and customer loyalty, helping businesses identify opportunities to increase their revenue streams.

SOW is calculated by dividing the total amount spent by a customer on a specific product or service category by the total amount spent by the customer across all companies within that category. This calculation provides a measure of the customer's loyalty and purchasing power within the market.

Shopper Experience

Shopper Experience refers to the overall perception and interaction of a consumer or potential buyer with a brand, product, or service during the process of making a purchase decision. It encompasses the various touchpoints and interactions that occur throughout the customer journey, from initial awareness and consideration to the actual purchase and post-purchase experiences.

In the context of Marketing Management, Shopper Experience is a crucial element that heavily influences consumer behavior and purchase decisions. It encompasses both online and offline channels, including physical retail stores, e-commerce websites, mobile apps, and social media platforms. The goal of managing the Shopper Experience is to create positive, seamless, and memorable interactions that effectively engage and satisfy the customer, ultimately leading to increased brand loyalty, repeat purchases, and positive word-of-mouth.

The discipline of Marketing Management focuses on understanding and strategically managing the Shopper Experience to enhance customer satisfaction and drive business growth. This involves analyzing consumer behavior, preferences, and expectations at each touchpoint, identifying pain points or areas of improvement, and implementing appropriate marketing strategies, tactics, and technologies to optimize the overall Shopper Experience.

Effective Shopper Experience management involves various aspects such as personalized marketing communications, user-friendly interfaces, intuitive navigation, streamlined checkout processes, prompt and efficient customer support, and relevant and compelling product information. It also involves measuring and tracking key performance indicators, conducting market research, and continuously adapting and optimizing strategies based on consumer feedback and market trends.

In summary, Shopper Experience in the Marketing Management discipline refers to the holistic management of consumer interactions and perceptions throughout the customer journey, with the aim of creating positive, engaging, and satisfying experiences that drive customer loyalty and business growth.

Shopper Marketing Insights Tools

Shopper Marketing Insights Tools refer to a set of strategies, methodologies, and techniques utilized by marketing management professionals to gain a comprehensive understanding of consumer behavior and purchase decision-making within retail environments. These tools enable marketers to analyze and interpret data, identify consumer trends and patterns, and subsequently develop effective marketing strategies to influence shopper behavior and drive sales.

Shopper Marketing Insights Tools encompass various analytical approaches and market research techniques that aid in understanding the psychology of consumers and their shopping experiences. This includes methods such as consumer surveys, focus groups, observational studies, and data analysis of purchasing patterns and shopping habits. These tools help marketers gain insights into shopper motivations, preferences, and shopping journeys, allowing businesses to tailor their marketing strategies accordingly.

Shopper Marketing Insights

Shopper marketing insights refer to the information and knowledge gained through the systematic analysis of consumer behavior and purchasing patterns within the context of the marketing management discipline. This field focuses on understanding and influencing the decision-making process of shoppers, with the objective of maximizing sales and creating meaningful connections between shoppers and brands.

Shopper marketing insights help marketers identify the various factors that affect a shopper's decision-making process, such as product packaging, pricing, promotions, and the overall shopping experience. By analyzing and interpreting these insights, marketers can tailor their strategies and tactics to effectively engage with shoppers and drive sales growth.

Shopper Marketing

Shopper Marketing refers to a strategic approach in marketing management that involves understanding and influencing the purchasing decisions of consumers during their shopping experiences. It aims to create targeted and personalized marketing campaigns that effectively connect with shoppers at various touchpoints and encourage them to make purchase decisions.

In this discipline, the focus is on analyzing consumer behavior and developing strategies that align with the shoppers' preferences, needs, and shopping journeys. Shopper Marketing goes beyond traditional marketing practices by considering the entire shopping ecosystem, including physical stores, online platforms, and the interaction between consumers and brands.

The key objectives of Shopper Marketing include enhancing brand awareness and loyalty, increasing sales, and improving the overall shopping experience for consumers. It involves gathering insights about the target audience, including their demographics, psychographics, and shopping habits. With this information, marketers can design personalized marketing campaigns that resonate with shoppers and influence their purchasing decisions.

Effective shopper marketing strategies often incorporate elements such as point-of-sale displays, special promotions, product demonstrations, interactive experiences, and targeted advertising. By integrating these tactics, marketers can create a seamless and engaging shopping experience that encourages consumers to choose their brand over competitors.

Overall, Shopper Marketing is a dynamic and evolving discipline within marketing management that recognizes the importance of understanding and influencing consumer behavior during the shopping process. It requires a deep understanding of consumer preferences, the ability to create personalized marketing campaigns, and the use of various touchpoints to connect with shoppers effectively.

Social Commerce

Social commerce refers to a business strategy that combines social media and online shopping platforms to enable direct selling of products or services to consumers. It is a subset of e-commerce that leverages social networks, such as Facebook, Instagram, and Pinterest, to facilitate transactions and drive customer engagement.

With the rise of social media, consumers now spend a significant amount of time online, browsing and interacting with content on various social platforms. Social commerce takes advantage of this trend by providing a seamless shopping experience within these social media environments. It allows businesses to showcase their products or services, engage with customers, and ultimately drive sales, all within the social media ecosystem.

One of the key aspects of social commerce is the integration of social media features and functionalities into the online shopping experience. For example, businesses can create shoppable posts or advertisements that allow users to make a purchase directly from their social media feed. Additionally, social commerce often incorporates user-generated content, such as reviews, ratings, and testimonials, which helps build trust and credibility among potential customers.

Furthermore, social commerce enables businesses to leverage social networks as a powerful marketing tool by using targeted advertising, influencer marketing, and social recommendations to reach and engage with their target audience. By tapping into the vast user base and extensive data available on social media platforms, businesses can deliver personalized and relevant product offerings, promotions, and recommendations to individual users.

Social Listening

Social listening is a marketing management practice that involves monitoring and analyzing social media platforms and online channels to gather insights and understand customer opinions, preferences, and sentiment. It helps businesses gain a deep understanding of customer needs, interests, and behaviors, and provides valuable market intelligence.

By systematically monitoring and analyzing conversations, mentions, and interactions on platforms like Facebook, Twitter, Instagram, and online forums, businesses can identify emerging trends, track brand reputation, and measure the impact of marketing efforts. Through social listening, companies can stay informed about customer perceptions, their satisfaction levels, and the effectiveness of their marketing campaigns.

Social Media Advertising Metrics Software

Social Media Advertising Metrics Software is a tool used in the field of Marketing Management to measure and analyze the performance and effectiveness of social media advertising campaigns. It is a software application designed to collect, track, and interpret data related to various metrics specific to social media advertising, such as impressions, clicks, conversions, reach, engagement, and ROI (Return on Investment).

This software helps marketers and advertisers to understand the impact of their social media advertising efforts and make informed decisions to optimize performance. It provides a comprehensive view of campaign performance by aggregating data from multiple social media platforms, such as Facebook, Twitter, Instagram, LinkedIn, and YouTube, into a single dashboard or interface.

By using Social Media Advertising Metrics Software, marketers can gain real-time insights into key performance indicators (KPIs) to evaluate the success of their campaigns. They can track the reach and visibility of their ads, measure audience engagement and interactions, assess the conversion rates and return on ad spend (ROAS), and identify trends or patterns that can inform future strategies.

Furthermore, this software allows marketers to compare the performance of different social media channels, A/B test their ad creative and messaging, and monitor the effectiveness of their targeting and segmentation strategies. It helps them to identify high-performing ads, target specific customer segments, identify opportunities for improvement, and allocate their advertising budget effectively.

Social Media Advertising Metrics Tools

Social media advertising metrics tools are software applications used by marketing managers to track, analyze, and measure the effectiveness of their social media advertising campaigns. These tools provide valuable insights and data that help marketing managers make informed decisions about their advertising strategies in real-time.

Marketing managers use social media advertising metrics tools to monitor various key performance indicators (KPIs) related to their social media ad campaigns. These KPIs include reach, engagement, impressions, click-through rate (CTR), conversion rate, cost per click (CPC), return on ad spend (ROAS), and overall return on investment (ROI).

Social Media Advertising Metrics

Social Media Advertising Metrics refers to the quantitative and qualitative measurements used to evaluate the performance of social media advertising campaigns. These metrics are vital in the field of Marketing Management as they help marketers assess the effectiveness and success of their social media advertising strategies.

Quantitative metrics provide numerical data about various aspects of a social media advertising campaign. These metrics include reach, impressions, click-through rates (CTR), conversion rates, cost-per-click (CPC), cost-per-acquisition (CPA), and return on investment (ROI). Reach measures the number of unique users who see an advertisement, while impressions represent the total number of times an advertisement is displayed. CTR measures the percentage of users who click on an advertisement after viewing it, and conversion rates determine the number of users who complete a desired action, such as making a purchase or filling out a form. CPC and CPA metrics measure the cost incurred per click and acquisition, respectively, and ROI assesses the profitability of the advertising investment.

Social Media Advertising

Social Media Advertising refers to the process of promoting products or services through the use of various social media platforms such as Facebook, Instagram, Twitter, and LinkedIn. It involves creating and delivering persuasive messages to a specific target audience in order to generate awareness, engagement, and conversion.

In the context of Marketing Management, social media advertising plays a crucial role in reaching and engaging with the target market. It allows businesses to leverage the popularity and wide user base of social media platforms to effectively communicate their brand message and offerings.

Social media advertising offers several advantages for marketers. Firstly, it provides a cost-effective way to reach a large audience, as many social media platforms offer options to target specific demographics and interests. Secondly, it allows for real-time interaction and feedback between businesses and customers, fostering engagement and building brand loyalty. Thirdly, it offers valuable insights and data on consumer behavior, allowing marketers to analyze and optimize their campaigns for better results.

Despite its advantages, social media advertising also presents challenges for marketers. The competition for audience attention is intense, and standing out from the crowd requires creative and compelling content. Additionally, the ever-changing algorithms and rules of social media platforms can impact the visibility and effectiveness of ads, requiring marketers to stay up-to-date and adapt their strategies accordingly.

Social Media Algorithm

A social media algorithm is a set of rules or calculations used by social media platforms to determine which content is displayed to users in their newsfeeds or search results. This algorithm is designed to optimize the user experience by presenting them with content that is most relevant, engaging, and valuable to them.

In the context of Marketing Management, social media algorithms play a crucial role as they determine the reach and visibility of a brand's content on social media platforms. Understanding and adapting to these algorithms is essential for effective social media marketing strategies.

Social media algorithms consider various factors when deciding what content to display to users. These factors may include the user's past interactions, interests, demographics, and the popularity or engagement levels of the content. The goal of the algorithm is to present users with content that is likely to resonate with them and keep them engaged on the platform.

For marketing management professionals, it is important to stay updated with the changes in social media algorithms to ensure that their content reaches the target audience. By understanding the preferences and behavior of their target market, marketers can create content that aligns with the algorithm's criteria and improves visibility.

Social Media Engagement Strategies

Social media engagement strategies refer to the planned and organized efforts of a company or brand to interact, connect, and build relationships with its target audience through social media platforms. As a key component of marketing management, these strategies aim to foster engagement, increase brand visibility, and ultimately drive desired actions such as conversions and customer loyalty.

Effective social media engagement strategies involve several key elements. Firstly, understanding the target audience is crucial. By gaining insights into their demographics, interests, and behaviors, marketers can tailor their content and messaging to resonate with the audience and spark meaningful interactions. Additionally, thorough research and analysis of the social media landscape can help identify the most appropriate platforms and channels for engagement, ensuring that resources are allocated efficiently.

Creating valuable and engaging content is another essential aspect of social media engagement strategies. This can include a mix of informative articles, compelling visuals, entertaining videos, and interactive posts that encourage audience participation. By providing relevant and interesting content, brands can capture the attention of their target audience and prompt them to like, comment, share, and follow, thereby increasing brand reach and visibility.

Furthermore, actively monitoring and responding to audience feedback and comments is vital for building and maintaining relationships. Engaging in two-way conversations not only demonstrates that the brand values its customers but also provides opportunities for gathering insights, addressing concerns, and resolving queries or issues in a timely manner.

Overall, by employing effective social media engagement strategies, marketers can leverage the power of social media to enhance brand awareness, foster meaningful connections, and drive business growth.

Social Media Engagement Strategy Platforms

Social media engagement strategy platforms are tools or platforms used by marketing professionals to create and implement effective strategies for engaging with their target audience on social media platforms. These platforms provide features and functionalities that enable marketers to plan, execute, and measure the effectiveness of their social media engagement efforts.

With the increasing popularity and influence of social media, it has become crucial for businesses to establish a strong presence on these platforms and actively engage with their audience. Social media engagement refers to the interaction between a brand and its followers, which includes likes, comments, shares, mentions, and direct messages. It is an essential element of successful social media marketing as it helps build brand awareness, drive website traffic, increase customer loyalty, and boost sales.

Social media engagement strategy platforms offer a wide range of tools and features that facilitate effective engagement with the target audience. These platforms provide features such as content scheduling, social media monitoring, analytics, campaign tracking, and audience segmentation. Marketers can use these features to plan and schedule their social media content, monitor and respond to customer interactions, analyze the performance of their campaigns, and segment their audience based on demographics, interests, and behaviors.

Furthermore, social media engagement strategy platforms allow marketers to collaborate with team members, manage multiple social media accounts, and track the performance of their competitors. They provide comprehensive dashboards and reports that help marketers make data-driven decisions and optimize their social media engagement strategies.

Social Media Engagement

Social media engagement refers to the level of interaction, involvement, and attention that a brand or organization receives from its target audience on social media platforms. It is a measure of how effectively a brand is able to connect and engage with its followers, fans, and customers in the online space.

In the context of marketing management, social media engagement plays a crucial role in building brand awareness, generating leads, and fostering customer loyalty. It encompasses a range of activities such as likes, shares, comments, mentions, retweets, and direct messages that indicate the level of interest and engagement from users.

Effective social media engagement requires strategic planning and implementation of various tactics such as creating relevant and compelling content, responding to customer inquiries and feedback, and actively participating in online conversations. By actively engaging with their target audience on social media, brand managers can build a positive brand image, gain insights into customer preferences, and create a loyal and supportive customer base.

Monitoring and analyzing social media engagement metrics such as reach, engagement rate, and sentiment can provide valuable insights into the effectiveness of a brand's social media efforts. These metrics help marketing managers understand the impact of their social media campaigns, make data-driven decisions, and optimize their strategies to achieve better business outcomes.

Social Media Influencer

A social media influencer is an individual who has established a significant presence and following on social media platforms, such as Instagram, YouTube, or TikTok. They are considered authoritative figures and are able to influence the opinions, behaviors, and purchasing decisions of their followers.

In the context of marketing management, social media influencers have emerged as powerful tools for brands to reach and engage with their target audiences. These influencers typically have a niche or expertise in a specific industry or topic, and their followers trust and value their opinions and recommendations. Marketers can leverage this trust and credibility to create brand awareness, generate leads, and drive sales.

Social Media Listening Tools

Social media listening tools refer to software applications or platforms that enable marketing managers to monitor, track, and analyze conversations, mentions, and discussions happening on various social media channels. These tools assist in gathering valuable insights and data about consumers' opinions, preferences, and behaviors, which can be leveraged to inform marketing strategies and decision-making processes.

In the field of marketing management, social media listening tools play a crucial role in understanding and engaging with the target audience. By monitoring social media platforms such as Facebook, Twitter, Instagram, and LinkedIn, these tools provide a comprehensive view of customers' sentiments, trends, and influencers within the digital landscape.

Marketing managers can utilize social media listening tools to:

- Track brand mentions and sentiment: By monitoring social media conversations, marketing managers can gauge the overall perception of their brand and identify any emerging positive or negative sentiments.
- Monitor competitors: These tools enable the identification and analysis of competitor activities and strategies, helping marketing managers to benchmark their own performance and identify areas of improvement.
- Identify customer trends and preferences: Social media listening tools allow marketing managers to track discussions about products, services, and industry trends, helping them identify evolving customer needs and preferences.
- Identify and engage with influencers: By identifying influential individuals within specific niches, marketing managers can develop relationships and partnerships with these influencers to amplify their brand message and reach a broader audience.

Overall, social media listening tools provide marketing managers with invaluable insights into consumer behavior, allowing them to make informed decisions and tailor their marketing strategies to effectively engage with their target audience.

Social Media Marketing

Social Media Marketing refers to the use of social media platforms and websites to promote a product or service. It is a form of digital marketing that utilizes social media channels such as Facebook, Instagram, Twitter, LinkedIn, and YouTube to reach and engage with the target audience.

As part of the Marketing Management discipline, Social Media Marketing focuses on using social media platforms strategically to build brand awareness, increase website traffic, generate leads, and ultimately drive sales. It involves creating and sharing content that is relevant and valuable to the target audience, with the goal of fostering meaningful relationships and interactions.

Social Media Marketing is an essential component of a company's overall marketing strategy. It allows businesses to connect with their customers on a personal level, enabling them to understand their needs and preferences better. By leveraging social media platforms, companies can create targeted advertising campaigns, track and analyze customer behaviors and preferences, and make data-driven decisions to optimize their marketing efforts.

Furthermore, Social Media Marketing enables businesses to establish themselves as thought leaders in their industry by sharing valuable insights and expertise. It also provides a platform for customers to provide feedback, ask questions, and engage in conversations, creating a sense of community and fostering brand loyalty.

Social Media Optimization (SMO)

Social Media Optimization (SMO) is a marketing strategy that aims to enhance a company's online presence and visibility through various social media platforms. It involves the systematic utilization of social media channels to promote a brand, boost brand awareness, engage with target audiences, and drive traffic to websites. SMO encompasses different techniques and tactics to optimize a company's social media profiles, posts, and content to effectively reach and connect with the target audience.

In the field of marketing management, SMO plays a crucial role by leveraging the power of social media in building a strong brand image and fostering brand loyalty. By strategically utilizing social media platforms such as Facebook, Twitter, Instagram, LinkedIn, and YouTube, companies can effectively communicate with their audience, establish a positive brand reputation, and develop a loyal customer base. SMO also involves the use of social media analytics tools to monitor and analyze the performance of social media campaigns, allowing companies to track their online presence and make data-driven decisions.

Social Proof

Social proof, in the context of marketing management, refers to the psychological phenomenon wherein people tend to make decisions and adopt behaviors based on the actions and opinions of others. It is a powerful marketing concept that leverages the influence of social validation to shape consumer behavior and increase conversions.

When consumers see that others have already purchased or endorsed a product or service, they perceive it as more trustworthy and valuable. This perception is especially influential in situations where individuals lack personal experience or knowledge about a particular offering. Social proof can be manifested in various forms, such as customer reviews, testimonials, case studies, celebrity endorsements, social media likes and shares, and even numerical indicators like ratings and popularity metrics.

Marketers strategically use social proof to build credibility, foster trust, and reduce perceived risks associated with a purchase decision. By showcasing positive experiences and emotions of previous customers or influential individuals, companies can influence potential buyers to align their actions with the behavior of the majority. This helps create a sense of safety, as consumers feel they are making an informed choice that aligns with the crowd's preferences.

The concept of social proof aligns with the principles of social influence theory, which suggests that individuals are more likely to conform when they perceive others' behavior as desirable or correct. By effectively utilizing social proof, marketing managers can tap into the innate human need to belong and use it to drive sales, increase brand loyalty, and shape consumer attitudes in a desired direction.

Sponsored Content Strategies

Sponsored Content Strategies refers to the techniques and approaches employed by marketers in creating and distributing sponsored content that is designed to promote their brand, products, or services. Sponsored content is content that is created and shared by an individual, organization, or brand, and is paid for by another entity to promote their offerings.

Successful sponsored content strategies involve careful planning and execution to ensure that the content aligns with the brand's objectives and resonates with the target audience. It requires a deep understanding of the target market, as well as knowledge of the platforms and channels on which the content will be distributed.

Sponsored Content Strategy Platforms

A sponsored content strategy platform is a technology-based solution that helps marketers plan, execute, and manage their sponsored content campaigns. It provides a centralized platform where marketers can research, build, distribute, and measure the success of their sponsored content initiatives.

Such platforms often offer a variety of features and tools that facilitate the entire process of creating and promoting sponsored content. They typically include capabilities such as audience targeting, content recommendation, campaign management, and performance tracking.

Sponsored Content

Sponsored content refers to marketing messages or advertisements that are created and paid for by a third-party advertiser but are designed to blend seamlessly into the regular, non-promotional content of a particular medium or platform. This type of content is typically used as a way to engage and inform the target audience without directly selling or promoting a product or service.

The goal of sponsored content is to provide valuable and relevant information to the audience, while also promoting the advertiser's brand or message. It often takes the form of articles, videos, infographics, or other formats that resemble the regular content found on the platform. By presenting the content in a non-intrusive and organic way, sponsored content aims to capture the attention and interest of the audience, leading to increased brand awareness, engagement, and ultimately, conversion.

Sponsored Post

Marketing Management is a discipline that involves the planning, organizing, directing, and controlling of the marketing activities of an organization. It is a strategic process that aims to understand, influence, and satisfy the needs and wants of customers in a profitable manner.

Marketing Management encompasses various activities such as market research, product development, pricing, promotion, and distribution. These activities are carried out with the goal of creating, communicating, delivering, and exchanging value with customers.

The discipline of Marketing Management involves the analysis of market opportunities, identification of target markets, and the development of marketing strategies to reach and engage these target markets. It also includes the implementation and monitoring of marketing programs and campaigns to achieve the organization's marketing objectives.

Marketing Management requires an understanding of consumer behavior, market dynamics, competitive landscape, and marketing metrics. It involves making strategic decisions based on market insights and customer feedback, and continuously adapting and optimizing marketing efforts based on the changing business environment.

Overall, Marketing Management plays a crucial role in driving business growth and profitability. It involves the application of various marketing concepts, principles, and tools to create and deliver superior customer value, build strong customer relationships, and achieve sustainable competitive advantage in the marketplace.

Storytelling Marketing

Storytelling marketing refers to the strategic use of storytelling techniques and narratives to engage and connect with consumers in the context of marketing management. It involves crafting and sharing compelling stories that resonate with target audiences to effectively communicate brand messages, values, and offerings.

Through storytelling marketing, organizations aim to create an emotional connection with consumers by tapping into their desires, fears, dreams, and aspirations. By integrating narratives into marketing campaigns and brand communications, companies can differentiate themselves from competitors and capture the attention and loyalty of consumers.

Storytelling In Marketing Technique Tools

Storytelling in marketing refers to the strategic use of narratives and storytelling techniques to engage and connect with consumers, with the objective of enhancing brand awareness, promoting products or services, and influencing purchasing decisions. It is a powerful marketing technique that leverages the emotional and psychological impact of well-crafted stories to effectively communicate brand messages, values, and offerings to target audiences.

Storytelling in marketing management involves the skillful integration of storytelling elements such as characters, plot, conflict, and resolution into various marketing strategies and campaigns. Marketers use narratives to create a compelling brand story that resonates with consumers, connects on a deeper level, and establishes a memorable and meaningful brand identity.

Storytelling In Marketing Techniques

Storytelling in marketing techniques refers to the strategic use of narratives to engage and connect with target audiences in order to achieve marketing goals. It involves incorporating storytelling elements in marketing messages and campaigns to captivate, inspire, and influence consumers.

Storytelling is an essential tool in marketing management, enabling brands to differentiate themselves in a crowded marketplace while forging emotional connections with consumers. By crafting narratives that resonate with the target audience, marketers can effectively communicate brand values, capture attention, and build brand loyalty.

Storytelling In Marketing

Storytelling in marketing refers to the strategic use of narratives to communicate a brand's message, engage consumers, and drive conversions. It involves crafting compelling stories that resonate with the target audience, highlighting the brand's values, unique selling propositions, and emotional appeal.

In marketing management, storytelling is a powerful tool that enables companies to create a coherent and memorable brand identity. By using storytelling techniques, marketers can captivate their audience, establish an emotional connection, and differentiate their brand from competitors.

Storytelling

The marketing management discipline involves the practice of storytelling, which can be defined as a strategic communication process that aims to convey a message or information to a target audience by using narrative techniques.

In the context of marketing management, storytelling refers to the use of storytelling techniques to create and communicate a brand's story or narrative to its target customers. It is a powerful tool that helps businesses in building and maintaining their brand image, engaging and connecting with their audience, and influencing their perception and behavior.

Storytelling in marketing management is not merely about telling stories for entertainment purposes; it is a strategic approach that serves specific marketing objectives. It involves identifying and understanding the needs and desires of the target audience, crafting a narrative that resonates with those needs, and delivering the message through various marketing channels.

By incorporating storytelling into their marketing strategies, businesses can create a more meaningful and memorable brand experience for their customers. It allows them to communicate their brand values, differentiate themselves from competitors, and establish an emotional connection with their audience. Effective storytelling can evoke emotions, capture attention, and ultimately drive customer engagement, loyalty, and conversion.

Strategic Marketing Planning Software

Strategic Marketing Planning Software refers to a specialized tool or platform designed to facilitate the strategic planning process within the marketing management discipline. It enables marketing professionals to develop, implement, and evaluate marketing strategies through a structured and systematic approach.

This software encompasses various features and functionalities that help marketers analyze market trends, identify target customers, set marketing objectives, allocate resources, and define marketing tactics. It allows for the creation of comprehensive marketing plans by integrating different components such as market research, competitive analysis, segmentation, positioning, pricing, promotion, and distribution strategies.

By leveraging strategic marketing planning software, marketing managers can streamline their planning efforts, enhance collaboration among team members, and ensure alignment with overall business objectives. The software provides a centralized platform where all relevant data, insights, and metrics can be accessed and utilized for decision-making purposes.

Furthermore, strategic marketing planning software often includes forecasting and performance tracking capabilities that enable marketing professionals to monitor and measure the effectiveness of their strategies over time. This allows for continuous optimization and refinement of marketing efforts, ultimately leading to improved business performance, customer satisfaction, and market competitiveness.

Strategic Marketing Planning Tools

Strategic marketing planning tools encompass a variety of frameworks, models, and techniques that assist marketing managers in developing effective strategies to achieve organizational goals. These tools provide a structured approach to analyzing the market, identifying target customers, and formulating marketing plans.

The first set of tools focuses on analyzing the external environment, including the macro-environmental factors such as political, economic, social, technological, environmental, and legal forces (PESTEL analysis). This analysis helps marketing managers understand the opportunities and threats present in the market, allowing them to make informed decisions about market entry, new product development, and strategic alliances.

The next set of tools revolves around understanding the competitive landscape, typically through a competitive analysis. This involves conducting a thorough examination of competing firms' strengths, weaknesses, opportunities, and threats (SWOT analysis) and identifying the key success factors within the industry. By assessing the competition, marketing managers can identify their company's competitive advantages and develop strategies to exploit them.

Another set of tools focuses on understanding customer behavior, needs, and preferences. This includes conducting market research, segmentation analysis, and targeting strategies. Market research involves collecting and analyzing data on customer preferences, usage patterns, and demographics to identify opportunities and understand consumer behavior. Segmentation analysis helps marketers divide the market into distinct groups based on demographic, psychographic, and behavioral characteristics, enabling them to tailor marketing strategies to specific segments. Targeting strategies involve selecting the most attractive segments and positioning the organization's offerings to meet their needs and desires.

Finally, strategic marketing planning tools include tools for setting marketing objectives, developing marketing plans, and evaluating and controlling marketing efforts. These tools help marketing managers define clear marketing objectives, set budgets, allocate resources, and determine strategic priorities. Through ongoing measurement and evaluation, marketing managers can monitor the performance of their marketing plans and make necessary adjustments to ensure success.

Strategic Marketing Planning

Strategic marketing planning is a crucial component of marketing management, involving the process of developing an effective and well-structured marketing plan to achieve the organization's goals and objectives. It encompasses the identification of target markets, analysis of competitors, and the formulation of strategic initiatives and tactics to gain a competitive edge in the market.

The goal of strategic marketing planning is to align the organization's marketing activities with its overall business objectives. It involves a systematic approach to understanding the market environment, the target customers, and the internal capabilities of the organization. This enables marketers to make informed decisions about product development, pricing strategies, distribution channels, and promotional activities.

The process of strategic marketing planning typically begins with a thorough analysis of the external environment, including market trends, customer needs, and competitive forces. This helps identify opportunities and threats in the market and allows marketers to position their products or services effectively. The next step involves conducting a detailed analysis of the organization's internal capabilities, such as its strengths, weaknesses, resources, and competencies. This provides insights into the organization's ability to meet customer needs and create value in the market.

Based on the external and internal analysis, marketers develop marketing objectives and strategies that are aligned with the overall business objectives. These strategies define how the organization will compete in the market and differentiate its offerings from competitors. Tactical plans are then developed, outlining the specific actions and initiatives required to implement the strategies effectively.

Overall, strategic marketing planning is a proactive and dynamic process that guides organizations in making informed decisions about their marketing efforts. It ensures that marketing activities are focused, well-coordinated, and aligned with the organization's long-term goals. By effectively utilizing strategic marketing planning, businesses can maximize their market share, profitability, and overall success in today's competitive business environment.

Strategic Marketing

Strategic marketing is a vital component of marketing management that focuses on long-term planning and decision-making to achieve a competitive advantage in the market. It involves the development and implementation of a well-defined marketing strategy that aligns with the overall business objectives and mission.

The primary objective of strategic marketing is to position a company or brand effectively in the market to attract and retain customers, while also driving profitability. This requires a deep understanding of the target market, including their needs, preferences, and behaviors, as well as a thorough analysis of the competitive landscape.

Strategic marketing involves a systematic process of market segmentation, targeting, and positioning to create a unique value proposition for the target customers. It encompasses various activities such as conducting market research, analyzing consumer trends, identifying potential markets, and developing effective marketing campaigns.

A well-developed strategic marketing plan includes clear objectives, actionable strategies, and measurable outcomes. It outlines the marketing initiatives and tactics that need to be implemented to achieve the desired results. The plan also considers factors such as pricing, distribution channels, promotional activities, and customer relationship management.

Overall, strategic marketing plays a crucial role in shaping the success of a company or brand. It helps companies adapt to changing market conditions, leverage opportunities, and minimize risks. By aligning marketing efforts with business goals, strategic marketing enables companies to stay competitive, build strong customer relationships, and ultimately drive growth and profitability.

Sustainability Marketing

Sustainability Marketing is a marketing approach that focuses on the integration of environmental, social, and economic considerations into all marketing strategies, activities, and practices. It involves promoting products, services, and brands that demonstrate a commitment to sustainable practices, while also addressing the needs and desires of consumers.

This approach recognizes that consumers are increasingly aware of and concerned about sustainability issues, such as climate change, resource depletion, and social inequality. Therefore, sustainability marketing aims to align the values and aspirations of consumers with the values and actions of companies, in order to create mutual benefits for both parties. It involves the development and communication of sustainable marketing messages and claims, as well as the implementation of sustainable practices throughout the entire marketing value chain.

Sustainability marketing encompasses a range of strategies, including the use of sustainable packaging materials, the promotion of energy-efficient and eco-friendly products, the support of fair trade and ethical sourcing, and the engagement in corporate social responsibility initiatives. Key objectives of sustainability marketing include building brand reputation and trust, enhancing customer loyalty and satisfaction, and gaining a competitive advantage in the marketplace.

In conclusion, sustainability marketing is a critical component of the marketing management discipline, as it addresses the increasing societal expectations for businesses to operate in an environmentally and socially responsible manner. By embracing sustainability marketing, companies can contribute to the achievement of sustainable development goals, while also driving business growth and profitability.

Target Audience

A target audience refers to a specific group of individuals or customers that a business or organization aims to attract and serve through its marketing efforts. In the field of marketing management, identifying and understanding the target audience is crucial for developing effective marketing strategies and campaigns.

The target audience is typically defined based on various demographic, psychographic, and behavioral characteristics. Demographic factors include age, gender, income, education, occupation, and location. Psychographic factors delve into the audience's attitudes, beliefs, values, interests, and lifestyles. Behavioral factors encompass the audience's purchasing behaviors, brand preferences, usage patterns, and satisfaction levels.

By clearly defining the target audience, marketers can tailor their marketing mix (product, price, place, and promotion) to meet the specific needs and wants of the identified audience segments. This enables them to deliver personalized and targeted marketing messages, products, and experiences that resonate with the intended audience, leading to higher customer satisfaction, loyalty, and ultimately, business success.

Moreover, knowing the target audience helps marketers in selecting the most appropriate marketing channels and platforms to reach and engage with their audience effectively. Whether it's through traditional advertising mediums, digital and social media channels, or direct marketing approaches, understanding the target audience enables marketers to allocate their resources efficiently and optimize their marketing efforts for maximum impact and return on investment.

Target Market Expansion Approaches

Target market expansion approaches refer to the strategies and methods used by businesses to broaden their customer base and reach out to new segments of the market. These approaches aim to identify and target new customer groups that are likely to be interested in the company's products or services.

There are several target market expansion approaches that marketing managers can utilize. The first approach involves conducting market research to identify new segments with unmet needs.

By analyzing market trends, customer preferences, and competitor strategies, companies can identify potential new segments that align with their offerings.

The second approach is to modify the marketing mix to appeal to new target markets. This includes developing new products or services that cater to the specific needs and preferences of the identified segments. Companies may also adapt their pricing, distribution, and promotional strategies to better target these new customer groups.

Target Market Expansion Strategies

Target market expansion strategies refer to the set of approaches and tactics implemented by a company or organization to broaden its customer base and reach new markets. These strategies are a crucial part of marketing management and involve identifying and targeting new customer segments, exploring untapped geographies or demographics, and creating marketing initiatives to attract and retain these new customers.

There are various methods that companies can employ to expand their target market. One common approach is through demographic expansion, which involves identifying new customer groups based on factors such as age, gender, income level, or occupation. By analyzing consumer behavior and market trends, companies can develop tailored marketing strategies to appeal to these new segments.

Target Market Expansion

Target market expansion refers to the strategic effort undertaken by a business to widen its reach and attract new customers. It involves identifying and tapping into new market segments or geographical areas that offer potential growth opportunities for the company. This strategy is employed to increase market share, boost sales, and improve overall profitability.

The process of target market expansion begins with conducting thorough market research and analysis to identify untapped customer segments or new markets where the company's products or services can be well-received. This may involve studying customer demographics, preferences, behaviors, and purchasing patterns to gain insights into their needs and wants.

Once the potential customer segments are identified, the company develops marketing strategies and campaigns specifically tailored to target and attract them. This may include changes in product features, pricing, distribution channels, or promotional activities to resonate with the needs and preferences of the new market segment.

Target market expansion also requires careful consideration of the competition in the new market segments. Companies must assess their competitive advantage and develop strategies to differentiate themselves from existing players in order to successfully penetrate the new market.

Overall, target market expansion is a strategic approach aimed at growth and diversification. It allows businesses to tap into new customer segments and geographical areas, which can lead to increased market share, higher sales, and improved financial performance.

Target Market

A target market refers to a specific group of individuals or businesses that a company aims to sell its products or services to. In the context of marketing management, defining a target market is a crucial step in developing a marketing strategy.

Identifying a target market enables a company to focus its marketing efforts and resources on the most promising customer segments. By understanding the characteristics, needs, and preferences of the target market, a company can tailor its marketing mix (product, price, promotion, and place) to effectively reach and satisfy the target customers.

Targeted Advertising

Targeted advertising, within the context of Marketing Management discipline, refers to the practice of delivering advertisements specifically tailored to reach a specific audience based on their characteristics and preferences. This approach involves gathering and leveraging data on consumers' demographics, behavior, interests, and purchase history to optimize the effectiveness of advertising campaigns.

The objective of targeted advertising is to minimize marketing waste by ensuring that ads are shown to the most relevant and receptive individuals. By understanding the target audience's interests and behaviors, marketers are better equipped to craft compelling and personalized messages that align with their needs and desires. This helps to enhance brand perception, increase customer engagement, and ultimately drive sales and revenue growth.

Targeted Marketing

Targeted marketing, in the context of marketing management, refers to the strategy employed by organizations to reach a specific audience or customer segment with tailored marketing messages and promotional efforts. It involves identifying and understanding the unique characteristics, needs, preferences, and behaviors of a particular group of consumers in order to create and deliver marketing campaigns that resonate with them.

Targeted marketing utilizes various tactics and approaches to maximize the effectiveness of marketing efforts. This includes conducting research and analysis to segment the market based on factors such as demographics, psychographics, geography, and buying behaviors. By narrowing down the target audience, organizations can develop customized marketing strategies that directly address the needs and interests of the identified segment.

This approach allows marketers to optimize resources and minimize wastage by focusing their efforts on the most potential customers who are likely to respond positively to their marketing initiatives. By understanding the specific requirements and preferences of the target audience, organizations can create tailored marketing messages, products, and services that are more likely to resonate with them. This results in higher conversion rates, increased customer satisfaction, and ultimately, improved business performance.

Effective targeted marketing requires organizations to continuously monitor, analyze, and track the effectiveness of their marketing efforts. By collecting and utilizing data and insights, marketers can refine their strategies, adjust their messaging, and adapt their approaches to ensure that they are consistently engaging and meeting the needs of the target audience.

Test Marketing

Test marketing refers to the process of introducing a new product or service to a limited market in order to gather feedback and evaluate its potential success before a full-scale launch. It is a crucial step in the marketing management discipline, allowing companies to test various aspects of their offering such as the product itself, pricing, distribution, and promotional activities. This test phase helps companies make informed decisions and minimize risks associated with launching an untested product or service to a broader market.

During test marketing, companies select a specific geographic location or target market segment to test their product or service. They then monitor customer reactions, collect data, and evaluate the effectiveness of their marketing strategies. Companies may use different methods to gather feedback, such as surveys, interviews, and observing customer behavior. The insights gained from this testing phase inform decision making and enable companies to make adjustments or refinements to their marketing mix before scaling up.

Testimonial Marketing

Testimonial marketing is a strategic marketing approach that involves the use of customer testimonials to promote a product or service. It is a powerful tool in the field of marketing management that aims to build trust, credibility, and social proof, by leveraging the experiences and opinions of satisfied customers.

Testimonials, in the form of written statements, videos, or audio recordings, provide proof of the value and effectiveness of a product or service, and serve as a persuasive tool to influence potential customers. They are typically sourced from happy customers who have had a positive experience with the brand, and are willing to share their thoughts and recommendations with others.

This marketing technique is rooted in the psychological principle of social proof, which suggests that people are more likely to adopt a behavior or make a purchase if they see others doing the same. By showcasing testimonials from satisfied customers, businesses can tap into the power of social proof to influence consumer behavior.

Testimonial marketing can be implemented through various channels, including websites, social media, advertisements, and offline marketing materials. It is often used in conjunction with other marketing strategies, such as influencer marketing, content marketing, and digital advertising, to maximize its impact.

In summary, testimonial marketing is a key practice in marketing management that utilizes the positive experiences and opinions of customers to build trust and credibility, and persuade potential customers to purchase a product or service.

Thought Leader

A Thought Leader in the context of Marketing Management discipline is a recognized expert who has a deep understanding and influential perspective on marketing trends, strategies, and best practices. They are individuals who consistently create and share valuable insights, innovative ideas, and thought-provoking content that challenges traditional thinking in the field of marketing.

These thought leaders have a strong presence and following in the marketing community, both online and offline. They possess exceptional knowledge and expertise in various areas of marketing, such as consumer behavior, brand management, digital marketing, social media, and market research. They have a unique ability to analyze complex marketing problems and provide effective solutions that drive business growth and success.

Thought Leadership Marketing

Thought leadership marketing refers to a strategic marketing approach adopted by organizations to establish themselves as industry experts and leaders in their respective fields by consistently providing valuable and authoritative insights, ideas, and opinions. It involves thoughtfully crafting and distributing high-quality content that not only educates and engages the target audience but also positions the organization as a trusted resource and go-to authority.

As a marketing management discipline, thought leadership marketing aims to build brand credibility and gain a competitive edge by focusing on creating and distributing thought-provoking content that addresses industry challenges, trends, and innovative solutions. It not only showcases the organization's expertise but also stimulates discussions, influences industry conversations, and attracts attention from key stakeholders, including customers, prospects, influencers, and media.

Effective thought leadership marketing requires in-depth industry knowledge, market research, and a deep understanding of the target audience's pain points, needs, and aspirations. It involves developing a content strategy that aligns with the organization's overall marketing objectives and brand positioning. This strategy may entail creating various content formats, such as articles, whitepapers, research reports, case studies, videos, and webinars, and leveraging different channels and platforms to reach the target audience.

By positioning themselves as thought leaders, organizations can enhance their brand reputation, increase visibility and awareness, establish long-lasting relationships with customers, and drive business growth. Thought leadership marketing goes beyond traditional marketing tactics and focuses on thoughtfully crafting content that genuinely adds value to the industry, establishes trust, and positions the organization as a trusted advisor and industry leader.

Thought Leadership

Thought Leadership in the context of Marketing Management refers to the position of an

271

individual or organization as an industry expert or authority in a specific field or area of knowledge. It involves consistently providing valuable insights, innovative ideas, and unique perspectives that challenge existing norms, inspire others, and shape the industry's direction.

A thought leader in Marketing Management is recognized for their deep understanding of market trends, consumer behavior, and industry dynamics. They possess the ability to anticipate emerging trends, identify new opportunities, and offer strategic guidance based on their expertise. Thought leaders often lead the way in introducing novel approaches, methods, or technologies that drive marketing innovation and effectiveness.

Through their thought leadership, these individuals or organizations establish themselves as trusted sources of information, thought-provokers, and reliable guides for industry professionals and decision-makers. They publish research papers, whitepapers, articles, or speak at conferences, webinars, and other industry forums to share their knowledge and insights. They may also engage in networking and mentoring activities to foster collaboration and development within the industry.

Being a thought leader in Marketing Management requires not only possessing deep subject matter knowledge but also having the ability to communicate complex ideas in a concise and accessible manner. They possess strong analytical skills, critical thinking, and a forward-thinking mindset. By influencing and shaping the thoughts and practices of others, thought leaders drive progress, innovation, and change within the marketing industry.

Top Of Mind Awareness (TOMA)

Top of Mind Awareness (TOMA) refers to a marketing concept that measures the level of brand awareness and recognition among consumers. In the context of marketing management, TOMA plays a crucial role in determining a brand's success in the marketplace.

When a brand achieves TOMA, it means that it is the first brand that comes to consumers' minds when thinking about a particular product or service category. This mental availability of the brand ensures that it is considered before any other competitor brand during the purchase decision-making process.

Top-Of-Mind Awareness (TOMA)

Top-of-Mind Awareness (TOMA) is a marketing concept used in the discipline of Marketing Management that refers to the extent to which a brand or product is the first to come to consumers' minds when they think about a particular product category. It represents the highest level of brand awareness, indicating that a brand is the first choice or the most memorable among consumers.

TOMA is crucial for brands as it is directly linked to brand preference and purchasing behavior. Brands that have high TOMA are more likely to be considered and chosen by consumers when making purchasing decisions. It is a measure of a brand's ability to occupy a prominent space in consumers' minds, allowing it to stand out from competitors and maintain a competitive advantage.

Touchpoint Analysis

Touchpoint Analysis, in the context of Marketing Management, refers to the process of identifying and analyzing all the points of contact or interactions that a customer has with a company or brand during their customer journey. These touchpoints can be both online and offline, and may include interactions through various channels such as websites, social media, phone calls, emails, physical stores, and customer service.

The purpose of conducting a touchpoint analysis is to gain a comprehensive understanding of how customers engage with a brand at each touchpoint, as well as to evaluate the effectiveness of these touchpoints in terms of creating positive customer experiences and driving customer loyalty. By identifying and analyzing these touchpoints, companies can make informed decisions about how to improve their customer interactions and enhance the overall customer journey.

Trade Show Marketing

Trade Show Marketing refers to the strategic planning and execution of promotional activities at trade shows and exhibitions to achieve marketing objectives. It is a specialized area within the Marketing Management discipline that focuses on leveraging trade shows as a platform to generate leads, build brand awareness, and engage with target audiences.

The primary goal of Trade Show Marketing is to maximize the return on investment (ROI) by effectively showcasing products, services, and solutions to potential customers. This involves designing visually appealing booths, creating compelling marketing collateral, and training sales representatives to effectively communicate key messages to attendees. Additionally, Trade Show Marketing involves pre-event, during-event, and post-event activities to ensure a comprehensive approach to generating leads and driving business growth.

This marketing discipline requires careful planning and coordination with various internal and external stakeholders, including marketing teams, event organizers, and sales representatives. It also involves conducting market research to identify relevant trade shows and target audiences, as well as tracking and analyzing metrics to evaluate the success of the trade show marketing efforts.

Overall, Trade Show Marketing plays a crucial role in the overall marketing strategy of a company, as it provides a valuable opportunity to interact with potential customers in a face-to-face environment and establish brand credibility and industry presence.

Traditional Marketing

Traditional marketing refers to the conventional methods and strategies employed by organizations to promote their products or services to a target audience. It involves the use of offline channels such as print media, television, radio, direct mail, and billboards to reach and influence consumers.

In traditional marketing, companies focus on mass communication and one-way messaging to convey their brand message and persuade consumers to purchase their offerings. They often rely on interruptive advertising techniques, such as commercials during TV shows or radio programs, to capture the attention of potential customers.

Traditional marketing also encompasses events and exhibitions, where companies showcase their products or services in a physical setting and engage with customers face-to-face. Additionally, it includes public relations efforts, such as press releases and media relations, to shape a positive image of the brand in the eyes of consumers.

While traditional marketing methods have been widely used for many decades and have proven to be effective, they are now facing challenges due to the increasing popularity of digital marketing. The rise of the internet and social media platforms has altered consumer behavior and created new opportunities for marketers to engage with their target audience in a more interactive and personalized manner.

To remain competitive in today's digital world, organizations often integrate traditional marketing techniques with digital marketing strategies to create a cohesive and comprehensive marketing campaign.

Transactional Data

Transactional data refers to the information collected during the processing of transactions in a business. In the context of marketing management, transactional data is crucial as it provides insights into customer behavior and helps in making strategic decisions.

The data encompasses various types of transactions, such as purchases, returns, exchanges, and inquiries, as well as the associated details such as time, date, location, and payment method. It typically includes information about the customer, such as their name, contact details, and purchase history.

UGC Marketing

UGC Marketing refers to User Generated Content Marketing, which is a marketing strategy that involves the use of content created by consumers or users to promote a brand or product.

This type of marketing relies on the idea that consumers are more likely to trust and engage with content that is created by other consumers rather than by the brand itself. UGC can take various forms, such as customer reviews, social media posts, videos, photos, and blogs.

Unaided Recall

Unaided recall refers to the ability of a consumer to remember a particular brand or product without any prompts or assistance from external sources. In the field of marketing management, unaided recall is considered as a measure of brand awareness and brand recognition.

Marketers often conduct unaided recall surveys or tests to assess the effectiveness of their branding and advertising strategies. These tests involve asking consumers to recall brands or products within a specific category, without providing any cues or prompts. Consumers are expected to spontaneously recall the brands that come to their mind.

Unique Selling Proposition (USP)

A Unique Selling Proposition (USP) is a distinctive and compelling factor that sets a product or service apart from its competitors in the market. In the context of Marketing Management, USP is a strategic concept that focuses on creating a competitive advantage by offering consumers something unique and valuable.

The USP serves as the foundation for a brand's marketing strategy and helps to communicate its value proposition to the target audience. It identifies the key benefits or features that differentiate a product or service from others available in the market, highlighting why customers should choose it over alternatives.

There are several components that contribute to the development of a strong USP. Firstly, it must be clear and concise, ensuring that consumers can easily understand the unique offering. Secondly, it should be relevant to the needs and desires of the target market, addressing a specific pain point or fulfilling a specific desire. Thirdly, the USP must be sustainable and difficult for competitors to replicate, providing a long-term advantage in the marketplace.

Effective USPs can take various forms, such as offering superior quality, lower price, faster delivery, exemplary customer service, or innovative features. By successfully promoting and delivering on its USP, a company can differentiate itself from the competition, attract new customers, and retain existing ones.

Unique Visitor

A unique visitor, in the context of marketing management, refers to a person who visits a website, application, or online platform within a specified period of time, such as a day, week, month, or year. The term "unique" implies that each visitor is counted only once, regardless of how many times they visit or interact with the website.

Marketing professionals use the concept of unique visitors to measure the reach and effectiveness of their online marketing campaigns. By tracking the number of unique visitors, they can evaluate the success of their strategies and make informed decisions to optimize their marketing efforts.

Upselling

Upselling refers to the sales technique employed by marketers to persuade customers to purchase a more expensive or upgraded version of a product or service or to add on additional items to their original purchase. It involves the process of convincing customers to invest in a higher-priced offering, often by showcasing the additional benefits, features, or value that the upgraded version provides.

In the field of marketing management, upselling is a strategy used to increase revenue and profit margins through customer persuasion. It is based on the understanding that once a customer has made a buying decision, they are more inclined to consider additional options. By using effective upselling techniques, marketers seek to maximize the customer's spending potential and increase the overall revenue generated from a single transaction.

User Acquisition

User acquisition, in the context of marketing management, refers to the process of attracting and converting new customers to a product or service. It involves identifying and targeting potential customers, creating awareness of the product or service, and persuading them to make a purchase or take a desired action.

The first step in user acquisition is understanding the target audience and their needs. This involves conducting market research and segmentation to identify the specific customer groups that are most likely to be interested in the product or service. Once the target audience is defined, marketing efforts can be tailored to effectively reach and engage them.

To create awareness and generate interest, various marketing channels and tactics can be employed. These may include advertising, content marketing, social media marketing, search engine optimization, email marketing, and influencer partnerships. The goal is to reach potential customers through the channels they frequent and deliver a compelling message that captures their attention.

Once potential customers are aware of the product or service, the next step is to persuade them to take action. This could be making a purchase, signing up for a trial, or subscribing to a newsletter. Effective sales and marketing techniques, such as persuasive messaging, targeted promotions, and personalized offers, can help to drive conversions.

User acquisition is an ongoing process that requires continuous monitoring, analysis, and optimization. Marketing campaigns and strategies should be regularly assessed and adjusted to ensure maximum effectiveness. By successfully acquiring new users, businesses can grow their customer base, increase revenue, and achieve their marketing objectives.

User Experience (UX)

User Experience (UX) in the context of Marketing Management refers to the overall experience that a customer has when interacting with a company, brand, product, or service. It encompasses every aspect of the customer's interaction, including their initial exposure to the brand, their perception of its value, the ease with which they are able to access and use the product or service, and their overall satisfaction with the experience.

UX is crucial in Marketing Management as it directly influences a customer's perception of a brand and its offerings. A positive UX can lead to increased customer loyalty, higher levels of customer satisfaction, and ultimately, higher sales and profitability for the company. On the other hand, a negative UX can result in dissatisfied customers, negative word-of-mouth, and decreased sales and market share.

Effective UX in Marketing Management requires a deep understanding of the target audience and their needs, preferences, and behaviors. It involves designing and delivering an experience that is intuitive, user-friendly, and aligns with the brand's values and promises. This can be achieved through extensive market research, user testing, and continuous refinement of the customer journey.

Furthermore, UX should also take into account the omni-channel nature of modern marketing, ensuring a consistent and seamless experience across various touchpoints, including websites, mobile apps, social media platforms, and physical stores.

User-Generated Content (UGC) Strategies

User-Generated Content (UGC) refers to any form of content, such as text, images, videos, or reviews, that is created and shared by consumers or users of a product or service. In the context of Marketing Management discipline, UGC strategies are techniques employed by marketers to leverage and harness user-generated content for promotional purposes, brand building, and engagement with the target audience.

UGC strategies involve encouraging and incentivizing consumers to create and share content related to a brand or its offerings. This content can be in the form of testimonials, product reviews, social media posts, blog articles, or any other user-generated material. Marketers can actively invite and solicit UGC through contests, giveaways, or branded hashtags, or they can simply monitor and curate existing UGC that consumers voluntarily create.

By utilizing UGC strategies, marketers can achieve several marketing objectives. Firstly, UGC provides social proof and authenticates a brand's claims or promises by showcasing real experiences and opinions of consumers. It helps to build trust, credibility, and enhances the brand's reputation. Secondly, UGC provides valuable insights into consumer preferences, behaviors, and trends, which can be used to tailor marketing campaigns and offerings. Thirdly, UGC acts as a powerful word-of-mouth marketing tool, as consumers are more likely to trust and be influenced by content created by their peers or fellow consumers. Lastly, UGC strategies foster engagement and interaction with the target audience, as consumers feel more involved and connected when their content is shared or featured by a brand.

User-Generated Content (UGC) Strategy Platforms

User-Generated Content (UGC) Strategy Platforms refer to digital tools and platforms that enable marketers to effectively harness and leverage user-generated content for marketing purposes within the context of Marketing Management discipline.

These platforms provide marketers with the necessary infrastructure and features to facilitate the collection, curation, and amplification of user-generated content. By leveraging user-generated content, marketers can tap into the power of their audience to create authentic and engaging content that resonates with their target market.

User-Generated Content (UGC)

User-Generated Content (UGC) is a significant aspect of the modern marketing landscape. It refers to any content created and shared by users of a brand, product, or service. Such content can include text, images, videos, and reviews that are voluntarily shared by consumers on various online platforms, such as social media, review websites, forums, or blogs. UGC is considered invaluable for marketing management as it provides authentic and unbiased testimonials about a brand, influencing the opinions and decision-making of other consumers.

Marketers leverage UGC to strengthen their brand reputation, increase engagement, and drive conversions. By encouraging users to share their experiences and opinions, brands gain access to a continuous stream of user-generated content that can be repurposed for promotional activities. UGC also fosters a sense of community and social proof, as consumers tend to trust and relate more to content created by their peers rather than traditional advertising methods. Additionally, UGC generates a buzz around a brand, enhancing its visibility and reach through word-of-mouth marketing.

Value Proposition

A value proposition in the context of Marketing Management is a statement that describes the unique value or benefits that a product or service offers to its target customers. It outlines how the product or service solves a problem, meets a need, or provides a desirable outcome better than the competition.

A strong value proposition clearly communicates the key features, advantages, and benefits of the product or service, and differentiates it from others in the market. It is a concise and compelling message that resonates with the target audience and influences their purchasing decisions.

Value-Based Pricing

Value-Based Pricing is a pricing strategy utilized in the field of marketing management that focuses on the perceived value of a product or service to customers. This strategy involves setting the price based on the value that customers are willing to pay for the benefits or satisfaction they receive from the product or service.

Value-Based Pricing takes into consideration the unique needs, preferences, and perceptions of different customer segments. It acknowledges that customers are willing to pay different prices for products or services based on the value they derive from them. This value can be determined by factors such as the quality, features, performance, convenience, and reputation of the offering.

Video Marketing Technique Tools

A video marketing technique tool refers to any software or platform that enables marketers to create, analyze, and optimize videos as part of their marketing strategy. These tools are designed to help marketers leverage the power of visual content to engage and connect with their target audience effectively.

Video marketing has become an integral part of the marketing management discipline as it allows businesses to communicate their brand messages, showcase their products or services, and tell compelling stories in a more engaging way. The use of video has proven to be highly effective in capturing audience attention, increasing brand awareness, and driving customer conversions.

There are various types of video marketing technique tools available in the market. Some tools focus on video creation, providing features such as video editing, adding captions or subtitles, and incorporating special effects. Others offer video hosting and distribution capabilities to ensure that videos are easily accessible across multiple platforms and devices.

Additionally, video marketing tools also provide analytics and tracking features, allowing marketers to measure the success of their video campaigns. These tools enable marketers to monitor key metrics such as views, engagement rate, click-through rate, and conversion rate, providing valuable insights into the effectiveness of their videos and helping to optimize future efforts.

In summary, video marketing technique tools play a vital role in the marketing management discipline by empowering marketers to create, measure, and optimize video content. These tools enable businesses to effectively communicate their brand messages and engage with their target audience, ultimately driving positive marketing outcomes.

Video Marketing Techniques

Video marketing techniques refer to the various strategies and tactics used by marketers to promote their products, services, or brand through the use of videos. Videos have emerged as a powerful tool in the marketing realm due to their ability to capture and engage the attention of audiences effectively.

In the context of marketing management, video marketing techniques involve the creation, distribution, and optimization of video content to achieve marketing objectives. These techniques encompass activities such as conceptualizing and scripting compelling video concepts, filming and producing high-quality videos, and strategically distributing them across relevant platforms.

Video marketing techniques aim to engage and connect with target audiences by utilizing the visual and auditory elements of videos. This medium allows marketers to convey messages, emotions, and information in an engaging and easily digestible format. Through videos, marketers can communicate product features, demonstrate product usage, share customer testimonials, or tell compelling brand stories.

Furthermore, video marketing techniques also involve optimizing videos for search engines and social media platforms to enhance their reach and visibility. This may include incorporating relevant keywords, creating enticing video thumbnails, and sharing videos on platforms that align with the target audience's preferences and behaviors.

Overall, video marketing techniques play a vital role in the marketing management discipline by enabling marketers to drive brand awareness, engage audiences, and ultimately, convert viewers into customers. By leveraging the power of videos, marketers can create impactful marketing campaigns that resonate with their target audience and achieve their marketing goals.

Video Marketing

Video marketing refers to the strategic use of video content for promotional and marketing purposes. It involves creating and sharing videos that engage, inform, and persuade target audiences to take desired actions. Video marketing has become an integral part of the marketing management discipline as it offers various benefits and opportunities to businesses.

Video marketing allows businesses to convey their brand message, product information, and value proposition in a dynamic and compelling way. By leveraging the power of audiovisual storytelling, businesses can create emotional connections with their target audience, establish brand credibility, and differentiate themselves from competitors. Additionally, videos can be easily shared and have the potential to reach a wide range of viewers, increasing brand visibility and exposure.

In the context of marketing management, video marketing plays a crucial role in the customer journey. It can be used at different stages of the marketing funnel, from creating awareness and generating interest to driving conversions and fostering customer loyalty. Video content can be utilized across various digital channels, including websites, social media platforms, email marketing campaigns, and video-sharing platforms like YouTube.

Furthermore, video marketing enables businesses to track and measure the performance of their videos, allowing them to optimize their marketing strategies and improve their return on investment. By analyzing metrics such as views, engagement rates, and conversions, marketers can gain valuable insights into the effectiveness of their video campaigns and make data-driven decisions.

Viral Content Marketing

Viral content marketing refers to the strategic promotion and distribution of content with the goal of creating a significant buzz and rapidly spreading among a large audience. It involves creating content that is shareable, engaging, and relevant, with the intention of maximizing its reach through social media platforms, email campaigns, and other digital channels.

The primary objective of viral content marketing is to leverage the power of word-of-mouth advertising, where consumers become the catalysts for sharing and promoting the content within their networks. By creating content that resonates with the target audience and elicits strong emotions or reactions, brands aim to generate organic and exponential growth in brand awareness, reach, and ultimately, conversions.

In order to achieve viral success, marketers need to carefully craft and optimize their content for various platforms and formats, considering the preferences and behaviors of their target audience. Additionally, the use of storytelling techniques, humor, emotional triggers, and captivating visuals can enhance the shareability and virality of the content.

Viral content marketing can yield numerous benefits for a brand, including increased brand exposure, enhanced brand reputation, improved customer engagement, and higher conversion rates. However, it also requires continuous monitoring, analysis, and adjustment to ensure that the content resonates with the intended audience and delivers the desired outcomes. Moreover, marketers need to be mindful of potential risks and negative impacts associated with viral content, such as backlash or unintended misinterpretation.

Viral Content

Viral content refers to online material, such as articles, videos, or images, that spreads rapidly and extensively through social media platforms and other digital channels. It is characterized by its ability to capture the attention and interest of a large audience, generating high levels of engagement, sharing, and exposure.

In the context of marketing management, viral content plays a crucial role in brand promotion and communication. By creating and distributing captivating and shareable content, marketers aim to increase brand visibility, reach, and awareness. When content goes viral, it has the potential to reach millions of people within a short period, amplifying its impact and enabling brands to reach a wider audience than through traditional marketing methods.

Viral content often possesses certain qualities that make it highly shareable and engaging. These qualities include being emotionally appealing, amusing, informative, or even controversial. It may also rely on influencers or celebrities to catalyze its spread. The content itself may be in the form of entertaining videos, compelling stories, thought-provoking articles, or visually stunning images. Additionally, viral content often takes advantage of current trends, hashtags, or timely events to capture attention and foster engagement.

While the primary goal of viral content is to increase brand exposure, it can also lead to other benefits such as improved brand reputation, enhanced customer loyalty, and increased website traffic. By leveraging the power of viral content, marketers can tap into the immense potential of social sharing and user-generated promotion, creating opportunities for organic growth and building strong brand communities.

Viral Loop

A viral loop in the context of marketing management is a strategy used to drive exponential growth by leveraging the power of word-of-mouth referrals and social sharing. It involves creating a feedback loop where satisfied customers not only continue to use and promote a product or service but also encourage others to do the same.

The viral loop process typically begins with a company delivering exceptional value and an outstanding user experience. This prompts customers to naturally spread the word about their positive experience, either through personal recommendations or by sharing their experiences on social media platforms.

As these recommendations and shares reach new potential customers, they become aware of the product or service and are compelled to try it out based on the positive reviews. If these new customers also have a positive experience, they are then motivated to share their own feedback and recommend the product or service to their own network of contacts. This cycle continues, creating a self-sustaining loop of growth as new customers are constantly brought into the fold.

The success of a viral loop relies heavily on two key factors: the uniqueness and quality of the product or service, and the ease with which it can be shared or recommended. A product that provides exceptional value or solves a pressing problem is more likely to generate viral growth, as satisfied customers will naturally want to share their discovery with others. Additionally, the process of sharing or recommending should be seamless, whether through social media integration, referral programs, or other incentives.

In implementing a viral loop strategy, a company must carefully design and optimize its product or service to encourage sharing and referrals. Monitoring and analyzing user behavior and feedback is crucial to identify areas for improvement and to ensure the loop continues to generate growth. By harnessing the power of word-of-mouth and social sharing, a viral loop can become a powerful marketing tool in driving exponential growth for a business.

Viral Marketing Campaign

Viral marketing campaign is a strategic marketing approach that leverages social networks and online platforms to generate buzz, increase brand awareness, and enhance customer engagement through the rapid spread of content.

This type of campaign relies on creating highly shareable content, such as videos, memes, or interactive campaigns, that resonate with the target audience and encourage them to share with their social networks. The goal is to spark conversations and encourage individuals to voluntarily distribute the content to their connections, resulting in exponential reach and exposure for the brand.

Viral marketing campaigns often tap into emotions, humor, or novelty to capture the attention of the audience and motivate them to share. The key to success lies in designing content that is easily shareable, relatable, and aligns with the brand's values and objectives. By harnessing the power of social sharing, viral campaigns can achieve significant organic reach and engagement, potentially reaching millions of people within a short span of time.

While the primary objective of viral marketing campaigns is to increase brand visibility, they can also drive other marketing outcomes such as increased website traffic, lead generation, and sales. To maximize the impact of a viral campaign, marketers often use social media platforms, influencers, and online communities to amplify the content's reach and engagement.

Viral Marketing

Viral Marketing can be defined as a marketing strategy that aims to create a significant buzz and increase brand awareness by encouraging individuals to spread a brand's message or content through social media platforms, email, or other online channels.

This form of marketing relies heavily on word-of-mouth and peer-to-peer sharing to reach a large audience, often surpassing the reach of traditional advertising methods. When a marketing campaign goes viral, it means that it has gained immense popularity and has been shared by a large number of people in a short period.

Visual Content Marketing

Visual Content Marketing refers to the strategic use of visually appealing and engaging content to promote a brand or product and attract target audiences. It is a key component of marketing management that utilizes various forms of visual media, such as images, videos, infographics, and animations, to convey brands' messages effectively.

In today's fast-paced digital world, where consumers are overloaded with information, visual content plays a crucial role in capturing their attention and delivering messages in a more memorable and impactful way. By incorporating visual elements into marketing campaigns, businesses can enhance their brand storytelling, evoke emotions, and establish a stronger connection with their target audience.

Visual content marketing allows companies to create a cohesive and visually consistent brand image across different platforms, such as websites, social media, and advertisements. By utilizing colors, typography, and striking visuals, companies can effectively communicate their brand values and differentiate themselves from competitors.

Moreover, visual content marketing can also enhance SEO (Search Engine Optimization) efforts by increasing website traffic and engagement. Search engines prioritize websites that offer visually appealing and user-friendly experiences, leading to higher search rankings and organic visibility. Engaging visual content also encourages social sharing, which can lead to increased brand exposure and user-generated content.

In conclusion, visual content marketing is a powerful strategy within the realm of marketing management that utilizes visually captivating content to attract and engage target audiences, effectively convey brand messages, and enhance overall brand visibility and recognition.

Visual Merchandising Concepts

Visual merchandising refers to the strategic use of design elements and displays to create an inviting and visually appealing shopping environment that enhances the overall shopping experience and drives sales. It is an essential aspect of marketing management as it directly impacts a company's brand image, customer perception, and ultimately, its bottom line.

The concept of visual merchandising encompasses various elements such as product placement, store layout, signage, lighting, and displays. These elements are strategically used to showcase products, highlight their features, and create an emotional connection with customers. By creating an aesthetically pleasing and well-organized shopping environment, visual merchandising aims to attract customers, engage them, and ultimately influence their purchasing decisions.

Visual Merchandising

Visual merchandising is a marketing management discipline that focuses on creating a visually appealing and enticing display of products in retail spaces. It involves the use of various design elements, such as color, lighting, layout, and signage, to enhance the overall customer experience and drive sales.

The primary objective of visual merchandising is to capture the attention of potential customers and encourage them to make a purchase. By strategically arranging products, highlighting key features, and creating visually appealing displays, retailers can create a positive environment that stimulates customer interest and influences their buying decisions.

Visual Storytelling

Visual storytelling refers to the strategic use of visual elements, such as images, videos, and infographics, to convey a brand's narrative, message, or information to its target audience. It is an effective marketing management technique that aims to engage and resonate with consumers by leveraging the power of visual communication.

In the field of marketing management, visual storytelling plays a crucial role in capturing the attention of consumers in an increasingly visually-driven world. It allows brands to communicate their unique value proposition, evoke emotions, and create memorable experiences that differentiate them from competitors.

By utilizing visuals, marketers can effectively convey complex ideas and information in a concise and engaging manner. Visual storytelling enables brands to simplify messages, making them easier to understand and remember. This approach also appeals to the human brain's preference for visual processing, enabling consumers to absorb information more quickly and effectively.

Furthermore, visual storytelling helps marketers establish a deeper connection with their target audience. By telling stories through captivating visuals, brands can elicit emotions, evoke empathy, and generate a sense of authenticity. This emotional connection drives consumer engagement, loyalty, and ultimately, conversion.

Voice Search Optimization Strategies

Voice search optimization strategies refer to a set of techniques used to improve the visibility and ranking of a website or web content in voice search results. With the growing popularity of voice-enabled devices and virtual assistants like Siri, Google Assistant, and Amazon Alexa, voice search has become an increasingly important aspect of digital marketing.

Marketing management professionals need to understand and implement effective voice search optimization strategies to stay ahead in the digital landscape. These strategies involve optimizing website content, structure, and technical elements to ensure that they are easily discoverable and comprehensible by voice search algorithms.

One key aspect of voice search optimization is optimizing content for conversational queries. Voice searches often involve longer and more conversational phrases compared to textual searches. Understanding the natural language and context behind user queries can help marketers create content that is more aligned with user intent and more likely to show up in voice search results. In addition, structuring content with clear headings, subheadings, and concise summaries can enhance the chances of appearing in featured snippets, which are often read aloud by virtual assistants in response to voice queries. Optimizing for local search is also crucial, as voice searches are often used for finding local businesses and services. This includes optimizing business listings, using schema markup, and providing accurate and up-to-date location information.

Voice Search Optimization Strategy Platforms

Voice search optimization strategy platforms refer to tools or technologies used in the field of marketing management to optimize websites and content for voice search. With the rise in popularity of voice assistants and smart speakers, more and more people are utilizing voice search to find information or make purchases online.

These platforms enable marketers to understand user search behavior and optimize their website and content to better align with the way people use voice search. This involves making adjustments to the website's structure, content, and technical elements to improve visibility and relevance in voice search results.

Voice Search Optimization

Voice search optimization refers to the process of optimizing a website or online content to enhance its visibility and relevance in voice-based search queries. With the growing prevalence of voice assistants and smart speakers like Amazon Alexa, Google Assistant, and Apple Siri, voice search has become an integral part of consumers' digital experience.

From a marketing management perspective, voice search optimization involves understanding and adapting to the nuances of voice-based queries. This includes optimizing website content and structure to align with how people speak and ask questions, as opposed to typing search queries.

Implementing voice search optimization strategies can help businesses improve their visibility and rankings in voice search results, thus increasing their chances of being discovered by potential customers. This involves considering factors such as conversational language, long-tail keywords, and the context of search queries.

Furthermore, voice search optimization also encompasses improving website loading speed, mobile-friendliness, and user experience, as these factors are crucial for voice search rankings. Additionally, businesses should focus on creating relevant and concise answers to commonly asked questions, as voice search queries tend to be more specific and intent-driven.

In conclusion, voice search optimization within the marketing management discipline involves optimizing online content, website structure, and user experience to align with the increasing reliance on voice-based search queries. It aims to improve search visibility, rankings, and ultimately, enhance the overall digital presence and accessibility of a business.

Web Analytics

Web analytics, within the context of Marketing Management, refers to the practice of collecting, measuring, analyzing, and reporting website data to understand and optimize online marketing efforts. It involves the systematic measurement of website visitor behavior and interactions to gain insights into user preferences and drive data-driven marketing strategies.

The primary goal of web analytics is to track and measure various key performance indicators (KPIs) related to website performance, user engagement, and online marketing campaigns. These KPIs can include metrics such as website traffic, conversion rates, bounce rates, click-through rates, average session duration, and more. By analyzing these metrics, marketing managers can evaluate the effectiveness of their online marketing initiatives and make informed decisions about where to allocate resources for maximum impact.

Webinar Marketing Campaign Platforms

A webinar marketing campaign platform is a digital tool or software used by marketers to plan, create, and manage webinars as part of their marketing strategy. Webinars are online seminars or presentations that allow businesses to connect with their target audience and deliver valuable content or information.

These platforms provide a range of features and functionalities that help marketers effectively promote, host, and analyze the success of their webinars. They typically offer tools for creating and designing webinar landing pages, registration forms, and email invitations to attract and capture leads. Additionally, these platforms usually provide options for integrating with other marketing tools, such as email marketing software or customer relationship management (CRM) systems.

During the actual webinar, the platform enables marketers to host live presentations, including features like video streaming, screen sharing, and chat capabilities to engage with attendees. Some platforms also offer interactive features, such as polls, surveys, and Q&A sessions, to enhance audience participation and gather valuable feedback.

Furthermore, webinar marketing campaign platforms often provide analytics and reporting features to measure the success of a webinar campaign. Marketers can track metrics like attendance rates, engagement levels, and conversion rates to evaluate the effectiveness of their webinars and make data-driven decisions for future campaigns.

Webinar Marketing Campaigns

A webinar marketing campaign refers to a strategic approach adopted by businesses to promote their products or services by using webinars as a marketing tool. It is a form of digital marketing that involves hosting live online seminars or presentations to engage with a target audience and generate leads. Webinars are typically interactive and educational sessions that allow businesses to share valuable information, demonstrate their expertise, and build brand awareness.

The objective of a webinar marketing campaign is to attract potential customers, nurture existing leads, and ultimately drive conversions. It involves various marketing activities such as creating compelling webinar content, promoting the event through different digital channels, and managing registrations. During the webinar, businesses have the opportunity to engage with participants through Q&A sessions, polls, and interactive features, creating a personalized experience for attendees.

Webinar marketing campaigns have become increasingly popular due to their cost-effectiveness, convenience, and ability to reach a global audience. They provide businesses with an opportunity to showcase their thought leadership, establish credibility, and build relationships with prospects. By leveraging webinars, companies can gather valuable data about their target audience, gather feedback, and refine their marketing strategies.

In conclusion, a webinar marketing campaign is a powerful tool in the marketing management discipline that allows businesses to engage with their target audience, promote their offerings, and drive conversions through interactive online seminars. It is an effective digital marketing strategy that can help companies build brand awareness, establish credibility, and generate leads.+

Word Of Mouth Marketing (WOMM)

Word of Mouth Marketing (WOMM) refers to a marketing strategy that focuses on promoting a product, brand, or service through organic conversations and recommendations among consumers.

In the context of Marketing Management, WOMM plays a crucial role in building brand awareness and driving customer acquisition. It harnesses the power of positive word of mouth to generate buzz, create brand advocates, and ultimately increase sales.

WOMM relies on the simple concept that people are more likely to trust recommendations from friends, family, or colleagues than traditional advertising. It leverages the interpersonal relationships and networks that individuals have to generate positive brand associations and influence purchasing decisions. Therefore, it is crucial for marketers to understand and encourage these conversations to work in favor of their brands.

There are several strategies that can be employed to capitalize on WOMM in Marketing Management. These include providing exceptional customer experiences to inspire positive conversations, incentivizing customers to refer their friends or share their experiences, and utilizing social media platforms to amplify the reach and impact of word of mouth. Additionally, it is important for marketers to actively listen and respond to customer feedback to further foster positive brand perception.

Overall, WOMM is a powerful and cost-effective tool in the marketer's arsenal. By harnessing the power of word of mouth, brands can tap into the trust and influence of existing customers to attract new customers and build long-lasting relationships.

Word-Of-Mouth Advertising

Word-of-mouth advertising refers to the spread of information and recommendations about a product, service, or brand, primarily through interpersonal communication. It is a form of organic marketing which relies on individuals sharing their positive experiences with others, such as friends, family, colleagues, or social media followers.

In the marketing management discipline, word-of-mouth advertising is recognized as a highly influential and effective tool for businesses. It is often considered as one of the most powerful forms of advertising due to its ability to generate trust and credibility among consumers. This form of advertising can significantly impact consumer behavior, brand perception, and purchase decisions.

Word-of-mouth advertising can occur both offline and online. Offline word-of-mouth may involve personal conversations, recommendations, or reviews shared by individuals in social gatherings, workplaces, or casual interactions. On the other hand, online word-of-mouth advertising takes place through various digital channels, including social media platforms, review websites, forums, or blogs.

Word-of-mouth marketing can be spontaneous, generated by satisfied customers sharing their personal experiences, or it can be strategically stimulated by businesses through different means. Some businesses actively encourage word-of-mouth advertising by implementing referral programs, loyalty schemes, or by offering incentives to customers who refer others. This approach aims to amplify positive word-of-mouth and leverage the influential power of interpersonal communication.

In conclusion, word-of-mouth advertising plays a crucial role in marketing management as it can significantly impact brand reputation, consumer trust, and purchase decisions. It is a valuable tool that businesses should embrace and leverage in order to create positive buzz and cultivate a strong customer base.

Word-Of-Mouth Marketing Strategy

Word-of-Mouth marketing is a strategic approach to promoting a product or service that relies on individuals sharing positive information and recommendations about the brand to others. It is a form of organic, unpaid promotion that harnesses the power of interpersonal communication.

In the field of Marketing Management, Word-of-Mouth marketing is considered one of the most effective and influential tactics for generating brand awareness, building credibility, and ultimately driving customer acquisition and retention. The key premise behind this strategy is that people are more likely to trust recommendations and personal experiences shared by friends, family members, or acquaintances, rather than traditional advertising messages.

Word-of-Mouth marketing typically occurs through various channels, including face-to-face conversations, phone calls, text messages, social media platforms, online forums, and review websites. Companies can facilitate and encourage Word-of-Mouth marketing by creating exceptional customer experiences, providing high-quality products or services, and implementing referral programs or incentives to motivate their customers to share their positive experiences.

Furthermore, online Word-of-Mouth marketing has gained significant importance in the digital era. Social media platforms, online reviews, and influencers have become vehicles for consumers to share their opinions and recommendations widely. Marketers can leverage these platforms by actively engaging with customers, monitoring and responding to online feedback, and collaborating with influencers to amplify positive word-of-mouth.

284

Word-Of-Mouth Marketing Tactic Tools

Word-of-mouth marketing tactic tools are a set of strategies and methods employed by marketers to amplify and harness the power of positive word-of-mouth referrals and recommendations from customers. This marketing approach leverages the influence of satisfied customers to spread awareness, generate buzz, and ultimately drive sales for a product or service.

These tools encompass various techniques and platforms that enable businesses to encourage and facilitate word-of-mouth marketing. They typically include:

1. Influencer marketing: Collaborating with influential individuals who have a large following and credibility in a specific niche to promote a product or service.

2. Referral programs: Implementing structured systems that incentivize customers to refer friends, family, or colleagues to try the brand's offerings.

3. User-generated content: Encouraging customers to create and share content related to the brand, such as reviews, testimonials, or social media posts.

4. Brand advocacy programs: Cultivating a community of passionate brand advocates who actively promote the brand through various channels.

5. Social media marketing: Utilizing social media platforms to engage with customers, foster meaningful interactions, and encourage positive word-of-mouth recommendations.

These tools serve as a catalyst for organic, genuine conversations about a brand, as recommendations and referrals from friends, family, and influencers are generally trusted more than traditional advertising. By tapping into the power of word-of-mouth marketing, businesses can leverage the enthusiasm and loyalty of their customers to expand their reach, build credibility, and ultimately drive sales and growth.

Word-Of-Mouth Marketing Tactics

Word-of-mouth marketing tactics refer to a set of strategies and techniques implemented by organizations to encourage and leverage positive recommendations and referrals from satisfied customers and individuals within their social networks. This form of marketing relies heavily on encouraging individuals to spread positive information about a brand, product, or service through personal conversations and online interactions.

Word-of-mouth marketing is considered highly influential as it is based on trust and relies on the credibility of the individuals sharing their experiences. It is an organic and spontaneous form of promotion that can significantly impact a brand's reputation, growth, and customer acquisition efforts.

There are various word-of-mouth marketing tactics that organizations can employ. These may include:

- Creating exceptional customer experiences to generate positive conversations and recommendations.

- Encouraging customers to provide reviews and testimonials that can be shared with others.

- Implementing referral programs that incentivize existing customers to refer new customers.

- Leveraging social media platforms to engage with customers and enable them to share their positive experiences.

- Collaborating with influencers and brand advocates to amplify positive word-of-mouth recommendations.

Effective word-of-mouth marketing tactics involve understanding the target audience and identifying strategies to incentivize and facilitate the sharing of positive experiences. Organizations need to continuously monitor and manage these tactics to ensure that the conversations and recommendations align with their overall marketing objectives.

Word-Of-Mouth (WOM) Advertising

Word-of-Mouth (WOM) Advertising is a marketing strategy that relies on individuals or consumers spreading information about a product, service, or brand through personal conversations or recommendations. It is considered to be one of the most effective forms of marketing as it leverages the trust and credibility between individuals.

WOM advertising can occur both offline and online. Offline WOM advertising involves individuals sharing their positive experiences or opinions about a product or service with their friends, family, or colleagues through face-to-face conversations, phone calls, or written communication. This can happen spontaneously or as a result of deliberate efforts made by marketers to stimulate positive word-of-mouth.

Word-Of-Mouth (WOM) Marketing

Word-of-Mouth (WOM) Marketing refers to the organic, informal communication and sharing of information about a product, service, or brand between individuals. It involves customers voluntarily recommending or endorsing a particular offering to their friends, family, colleagues, or other acquaintances.

WOM marketing is a powerful tool in the field of marketing management as it taps into the influence and credibility of personal relationships to promote a product. It relies on the trust and perception of consumers in the opinions and recommendations of those they know and trust, rather than traditional advertising or promotional messages.

WOM marketing can take various forms, including personal conversations, social media interactions, online reviews, and testimonials. It can be both offline and online, creating a virtual network of interconnected consumers who share their experiences and opinions with others.

The impact of WOM marketing is significant as it is often perceived as a more authentic, unbiased source of information compared to traditional advertising. It can generate positive and negative WOM, which can have long-lasting effects on a brand's reputation and sales. Businesses can leverage WOM marketing by providing exceptional customer experiences, encouraging customer feedback and reviews, and fostering brand loyalty.

In summary, WOM marketing is the process of leveraging the power of interpersonal communication and personal connections to spread information and recommendations about a product, service, or brand. It plays a vital role in marketing management by harnessing the influence of word-of-mouth to create brand awareness, build trust, and drive customer engagement and loyalty.

Zero Moment Of Truth (ZMOT) Strategies

The Zero Moment of Truth (ZMOT) is a concept in marketing management that refers to the critical moment when a consumer actively searches for information about a product or service online before making a purchasing decision. It is the moment when a consumer moves from being aware of a product or service to actively considering it. The ZMOT strategies are the marketing tactics used by companies to influence and optimize this consumer decision-making process.

Companies can employ various ZMOT strategies, including search engine optimization (SEO), content marketing, social media marketing, online advertising, and user-generated content. By ensuring that their brand and products appear prominently in search engine results and providing helpful and relevant content, companies can increase their chances of influencing consumers during the ZMOT.

Zero Moment Of Truth (ZMOT)

The Zero Moment of Truth (ZMOT) is a concept in the field of Marketing Management that refers to the point in the buying cycle where a consumer researches a product or service online before making a final purchasing decision. It is a critical moment that occurs before the First Moment of Truth (FMOT), which is when the consumer encounters the product in-store.

ZMOT is driven by the increasing use of the internet, search engines, and online reviews as key sources of information during the consumer decision-making process. During this phase, consumers actively seek out reviews, compare prices, read product descriptions, and view images and videos to gather information and evaluate options.

Marketing professionals recognize the importance of the ZMOT and have adapted their strategies to reach consumers during this phase. They strive to create a positive online presence, ensuring their products or services are easily discoverable, have an appealing online presence, and provide relevant and useful information to potential customers.

Understanding the ZMOT allows marketers to develop targeted content and advertising strategies to effectively engage with consumers during their online research. By providing valuable information and addressing their needs and concerns, marketers can influence the consumer's decision-making process and increase the chances of converting a lead into a sale.

In summary, the Zero Moment of Truth is a crucial stage in the consumer buying cycle where consumers research and gather information online before making a final purchasing decision. Effective marketing strategies that cater to this stage can greatly influence consumer decisions and increase the likelihood of conversion.

Zero-Sum Game

A zero-sum game, in the context of marketing management, refers to a situation where the gains of one participant or organization are exactly balanced by the losses of another participant or organization. In other words, the total amount of benefits and losses remains constant, resulting in no net gain for the participants involved.

In marketing, zero-sum games often occur in competitive scenarios, where each competitor aims to maximize their market share and profitability at the expense of their rivals. The concept aligns with the notion of a finite market, where the total demand for a particular product or service remains relatively stagnant over time.